Teaching Literature with Digital Technology

Teaching Literature with Digital Technology

ASSIGNMENTS

Tim Hetland

North Seattle Community College

bedford/st.martin's
Macmillan Learning
Boston | New York

For Bedford/St. Martin's

Vice President, Editorial, Macmillan Learning Humanities: Edwin Hill
Editorial Director, English: Karen S. Henry
Executive Editors: Karita France dos Santos, Vivian Garcia, Ellen Thibault
Assistant Editor: Sydney Hermanson
Production Editor: Lidia MacDonald-Carr
Production Supervisor: Robert Cherry
Marketing Manager: Joy Fisher Williams
Project Management: DeMasi Design and Publishing Service
Director of Rights and Permissions: Hilary Newman
Permissions Editor: Angela Boehler
Senior Art Director: Anna Palchik
Text Design: DeMasi Design and Publishing Service
Cover Design: John Callahan
Composition: Achorn International, Inc.
Printing and Binding: RR Donnelley and Sons

Manufactured in the United States of America.

0 9 8 7 6
f e d c b a

For information, write: Bedford/St. Martin's, 75 Arlington Street, Boston, MA 02116
    (617-399-4000)

ISBN 978-1-4576-2948-8

ACKNOWLEDGMENTS
Acknowledgments and copyrights appear on the same page as the text and art selections they cover; these acknowledgments and copyrights constitute an extension of the copyright page. It is a violation of the law to reproduce these selections by any means whatsoever without the written permission of the copyright holder.

At the time of publication all Internet URLs published in this text were found to accurately link to their intended Web site. If you do find a broken link, please forward the information to BedfordEnglishSurvey@macmillan.com so that it can be corrected for the next printing.

To Theodore

Who will learn with tools not yet invented

About the Author

Timothy Hetland holds a Ph.D. in English Literature and Film from Washington State University. Hetland has taught literature, film, writing, and technical communication courses at universities and community colleges throughout the state of Washington, including Washington State University and the Seattle Community College system. Previously, he has contributed to Bedford's *LitBits*, where he has blogged about teaching literature. Now pursuing a career in technology, Hetland has founded multiple startup companies and currently oversees marketing and content initiatives at a digital agency in Seattle.

Contents

SOCIAL MEDIA   1

PART THREE ASSIGNMENTS

PODCASTS   235

PART FIVE ASSIGNMENTS

ARCHIVES 451

Teaching Literature
with Digital Technology

PART ONE ASSIGNMENTS

Social Media

1

1

Shaking the Magic 8 Ball: Social Media for Readers and Writers

Laura Madeline Wiseman
University of Nebraska–Lincoln

AND

Adam Wagler
University of Nebraska–Lincoln

COURTESY OF LAURA
MADELINE WISEMAN

Laura Madeline Wiseman is the author of eleven collections of poetry, including *Queen of the Platform* (2013) and *Sprung* (2012) and the chapbook *Stranger Still* (2013), and is the editor of *Women Write Resistance: Poets Resist Gender Violence* (2013). Her work has appeared in *Prairie Schooner, Margie, Collagist, Valparaiso, Arts & Letters, Poet Lore, Feminist Studies*, and elsewhere. Wiseman has received an Academy of American Poets award, a Mari Sandoz/Prairie Schooner Award, a Susan Atefat Peckham Fellowship, and the Wurlitzer Foundation Fellowship. She has a doctorate from the University of Nebraska–Lincoln. Wiseman maintains a Web site and a blog, and posts content on YouTube, Facebook, Twitter, and other social media sites. www.lauramadelinewiseman.com

COURTESY OF ADAM WAGLER

Adam Wagler is an assistant professor of advertising and public relations at the University of Nebraska–Lincoln's College of Journalism and Mass Communications. He teaches design, development, and creative strategy courses using interactive and traditional media. His professional and research interests revolve around interactive media and technology in communications, advertising, and education. An Apple Distinguished Educator (2011), Wagler was a visiting professor at Colle + McVoy in Minneapolis (2010), and received the American Advertising Federation's Most Promising Minority Student Nominator award (2012). He is a doctoral candidate at UNL in instructional technology with an emphasis in informal learning using emerging technologies. www.adamwagler.com

1. OVERVIEW

- **Assignment:** Students follow an author on a social network and create a portfolio of writing in which they reflect on the ways in which the author used the site to engage rhetorically with readers.
- **Courses:** Composition; introduction to literature; fiction; creative writing; journalism; communications.

- **Literature:** Social media posts written by contemporary authors.
- **Technology:** A computer or smartphone with access to social media sites.
- **Time:** Can be a brief one-week assignment or an extended six-week assignment.

2. GOALS OF THE ASSIGNMENT

We created this assignment to help students develop a rhetorical understanding of how readers, writers, and published literary authors use social media. Through a hands-on, real-world project, they develop critical thinking skills about media consumption as they participate in literary communities and explore new venues for writing.

The goals of this assignment are based on University of Nebraska–Lincoln and English Department outcomes, aims, and scope, and meet the criteria for the university's Achievement-Centered Education (ACE) program. To meet the first ACE outcome, students

> write texts, in various forms, with an identified purpose, that respond to specific audience needs, incorporate research or existing knowledge, and use applicable documentation and appropriate conventions of format and structure.

Furthermore, we created this assignment to primarily address the first two goals outlined by our department's aims and scope for English 101:

- "Students will gain extended practice with composing processes (including invention, drafting, revision, and final editing) and explore a range of forms and purposes for their writing. Students will write *at least* 3 sustained finished texts (the equivalent of 25 typed, double-spaced pages) in addition to a series of shorter writing assignments that lead (directly or indirectly) to the finished pieces.
- Students will develop their capacities for critically reading and responding to texts. Particular attention will be paid to helping students develop a working knowledge of rhe-

> "Integrating mobile and social media into instruction creates opportunities for students to use technologies that many are comfortable with. [It also allows] instructors to extend the classroom beyond the scheduled meeting time. The result provides a space to explore the professional side of interactive media including concepts of audience, strategy, and communications."
>
> **Adam Wagler**
> University of
> Nebraska–Lincoln

> "Our assignment merges several assignments from two different disciplines, English and Communications. After teaching courses in women's studies and consumerism at the University of Arizona, I began teaching English courses in composition, literature, and creative writing in 2006 at the University of Nebraska–Lincoln (UNL). At UNL I developed assignments to teach students skills in critical thinking and the rhetorical analysis of literature, popular culture, and creative writing."
>
> **Laura Madeline Wiseman**
> University of
> Nebraska–Lincoln

torical concepts (audience, purpose, cultural context, genre and style) that students can apply to their own writing as well as other texts."

Following is the assignment sheet that we provide to our students.

"I began teaching interactive media and creative advertising courses at UNL in 2006. My assignments integrate new technology and emerging media to address communications concepts and challenges. My research focuses on the integration of interactive media as a teaching tool. After discussions with Laura Wiseman on social media, audience, and emerging platforms for publications, we combined our assignments to create the one outlined in this chapter. This assignment was taught in four sections of English 101: Writing: Rhetoric and Reading and in one section of English 254: Writing and Communities in the English Department at UNL in 2012."

Adam Wagler

3. ASSIGNMENT SHEET

Shaking the Magic 8 Ball: Social Media for Readers and Writers

Course: _____

Instructor: _____

Date: _____

Part 1: Choose a contemporary literary author you like and follow that author on a social media site.

In Part I of this assignment, you will begin to research, participate in, and evaluate a social media site and your author's presence there. You'll also start to draft an essay — presenting your experience, recommendations, and analysis — that will become part of a final portfolio and presentation.

Social media can be used as a powerful marketing platform for promoting literary authors. In fact, publishers now use social media to help inform their decision-making processes (PBS Mediashift). The rise of social media sites has created individual writing, publishing, and reading platforms for individuals to share information, publish work, and connect with other writers. Each network has a unique audience, social norms, and niches that attract users to join and interact.

Authors, poets, and other writers look for ways to engage their audiences and distribute their writing (in all its forms) to interested parties. For example, *Poets & Writers'* public relations representative Lauren Cerand writes, "You can use Twitter to promote yourself and your writing, to engage your readers, or to stay current on the publishing and literary scenes" (79). Knowing the social media landscape is necessary if authors are to effectively convey their work and themselves. How one approaches, joins, and interacts with others online should be based on the rhetorical strategies of audience, purpose, cultural context, genre, and style, and for authors, delivering relevant content to readers is key.

Imagine you are working at a publishing company and your boss says: "We need to expand our social media efforts." She asks you to research a particular social media site and evaluate how literary authors present themselves (or are presented) there. Might that site be appropriate for promoting the authors your company publishes? Why or why not?

For this project, your task is to select a published literary author, follow that author on a social media site, participate at site, and write about it. Your finished product will be a portfolio that will include 8 to 10 pages of polished prose in which you document, reflect on, and describe the social media site, the opportunities it may create, the ways in which your author presents himself/herself rhetorically, and your own evaluation of your experience posting content and interacting with others at the site. Your portfolio will also include screenshots or other artifacts that support your recommendation; ultimately you will translate your portfolio into a PowerPoint presentation to share with your class.

This project will give you a hands-on, real-world experience in which you analyze how a real author uses a real social media site for networking and promotion. As a participant and researcher, you will also develop your own rhetorical writing skills.

In order of preference, select your top 5 social media sites and authors of choice and submit them to your instructor. *No student may do the same author on the same network.* I will approve your choices and assign your author and network. Once approved, you will join and interact with others at the site by posting video, audio, photos, content, links, ideas, and whatever else is relevant to your network. You will follow what your author does, noting how he/she uses the site. Meanwhile, you will begin drafting and workshopping your essay in peer groups during class.

Part 2: In an 8- to 10-page essay, analyze your author's chosen social media site, your author's presence on that site, and your experience as a participant at the site.

In Part 2 of this assignment, ask yourself: What rhetorical concepts are at work at the site? How does your author use these concepts? How do you use them? How engaging is your experience?

In your 8- to 10-page essay, you will include information on three key areas (see below), paying particular attention to and incorporating the rhetorical concepts of purpose, audience, genre and style, and cultural context. Use these questions to guide your writing, citing your observations and descriptions in appropriate stylistic conventions (e.g., MLA, APA, etc.).

1. **Analyze the social media site that your author uses.**

   Purpose. What are the basic functions of the site? What is the purpose of the site? What is it attempting to do or accomplish (invite, teach, inform, persuade, entertain, encourage reflection or introspection, scare, urge action, woo)?[1]

   Audience. What is the estimated total number of users? How many are active? Passive? Who are some of the literary authors using the site? How do they use it, generally? Specifically? How do these authors identify themselves at the site? Gather any demographic and psychographic information that you can. Who is the audience for the site? Generally?

---

[1] Rhetorical questions and portfolio rubric adapted from *The 2006 Writing Teachers' Sourcebook*, edited by Dana Kinzy.

(*continued*)

ASSIGNMENT SHEET *(continued)*

Specifically? What do the participants on the site assume about their audience and how do you know?

Genre and Style. What genres of writing does the site feature? What types of media are native to the site — text, video, audio, photo? What isn't on this site? What types of analytics or marketing tools are available on this site? What composing style does the site use? What is its design? What niche does the site fill? What activities show this? When listening to or reading conversations on the site, ask yourself, what is the style of this communication? What persona, manner, spirit, or tone does the social media site project and use to attract an audience?

Cultural Context. What is the cultural context of the site? Why was the site constructed? What do you know or what can you learn about this site by examining the context in which it occurs — physically, historically, socially, geographically? One way to understand a site's cultural context is by comparing the site to other social media sites. On what other sites might similar information be found? Why? On what sites would it be very unlikely or never be found? Why?

2. **Analyze your author's use of the social media site.**

Purpose. What do you believe is the author's purpose for using the site? What does she/he attempt to do or accomplish (invite, teach, inform, persuade, entertain, encourage reflection or introspection, scare, urge action, woo)? What do you think your author's main goals are in using the site? What topics or ideas seem to be the author's main concern? How does your author's approach compare with and/or connect to other authors you've read?

Audience. What is your author's point of view? What does the author assume about his or her audience and how do you know? How does this audience influence the rhetoric (style of writing, etc.) that the author uses? What is the relationship between author and audience on this site? Where do you see these influences in the descriptions and observations you've collected? Where and how does the writer of the text establish authority in relation to the audience? What kinds of groups/functions do authors have on this site?

Genre and Style. What writing genres does your author seem to prefer or embrace on the site? What types of media does the author use (text, video, audio, photo)? What doesn't your author use on this site? What types of analytics or marketing tools has the author chosen to include on this site? What style does the author write in? What niche does the author's social media activity seem to fill? What activities show this? When reading the author's posts, notice the style of communication she/he uses. What persona, manner, spirit, or tone does the author project in order to draw in an audience and other participants? Do you see any recurring themes or discontinuities in your author's point of view?

Cultural Context. What do you know or what can you learn about this author by examining the cultural context in which she/he is using this social media — physically, historically, socially, geographically? Why is the author using this social network rather than another? Where else does the author post content on the Internet (e.g., personal Web site, blog, other social networking sites)? Is the content the same? Different? Why?

3. **Reflect on and analyze your participation as a writer and reader at the site.**

Rhetorical Analysis. Based on your analysis and experience with this social network for this assignment, describe what suggestions you have for participants, including authors and publishers, who might just be getting started on this network. What groups did you join, follow, or participate in? What was your role as a user? Would you have done anything differently? How can this network integrate with other media (e.g., e-books, books, journals, other networks, e-mail)? Describe your sense of your own use in terms of audience, purpose, cultural context, and genre and style.

Emotional Reaction, Intellectual Reaction, and Response as a Writer/ Participant.

Emotional: How did engaging on this site make you feel? Were there posts that made you feel left out — either because the vocabulary was difficult or the ideas were new or the authors/users were assuming knowledge about events, ideas, or theories that were unfamiliar to you? Does your engagement at the site remind you of other experiences? What do you already know that can contribute to your understanding of this site? How are the ideas in this site or the style of writing different from what you already know or have experienced online on other networks?

Intellectual: What ideas came to mind as you engaged at the site? What questions does this raise about you, other humans, life, the state of the world, the relationship between participant readers and writers, social media, and technology, and so on?

Writer/Participant: What did you notice about the way posts were written, the choices your author, you, and other users made in terms of details, organization, voice, point of view, argument? What appeals to you about the style of the site and the posts? What does not?

Reflection. What do you feel has been most and least effective in your experience on the site? What is your assessment of the responses you've received to your posts? What would you have done differently? What do you understand better about yourself as a writer and a user of social media? What have you learned about your literary author and your own writing through this assignment? What writing issues would you like to

(*continued*)

ASSIGNMENT SHEET (*continued*)

continue examining or learning about in the remainder of the semester? What roles have you played on the site and in your peer workshopping group for this assignment? What is your assessment of your overall participation in this assignment, in your peer group, and in the class so far? What areas do you plan to improve on for the remainder of the semester?

Part 3. Finalize your essay, organize your appendix of screenshots, assemble your portfolio, and create and give a presentation.

In Part 3 of this assignment you will:

1. Draft, workshop, and revise your essay. Make sure that in your essay you draw on five (5) sources and include an annotated MLA bibliography.

2. Create and share with the class a 5- to 7-minute PowerPoint presentation.

PROJECT CHECKLIST:
- ❏ All in-class/prewriting and brainstorming (untyped)
- ❏ Draft 1 of 4 with author's note, Track Changes off, 3–4 pages, 2 annotated sources for MLA bibliography
- ❏ Workshop comments and edits from peers
- ❏ In-class revision work of draft 2 of 4, Track Changes on with author's editing notes in comment bubbles, 5–6 pages, 4 annotated sources for MLA bibliography
- ❏ Workshop comments and edits from peers
- ❏ Peer response letter
- ❏ Draft 3 of 4, Track Changes on with author's editing notes in comment bubbles, 7–8 pages, 5 annotated sources for MLA bibliography
- ❏ Workshop comments and edits from peers
- ❏ In-class revision work
- ❏ Appendices beyond the final essay
- ❏ Screenshot of your profile with relevant information
- ❏ 5 relevant posts you made
- ❏ 3 additional examples of your interactions with others
- ❏ Screenshot of your case study author's profile
- ❏ 5 examples of relevant posts the author made
- ❏ 5 additional examples of the author's interactions with others
- ❏ Other charts, graphs, or other visuals that support your findings

4. TIME AND TECHNOLOGY

TIME. The assignment asks students to participate on a social media site of their choice as they follow an author over six weeks and work through at least four drafts of a paper documenting their findings, reflections, and analyses. First, students research and select an author using a social network during the first week. We are actively involved with the selection process to ensure that students choose well. We encourage students to look for an author who frequently posts content, is a member of several social networks, and has many active followers. Students submit their authors and social networks for approval, also during the first week of the assignment. Once approved, students begin following their author on social media, participate on the site, reflect on their interactions, and evaluate their site rhetorically (purpose, audience, genre and style, and cultural context).

Second, we build all class readings, materials, discussions, and workshops around the goals of the assignment. For example, during week two and week three we offer guided, in-class writing on what students are noticing rhetorically on their site. During week three we engage in small and large group discussions about determining, and thus narrowing down, an audience, gauging the cultural context, and exploring the site's purpose as students draft their paper. The in-class writing, discussions, workshops, and sharing build a collective knowledge that gives students the opportunity to relate their peers' findings to their own during weeks four and five. After a final workshop during week five or six, students conclude the assignment in week six by giving a five- to seven-minute presentation of their portfolio on the day it's due.

Though this assignment is designed for a six-week time period, other versions could be developed to fit the needs of a particular course or focus.

> **Example 1:** Ask for an analysis of a specific aspect of rhetorical use (e.g., purpose, audience, genre and style, and cultural context). Such an assignment may ask students to write a one- to two-page analysis of a given aspect of a social network site or an author's use of that site.

> **Example 2:** Run an analysis as an in-class activity. Use small groups to discussion purpose, audience, genre and style, and cultural context, then share findings as a class. This approach is simply an overview to introduce how authors use social media as a marketing platform.

Such activities may be a preparatory assignment for analyzing the rhetoric in other social settings and/or other historical time periods.

TECHNOLOGY. The structure of the assignment is flexible, giving you the ability to integrate it into your course schedule. This section outlines the technology needed and provides examples of different time frames for activities.

As noted at the beginning of this chapter, students will need a computer or smartphone with Internet access.

Students will also need a flexible list of social media sites and literary authors. You could develop a list of networks and/or authors, perhaps drawing on sources used by past students. You could also conduct a class discussion, asking students to generate a list, and/or ask students to suggest other sites not on the list. We encourage our students to think about their reading and writing interests and the authors they admire. For example, a Harry Potter fan might enjoy exploring Pottermore, whereas a vampire series addict might benefit from analyzing Goodreads. For students who find their own social network and author, it is important to have them present a quick analysis to check that enough material is available to complete the project. We recommend looking at the number of posts, examples, and interactivity with followers as a baseline for students to consider when choosing an author and corresponding social media site.

5. ANTICIPATING STUDENT NEEDS

The majority of students arrive in class already using social media. They may have more digital expertise than their instructors, a situation that allows for a decentralized classroom. Feminist pedagogy often works to decenter the classroom, to question power structures, and to challenge traditional teaching models, including refocusing attention onto students themselves to see what they know, what new knowledge they bring to the classroom, and what excites them about reading and writing. bell hooks writes, "As a classroom community, our capacity to generate excitement is deeply affected by our interest in one another, in hearing one another's voices, in recognizing one another's presence" (8).

Activities, such as this one, shift the authority from you to the student and offer an exciting place to learn together about contemporary uses of media by authors and readers. As Mary Rose O'Reilley says in *The Peaceable Classroom*, "For the teacher, it is terrifying to cede control ... yet I believe that by giving students their autonomy we win our own. We expect our student to 'change' in the course of a semester. If we ourselves are not changing, I suspect we are not permitting ourselves to be put at risk by our students" (30).

In one of his courses, Adam Wagler (coauthor of this chapter) offered students the option to create mood boards using Pinterest. At the time, Pinterest was relatively new and potential users needed to be invited to use it. In class, Wagler asked students who were already on Pinterest to invite and help those who wanted to learn about and use the site to create their mood boards. In no time, a handful of heavy Pinterest users were jumping around class inviting classmates and teaching each other how to use the site. This was not only a learning experience for the students, but also for Wagler, which would not have been possible without allowing students to share their expertise.

It's also beneficial to define for students the terms *author* and *social media* at the outset. In the assignment, we defined an author as one who has published book(s) (e.g., chapbooks, e-books, self-published, small press, or commercial press), one who is alive, and one who uses social media to promote his/her work. We defined social media as a site where all visitors have the opportunity to engage, post content, create a profile, and interact with other users. Students generate a list of their favorite authors and the social media sites they use regularly. We also discuss sites not usually noted by students where readers and writers interact (e.g., LibraryThing, Goodreads).

Additionally, it can be helpful to do an activity at the beginning of the assignment that physically separates students from their technology. For example, for Valentine's Day, Laura Wiseman (coauthor of this chapter) began a class by asking students to line up all their devices (e.g., smartphones, laptops, tablets) on the table at the front of the classroom. Students returned to their desks and wrote love poems or anti-love poems to their devices. They then shared what they'd written. For the entire period, their devices remained on the front table while they talked through an article on social media. During the last twenty minutes of the period, students were asked to write about the experience of being separated from their devices and the Internet, and to share their writing with the class, which led to a thoughtful discussion.

6. ASSESSMENT TOOLS

To encourage deep student engagement with a social media site, this assignment requires students to create a profile, post content, and interact with others at the site while following their chosen literary author. The paper and presentation require students to create a PowerPoint and an appendix that showcase their engagement and participation, their author case studies, research, and reflection on their (and their author's) media and rhetorical literacy.

We use a checklist (see the Assignment Sheet on p. 10) to note what items may be missing or incomplete in the portfolio. We also use the following portfolio rubric.

RUBRIC for Evaluating Student Portfolios	(50 points total)

Polished Prose (8–10 pages)	____/10

Uses of rhetorical concepts? Writes in genres? Thoughtful analysis of social network? Experiments with new structures and genres? Avoids clichés? Uses new and interesting word choice? Showing and telling?

Does the final essay display a coherent and original (creative!) argument with a clear introduction, thesis, and conclusion and a well-organized body with a balance between argumentative points and textual illustrations? Does it articulate a clear audience, purpose, and context for the project? Does it develop an idea, explore a significant question, or make a point about the topic through the strategic use of detailed descriptions and careful analyses? Is the writing—punctuation, spelling, sentence structure—of excellent quality?

Revision/Writing Process	____/10

Has the student reevaluated, reworked, and developed the project fully? Has he/she applied writing techniques and concepts discussed in class? Are all the workshop drafts here? Does the student engage with revision suggestions from peers and instructor? Does the student fix errors in paper drafts? Does the portfolio contain all in-class, out of class, pre- and brainstorming writings that lead up to the final paper? Is Track Changes used?

Does the student's author's note and comment bubbles outline what was taught in class? Does he/she point to examples to support claims made? Has the student thought about his/her writing process? Shown examples of progress? Identified strengths? Weaknesses? Articulated why revisions were made?

Research and Stylistic Conventions	____/10

Is the use of research apparent in the student's work? Is the research thorough, well done, and thought out? Is the research applicable to the essay's topic? Are social media artifacts used appropriately? Does the essay focus around some central idea/question that grows out of the research? Does it describe this research and artifacts? Does it include an appendix, when appropriate (posts, charts, followers, visuals, graphics, etc.)? Are there appendices that include 5 relevant posts made by the student, 3 additional examples of interactions with others, 5 examples of relevant posts the author made, 5 additional examples of the author's interactions with others, other charts/graphs/visuals that support the student's findings? Is there an annotated MLA bibliography with at least 5 sources? Does the annotated bibliography follow MLA formatting on the works-cited page and within the paper?

Follows Assignment and Organization	/10
Is the student's portfolio organized? Is it neatly done and structured in a logical, organized fashion? Does it show focus and attention to detail and precise language that involves showing, not telling? Does it demonstrate that the student has applied knowledge of style and skillful language? Does it meet assignment requirements? Is it 8–10 pages? Are the grammar and mechanics consistent? Has it been proofed? Does it avoid passive voice and forms of "to be"?	
Final Presentation	/10
Does the final presentation show poise, maturity, and practice? Does the 5- to 7-minute PowerPoint presentation demonstrate the writer's research? Does it show her/his writing process? Does it give examples of revision and a writer's strategies?	
Total	/50

7. THEORETICAL BASIS FOR THE ASSIGNMENT:
Shaking the Magic 8 Ball: Social Media for Readers and Writers

After my [Laura Madeline Wiseman's] sister's wedding, family gathered at the newlyweds' brick home under a canopy of established elm, oak, and pine. Between cake and photo ops, we nibbled pineapple, green grapes, and strawberries. When conversation lagged or someone's squalling child was sequestered with teat and clean diapers in a back bedroom, I watched my other, younger sister and her husband with their mobile phones, those black plastic boxes they cradled in one hand, a finger sweeping blithely over the shiny surface or two thumbs tapping and reaching as it dimmed and flashed before them. I watched their eyes, the glitter of the small box reflected there. I watched their faces, their skin, as they read—a crinkled brow, a clucked tongue, a gentle snorting laugh, more puff of air than sound escaping. I watched the ease of their shoulders, the shift of weight as they leaned back in their chair. I didn't have a mobile phone with a data plan. I had a cell phone, of course, and at home, a laptop, but how strange I thought—those black boxes of light and words, like a Magic 8 Ball. You shake it and answers rise to the surface from that swirling, purple-black water. You read, consider, and shake it again.

A year earlier, we [the coauthors of this chapter] led a study abroad to Russia and encountered the same thing—students with tablets and smartphones, eyes bright and intent with the flicker from their screens. Behind them, unseen, was the red-walled fortress of the Kremlin, topped with jeweled and glowing red stars. We'd also seen this at academic conferences in Chicago, D.C., and Toronto — a hotel lobby swimming with dresses and suits, expensive haircuts and muted leather loafers, fingers communing with small black boxes in the roar of conversation, a white noise in which to meditate. And we'd seen this in our classrooms, the furtive thumbs and sleek, plastic boxes between the jeaned thighs of students, mid-class — assignments and notebooks open on their desks, yes, but below their desks, that Magic 8 Ball summoning the real answers they sought. And it is here that this assignment came to be and rose from the darkness to light, because we wanted to know why.

In a recent issue of *Poets & Writers*, Jami Attenberg offers tips for writers who use social media. In her article, "Network: How to Use Tumblr to Connect With Readers," Attenberg writes, "A savvy young friend of mine pushed me to launch a Tumblr page because my fourth book was coming out and she believed it would expose me to a new audience. . . . [Now] I have close to two thousand followers" (79). Many writers are using social media to connect. In the United States, 275,000 books are published annually, with self-published/e-books at 765,000 (Goldfarb 53). In "What Writers Need to Know About Electronic Publishing," Ronald Goldfarb writes, "A year ago, there were fifteen million electronic readers; today they number forty million. . . . [In 2009] electronic publishing comprised about 3% of all new books; today it is 15% and it has been predicted . . . by 2020, it will be as much as 50%" (53-54). Given the growth of e-publishing and new media, social media provides a powerful pedagogical space, in part because our students are already using it to connect, research, and write. Eighty-seven percent of Internet users, ages 18-29, use online social networking sites (Purcell, slide 10). If writers are using social media and if our students are too, than how does a teacher incorporate social media into the goals, aims, and scope of their classroom?

Wait, maybe we should back up. Both of us grew up in a pre-Internet world. We both went to college when e-mail and the Internet were in its infancy, the time when Web sites were static pages of information. We both have watched the evolution of the Internet to platforms where people interact in virtual communities. Facebook, where we both have pages, is still the largest social network (Experian) with 1.15 billion active users as of June 2013 (Facebook). Denis McQuail defines social media participation as "two-way and interactive" forms of speaking, writing, and communicating that are integral to its appeal (542). As Kim Sheehan and Deborah Morrison note, such "interactive creativity is built around engagement, and it recognizes that people are inherently social and look to create and maintain relations" (41). Compare new media (e.g., Facebook, Twitter, Google+) that use the new communication model of individual messages, personalized responses, and audience participation to traditional media outlets (e.g., NPR, *The New York Times*, local news broadcasts) that use numerous communication models and one has a curious conundrum. If traditional media outlets and new media outlets are using different means of engagement, how do students view these sites? Are they doing so rhetorically? Critically? Can media be studied in the English classroom, especially given that authors and readers are using social media at least at the rate of the students we teach?

In her book *Teaching to Transgress*, bell hooks writes: "One way to build community in the classroom is to recognize the value of each individual voice" (40). In our teaching a shared goal is to create a classroom community that will generate excitement about the course material; we do this by listening to — and teaching students to listen to — the ways community members speak, with a focus on rhetorical concepts. In such a community, we stress that each individual rhetorical voice adds to the conversation. Assignments such as the one we've presented in this chapter (see p. 6), round-robin activities that ask students to share observations, peer review sessions that get students to share constrictive criticism — all of these contribute to create a space where students can learn, appreciate, and think critically about various viewpoints, ideas, and arguments. Any assignments that ask students to think critically and to consider rhetorical strategies improves student writing. The National Writing Project suggests the following:

> An effective writing assignment does more than ask students to write about what they have read or experienced. It engages students in a series of cognitive processes, such as reflection, analysis, and synthesis, so that they are required to transform the information from the reading material in order to complete the writing assignment. (47)

Social media creates a learning environment where students can interact with other readers and writers and with each other in and beyond the classroom as they discuss and analyze their experiences. Teaching students to think critically about their surroundings, their popular culture consumption, and their social media habits helps them to become savvier citizens, thinkers, and learners. In *Here Comes Everybody: The Power of Organizing Without Organizations*, Clay Shirky writes, "It's when a technology becomes normal, then ubiquitous, and finally so pervasive as to be invisible, that the really profound changes happen, and for young people today, our new social tools have passed normal and are heading to ubiquitous, and invisible is coming" (105). If social media is not invisible yet, then as teachers we have an opportunity to encourage students to critically investigate social media by creating assignments that are framed around social media and the goals of our classes. Many students are experienced social media users, but it's likely that few have thought about social media as a professional communication tool. The ubiquity of technology in the classroom makes this an exciting place for us and our students to focus on thoughtful, critical, and analytical inquiries.

This assignment challenges students to reflect as they analyze their own use of social media. It prompts them to learn more about the authors they already admire and to discover new ones. Most importantly, it asks students to apply rhetorical analysis over several weeks in a researched essay that is workshopped and peer-edited. Taught in a composition course, this assignment fulfills, in part, the aims and scope that ask students to produce twenty-five pages of polished prose by the end of the course. Workshopping the assignment allows students to think through their ideas by learning from their classmates as they develop skills in revision, argument, and peer feedback.

Recommended Scholarship on Social Media

"Generation Why?" from the New York Review of Books by Zadie Smith offers a critical look at how Facebook and technology are shaping a generation.

Here Comes Everybody: The Power of Organizing Without Organizations by Clay Shirky explores how traditional forms of communication and media are changing by people connecting, collaborating, and organizing online.

Mashable (mashable.com) is a news source that covers social media and provides current information, trends, tips, tricks, and how-tos. For example, the article by Leyl Master Black looks at "5 Low-Cost Social Media Marketing Strategies for Authors."

Poets & Writers runs "The Practical Writer" series on "Network" offering tips for writers getting started on social media. For example, the November/ December 2011 issue focuses on LinkedIn. They also feature pieces such as Lauren Cerand's "Social Media for Authors" and the interview "A Social Approach" with Richard Nash by Gabriel Cohen on Redlemona.de.

8. CONCLUSION

When I [Laura Madeline Wiseman] was in middle school, I had a Magic 8 Ball. As I did with other fortune-seeking tools—Ouija Board, tarot cards, horoscopes, and palm readers at the fair—I asked questions hoping some truth would float up from the inky nebula. Later, I had a computer, a large charcoal metal box with a black screen, ghoulish letters, and a blinking green cursor. When I saved something on a floppy disk or opened up a file, it churned and grunted like it was engraving silver. Today I have an iPad, and as a writer, I use social media and follow my peers and the writers and literary authors I admire. I'm not sure what I'm searching for as I tap my screen or sweep a finger to scroll through the recent tweets, but I do know that I feel a sense of community, a connection to what's going on in the literary world, and an astonishment at what other writers and my students teach me about social media.

The assignment presented here (beginning on p. 6) provides an opportunity for you and your students to investigate current ways that authors, presses, journals, and readers are using new technologies to communicate, discuss, and explore literature. Through the rhetorical analysis of social media, this assignment builds new knowledge in the classroom by offering a snapshot of what is happening in digital reading and writing communities and gives students the tools to critically think and become rhetorically savvy as they consume and produce content in an online, social environment. Future iterations of this assignment could develop an online course wiki from student work, potentially connecting multiple sections or other courses (e.g., creative writing, literature, journalism). I am no soothsayer. I have no smartphone, no Magic 8 Ball, but what an opportunity we have to shake up social media, to shake up our classrooms and see what truths float to the surface, bright and buoyant and filled with the exuberance of student insight.

9. WORKS CITED

Attenberg, Jami. "Network: How to Use Tumblr to Connect with Readers." *Poets & Writers*, vol. 40, no. 4, July-Aug. 2012, p. 79.

Bandura, Albert. "Social Cognitive Theory." *Annals of Child Development*. Edited by R. Vasta, vol. 6, 1989, pp. 1-60.

Black, Leyl Master. "5 Low-Cost Social Media Marketing Strategies for Authors." *Mashable Business*, 4 Aug. 2012, mashable.com/2012/08/04/author-social -media/.

CaseStudiesOnline. "Jay-Z Teams Up with Bing to Dethrone Google for a Few Days." *Tod Mafin's CaseStudiesOnline.com*, 2011, www.casestudiesonline.com /jayz. Accessed 6 Aug. 2012.

Cerand, Lauren. "Network: How to Use Twitter to Connect with Readers." *Poets & Writers*, vol. 39, no. 4, July-Aug. 2011, 79.

- - -. "Social Media for Authors." *Poets &* Writers, vol. 39, no. 3, May-June 2011, pp. 71-76. Print.

Cohen, Gabriel. "A Social Approach: An Interview with Innovative Publisher Richard Nash." *Poets & Writers*, vol. 39, no. 6, Nov.-Dec. 2011, pp. 66-72.

Experian. "The 2012 Digital Marketer Trend and Benchmark Report." *Experian Marketing Services*, go.experian.com/forms/experian-digital-marketer-2012. Accessed 1 Aug. 2012.

Facebook. "Key Facts — Facebook Newsroom." *Facebook Newsroom*, newsroom
.fb.com/content/default.aspx?NewsAreaId=22. Accessed 20 Oct. 2013.

Goldfarb, Ronald. "What Writers Need to Know About Electronic Publishing."
The Writer's Chronicle, vol. 44, no.6, May-Summer, 2012, pp. 52-54.

hooks, bell. *Teaching to Transgress: Education as the Practice of Freedom*. Routledge,
1994, p. 8, p. 40.

Hopkins, Thomas Israel. "Network: How to Use LinkedIn to Connect with Your
Community." *Poets & Writer*, vol. 39, no. 6, Nov.-Dec. 2011, p. 107.

Kinzy, Dana, editor. *The 2006 Writing Teachers' Sourcebook*. U of Nebraska–Lincoln
Composition Program, 2006.

McLuhan, Marshall. *Understanding Media: The Extensions of Man*. MIT P, 1994.

McQuail, Denis. *Mass Communication Theory*. 6th ed., Sage, 2010, p. 542.

National Writing Project, and Carl Nagin. *Because Writing Matters: Improving
Student Writing in Our Schools*. Jossey-Bass, 2006, p. 47.

O'Reilley, Mary Rose. *The Peaceable Classroom*. Boynton/Cook, 1993, p. 30.

PBS Mediashift. "10 Social Media Tips for Authors." *PBS Mediashift*, 14 Feb.
2013, www.pbs.org/mediashift/2013/02/guy-kawasakis-10-social-media
-tips-for-authors045/.

Purcell, Kristen. "Teens 2012: Truth, Trends, and Myths About Teen Online
Behavior." Pew Research Center, 11 July 2012, www.pewinternet.org
/Presentations/2012/July/Teens-2012-Truth-Trends-and-Myths-About-Teen
-Online-Behavior.aspx. Slide presentation.

Sheehan, Kim, and Deborah Morrison. "The Creativity Challenge: Media Conflu-
ence and Its Effects on the Evolving Advertising Industry." *Journal of Interactive Advertising*, vol. 9, no. 2, 2009, pp. 40-43.

Shirky, Clay. *Here Comes Everybody: The Power of Organizing Without Organizations*. Penguin, 2008, p. 105.

Smith, Zadie. "Generation Why?" *The Best American Essays 2011*. Edited by
Edwidge Danticat and Robert Atwan, Mariner, 2011, pp. 185-99.

Socialnomics. "Social Marketing: The Spokes to the American Cancer Society
Hub, Interview with Karen Rose." *Socialnomics Case Studies*, Dec. 2011, www
.socialnomics.net/2011/12/27/social-marketing-the-spokes-to-the-american
-cancer-society-hub-interview-with-karen-rose/.

University of Nebraska–Lincoln. "General Education at UNL: Achievement-
Centered Education (ACE)." *General Education at UNL*, Jan. 2008, ace.unl
.edu.

University of Nebraska–Lincoln, Department of English. "English 101 Aims and
Scope — Writing: Rhetoric and Reading." *UNL*, Fall 2009.

2

Writing on the Wall: Using Facebook's Timeline for Literary Analysis

Jennifer Parrott
Clayton State University

Jennifer Parrott earned her PhD in English from Southern Illinois University Carbondale. She specialized in Irish studies with a focus in contemporary Irish fiction and drama. She holds an MA in English from DePaul University and a BA in English from Furman University. Her research interests include portrayals of domestic life in contemporary Irish drama, representations of post–Celtic Tiger Ireland, and technology in composition and literature classrooms. Parrott taught first-year composition at the Georgia Institute of Technology for four years. Additionally, she worked on a digital scholarship initiative at Bucknell University through a postdoctoral fellowship from the Council of Library and Information Resources. She is assistant professor of English at Clayton State University. Her teaching interests include the rhetoric of food, travel literature, and contemporary Irish literature.

COURTESY OF
JENNIFER PARROTT

1. OVERVIEW

- **Assignment:** Students conduct a group literary analysis project using Facebook.
- **Courses:** Introduction to literature; literature survey; themes in literature; composition; courses that incorporate multimodal assignments.
- **Literature:** Short fiction or other literature.
- **Technology:** Facebook.
- **Time:** Can be conducted in a single class period or extended over one to two weeks.

2. GOALS OF THE ASSIGNMENT

After completing this assignment, students will be able to

- use Facebook to create a supplement to works of literature;
- work collaboratively with peers in the construction of this social network;

21

- understand the sociohistorical context of a literary text and translate that context into social media;
- analyze the relationships among narrative, identity, and social media;
- discuss issues of public and private spaces in relation to social media; and
- generate project statements and other artifacts demonstrating student reflection on the process.

"Facebook allows students to connect with unfamiliar material using familiar technology, to consider the private and public identities of literary characters, and to think about the complex issues surrounding their own public identities in the digital age."

Jennifer Parrott
Clayton State University

3. ASSIGNMENT SHEET

Writing on the Wall: Using Facebook's Timeline for Literary Analysis

Course: _____

Instructor: _____

Date: _____

Task: Working in groups of three, use Facebook to create a social network for the characters in one of our assigned texts. You may choose as many or as few of the characters as you wish to include in the network, but be sure to have logical reasons to support your choices. You will explain your character choices and the design and interactions of your network in a project statement (see description below); therefore, you should make decisions thoughtfully, and document your decision-making process, which will help you generate the content for the justification essay.

Materials: You will need a Facebook account for this assignment. You can create an account at www.facebook.com. If this is a problem for you, please contact me.

Instructions: If you need step-by-step instructions for creating a fictional character page for each character in the social network, see the final section of this handout.

Consider the following as you build your social network:

- **Start with the basics.** Consider the timeline for the various characters you will include in your social network, demarcating important events for each character. This will help you structure the characters' interactions and wall posts. Another good place to start is the information section, which allows you to input factual information about each character. Once you map out these basic elements, you can move to more advanced interactions.

- **Keep perspective in mind.** Be sure that your character's Facebook wall represents the character's perspective based on textual evidence. It is easy to impose your own perspective as an outside reader, but you should return to the text frequently for evidence of your character's take on an event or situation.

- **Use images and videos thoughtfully.** When posting images, make sure that you are either creating original images or using images that permit public use. You will need to cite all outside materials in your project statement.

- **Don't forget to "Like."** Be sure to consider pages that your character might Like.

- **Think carefully about language.** Is your character shy, bold, self-centered? How would he or she craft a public identity? Again, use evidence from the text to support your decisions.

(continued)

ASSIGNMENT SHEET *(continued)*

Project Statement: Along with the completed Facebook project, each group will submit a project statement that accomplishes two tasks:

1. **Explain the choices** that you made in creating the social network for your assigned text.

2. **Offer a reflection** on what you learned about the text through the creation of your social network.

Divide your project statement into distinct sections that deal with the following elements:

- **Overall Approach:** In this section, you should address the general principles governing the choices that you made. Why did you choose particular characters and events? Why did you exclude others?

- **Written Communication:** How did you determine each character's voice? Did you stick closely to the text, using quotations, or did you modernize it to appeal to a modern audience? What about decisions regarding spelling and grammar? Did you consider the character's education level and dialect, or did you standardize these elements for your audience?

- **Visual Rhetoric:** Discuss your decisions regarding the visual aspects of the assignment. Did you create your own photos or use images from Creative Commons or another source? What is the significance of your cover photo? Did you choose historic images to include in your timeline? Why or why not? What led you to this decision and how do you think it affects your audience's understanding of the work?

- **Division of Labor:** How did your group distribute the work? Did each person assume the role of a character? How did you coordinate wall posts, messages, and so on? Did you work together in person or virtually? Why did you decide to approach the project in this way? Which aspects of this approach were successful, and which would you change? Finally, for which aspects of the project was each group member responsible?

- **Logistical Challenges:** How did you handle challenges related to the Timeline or the restrictions of Facebook Pages? What about cultural references and Likes? Did you try to keep these simple and consistent with what would have been possible for characters during the period in which the work is set, or did you present characters as you believe they would have presented themselves if they existed during the Facebook age? Explain your decisions thoroughly. Finally, what other challenges did you face and how did you overcome them?

STEP-BY-STEP INSTRUCTIONS FOR CREATING CHARACTER PAGES ON FACEBOOK

1. Create a fictional character page on Facebook for each character that you plan to include in the social network.
2. Log in to your Facebook account and scroll to the bottom of your home page, where you will see the option to Create a Page. Or go to www .facebook.com/pages/create.php.
3. Choose Artist, Band, or Public Figure.
4. From the drop-down menu choose Fictional Character.
5. Enter the character's name, agree to the terms, and click Get Started.
6. Now you can begin to create your page.

4. TIME AND TECHNOLOGY

TIME. This assignment can be done in one class period or over the course of one to two weeks.

TECHNOLOGY. At a minimum, students will need a computer or smartphone, Internet access, and a Facebook account. If the project is completed in class, students will need laptops or other computer access within the classroom. Beyond that, a working knowledge of Facebook is helpful but not required, as it is easy enough to put any Facebook outliers in groups with students who are more comfortable using it. Furthermore, fresh perspectives on Facebook's interface are actually welcome — they provide refreshing new insights on how to best use the site and how to reflect the characters and events being explored.

FACEBOOK PAGE CREATION. The Create a Page button allows users to set up pages for a variety of real and imagined figures. In modeling the creation of this page for your class, you can easily demonstrate any lesser-known aspects of the Timeline that you would like students to engage with in their projects, or point out some of the limitations that are put on pages created for fictional characters. Similarly, you can explain any suspension of disbelief (see the "Anticipating Student Needs" section) in which you might ask students to engage.

Facebook's Timeline feature allows students to recreate the identities of their characters using a variety of options.

Status Updates. The use of Status Updates gives students a forum in which specific scenes, conversations, and events from within the text can play out in real time. By engaging in conversations through and within these updates, multiple characters can participate in explicating key events from the text. These interactions create a unique perspective from which students can explore the psychologies of their characters. Furthermore, the unfolding of these updates over time allows students to demonstrate character development throughout the course of a text.

Friends. In a group project where students create a number of character profiles and timelines, it is possible for them to thoughtfully select how and to what extent various characters interact with each other. Logistically, since they are set up as Pages (rather than Accounts), characters have to be Friends to interact at all on Facebook, which can open up a discussion about social circles (or as our students might know them, "frenemies") and the politics of Friending, Blocking, and Unfriending. While some of these choices are unavailable to character pages, students must find other ways to demonstrate antipathy among characters.

Photos/Videos. Facebook's photo feature allows students to upload images associated with characters, authors, and historical events. These images can be arranged in specific order, and students can use scale to demonstrate significance with the use of the Cover option. Choosing a cover photo is a particularly important decision for students, as it provides the public face of the characters' Timelines. This section also allows substantial space for creativity, as students can reimagine their characters in the twenty-first century by filming scenes or staging photo shoots in an attempt to either recreate period dress according to information from the text, or to imagine how the characters would dress and talk if they existed in the twenty-first century.

Linking to or uploading videos is also possible within the Timeline. In the past, I have had students create their own photos and videos where they adopt the guises of the characters. Students have fun acting out scenes, either for still photos or videos, and the process allows them to think concretely about the logistics of situations and the characters' appearances, style of dress, and verbal and nonverbal communication styles. This would also be an excellent opportunity for students to develop the technical skills required in video and photo editing.

Info. The information section of a character's Profile provides an opportunity to engage with a variety of concrete facts and information about that character. The elements presented in the Info section include: Basic Info (birthday, sex, religious views, political views, languages), Work and Education, History by Year, About You (similar to a Twitter bio, this is a general statement about the character that is visible to all viewers), Living (this section allows students to trace where the character lived at various points), Relationship Status ("It's Complicated" is a perennial favorite), and Favorite Quotations.

Cumulatively, the Info section provides an opportunity for students to identify concrete elements of a character's life and consider how those would be presented using the categories provided by Facebook. Additionally, in certain instances it provides an opportunity to discuss the limitations of those options (the strict male/female distinction would be interesting to teach with Virginia Woolf's *Orlando*, for example).

Students can decide which elements a character would choose to fill out in his/her Profile and what information the character would state there. For example, characters might not state their political affiliations if they are living in a time when doing so might endanger them. Similarly, characters engaged in illicit behavior would not present that on their information page, though we might find evidence of it in other private communication methods; for example, one character may expose another by tagging him/her in an incriminating photo or posting on the character's wall.

Likes. Because of Facebook's billion-plus users, pages exist for nearly every person, place, or entity that students can imagine. Deciding what their characters would Like (the capital *L* here is important, of course, because like nearly every aspect of Facebook, the decision to Like something is a public, political act) provides students with another avenue for considering identity construction and presentation in a public space. The Profile also includes places to list a variety of Favorites, including books, activities, admired individuals, sports, movies, and music.

Events. Planning Events is a way for students to enact plot points from the text that are difficult or impossible to cover through Status Updates. The invitation or exclusion of various characters demonstrates an awareness of interaction among multiple perspectives, and the ability to schedule Events at specific times provides one of the most concrete ways to represent plot points unfolding over a range of time.

Milestones. Creating Milestones is one of the most direct ways that students can present information from the lives of their characters. While status updates allow students to enact events as they are occurring, Milestones give them the opportunity to explore and present a broad range of time in the lives of their characters.

5. ANTICIPATING STUDENT NEEDS

Unless you are working with contemporary texts, there is a certain anachronistic element to this assignment. Obviously Facebook is a fairly recent technological innovation, so students must willingly suspend their disbelief in imagining characters from previous centuries posting their statuses online for their friends to read. With that being said, I find that students typically enjoy this element, because it allows creative license and opens up exciting discussions. It is interesting to consider, for example, how characters from Victorian texts would present themselves; might Facebooking have been an inherently subversive act at that time, or would the Victorian culture have been as drawn to it as we are?

One logistical problem that can be difficult to overcome is that Facebook's Timeline only allows users to go back to 1800. As a result, if your students are working with texts set prior to the nineteenth century, viewers will have to suspend their disbelief in the dates that events are tagged, and the group will be forced to be creative in finding ways to reflect events within those limitations.

The most significant logistical problem, though, is that students are creating Pages, rather than Accounts. In other words, they are not creating wholly new Facebook identities (which is not allowed), and there are a variety of limitations placed on the Pages that they can create. Pages do not give users the option to send private messages to other characters, which limits private, character-to-character communication. This is frustrating because those exchanges would provide a way to distinguish between public and private interactions. Additionally, other features (like inviting other characters to Events) are limited in terms of their functionality when creating links between two characters. The limitations, however, provide opportunities for students to be creative in finding ways to work within the parameters, and it opens up an avenue for an interesting discussion about why the Pages are limited in these ways.

Furthermore, students are essentially functioning in an administrative role in relation to their character Pages. On one hand, this is negative because it prevents them from slipping completely into the identity of their characters and limits some of the page-to-page interactions with other characters. On the other hand, by functioning in an administrative capacity, students are empowered as advanced users of a technology and inclined to think metacognitively about constructing Pages and the limitations and opportunities that it provides. This also provides a great space to discuss Privacy settings and other advanced features.

By scrolling to the bottom of the Timelines, students can access a menu of links, including Privacy, which provides a convenient opportunity to discuss issues of how to monitor who can access which elements of a character's Profile, how to determine whether something is or is not appropriate to post on Facebook, and how to maintain control of their identity. For example, it would be appropriate to have a discussion about privacy controls. For a character it might make sense for students to allow Friends to tag the character in a photo, but it might be worth discussing the potential problems in giving that permission for a student's personal Page. Similarly, this project provides an opportunity to discuss issues of copyright and fair use, particularly how to use sites such as Flickr and Creative Commons, and develop strategies for conducting searches that yield images that students can use without violating copyright.

A final difficulty is that Facebook is constantly changing. Part of why Facebook has remained the dominant social media site is because of their executives' willingness to embrace large structural changes. Despite the possibility that Facebook will overhaul the Timeline structure in the years ahead, the good news is that it now seems committed to retaining this sort of imaginative and potentially pedagogical functionality. Specific instructions for creating Pages, in addition to the list of available options for those Pages, will have to be updated as Facebook continues to evolve.

6. ASSESSMENT TOOLS

Because most students have a high level of familiarity with Facebook, I have high expectations for the quality of these projects. While the focus and scope will likely play some part in determining the point value and expectations in each of the following categories, these are the key areas to consider when grading these projects:

- **Accuracy of Their Facebook Character Profiles and Timeline:** At a minimum, students need to present the available information for the characters in the About and Information sections. Completing this section ensures that students understand the concrete details of the plot.

- **Quality of Textual Insights:** I look for students to use the available features to make clear insights into the characters and the events of the texts. Students should read beyond what is explicitly stated in the text, making arguments about the characters through the choices they make in creating their profiles and interactions.

- **Number of Facebook Tools Incorporated in Project and Depth of Usage:** Students should engage with a variety of tools at their disposal, though there should also be depth. Particularly for projects that take a significant amount of time and have several people working on them, the social network created among these characters should be rich and interesting.

- **Creativity of Interactions and Use of Tools:** Students are constantly surprising me in terms of how they incorporate various aspects of Facebook into their projects. Furthermore, the constant reinvention of Facebook will make these innovative responses continue to evolve each time you assign the project.

- **Consistent Representation of Characters and Events:** Students can choose to represent a character faithfully, using quotations from the text for posts, they can modify the quotations slightly, or they can choose to modify the language to address a contemporary Facebook audience. Either way, students should consistently represent characters across a text.

- **Project Statement:** Students are graded on the depth and quality of their project statement, as well as the technical aspects of the writing. I explain the project statement as the students' opportunity to demonstrate how carefully they thought about the construction of their page. I encourage them to clearly explain all of their major decisions regarding the construction of the character within the Facebook platform.

7. THEORETICAL BASIS FOR THE ASSIGNMENT:
Writing on the Wall: Using Facebook's Timeline for Literary Analysis

Regardless of whether you appreciate its pedagogical potential, Facebook has more than a billion users and is impossible to ignore. As you may have experienced in your own classrooms, it is difficult to engage your students in a rich discussion of a literary text while they are smiling at their screens, typing short messages, pausing briefly, and typing again. With Facebook-blue reflected in their eyes, the smiles clearly call out those students not taking notes on the discussion. Any instructor with even the least bit of teaching experience will recognize those students who are on Facebook, chatting with their friends or posting status updates about their thoughts on any number of topics, though likely not those related to class. As a result, Facebook has been explicitly banned from many college classrooms, including mine.

But no longer. As more and more educators are tuning in to the ways in which Facebook and other social media can enhance what happens in the classroom, more blog posts, articles, and tweets are appearing with ideas about how we, as instructors, can use Facebook to connect with our students. We can do this by answering their questions, reminding them of deadlines, linking to relevant resources and events, and encouraging them to collaborate on academic projects outside class time. While most strategies for incorporating Facebook into the classroom address how to create a page that functions as some version of a course management system—which can be very helpful—the focus of the assignment I've presented here (see p. 23) and this essay, is how and why to use Facebook, particularly the Timeline feature, as a way to engage students in literary analysis.

The assignment presented in this chapter asks students to use Facebook to create a social network that will serve as a supplementary guide to a specified literary text. What they create will be used by students in my course in future semesters. I have students work in small groups of two to five, depending on the class size, literary work, and scale of the assignment, to create character profiles and interactions for the assigned text. Part of my goal for this assignment is to give students a specific rhetorical context for their work: they are being asked to write and design for a specific academic audience—future students of the course. Likewise, students are asked to think in terms of any contextual information they wish they had known during their initial reading of a literary work, such as author, setting, historical period, and character background.

Furthermore, the existence of these Facebook character Profiles outside of the literature classroom, in the larger virtual environment (they can be viewed and Liked by anyone, unless they are created in a way that doesn't allow for public viewing), gives the project a life beyond the classroom. Students' classmates, relatives, friends, and other audience members may view and discuss students' Facebook projects. This factor ups the enthusiasm and comfort level for my students. This effect would be hard to replicate through traditional projects. Further, Facebook functions as a learning tool, providing a common ground for multiple generations of users.

> "The existence of these Facebook character profiles gives the project a life beyond the classroom."
>
> **Jennifer Parrott**

This assignment grew out of a multimodal, literature-themed composition course that I developed at Georgia Tech.[1] Our topic was the haunted figure in Irish literature, and we used the university's WOVEN (Written, Oral, Visual, Electronic, and Nonverbal) approach to communication. I developed this assignment to give students the opportunity to choose one literary text and explore it in depth; the assignment also provides students with the opportunity to develop strategies for communication in written, visual, and electronic modes.

Initially, the assignment allowed each group to choose which technology/social media site students would use to create a student guide to one of our course texts, which consisted of contemporary British and Irish drama. Facebook was a popular option, and the groups that used it had varying success in terms of taking advantage of the site's features to examine the text and its context more closely. At this point I recognized that Facebook had potential as a tool in the literature classroom, but that students needed more guidance on how to use it for academic purposes. As I was revising the assignment to require the use of Facebook, the company released the Timeline feature, which is a fantastic tool that allows students to visualize events from the plot of a literary work, author's life, or historical period. This version of the assignment transforms the use of Facebook from an electronic version of a character sketch to a forum for analyzing characters, their interactions, significant plot developments, and the sociohistorical context of the literary work.

The January 2013 volume of *PMLA* presented a series of short essays, under "The Changing Profession" subheading, in which authors discussed aspects of "Reading in the Digital Age." Michael Cobb's "A Little Like Reading: Preference, *Facebook*, and Overwhelmed Interpretations" focuses on the Like button as being particularly relevant to Facebook's impact on reading: "[L]ikes are not quite random. People have generated these items, these virtual objects of interest, for rapid public consumption and, with the ubiquity of the Like button, for rapid public response. . . . Whatever our motivations or the nature of our interest in what we curate for the world on

---

[1]See the Georgia Tech Writing and Communication Program's Web site for more information: wcprogram.lmc.gatech.edu.

Facebook, these objects for consumption often go under the heading of like" (202). Concluding that Facebook and Twitter leave users "adrift at sea in the immediate," Cobb describes the process of constructing identity through Facebook likes: "the likable Facebook object is an object that has been taken out of context, forced into our feeds. And more often than not we attach the likable object to the Facebook subject who brought it to our attention" (202). Thus, when we ask students to consider these issues from the perspective of literary characters, we invite them to apply social media behaviors in an entirely new context. By considering what Dorian Gray would "like," how he would present himself, who he would interact with, students think about the literature from a different and important vantage point.

What this assignment essentially asks students to do is translate: students translate literary texts into a new medium, and this act of translation is particularly valuable for them, because (a) social and digital media are always asking us to do this and (b) it provides them with a familiar language to discuss often difficult and unfamiliar literary perspectives. Jim Collins discusses the complicated tension between public and private discourse that is at work in the shift from private reading (in the form of a book) to semipublic reading (in the form of an e-book): "This transformation has profound ramifications for how we imagine the act of reading because it foregrounds the interplay between socialization and intimacy, between public and private cultural space. As readers, we can engage in social networking, but we are also curators of our own archives, which have become a medium of personal expression that subsumes reading, watching, listening, and collecting" (211). Facebook pages and Twitter feeds function as similarly liminal cultural spaces, at the meeting point of public and private. Both Collins and Cobb find these spaces to be valuable sites of tension to explore in scholarship and in the classroom.

> "This assignment asks students to translate: students translate literary texts into a new medium, and this act of translation is particularly valuable for them, because (a) social and digital media are always asking us to do this and (b) it provides them with a familiar language to discuss often difficult and unfamiliar literary perspectives."
>
> **Jennifer Parrott**

Many educators have had successful experiences bringing Facebook into the classroom. Paulette Stewart, for example, describes the use of literature circles within Facebook to have collaborative reading experiences. Allen Webb's book *Teaching Literature in Virtual Worlds: Immersive Learning in English Studies* presents a series of case studies in teaching literature through digital media. Robert Rozema describes a series of classroom activities designed to allow students to act out *Brave New World* in discussion boards and other digital spaces. He lists Facebook as one of the technologies commonly believed to be preventing learning, arguing that these technologies would be wisely repositioned with the goal of "creating a *secondary world* that goes beyond the details provided by the text" because "readers *must* create this world if they are to understand the text at all" (84).

Ultimately, asking students to translate or recreate a literary work in the world of Facebook addresses all levels of Bloom's Revised Taxonomy: students are reviewing the content or plot of the literary works, demonstrating their understanding of these works, applying this understanding to the creation of their chosen character(s) in the Facebook Profile, and then analyzing the characters in order to recreate them in their Facebook Profiles. The assignment appeals to both visual and kinesthetic learners as students assume the role of a character and actively engage with the other characters from the chosen work in order to create a complete Profile and Timeline.

8. CONCLUSION

My goal for this assignment is to encourage students to think deeply about narrative, identity, and social media, and the relationship among these elements. Since I often teach Irish literary texts in first-year college composition classes, my students generally don't have background knowledge of the texts that we read. Therefore, I regularly design projects that have students use a familiar technology as a pathway into texts that are likely unfamiliar.

Additionally, this assignment gives students the opportunity to contextualize the events of a literary work within the sociohistorical conditions under which it was written and set. Using Facebook's Timeline feature, students can create posts that include relevant historical and biographical events. These events may affect their interpretation of the work and enable them to consider the work in a broader context. When students explore the typically difficult Irish literary texts that we read, or delve into complicated, unsettling historical details of Ireland's relationship with England, the familiarity of Facebook counterbalances any inherent timidity. In other words, most students feel so comfortable using Facebook that they forget to be intimidated by the literature and history. As a result, their expertise often manifests itself in thoughtful projects. Because students already know how to use Facebook and its features—the Timeline, the commenting and Liking, the posting of updates, links, photos, videos, and more—and they also understand how and why others use these features, it's fairly easy for them to transfer their knowledge of a text from the physical page to the Profile page.

> "Most students feel so comfortable using Facebook that they forget to be intimidated by the literature and history. As a result, their expertise often manifests itself in thoughtful projects."
>
> **Jennifer Parrott**

9. WORKS CITED

Cobb, Michael. "A Little Like Reading: Preference, *Facebook*, and Overwhelmed Interpretations." *PMLA: Publications of the Modern Language Association of America*, vol. 128, no. 1, Jan. 2013, pp. 207-12, *www.mlajounals.org/toc /pmla/128/1*.

Collins, Jim. "Reading, in a Digital Archive of One's Own." *PMLA: Publications of The Modern Language Association of* America, vol. 128, no. 1, Jan. 2013, pp. 207-12, *www.mlajounals.org/toc/pmla/128/1*.

Georgia Institute of Technology. *Writing and Communication Program*. School of Literature, Media, and Communication, wcprogram.lmc.gatech.edu. Accessed 29 Oct. 2013.

Rozema, Robert. "Building a Secondary *Brave New World.*" *Teaching Literature in Virtual Worlds: Immersive Learning in English Studies*. Edited by Allen Webb, Routledge, 2012, books.google.com/books/about/Teaching_Literature_in _Virtual_Worlds.html?id=3p3HBQAAQBAJ.

Stewart, Paulette. "Facebook and Virtual Literature Circle Partnership in Building a Community of Readers." *Knowledge Quest*, vol. 37, no. 4, 2009, *The Learning and Technology Library*, www.learntechlib.org/j/ISSN-1094/v/37/n/4.

Webb, Allen. *Teaching Literature in Virtual Worlds: Immersive Learning in English Studies*. Routledge, 2012. *Google Books*, books.google.com/books/about /Teaching_Literature_in_Virtual_Worlds.html?id=3p3HBQAAQBAJ.

3

Wiki Critical Editions: Collaborative Learning in the Literature Classroom

Angela Laflen
Marist College

Angela Laflen, PhD, is an associate professor of English at Marist College. She teaches in the areas of literature and gender, digital writing, and technical communication. Her published work focuses on online pedagogy, visual rhetoric, and gender issues. Laflen is author of *Confronting Visuality in Multi-Ethnic Women's Literature* (Palgrave Macmillan; forthcoming) and coeditor of *Gender Scripts in Medicine and Narrative* (2010).

COURTESY ANGELA LAFLEN

1. OVERVIEW

- **Assignment:** Students collaborate and contribute to a wiki critical edition or wiki annotated version of a literary text.
- **Courses:** Introduction to literature; literature and composition.
- **Literature:** Any short piece of literature or literary excerpt, particularly if the text is available on the Internet.
- **Technology:** Wiki software (for example using a course management system, such as Blackboard, that includes wikis or Wikispaces).
- **Time:** Can be conducted in one to four course periods of seventy-five minutes each or extended over a full semester.

2. GOALS OF THE ASSIGNMENT

- Situate a literary text in relevant social and historical contexts.
- Conduct Internet research to locate relevant secondary sources of information and cite the sources properly in MLA style.
- Discuss a literary text and secondary texts closely and clearly in writing.

- Gain experience using a wiki to produce course content in collaboration with classmates.
- Practice writing constructive and critical comments in a digital forum.

"Experimenting with new technologies and techniques in the literature classroom is an important way I relate to my students. They get a chance to see me — sometimes struggling, sometimes succeeding — learn something new, and I gain a helpful reminder about the difficulties and rewards they are facing as they confront new ideas and read unfamiliar texts."

Angela Laflen
Marist College

3. ASSIGNMENT SHEET

Wiki Critical Editions: Collaborative Learning in the Literature Classroom

Course: _____

Instructor: _____

Date: _____

Illuminating *Eurydice* Assignment

Medieval scholars created "illuminated manuscripts" by adding images to their manuscripts. You might be familiar with "critical editions" of well-known and important literary works that do something similar by providing additional information alongside the literary text. This additional information might define key terms, provide biographical or historical context, or sometimes include maps or images. The idea is that the extra material can help you to better understand the text. Even better than reading these notes, though, is adding them to the text yourself to give you a deeper understanding and appreciation for a piece of literature.

For this assignment, we will work together to create a wiki critical edition of Ovid's *Eurydice*. You are probably familiar with wikis from visiting *Wikipedia*, but our wiki will be quite different. Rather than writing encyclopedia-style entries, we will work together to define important terms in the poem, identify interesting phrases or passages and consider what they mean, add images that might help us visualize parts of the poem, and consider how feminist poets have reworked parts of the Eurydice story in their writing.

We will go over in class how exactly to add annotations and comments to the wiki, but for the assignment, you will add at least 5 annotations to the text of Ovid's *Eurydice*. You will also add comments to at least 3 of your classmates' annotations.

Your annotations should be well developed and well focused. Don't just include a link to an image or external link; instead, explain in 1–2 developed paragraphs how the link or image you reference relates to the poem. Provide some context for your sources and explain how they "illuminate" *Eurydice* for the reader. How do we understand *Eurydice* better from reading/viewing the text alongside these notes?

Your comments on your classmates' posts should also be thoughtful and thorough. The goal is to engage one another's ideas and to further expand on those ideas in writing. We will discuss some guidelines to use in responding to one another in class, but you should avoid simply complimenting your classmates' annotations and really respond to them by asking questions, adding additional information, or making connections between annotations on the wiki.

Assignment Resources

There are a number of resources available to you online to help you write interesting and well-informed annotations.

Several feminist revisions of the Eurydice story are freely available on the Internet.

"Eurydice" by H.D.
www.poetryfoundation.org/archive/poem.html?id=182485

"Orpheus and Eurydice" by Jorie Graham
www.poemhunter.com/poem/orpheus-and-eurydice/

Please remember to cite them properly when you use them in writing an annotation.

I also want you to gain experience working with some of the resources available online through the college library. I have listed some of the most relevant resources available below. Please note that you will need to be logged in to the college library to access most of these sources. If you receive a notice asking you to pay for any of these resources, that means you aren't logged in properly. You can use other resources available through the college library as well.

Image Banks (be sure you use images legally on the course wiki): *Oxford Art Online, Art Images for College Teaching, Flickr Commons, The Library of Congress Prints & Photographs Reading Room*, *Pics4Learning, Smithsonian Institution, U.S. Government Graphics and Photos*

Dictionaries: *New Oxford American Dictionary* and the *Oxford English Dictionary*

Encyclopedias: *The Cambridge History of English and American Literature* or *Encyclopedia Britannica Online*

Grading

For the purposes of grading, please copy and paste your annotations and your comments in a .doc file and print this out to submit in class. I will read the wiki while grading, but this will allow me to have a hard copy on which to add my own comments and feedback. Your annotations and comments to the wiki will be graded based on how thorough they are, how well you have developed them with specific details, and on their grammatical and stylistic correctness. I will use the following grading sheet to evaluate and provide feedback on your project.

Wiki Critical Edition Grading Sheet

Annotations: *At least 5* annotations are required.	Excellent	Good	Fair	Poor	Failing/ Incomplete
Thorough: The annotations you added provide detail about the historical, artistic, critical, or literary connection, and explain clearly how each connection helps us better understand *Eurydice*.					
Accurate: External sources are incorporated so that the source for details is clear, and the sources are credible.					
Correctly formatted: Your annotations are formatted correctly in wiki style and are free of grammatical errors. External sources are correctly cited in MLA format.					

Comments: *At least 3* substantive comments are required.	Excellent	Good	Fair	Poor	Failing/ Incomplete
Comments: The comments you added are *constructive and critical*, and help *advance online discussion* of *Eurydice*. Questions, connections, and positive critique are all acceptable.					

Final Grade: _____

Overall Comment: _____

4. TIME AND TECHNOLOGY

TIME. Creating a wiki critical edition has the potential to run for an entire semester or just a single course period. In my course, I dedicate one 75-minute class period to this assignment, and then follow up on it during three subsequent classes, though only for about 15–20 minutes. This assignment runs over the course of eleven days (it is assigned on Monday of the first week and annotations and comments are due by Thursday of the second week). It has been helpful to break the project into several steps.

During the first course period, it is ideal if students have a chance to work together in a computer classroom where they can be introduced to the wiki platform. During this time, you should show students how to add links using the wiki software, and you can discuss the kinds of material that would be suitable to include in a wiki critical edition, perhaps by bringing in strong examples of print critical editions. This is a good opportunity to discuss the credibility of Internet sources and to direct students to high-quality online sources as well as to discuss using images from the Internet in legally and ethically appropriate ways. I introduce the assignment during this course period as well, and students sometimes begin adding annotations to the text during the class.

During the following class, after students have begun posting annotations on their own, I set aside a few minutes to look at the wiki critical edition. I discuss which annotations are particularly well written or effective and discuss ways the students can expand on the annotations, other ideas for annotating the text, and any challenges they are having. There is no need to work in a computer classroom for this review; simply projecting the wiki critical edition from a classroom computer station or a laptop is sufficient.

By the third class — approximately one week after the assignment is given — students should finish posting their annotations so they can spend the remaining two–three days posting comments on one another's annotations. During this third class period, I show them how to add comments to a wiki, and this is a good time to discuss what kinds of comments are useful and constructive. Writing effective comments is increasingly important in online communication and can be challenging for students, who often want to simply compliment one another's writing and stop with "good job."

Finally, students compile their annotations and comments into a .doc file to print and submit in the fourth class period or submit via an online course management system. This makes grading much easier and ensures that I have a stable version of the annotations for grading and don't overlook any annotations.

TECHNOLOGY. This assignment requires a computer with a Web browser and access to wiki software, which is easily and freely available online if it is not provided by your university. Other required resources include a digital version of the text of the literary work(s) to be annotated and directions to any supplemental materials students should consult to write their annotations. This assignment also requires you to create and organize the wiki prior to introducing the assignment. More details about these requirements follow.

Wikis can be created using software provided by a college or university or by using a course management system (such as Blackboard) that includes wikis, but Wikispaces (www.wikispaces.com) is another popular choice for college instructors. The assignment can be completed on students' laptops, their personal computers at home, or in computer labs. I often use this assignment in a fully online course in which students never meet face-to-face, and because editing a wiki is so easy and often familiar to students, they require very little coaching in the actual use of the wiki, so most of the instruction focuses on the content of the assignment.

The assignment also requires you to create and set up the wiki prior to introducing the assignment to students. Students should find the text(s) to be already annotated on the wiki: it is helpful for you to add one or two annotations as models of the depth and quality of response expected of students.

This assignment requires the text of the work to be annotated. In many cases, text is available online. In my course, students annotate the text of Ovid's *Eurydice*, and the text of the poem is available online from the Internet Classics Archive (classics.mit.edu/Ovid/metam.10.tenth.html). When choosing texts to work with for this assignment it is important to choose ones you can find online or to factor in time for typing in the text yourself.

I also direct students to supplemental materials they should consult to write their annotations. For the critical edition of *Eurydice* these include feminist revisions of the Eurydice story, along with the dictionaries, encyclopedias, and image banks outlined in the Assignment Sheet on pp. 38 and 39.

For other types of literature, it might be helpful to include links to map banks, census data, alternative translations, or other online or print resources, depending on the work being annotated. You could also allow students to use freely available Internet resources including Google Books, *Wikipedia*, and *Dictionary.com*.

5. ANTICIPATING STUDENT NEEDS

In addition to the challenge of providing critical feedback on student contributions to a wiki critical edition, the other potential difficulty of using a wiki critical edition stems from the issue of how open the wiki will be to the public, a question that requires you to consider what kind of community you want to foster in the classroom. You have the option of making a course wiki open to the public or keeping it private, and, if the wiki is public, of determining whether it will be open to editing by the public or restricted to class members with a password. There is no clear consensus on which type of wiki is better for instructional purposes. Matt Barton argues, for instance, that an "ideal wiki" must be open since this is what makes wikis unique from other classroom technologies. He suggests that "the further you get from the ideal wiki . . . , the further you get from the 'wiki way' and the very features that make wikis exciting in the first place. Therefore, quit trying to make wikis do what you could do under the old paradigms, and try instead to think of ways to use 'pure wikis' effectively."

Natalie Jeremijenko, a faculty member in the Department of Visual Arts at UC San Diego, uses a public wiki called "How Stuff Is Made" in her courses. Her students visit factories — from fortune cookie bakeries to Toyota Prius plants — and observe how products are made. They then post photo essays about the manufacturing process to the HSIM site. Many of the students contact the manufacturers and invite them to read and even edit their articles. Jeremijenko finds educational value in public wikis because they can be used to get students involved in actively creating knowledge while holding them accountable for the information that they publish (Murphy). However, she also acknowledges that at times the course wiki has been vandalized so severely that the university has had to "close" it temporarily (Murphy). Mark Phillipson avoided the problem of vandalism of the Romantic Audience Project wiki by restricting the ability to edit to only class members on his public course wiki, but he still suggests that public wikis "burden students with the exposure of their writing to readers having nothing to do with the class" (Phillipson and Hamilton). He reveals that after an initial use of the public wiki, he subsequently moved to a private wiki in future courses (Phillipson and Hamilton). Despite Barton's contention that only publicly available wikis are "pure wikis," Amit Ray and Erhardt Graeff suggest that whether a wiki is public or private, "the basic principle of providing access to shared documents remains intact irrespective of the specific wiki platform. The ability to read, compose, and edit content, whatever the constitution of the group, allows for a very different form of written expression to take shape" (46).

Since students in my Literature and Gender course are primarily non-English majors new to writing and discussing literature, I have always kept my wiki critical editions closed to the public. The wiki is therefore open only to the class for reading or posting. I would consider making the critical edition visible to the public for an advanced literature course to give my students experience writing for a public audience. However, in the lower-level literature and gender course I want to foster a sense of community among my students and to provide a low-risk space within which they can practice and develop their skills at written academic discussion.

6. ASSESSMENT TOOLS

The primary challenge of using a wiki in class is offering students critical feedback on their work. Unless an instructor wants to add comments directly within the wiki, making the evaluative comments public to the class, there is no easy way to comment directly on a student's writing, which can be a serious obstacle to classroom use. To deal with this challenge, I ask students to copy and paste their annotations into a .doc to submit separately in class. Although I read the wiki while grading the annotations, having a hard copy of the students' annotations allows me to add comments during grading and to keep these comments private. If someone does use a completely inaccurate source or introduces some major inaccuracy I will post a comment on the wiki itself noting that other students should be wary of the information. I grade annotations and comments to the wiki based on how thorough they are, how well students have developed them with specific details, and on their grammatical and stylistic correctness, and I use the grading rubric included with the Assignment Sheet (see p. 40) to ensure that I address these points for each student.

> "The primary challenge of using a wiki in class is offering students critical feedback on their work."
>
> **Angela Laflen**

An alternative to having students submit their annotations separately is to use the history function of the wiki to track individual contributions. This is much more time-consuming for you, but wiki software does keep track of every edit saved to the wiki. In fact, this is how you can deal with accidents to the wiki as well. On occasion, I have had students accidentally delete all the content on the wiki. When that happens, I simply use the history function to revert to a previously saved version of the wiki. The history function makes it impossible for anyone to destroy a wiki; this is how *Wikipedia* and other public wikis handle vandalism as well.

7. THEORETICAL BASIS FOR THE ASSIGNMENT:
Wiki Critical Editions: Collaborative Learning in the Literature Classroom

Instructors new to wikis often wonder why they would choose to use a wiki in the classroom, questioning what advantages a wiki offers over a blog or an online discussion forum. Wikis differ from these other tools most obviously due to their fluidity and openness; whereas blogs and discussion forums allow instructors to tailor the tools for their specific courses and activities in very limited ways, wikis can seem infinitely malleable. Consequently, instructors can use them in any number of ways to facilitate course activities. However, most often, instructors choose to use wikis in the classroom because they foster collaboration, and they facilitate collaborative projects that can be difficult, or even impossible, to manage without a wiki.

In fact, collaborative authoring is *the* defining characteristic of wikis, distinguishing them from other applications such as blogs. Most people are familiar with wikis because of *Wikipedia*, the world's largest and best-known wiki. Nevertheless, wikis are not limited to the encyclopedia style of *Wikipedia*. Created in 1995 by Oregon programmer Ward Cunningham, who named them for the Wiki-Wiki, or "quick," shuttle buses at the Honolulu Airport, wikis are special Web sites on which anyone can post material without knowing programming languages. Likewise, anyone can edit them. In the workplace, groups frequently use wikis to plan meetings or coordinate projects. Some communities have created public wikis that resemble travel guides, and in 2007 Penguin Books and De Montfort University sponsored "A Million Penguins," a wiki-novel project to which 1,500 writers contributed. [The project ended on March 7, 2007 and the site was vandalized.—Eds.] Although wikis vary greatly from one another, some fundamental characteristics that apply to most wikis include the following:

> "Collaborative authoring is *the* defining characteristic of wikis, distinguishing them from other applications like blogs."
>
> **Angela Laflen**

- Wikis use simplified hypertext markup language.
- Anyone can change anything.
- Linking within wiki pages is easy.
- Content is always evolving and never finished.

As wikis have become integrated into larger organizations, wiki systems have evolved to include functionality such as restricted access, private workspaces, hierarchical organization, WYSIWYG (what you see is what you get) Web editing, and integration with centralized content management systems.

Early wikis were intended for multiple users to create knowledge repositories, and wikis can facilitate any class or group project that does not require individual authorship or protected documents. The assignment discussed in this chapter draws on the strengths of wikis to foster collaboration by asking students to contribute to a wiki critical edition, or a collaboratively annotated literary text. Wikis are well suited to projects that involve annotation, and this project promotes close reading of literature, facilitates written discussion among students, and provides an opportunity for students to practice conducting online research. The fact that wikis facilitate group editing makes the assignment possible, and whether or not students actually collaborate with one another in writing specific annotations, they collaborate with one another by reading one another's annotations to avoid duplication and add comments, therefore engaging them in online written discussion.

I have used this assignment in a sophomore-level core literature course called Literature and Gender in which students created a critical edition of

Ovid's *Eurydice* via the course wiki. Most of the students in this course are nonmajors, and my goals for the assignment include performing close reading, practicing written discussion with classmates, and using quality online sources via the college library and on the Internet. I frame this assignment as low-risk for students since I see the assignment more as an opportunity to foster critical reading and writing skills than demonstrating mastery of those skills and because I don't want students new to using wikis to be anxious about using a new technology. It counts as a short paper assignment in my course in order to encourage students to take it seriously and write as clearly and correctly as possible, but it does not comprise the majority of points in my course and runs for only two weeks, or four course periods.

A wiki critical edition incorporates the text for analysis into the wiki itself, capitalizing on the ability of students to add hyperlinks to the text. Using a wiki, any word or phrase of a literary work can be turned into a link, and students can add their own written comments on the links. Student comments can also be linked to one another. One of the best-known wiki critical editions, the Romantic Audience Project wiki, was created by Mark Phillipson for use in his Romantic Literature course. Phillipson documented the project online and describes it as a "publicly staged discussion of poetry" (Phillipson and Hamilton). He points out that during this project, "a Keats sonnet, for example, was suddenly open to student intervention: the foregrounding of certain words, the linking of Keats's text to other material he may not have approved or foreseen, the 'manhandling' and 'interrupting' of a readerly text (Barthes 15)" (Phillipson and Hamilton). Additionally, "after they were posted, student entries were themselves prone to citation, linkage, and recontextualization" (Phillipson and Hamilton).

This "public staging" of literary analysis and the ability of students to link to one another's comments makes the wiki critical edition a particularly valuable tool in the literature classroom. In one of the few published articles focused on using wikis in literature classrooms, Jennifer Riddle Harding identifies this attribute of wikis as particularly beneficial for literature instruction. She suggests that too often students do not see the written work they do in a literature class as part of a larger conversation. They gain experience verbally conversing via class discussion, but they continue to see their written work as a private reflection or analysis intended only for the teacher and do not think of it in terms of participating in a larger scholarly conversation so as to improve their thinking skills. Harding contends that "technologies that approximate co-presence," such as wikis, "provide shared spaces that blend aspects of class discussion with writing" (134) and are characterized by the "capacity for a quick accumulation of words, in a shared space, formerly experienced mainly through face-to-face interaction or through a time-consuming process of collabora-

> "The 'public staging' of literary analysis and the ability of students to link to one another's comments makes the wiki critical edition a particularly valuable tool."
>
> **Angela Laflen**

tion" (134). This is valuable because it helps students to gain practice in conversing in academic contexts via written communication — something that compositionist Kenneth Bruffee has argued is important to helping students improve not only their writing, but also their critical thinking.[1]

8. CONCLUSION

In conclusion, wiki critical editions offer literature instructors a relatively easy way to help students generate knowledge for the course and to foster a sense of community and collaboration, without many of the headaches of traditional group projects. In doing so, they help instructors to approach wikis with a clear sense of purpose — something that is essential when using an open-ended and malleable instructional tool like a wiki, even as they give students the opportunity to develop what Stuart Selber has referred to as "rhetorical literacy" (25) by critically reflecting on the impact that digital technologies are having on the writing process and even what writing means.

For instructors, the strong sense of purpose provided by the wiki critical edition assignment can be invaluable. As Heather James observed in describing a "failed" wiki experiment, "Being so open, a wiki does not have any inherent properties that will instantly make a knowledge-building community. It depends not only on the software configuration — for example whether certain areas are locked or whether you make templates for layouts — but also on the social norms and practices around the wiki. In a classroom setting, this means the practice of the teacher, and the interactions of the students." Wikis have the potential to greatly benefit the classroom, but those benefits certainly aren't automatic or guaranteed simply by adding a wiki to a course. Although there may be no limit to the types of activities that wikis can facilitate, already it is clear that particular types of activities are well suited to wikis, and wikis can make possible assignments, such as wiki critical editions, that would be much more challenging to coordinate without the use of group editing software.

Moreover, the wiki critical edition assignment has usefully helped my students to reflect on the impact of digital technologies, wikis in particular, on writing and knowledge production. In their reflections on the assignment, my students invariably end up discussing how their experience has changed their view of the way information is created and disseminated online. As one student explained,

> For a long time I lived under the assumption that the word "wiki" was just short for *Wikipedia*. I never even considered the idea of becoming a contributor.

---

[1]Bruffee explains that thinking is linked to conversation and to understanding how to converse appropriately in the context of a specific community. According to this view, helping students to improve their conversational ability also helps to improve their thinking skills.

Wikipedia was a one-way information stream: I took facts in but never gave any back. This, of course, completely defeats the purpose of a wiki, but I never knew any better. Being a contributor to a wiki page brings a very different perspective. It has always been drilled into our heads that *Wikipedia* is nothing but a plague on the credibility of a research paper, but after becoming a contributor myself, that all seems a bit overdramatic. During the process of collectively editing the Eurydice critical edition, there were never any glaringly inaccurate contributions. By the time the project was finished, our class had turned the page into a very reliable guide to the poem.

> "In their reflections on the assignment, my students invariably end up discussing how their experience has changed their view of the way information is created and disseminated online."
> **Angela Laflen**

Also common is for students to reflect on how the collaborative nature of the project changes the experience of writing: "Writing on a wiki didn't even feel like 'writing.' It felt like I was contributing, or giving advice to someone, which I enjoy. I was adding on to other people's contributions and beginning thoughts for others to finish. It was a group effort. The things I was posting about also interested me."

The kind of self-consciousness that these students exhibit in reflecting on their experience of using the wiki gestures toward what Selber refers to as "rhetorical literacy," or reflective praxis (25). Selber suggests that while rhetorical literacy is a vital component of the type of digital literacy that contemporary students need in order to participate as productive digital citizens, to cultivate it students need opportunities to practice using technology in critical, academic contexts. The wiki critical edition assignment, despite the limited time it runs and its restricted scope, clearly has the ability to provide this kind of a valuable reflective opportunity for students as they not only learn to work together to produce course content but also consider the larger implications of producing knowledge in this way.

9. WORKS CITED

Barthes, Roland. *S/Z*. Translated by Richard Miller. Hill and Wang, 1974, p. 15.

Barton, Matt. "Embrace the Wiki Way." *The Matt Chat Blog*, 21 May 2004 and 1 Nov. 2013, mattchat.us/?p=322.

Bruffee, Kenneth. "Collaborative Learning and 'The Conversation of Mankind.'" *College English*, vol. 46, no. 7, Nov. 1984, pp. 635-52.

Graham, Jorie. "Orpheus and Eurydice." *Poem Hunter*, www.poemhunter.com /poem/orpheus-and-eurydice/.

Harding, Jennifer Riddle. "Extending the Classroom Space: Wikis, Online Discussions, and Short Fiction." *Eureka Studies in Teaching Short* Fiction, vol. 8, no. 1, 2007, pp. 131-38.

H. D. "Eurydice." *Poetry Foundation*, www.poetryfoundation.org/poem.html?id =182485. Accessed 9 Jan. 2012.

James, Heather. "My Brilliant Failure: Wikis in Classrooms." *Kairosnews: A Weblog for Discussing Rhetoric, Technology, and Pedagogy*, 21 May 2004, kairosnews .org/my-brilliant-failure-wikis-in-classrooms.

Murphy, Paula. "The Topsy-Turvy World of Wikis." U of California Office of the President, Apr. 2006, archive.is/FIIa.

Ovid. *Eurydice.* Internet Classics Archive, classics.mit/edu/Ovid/metam.10.tenth .html. Accessed 9 Jan. 2012.

Phillipson, Mark, and David Hamilton. "The Romantic Audience Project: A Wiki Experiment." *Romantic Circles*, U of Maryland, 1 Dec. 2004, www.rc.umd .edu/pedagogies/commons/innovations/rap/.

Ray, Amit, and Erhardt Graeff. "Reviewing the Author-Function in the Age of *Wikipedia.*" *Originality, Imitation, and Plagiarism: Teaching Writing in the Digital Age.* Edited by Caroline Eisner and Martha Vicinus. U of Michigan P, 2008, pp. 39-47.

Selber, Stuart. *Multiliteracies for a Digital Age.* Illinois UP, 2004, p. 25.

4

Writing a Wiki Resource Guide for a Literature Survey Course

Rochelle Rodrigo
Old Dominion University

Rochelle (Shelley) Rodrigo is assistant professor of rhetoric and (new) media at Old Dominion University. She was a full-time faculty member for nine years in English and film studies at Mesa Community College in Arizona. At MCC she served as instructional technologist and faculty professional development coordinator. Rodrigo has coauthored *The Wadsworth Guide to Research* (2007; 2013), and coedited *Rhetorically Rethinking Usability* (2009), both with Susan K. Miller. Her scholarly work has appeared in *Computers and Composition, C&C Online, Teaching English*

in the Two-Year College, EDUCAUSE Quarterly, Journal of Interactive Technology & Pedagogy, Journal of Advancing Technology, and *Flow*. Rodrigo has served as co-chair on the EDUCAUSE Evolving Technologies Committee (2009–2012) and was elected to the Conference on College Composition and Communication Executive Committee (2010–2012). In 2010 she became a Google Certified Teacher. In 2012, she was awarded the Digital Humanities High Powered Computing Fellowship.

1. OVERVIEW

- **Assignment:** Students contextualize literature into a larger time period and across themes by creating annotated bibliographies and other optional multimedia to post to a class wiki.
- **Courses:** Introduction to literature; American literature; any literature survey course.
- **Literature:** Time period–specific literature, especially with texts out of copyright; the assignment in this chapter focuses on American literature before 1860.
- **Technology:** Wiki applications (for example, Google Sites or PBworks).
- **Time:** Can be conducted in two to three weeks or extended over a full semester.

2. GOALS OF THE ASSIGNMENT

After completing this assignment, students will be able to

- distinguish between major literary periods and themes;
- analyze literary texts using literary elements/characteristics; and
- research, critically read, and summarize secondary resources.

"If a literature survey course has taught students to be critical readers and consumers of texts as well as confident producers of their own thinking and analysis, that is a job well done."

Rochelle Rodrigo
Old Dominion University

3. ASSIGNMENT SHEET

Writing a Wiki Resource Guide for a Literature Survey Course

Course: _____

Instructor: _____

Date: _____

Introduction to the Assignment

In a course that is supposed to survey American literature before 1860, most instructors feel the need to get students to read as much as possible from the period. However, as you can see from the following site — www.lang.nagoya -u.ac.jp/~matsuoka/AmeLit.html (and this is just a listing of authors, most of them have multiple works) — it would be impossible to have you "read everything" in a full 16-week semester, let alone a condensed 5-week summer session.

I believe, instead, that it is more important to introduce you to the primary periods and themes within this span of American literature. Therefore, this course is structured around your exploration of the primary periods in American literature before 1860. Now, please recognize that there are a variety of ways to break up and define these periods; however, that is part of the fun of letting you explore them on your own. You will be responsible for constructing your own understanding/definition of the periods, themes, authors, and so on.

I also believe that there are more than enough reputable sources in library databases and on the Internet for you to construct this understanding of American literature. Therefore, as a class we will immerse ourselves in the discussion of American literature as it is currently raging on the Internet and scholarly journals. You will find resources, evaluate their authority and credibility, and work them into our class discussion.

Packets to Complete during This Course

To facilitate this personal exploration of the major periods and themes of American literature before 1860, *you will put together a packet for each period you explore*.

Within each of your 4 packets you will be responsible for finding resources to help you

- define the literary period,
- explore 2 authors from the period,
- read 2 texts from the period, and
- identify 2 themes of American Literature that were explored in the period.

For each packet you will also be responsible to do the following:

- Identify 2 specific literary elements (e.g., character, symbolism), using resources to help you explore them.

- Draft, peer-review, and finalize an insight paper for one of the texts you read.

Literary Periods

For each of the 4 deadlines, you must focus on 1 of the 5 periods listed below. By the end of the course you will have explored four of the five periods. Although they are listed in, more or less, chronological order, you do not need to complete them in that order.

1. Puritanism

2. Enlightenment

3. Romantic

4. Transcendentalism

5. Critique of slavery

For this part of the assignment you need to do the following:

- Identify two electronic resources that help to define and describe the literary period you are focusing on. NOTE: at least one of these resources must be from one of the library's databases.

- Once you have identified 2 good resources, you must construct an annotated bibliography to post to the course wiki on the page associated with the specific literary period. Your annotated bibliography should include the following elements:

  - A full MLA bibliographic citation for the resource.

  - A paragraph or two about the resource that answers the following questions:

    — What is the main point or purpose for the resource? (Summarize the Web site.)

    — What are the criteria this resource uses to define the specific literary period? In other words, based on this resource, what criteria would you use to check whether a specific author or a specific text fit into this literary period?

    — How/why was this resource helpful in reading, interpreting, and making meaning of your other elements (author, texts, themes, etc.) for this assignment period?

    — How/why is this a credible resource?

(continued)

ASSIGNMENT SHEET (*continued*)

You may not post annotated bibliographies for resources that your classmates have already posted. By the end of the course we should have a long list of great resources for each literary period.

Authors

For each of the periods you focus on, you will select and write about 2 specific authors.

- Please make sure you select American authors (for example, there was also a romantic period in British literature, however, we are not studying British literature in this class).
- You will want to use your exploration of the period as a way to identify major authors.
- By the end of the course you will need to have selected at least one female author and one author of color.

For this part of the assignment you need to do the following:

- Identify resources that help you explore the authors you have selected.
- Find at least one resource per author. NOTE: the resources need to come from a library database.
- Once you have identified a good resource for each author, you must construct an annotated bibliography to post to a wiki page for that author that is associated with the specific literary period your author belongs to. Your annotated bibliography should include the following elements:
  - A full MLA bibliographic citation for the resource.
  - A paragraph or two about the resource that answers the following questions:
    - What is the main point or purpose for the resource? (Summarize the Web site.)
    - What are the reasons that this author is an important person to know/read in the specific literary period? What about this author's writings is critical to an understanding of the literary period?
    - How/why was this resource helpful in reading, interpreting, and making meaning of your other elements (author, texts, themes, etc.) for this assignment period?
    - How/why is this a credible resource?

Don't forget, by the end of the class you will be responsible for responding to at least 2 classmates' postings about 2 different authors from each period within the discussion threads on the wiki page. You may select one posting on an author you wrote about; however, your other reply must be to a posting about an author you did not write about. The easiest reply would probably be a comparison of your Internet source with your classmate's Internet source. Also consider discussing how/why your classmate's resource got you thinking about the author and/or literary period in a different way.

Texts

For each author you focus on, you will select one of his or her texts to read.

- You will want to use your exploration of the period and authors as a way to identify the author's major texts.
- By the end of the course you will need to have selected at least one poem and one novel.
- Because all of these texts were written before current copyright laws, the vast majority of them are in the public domain and available on the Web. Just be sure to check that you are reading a version from a reliable source (so you know you are getting a good copy of the text). And if reading on the computer screen is too difficult, most of these texts can easily be found at a (used) bookstore.

For this part of the assignment you need to do the following:

- Identify resources that help you explore the texts you have selected.
- The text itself does not count as a resource; instead you need to find a resource about the text.
- Once you have identified a good resource for each text (these also must be from the library), you must construct an annotated bibliography to post to the forum in the discussion board associated with the specific literary period your author belongs to. Your annotated bibliography should include the following elements:
  - A full MLA bibliographic citation for the resource.
  - A paragraph or two about the resource that answers the following questions:
    — What is the main point or purpose for the resource? (Summarize the Web site.)
    — What are the reasons that this text is important to know/read in the specific literary period? What about this text is critical to an understanding of the literary period?
    — How/why was this resource helpful in your reading and understanding of the text?
    — How/why was this resource helpful in reading, interpreting, and making meaning of your other elements (author, texts, themes, etc.) for this assignment period?
    — How/why is this a credible resource?

(continued)

ASSIGNMENT SHEET (*continued*)

Don't forget, by the end of the class you will be responsible for commenting on at least 2 classmates' postings about 2 different texts from each period within the discussion threads on the wiki page. You may select one posting on a text you read and wrote about; however, your other reply must be to a posting about a text you did not write about. Consider discussing how/why your classmate's source got you thinking about the author, text, and/or literary period in a different way.

Themes

For each of the four deadlines, you must focus on 2 of the 8 American literary themes listed below. By the end of the course you will have explored all 8 of these themes.

1. Diversity
2. The American Dream
3. Identity
4. The frontier
5. Self-confidence
6. Discontinuity
7. Eccentricity
8. Experimentalism

For this section of the assignment you need to do the following:

- Identify electronic resources that help to define and describe the literary themes you are focusing on (one for each theme).
- Once you have identified good resources, you must construct an annotated bibliography to post to the wiki page in the course wiki associated with the specific literary period. Your annotated bibliography should include the following elements:
  - A full MLA bibliographic citation for the resource.
  - A paragraph or two about the resource that answers the following questions:
    — What is the main point or purpose for the resource? (Summarize the Web site.)
    — What are the criteria this resource uses to define the specific literary theme? In other words, based on this resource, what criteria would you use to check whether a specific author or a specific text fit into this literary theme?
    — How/why was this resource helpful in reading, interpreting, and making meaning of your other elements (author, texts, themes, etc.) for this assignment period?
    — How/why is this a credible resource?

Literary Elements

For each of the 4 deadlines, you must focus on 2 of the 8 literary elements listed below. By the end of the course you will have explored all of these elements:

1. Character
2. Imagery
3. Setting
4. Symbolism
5. Point of view
6. Rhythm (w/ poetry)
7. Tone and style
8. Word choice

For this section of the assignment you need to do the following:

- Identify a resource that helps to define and describe each of the literary elements you are focusing on.

- Once you have identified a good resource, you much construct an annotated bibliography to post to the course wiki page associated with that literary term. Your annotated bibliography should include the following elements:

  - A full MLA bibliographic citation for the resource.

  - A paragraph or two about the resource that answers the following questions:

    — What is the main point or purpose for the resource? (Summarize the Web site.)

    — How does the resource define the literary term? How does the resource describe analyzing texts using the literary term?

    — How does understanding this literary term help you better understand the texts you are reading for this deadline?

    — How/why is this a credible resource?

Critical Analysis Paper

Write a critical analysis paper focusing on one of your texts.

- In your paper, discuss how 1 of the 2 literary themes you focused on emerges in the text. In other words, what are the defining characteristics of the specific literary theme and how/where does the text exemplify those elements?

- You'll also want to discuss how the author's work reflects one of the literary elements (see above). You will want to refer to specific passages in the text as evidence of your analysis of the literary theme and element.

(continued)

ASSIGNMENT SHEET (*continued*)

To help avoid plagiarism, be sure to document any sources you use. Using MLA style, document your sources (1) as in-text citations in the body of your paper and (2) work cited entries at the end of your paper.

For this part of the assignment you will be responsible to do the following:

- Share your draft for peer review.
- Peer-review 2 of your classmates' papers.
- Revise and submit your final paper.

Hopefully after you have read 1 or 2 of your classmates' drafts, you will have some ideas on how to revise your own. Be sure to also read the comments your classmates left for you about your draft in the exchange. Please submit your final version as an attached word-processed document. You will also be required to post a final revised version of your paper in the course wiki under the appropriate thread for the author's wiki page.

Reflect on and Write about the "Unknown" Literary Period

After finishing the work outlined above, you will have focused on 4 out of the 5 literary periods identified in this assignment: puritanism; enlightenment; romantic; transcendentalism; and critique of slavery.

That means there's one literary period that you need to learn about from your classmates. To make sure you get some knowledge of this remaining period, go into the course wiki for that period and read all of your classmate's postings. Folks, this should take a while!

After reading through all of the postings (including your classmate's insight papers), write a reflection essay about this period. In your reflection essay, be sure to answer the following questions/prompts:

- How does understanding this period get you to better understand the other four periods?
- How does understanding this period affect your understanding of the various literary themes?
- If you had done this period, which authors would you have selected? Why?
- If you had done this period, which texts would you have selected? Why?

Comment on Wiki Posts by Other Students

Through your own research and by reading and the work posted at the wiki by other students, hopefully you will see that different people understand American literature in different ways. That is why it is so important for you all to dialogue with one another about the different periods, authors, texts, themes, and literary elements of American literature.

To get full credit for this assignment, you will need to complete the following replies:

- 2 replies to postings about each period you focused on (8 total),
- 1 reply to 2 different authors (1 not your own) under each period you focused on (8 total),
- 1 reply to 2 texts (1 not your own) under each period you focused on (8 total),
- 2 replies to postings about each theme (16 total), and
- 2 replies to postings about each literary term (16 total).

Although the replies are not due until the end of the course, you probably want to get working on them as early as possible. For each reply, discuss whether or not you agree with the authority/credibility of the source. Also discuss how/why the source improves your understanding of the period, theme, or literary term.

You must also submit a short reflection essay on how reading and replying to your classmates helped you to broaden your understanding of American literature before 1860. Be sure to refer to the specific students and wiki posts that you are responding to.

4. TIME AND TECHNOLOGY

TIME. I have only taught this assignment as an entire course (all the students completed this assignment in a five-week, online, asynchronous summer Early American Literature survey course). I can imagine typical semester (sixteen weeks) or quarter (ten–twelve weeks) literature survey courses integrating parts of or the entire assignment in two ways:

1. *Entire Course Synthesis Assignment*
   After covering a major section of the course, you could ask students to add texts, authors, and/or other information to the course wiki as a way to summarize and synthesize what they have learned. You would need to split up material and/or ask students to add new material (such as read other texts by authors already covered in the course). You would then repeat the process after each major section of the course.

2. *End-of-Course Final Project*
   You could ask students to complete this assignment as a final project demonstrating synthesis of the material from the entire semester.

TECHNOLOGY. Depending on the scale and complexity of the assignment, you and your students may need access to a variety of technologies and resources.

The assignment does not require any specific hardware beyond what students should have access to in a college library or computer lab: specifically a computer with an Internet connection and updated Web browser. You will need to initiate the assignment in an empty wiki, or another easy and collaborative web production space. You might consider using any of the following:

- Google Sites: sites.google.com (Campuses that have "gone Google" will have campus-specific instances of Google Sites.)
- Wikispaces: www.wikispaces.com
- PBworks: pbworks.com
- Weebly: www.weebly.com

Many learning management systems (LMSs) now offer wiki solutions as well. When deciding which application to choose, you should think about Web space longevity and exportability (you will need to research the archiving features of individual wiki applications).

A basic wiki or Web site space will allow students to incorporate texts and images. Most also allow for embedding video and a range of formatting options. Since most wikis allow users to embed outside resources, students can also produce timelines and geospatial maps to incorporate into the wiki pages. Google Maps is the predominant Web-based geospatial mapmaking application, and there are a variety of applications students might use to make timelines, including:

- Timeglider: timeglider.com
- TimeRime: www.timerime.com
- Timetoast: www.timetoast.com

If the assignment calls for students to produce timelines and geo-spatial maps (see the Assignment Variations box), the appropriate Web-based applications only work with more recent Web browsers.

To prepare students for the assignment, you will want to demonstrate the kind of work you're looking for, and how to use the technologies. You might do this during a class period (probably in a computer lab environment) and then have students do the majority of the work as homework (therefore students would need access to computers with updated Web browsers outside of class).

For a face-to-face course, I suggest you dedicate at least one hour of a class period to introduce the assignment and the technologies. If the class is an online, asynchronous course, like mine was, you will need to include videos to help students use the technologies (ideally include examples as well). In other words, both the technology and critical analysis skills needed for the assignment require that you scaffold assignments to help the students learn through the process.

To this end, I always develop introductory assignments that use the various technologies. For example, I have students construct an introduction wiki page that includes a picture; I also have them add information to a

---

ASSIGNMENT VARIATIONS: MULTIMODALITY, TEXTS, AND CONTEXTS

You may want to adapt this assignment to make it richer in contexts and media. For example, you might ask students to include one representative image for each wiki page or an embedded About video or slideshow for each page.

You might also ask students to construct contextual timelines (or maps) for each literary period. The timelines could include historical and cultural contexts for that period, for example, providing notes on major events, major authors, and any significant social, political, economic, philosophical, and religious thinking or movements of the time.

You may want to provide a list of authoritative resources, such as the Library of Congress's American Memory collection (memory.loc.gov/ammem/index .html) where students can find multimedia content and instructions on how to cite the material when they post it on the wiki.

collaborative timeline and a collaborative map that I've already set up. Especially if you want students to incorporate robust multimedia elements, you will want to develop an assignment framework that scaffolds how students work through the material and technologies.

Because many students will be working with some of the various technologies for the first time, I suggest that you develop technology support materials as well. Most Web applications have official help sites, some quite useful. Many of the various Web applications listed above also have a variety of unofficial help materials, including YouTube videos. You might also consider using screencasting software like Camtasia, Jing, or Screencast-O-Matic to make course-specific videos. Making course-specific videos can be useful if the assignment asks for specific Web page–formatting requirements. In other words, this assignment does require you to do a lot of preparation work in advance.

Similarly, students may not know how to locate and work with primary and secondary materials. It helps to provide them with lists of resource to work with. For example, you might want to introduce students to the specific library databases that contain the most relevant materials for the assignment, including images and video. I also suggest providing scaffolding activities to help students find and critically consume texts. Most of the learning in the course will come from students becoming more critical readers and producers of a variety of texts. I have found that most students have not done this kind of assignment before; therefore, I give them the option to revise and resubmit work from the first one or two units worth of work (if completed over an entire course term).

5. ANTICIPATING STUDENT NEEDS

The potential difficulties of this assignment fall into two categories: legalities and logistics.

LEGALITIES. As with any project where students are using outside sources, copyright is always a concern. However, in a course where the resulting work might be published in a live Web site for the world to see, intellectual property issues are more complex. First, not only do students need to be aware of what, how, and why to cite resources, they also need to be sure to cite any images or videos they incorporate as well. And if the site is live, the resulting work itself becomes a text with intellectual property rights for the students. In short, this project provides an opportunity to talk to students about these issues and possibly introduce the concepts of public domain and Creative Commons licensing.

A public Web site also faces FERPA (Family Educational Rights and Privacy Act) issues; students have a right for their academic work to remain private. I have found that most students are excited about sharing their work, especially if it includes multimedia, with their friends and family. My students who have been concerned about privacy have had no problem with the assignment as long as they could use a pseudonym. Some institutions have more conservative interpretations of FERPA policies; you may need to ask students to sign a waiver about publishing work to the Web. You may also want to check with your institution's legal advisors prior to implementing the assignment.

Finally, students have the right to equal access to their educational materials. Various Web-based applications, like timelines, may not have particularly good usability and accessibility for screen readers. Although I have not specifically run up against accessibility as an issue, I believe that this is a creative assignment and that I could work with any student to develop another creative assignment to fulfill the same learning objective. If you intend for the wiki Web site to be used over multiple class sessions, you may need to think about the accessibility of the site itself. Ideally you would ask that students provide alt-text descriptions for any images and transcripts for any audio or video they incorporate into the wiki.

LOGISTICS. As already mentioned, students will need scaffolded assignments and support with the technologies as well as the content. Another logistical concern comes after the student submits the assignment. If a quarter of the course is adding annotated bibliography entries to the same time period page, how do you know who submitted what work? Although most wiki software has page histories that track changes by user, I've found that it is infinitely easier to ask students to submit packet cover sheets that specifically identify which resources they added and what work they completed.

6. ASSESSMENT TOOLS

To help students accomplish the work, I ask them to submit their wiki postings and draft of the critical analysis paper and then have a peer-reviewed and final version of the paper due a bit later. Through the critical analysis paper, students are asked to synthesize what they learned when they were writing and posting on the wiki. I like to have them peer-review and revise their essays with the goal of composing the strongest paper possible—one that will receive a good grade.

To me, this assignment represents a radically different way to conduct a class. That is why I prefer to provide a lot of comments and suggestions for revisions while grading the first two units of assignments (each unit or packet focused on one period, two authors, two themes, etc.) so that students understand what I am looking for. I generally allow them to revise at least the first, if not the second, packet as well. By the time they are working

Assignment Distribution for an Entire Course Term	
Accounts Setup and Introduction	40 points
Packets (200 points total) — You will complete 4 of these during the course. • **Literary Periods**: definitions & descriptions wiki posts x 2 per literary period (10 points each, 20 points) • **Authors**: resources wiki posts x 2 authors, 1 per author (10 points each, 20 points) • **Texts**: resources wiki posts x 2 texts, 1 per text (10 points each, 20 points) • **Themes**: resources wiki posts x 2 themes, 1 per theme (10 points each, 20 points) • **Literary Elements**: wiki posts x 2 elements, 1 per literary element (10 points each, 20 points) • **Critical Analysis Paper** Draft (10 points) Peer Review x 2 classmates (10 points each, 20 points) Final (65 points) Revised posting to wiki (5 points) Tracking Sheet (–50 points if not submitted)	800 points
Reflective Essay on "Unknown" Literary Period	100 points
Comments on Wiki Posts by Others Students	60 points
Total	**1,000 points**

on the third and fourth set, they have a better understanding of what they are being asked to do.

7. THEORETICAL BASIS FOR THE ASSIGNMENT:
Writing a Wiki Resource Guide for a Literature Survey Course

In 1995, Robert Barr and John Tagg flipped the scholarly focus on pedagogy from faculty teaching to student learning; since then most "new" pedagogical strategies have focused on ways to better facilitate student learning, usually through a variety of active learning assignments. Mary Kalantzis and Bill Cope describe "new" ways of student learning in terms of "social cognition and collaborative learning as aspects of human nature" and from "distributed knowledge, with more people as active knowledge makers" (189). Maryellen Weimer, as well as Phyllis Blumberg, discusses five changes that many faculty need to make in their teaching:

1. change the focus on memorizing content to (socially) constructing knowledge and meaning;

2. shift the teacher's role from disciplinary expert and content deliverer to learning experience facilitator;

3. motivate and teach students how to take more responsibility for the learning, shifting from passive to active learners;

4. change from an exclusive use of summative assessment to more frequent formative, peer, and self-assessments, providing frequent feedback and space for revision/learning; and

5. shift the balance of power in the classroom, giving students more control over determining what and how they learn, as well as how they are assessed. (Weimer 8-17)

In short, faculty who care about student learning have a plethora of theory- and research-based strategies to rely on, most of them suggesting students need to be more actively engaged in the learning process. In *How People Learn*, John Bransford and colleagues specifically articulate that for students to learn they must "organize knowledge in ways that facilitate retrieval and application" (16). The *heart* of this assignment is facilitating learning by turning over the knowledge construction of what constitutes literary period and themes to the students. By asking students to write the wiki site as the course, students are not being told how any given text fits into the larger canon of literature; instead, they are doing research and making claims about how the texts they read fit into the survey period or theme.

> "The *heart* of this assignment is facilitating learning by turning over the knowledge construction of what constitutes literary period and themes to the students."
>
> **Rochelle Rodrigo**

At the same time faculty are being asked to be more accountable for student learning, they are also asked to address the "crisis" of twenty-first-century literacies. The heart of this crisis is wrapped up in various techno-literacies. Since the National Council of Teachers of English (NCTE) 1970 "Resolution on Media Literacy," a variety of other related lists about techno-, media, and twenty-first-century literacies, as well as position statements about various related literacies authored by groups and organizations, have emerged. Companies like AT&T and Intel, as well as groups primarily backed by companies, like the Partnership for 21st Century Literacies, have developed lists. Both interdisciplinary organizations like the National Education Association and American Association of Community Colleges and disciplinary organizations like NCTE, the Council of Writing Program

Administrators, and the Association of College and Research Libraries have developed various guidelines and position statements related to the crisis of twenty-first-century literacies. In a white paper for the MacArthur Foundation, Henry Jenkins and his colleagues provide a list of skills that students will need to successfully participate in our participatory twenty-first-century digital culture: play, performance, simulation, appropriation, multitasking, distributed cognition, collective intelligence, judgment, transmedia navigation, networking, and negotiation (4).

These skills closely resemble a mix of the desired learning objectives by many faculty in higher education, the higher-order thinking goals outlined in Bloom's Taxonomy of Cognitive Learning Domains, as well as the characteristics of active learning and knowledge making. Even though scholars like Marc Prensky and Don Tapscott claim that students are extremely technologically savvy, EDUCAUSE's annual student technology usage survey (Dahlstrom et al.) claims that "a surprising number of students say they are not fully confident that they have the technology skills to meet their needs" (20) and that "technology can make learning a more immersive, engaging, and relevant experience" (10). Collaboratively producing a wiki-based digital resource for the class allows students to continue developing their traditional alphabetical writing skills and to grow their twenty-first-century digital communications skills.

8. CONCLUSION

The first version of this assignment happened in student blogs. For each major "unit" of the course, they would select a time period, two authors, two texts, two themes, and two literary elements. The students would then need to find resources to define each and then write an analysis of one of the texts focusing on the characteristics of the time period, theme, and literary element. Although I did have students read and respond to one another's work, the blogs didn't work because the students still worked too much in isolation from one another.

The next year I had students use basically the same assignment to collaboratively build the course wiki; the following two years' worth of students continued to add content to the course wiki. After three years the course wiki consisted of numerous annotated bibliographies about various early American literary periods, authors, themes, and literary elements. The final time I taught the course, I had students critically revise the pages and required that they add images, videos, timelines, and maps. Once all of the students were working within the same wiki environment, they were not only learning from constructing their own knowledge but also from reading, responding, and revising one another's work.

I knew I was successful with this assignment one summer when I had a student visit my office after the course. He said that although I didn't teach him anything, he learned a lot. That response told me that through this assignment I had achieved Weimer's change of shifting my role as teacher "from disciplinary expert and content deliverer to learning experience facilitator" (8). Instead of telling students what and how to read, and what to think about the reading, I constructed an environment that helped students select their own variety of readings and make meaning of the texts themselves.

> "I constructed an environment that helped students select their own variety of readings and make meaning of the texts themselves."
>
> **Rochelle Rodrigo**

Teaching a survey of literature course this way is hard work. First, you must spend a lot of time in advance developing the course materials; then, you need to address student resistance to work that is radically different from anything they've ever done before. Finally, it requires hard work and critical thinking to complete. However, it is amazing to read papers where students focus on specific literary elements, like word choice and setting, and a specific theme, like the American Dream, and make an interesting claim about a text that I would have never considered. Although I did not explicitly consider this when I designed the online summer survey course, this type of assignment could work well to help students make the shift from undergraduate consumers of course content to undergraduate researchers developing their own learning agenda.

9. WORKS CITED

American Association of Community Colleges. "AACC Position Statement on Information Literacy." *American Association of Community Colleges*, 4 May 2008, www.aacc.nche.edu/About/Positions/Pages/ps05052008.aspx.

Association of College and Research Libraries. "Information Literacy Competency Standards for Higher Education." *Association of Colleges and Research Libraries*, 18 Jan. 2000, www.ala.org/acrl/standars/informationliteracycompetency.

AT&T. 21st Century Literacies Home Page. *Internet Archive Wayback Machine*, 16 July 2011, web.archive.org/web/20110716160829/http://www.kn.pacbell.com/wired/21stcent/.

Barr, Robert B., and Tagg, John. "From Teaching to Learning—A New Paradigm for Undergraduate Education." Change, vol. 27, no. 6, 1995, pp. 13-25. Print.

Bloom, Benjamin S., et al. *Taxonomy of Educational Objectives: The Classification of Educational Goals. Handbook I: Cognitive Domain*. Longmans, 1956.

Blumberg, Phyllis. *Developing Learner-Centered Teaching: A Practical Guide for Faculty*. Jossey-Bass, 2009.

Bransford, John, and the National Research Council (U.S.) Committees on Developments in the Science of Learning and on Learning Research and Educational Practice, et al. *How People Learn: Brain, Mind, Experience, and School.* National Acad. P, 2000.

Council of Writing Program Administrators. "WPA Outcomes Statement for First-Year Composition." *Council of Writing Program Administrators*, July 2008, wpacouncil.org/positions/outcomes.html.

Council of Writing Program Administrators, et al. "Framework for Success in Postsecondary Writing." *Council of Writing Program Administrators*, Jan. 2011, wpacouncil.org/framework.

Dahlstrom, Eden, et al. "The ECAR National Study of Undergraduate Students and Information Technology, 2011." *EDUCAUSE*, Oct. 2011, net.educause .edu/ir/library/pdf/ERS1103/ERS1103W.pdf.Researched report.

Intel. "Technology literacy." Intel, www.intel.com/education/technologyliteracy /index.htm. Accessed 16 Aug. 2012.

Jenkins, Henry, et al. "Confronting the Challenges of Participatory Culture: Media Education for the 21st Century." *MacArthur* Foundation, 2006, www .macfound.org/media/article_pdfs/JENKINS_WHITE_PAPER.pdf.

Kalantzis, Mary, and Bill Cope. *New Learning: Elements of a Science of Education.* Cambridge UP, 2008.

National Council of Teachers of English. "The NCTE Definition of 21st Century Literacies." *National Council of Teachers of English*, 15 Feb. 2008, www.ncte .org/positions/statements/21stcentdefinition.

- - - "Resolution on Media Literacy." *National Council of Teachers of English*, 1970, www.ncte.org/positions/statements/medialiteracy.

National Education Association. "Partnership for 21st Century Skills." *National Education* Association, nea.org/home/34888.htm. Accessed 16 Aug. 2012.

Partnership for 21st Century Skills. "Framework for 21st Century Learning." *P21.* Dec. 2009, www.p21.org/storage/documents/P21_Framework_Definitions. pdf.

Prensky, Marc. "Digital Natives, Digital Immigrants." *On the Horizon*, vol. 9, no. 1, 2001, pp. 1-6.

Tapscott, Don. *Growing Up Digital: The Rise of the Net Generation.* McGraw, 1998.

Weimer, Maryellen. *Learner-Centered Teaching: Five Key Changes to Practice.* Jossey-Bass, 2002.

5

More Perfect Unions: Literary Studies, Blogging, and the Multigenre Essay

Eric Reimer
University of Montana

Eric Reimer is an associate professor of English at the University of Montana, with research and teaching interests in Irish Studies, contemporary British literature, postcolonial literatures, and digital pedagogies. His work has appeared in the journals *Eire-Ireland, Irish Studies Review, Journal of Caribbean Literatures*, and in the edited collection *The Poetics of American Song Lyrics* (2011).

COURTESY OF ERIC REIMER

1. OVERVIEW

- **Assignment:** Students participate in a blog by responding analytically to literature, texts that represent multiple modes and genres, various types of personal posts and testimonies, the posts of classmates, and various Web resources. I ask students to use this digital and hypertextual writing that they do on the blog as a model (and staging ground) for a final (print) essay for the course.
- **Courses:** Music in literature; any literature course that includes music as text; interdisciplinary courses built around literature, music, and various diverse texts, genres, and modes.
- **Literature:** Any literature, especially a reading list that represents various genres, e.g., short and long fiction, poetry, personal essays, theory, and autobiography.
- **Technology:** Blogging software (e.g., Blogger).
- **Time:** This semester-long assignment involves two hours of class time in ten- to thirty-minute segments throughout the course, or as much time needed to introduce blogging conventions and protocols, model the prelude/ introduction for the multigenre essay, and discuss samples of multigenre writing (culled from the course reading list and from previous students).

2. GOALS OF THE ASSIGNMENT

- To make classroom inquiry, student writing, and pedagogy more coterminous.
- To instill associative thinking, thereby helping students to recognize links and to create conversations among the disparate writers and texts of the course.
- To give students multiple venues for situating their selves, their lives, and their interests within the inquiry of the course, thereby investing them in that inquiry.
- To translate students' sense of emergence and creativity afforded by blog writing to their nondigital writing and, in so doing, to authorize the blending of imaginative, analytical, and reflective writing.
- To help students sense how digital writing technologies suggest possibilities for new aesthetic and argumentative arrangements in their print essays.
- To reconceive the course's final essay as a work that is contemplated, composed, and distributed across the entire semester.

"As I reflect on this project, I feel especially grateful for my students, who continue to help me remove the boundaries we tend to construct between teaching and scholarship, and between literary criticism and more expressive forms of writing; despite the many laments circulating today about the state of the humanities and the consumerist ethos of the university, it remains an exciting time to be a teacher."

Eric Reimer
University of Montana

3. ASSIGNMENT SHEET

More Perfect Unions: Literary Studies, Blogging, and the Multigenre Essay

Course: _____

Instructor: _____

Date: _____

Description

This assignment asks you to assume multiple voices, to write in multiple genres and on multiple levels, and to consider the texts and contexts of our course from a variety of vantage points. You will not be writing a linear, thesis-bound argumentative essay, but rather something with a more episodic, anecdotal, fragmented, collage-like aesthetic — it will be, perhaps, an exercise in "controlled randomness."

The spirit of the assignment asks that you be serious and playful, analytical and exploratory, personal and objective. One way for you to think about this essay is as a kind of hypertext, with each paragraph or section implying certain clickable links that will lead you and your readers — perhaps in unexpected and, at first glance, digressive ways — to the next section. The "controlled" aspect of the randomness, though, is just as important in an *artful* multigenre essay. That is, there should be a webbed sensibility and a linked, associational logic to your essay. The best essays will contain threads, themes, and motifs that bind the various sections together.

Topic and Idea Generation

Your first strategic choice is to decide how to characterize and define your range of inquiry in this paper. After thinking about the content of the course, the nature of the questions raised, the suggestiveness of texts, and personal interests, you might decide to focus your essay on literature and music. Or you might think about how these arts intersect with such notions as time, memory, loss and grieving, community, love, faith, ethics, and so on.

Having settled on your general area of inquiry, you will write a prelude that provides the exposition for your composition (the thematic material, the questions that will be at issue, something that will nearly sound like a thesis or a binding motif; think of it, perhaps, as the equivalent of that four-note theme that begins and eventually unifies the disparate parts of the opening movement of Beethoven's Fifth Symphony). This should be an especially sharp, interesting, and burnished piece, something that both reveals your argumentative terrain and gives your readers an early sense of your essay's aesthetic.

At this point, you have embarked. As you engage in the material of the course, you might also think about how music pervades and flavors a (your!) life.

(continued)

ASSIGNMENT SHEET (*continued*)

One or more sections of your multigenre essay could be triggered by looking at the spines of the CDs in your personal collections or the thumbnails in your iTunes libraries, for example, which you might find suddenly morphing into libraries of lost sensations, lost ideas, lost emotions, lost theories about the nature of things. In discrete moments, your essay might nearly resemble a kind of soundtrack of your life and times. What are the anthems of your world? How are you in some sense stitched together and constituted by music? What knowledge does music impart? What does music teach us about living in time? These latter questions should be particularly resonant in terms of the poetry, fiction, and essays you'll encounter this semester, and should thus give you countless possibilities for integrating our musical and literary texts and contexts.

Length, Genres, and Formatting

Your essay should be a minimum of 3,000 words, which may involve somewhere between 12 and 16 pages. You must use at least 5 genres, which you might consider drawing from the following possibilities: literary criticism, the essay, the stream-of-consciousness narrative, poetry, the song lyric, the dramatic dialogue, the interview, capsulized short fiction, album liner notes, the letter, autobiography, diary entries, the journalistic profile or review, the bullet list, and the parable, among others.

You are free to use any structural and/or aesthetic embellishments you want (e.g., numbered sections, dated sections, section titles, multiple fonts, visual components, etc.). In general, this essay might look most appealing if the individual sections are single-spaced, with a double space between sections. Don't forget to give your essays a carefully considered and interesting title.

4. TIME AND TECHNOLOGY

The blogging components of the class require nothing more than a single, centralized class blog, which you can establish through a hosting service such as Blogger, a popular and free resource that requires only a Google account to get started. Having entered the Blogger Web site with your newly established username and password, click on New Blog and proceed to supply a series of identifying and design characteristics, including choosing (1) a blog name; (2) an address/URL (which will then be established as *yourname*.blog spot.com); and (3) a design template that will determine the aesthetic of the blog.

Once these initial steps are completed, you can explore a series of options and customizations that are available via an arrow pull-down. For example, choosing the Layout option, you can indicate how the archived posts should be organized (e.g., monthly, weekly, daily, etc.), add a Gadget (which most commonly might be a blog list and/or a link list), or rearrange the location of the components on the template; by choosing the Template option, you are able to customize the template's background, layout, color palette, and fonts, among other things. Moving then to the Settings option, and then the Basic selection, you can determine whether the blog will be open to all readers (or, alternatively, only to blog authors), whether there will be a password required for visitors to the blog, whether the wider public (or only registered users) can comment to blog posts, and so on.

On the first day of class, I collect active e-mail addresses from all of the students, at which point, returning to that Settings and Basic path and choosing Permissions, I proceed to "add authors" by entering my students' e-mail addresses. They should be made aware that they will subsequently receive an invitation from Blogger to join the class blog, and that they will need to follow the link in that invitation to create an account/username and password. I ask my students to use their first names for their screen names on the blog (rather than some more cryptic or anonymous moniker), so that their classmates (and I) will always know who is posting and commenting, but I also invite them to talk with me if they have any concerns about privacy and the potential public aspects of a blog.

After saving all template and layout changes, you can view the blog or click on New Post; the latter action creates a text entry field with a toolbar of options that will be familiar from word processors (bold, italicized, underlined text, etc.) and the ability to highlight keywords in the text and thereby create links to images and other sites around the Web. What elevates a blog from the threaded discussion board features of course management software is the ability to create an aesthetic for the course's online presence, which subsequently adds more luster and import to the sense of authorship. In this sense, not only should the template be chosen carefully (and perhaps modified by additional customizations), but you should also choose a striking name for the blog and provide a crisply worded and welcoming description in the blog's heading. In my case, although the templates did not provide an option particularly pertinent to a course on music and literature, my blog title ("Liner Notes") and my list of music-related blogs and Web sites give the blog, I hope, the sensibility of an online music journal.

I introduce both the blog and the multigenre essay during the first week of class, describing both as semester-spanning projects. I explain to students that the writing they do for the blog will provide material for their multigenre essays, help them begin to intuit the guiding aesthetic for those essays, and reify, in a sense, our classroom methodology. Encouraging students to supplement their blog writing with a reading and listening journal, I emphasize that even short, fragmented entries will inevitably provide valuable material for their multigenre essays. At about the midpoint of the semester, after modeling my own version of a "prelude," we use part of a class session to begin discussing possibilities for this crucial opening section of the multigenre essay. Then, some three weeks later, I require that the students post drafts of their preludes to the blog, which subsequently becomes a peer commentary space and an impetus for revision.

There are two other more general (but very significant) issues relative to time and planning. Ensuring that an appropriate, balanced, and purposeful tone and ethos prevail on the class blog can require some careful nurturing, as well as a discussion with your students—perhaps during the first week of class—about the conventions and expectations of blog writing. Those who are familiar and experienced with blogging (or writing in electronic venues, generally) will likely be more familiar with personal/expressive writing rather than academic/scholarly writing. If the blog is to extend the work of the class, the latter type of writing will have to figure prominently; however, blogs tend to work best when they are allowed to grow organically, with a lot of freedom, and with a judicious blend of serious and more playful discourses.

> "Blogs tend to work best when they are allowed to grow organically, with a lot of freedom, and with a judicious blend of serious and more playful discourses."
> **Eric Reimer**

This balance undoubtedly begins with the instructor, whose initial posts can alternately model scholarly inquiry and authorize levity (and even irreverence) on the blog. Instructors must also, in the early weeks of the class, produce the activation energy to impel student participation (e.g., through the occasional directed/assigned posting, such as a modest reading response or some other follow-up to a class discussion, etc.) so as to lessen the potential of the instructor's voice to dominate the blog. It's a delicate balance, especially since that participation can so easily and unwittingly be dampened, or since, as Kathleen Fitzpatrick worries, "students might begin to write to [the instructor], not to one another" (210). Secondly, since most students will likely have had no experience writing multigenre essays, you will need to be prepared to use class time (probably in multiple ways on multiple occasions) not only to articulate how the essay should operate and look, but to provide students with examples of essays and texts that approximate a multigenre aesthetic. That articulation will begin with the assignment handout you distribute, ideally, in the first two weeks of class, but the students will likely need you to renew and recast these efforts—even if only for five to ten minutes at a time—at least every few weeks.

As the semester begins to mature, your descriptions of the essay will gain traction to the extent you can provide some accompanying examples (for which you should always be on the lookout): for example, in the Music and Literature class, I share and discuss excerpts from Robert Grudin's wonderful multigenre book *Time and the Art of Living*, as well as sections from Rob Sheffield's book *Love Is a Mix Tape: Life and Loss, One Song at a Time* and Jonathan Lethem's essay "The Beards: An Adolescence in Disguise." In his foundational book on multigenre writing, *Blending Genre, Altering Style: Writing Multigenre Papers*, Tom Romano also suggests various examples of multigenre texts. Even more significantly, with multiple iterations of the multigenre essay behind me, I am able to share past examples of successful student essays with the class, which are especially relevant in the latter third of the semester as the students begin to become more fully involved in the writing of the essays.

5. ANTICIPATING STUDENT NEEDS

Although most students are comfortable writing for electronic venues, some percentage will have no experience writing for a blog. I address this problem (during the first week of class) by demonstrating how to log on to the blog and navigate through one's "dashboard," and by explaining the difference between adding a comment to an already existing post and creating a new post. I will then typically require that they comment on my initial posting, in which I provide a particularly accessible and invitational question or issue to consider (e.g., in the Music and Literature class I might ask them to share a song lyric that they think rises to the level of poetry, or to identify what they consider to be particularly melancholy songs or melodies, which becomes a simple icebreaker in the manner of Nick Hornby's "Top 5" lists in *High Fidelity*).

Once students are acclimated to the blog, subsequent directed postings might then be oriented toward creating a body of material for students' multigenre essays. For example, in the Music and Literature course I might assign a blog posting that asks students to cite an individual song capable of transporting them to another time and/or to a lost emotion in the ways only music can. These responses can then be rendered freshly relevant when the class proceeds to a discussion of a text like James Joyce's short story "The Dead," when, upon expectedly hearing "The Lass of Aughrim," Greta Conroy is carried far back in time to memories of Michael Furey and youthful love. The juxtaposition of the student testimonials with the discussion of the devastating mysteries at the end of Joyce's story will not only isolate two genres (autobiography and literary criticism), potentially, but also show the richly suggestive potential of what Jeff Rice calls the "choral moves" (43) of a collage-like writing aesthetic.

As they begin to work more determinedly on their multigenre essays later in the semester, students may face another significant challenge in their attempt to bring a properly argumentative sensibility to a form that will necessarily be governed by textual ruptures and a more diffused organizing logic. Potentially fixated on issues of pattern and style, of form and design, or perhaps too facilely seeking to engage multiply and broadly with the course texts, students may sacrifice the robust interpretive work necessary for the essay to succeed. Helping them to overcome these tendencies may hinge crucially on multiple occasions of in-class modeling (even if they take place in impromptu, five- to ten-minute segments); to this end, resolve to write your own prelude for a multigenre essay, one that can then be used, in a group discussion or workshop activity, to prepare a detailed outline and examples for multiple sections of the essay. Of course, a particularly strong student example from a previous class can also work especially well for these purposes.

6. ASSESSMENT TOOLS

Because the writing can get so productively diffused within a successful blog (especially in a large class), and because of the diverse registers in which such writing can appear, the assessment of student blog participation is always a difficult and necessarily individualized issue. Although I have a minimum threshold I expect students to reach, which begins with the three to five directed postings I might assign in any given semester, I prefer blog participation to be something that students feel is strongly encouraged rather than strictly required. I find that blogs are most successful and most productive when they are allowed to develop organically, and when the students associate them with freedom and serendipitous discovery.

Thus, blog participation becomes merely one element within a student's broader class participation grade, a grade that, for me, is always most dependent on attendance, classroom engagement, and various short writing tasks. I tell my students, then, that the blog will adversely affect their participation grade only to the extent they do not respond appropriately to those few assigned postings; beyond that, the blog is there only as a potential boost to their participation grade. I want them to understand that any more comprehensive buy-in will benefit them individually in terms of both their multigenre essays and their class participation grade, and will benefit the collective, as well, in that the efforts of our discourse community will be extended and deepened. Ultimately, then, the assessment becomes something I do holistically at the end of the semester, when I use my sense of a student's overall presence on the blog to serve either as a boost or as a non-factor in compiling his or her class participation grade.

Meanwhile, the multigenre essay, typically representing 40 percent of the final grade in my Music and Literature class, is another matter, and a tricky one itself. Although most of us can rally behind the idea that students should be given the opportunity to deploy "the visual artist's instinct for pattern, contrast, unity, balance, and a bit of the poet's ability to posit and juxta/pose" (Vielstimmig 109), and that they be invited to defy the expectations of the academic essay, they may also, in the process, defy our ability to assess and grade their compositions. The best I can do is to share what I tell my students: that turning in a paper that meets the basic requirements (i.e., hits the installment due dates [prelude and final essay], fulfills the minimum page length, includes the minimum number of different genres (i.e., five), includes a works-cited list), but that is otherwise variously mechanical, careless, and spiritless, will typically equate with an average grade of C+. Failing to meet any of the basic requirements will, in all probability, drop the grade below a C+. How far above that average grade an essay can go will depend on the students' ability to

- demonstrate that they have not only done the reading (and listening) throughout the semester, but that they've also contemplated it and assimilated it (whether theoretically, critically, aesthetically, etc.);
- cite and engage the required texts on the syllabus in other than token ways;
- show that musical vocabulary and metaphors are informing their sensibility;
- reveal that they've used the class to contemplate music within the context of their own lives;
- supplement the course materials with outside readings and sources (in other words, yes, to some extent this is a research paper);
- burnish this material over an extended period of time;
- take some chances and generally manage to combine critical rigor with a playful spirit; and
- attend to issues of structure, connective threads, and writerly cleanliness.

7. THEORETICAL BASIS FOR THE ASSIGNMENT:
More Perfect Unions: Literary Studies, Blogging, and the Multigenre Essay

I have created and moderated blogs in my literature classes for many years—at first, strictly in my upper-division undergraduate and graduate classes but, increasingly, as I have mentioned, in my lower-division undergraduate classes. I have done so for many of the usual and expected reasons: blogs serve to enhance and extend class discussions, in the process giving students another venue in which to participate in the inquiry; they enable students to compensate (at least partially) for absences by being accountable for the readings; they leaven the seriousness of that inquiry with a sense of playfulness (even, at times, a sense of frivolity); they facilitate a cross-fertilization of ideas, and encourage more student-to-student exchanges; they allow for academic and personal writing that is not shadowed by the anxiety of evaluation and grading; they provide an archive of the semester's conversations and thematic currents that becomes, finally, a useful resource for final papers and projects; they allow students to rehearse and seek assistance with ideas for those final papers; and they allow you to build upon (or sometimes to correct or revise) your own classroom offerings, especially as they emerge from or are inflected by student comments and insights.

Significantly, blogs also remove the opacity from the scholarly process, refuting the old paradigm that scholarship is something that happens in isolation and that only reaches students when it is finished (and published). Elaine Showalter, for one, argues that we must "reconceive our pedagogy to make it as intellectually challenging as our research . . . so that the same problems we deal with in our research, including performance and narrative, become part of our pedagogical vocabulary" (11, 12).

Two moments, though, in two different classes separated by three years, clarified how the use of blogs in literature classes might more significantly reflect and advance my pedagogical goals, and intimated how I might subsequently reformulate print-based writing assignments. The first occurred following a class discussion in an undergraduate class on the tender and inspiring conclusion of Toni Morrison's *Jazz*. Later that night, I posted to the class blog, seeking not only to continue a conversation that had been curtailed by time, but also to suggest parallels between the speaker's ethical challenge to readers of Morrison's novel, the old griot's lessons in Morrison's Nobel acceptance speech, and Barack Obama's powerful speech on race in Philadelphia in 2008. I suggested that each text urges its readers and its audience—in a phrase defamiliarized by Obama and thereby made freshly poignant—toward a "more perfect union." The blog venue, of course, allowed me to link to both speeches so that the students could immediately access the full text of each, and perhaps offered them possibilities for an enriched, transhistorical, and multivalent response to *Jazz*.

Later, in a British literature survey course that carries students—in one semester—from the romantic through the contemporary periods, I was impressed when, during a discussion of Matthew Arnold's "Dover Beach," a student raised his hand and noted that the speaker's idyll-breaking "Listen!" (l. 9) early in the poem was a suggestive echo of the very same admonition in Wordsworth's sonnet "It is a beauteous evening." Whereas Wordsworth's speaker hears the consoling presence of "the mighty Being" (l. 6), Arnold's speaker, nearly fifty years later and informed by the questions of geological science, fixates on "the grating roar / Of pebbles" (l. 9-10) and "the eternal note of sadness" (l. 14). The student's perceptiveness in tracking the exclamatory admonition led to an illuminating class discussion of romantic versus Victorian engagements with Nature, Darwinian science, and ontological uncertainty, and the diverse connotations of the sea.

My student's observation was gratifying in that it actualized, however modestly, my goal of making associational thinking the basis of my pedagogy—certainly in survey courses that defy attempts to achieve rich historical "coverage," but also in courses like my Music and Literature that are built around especially diverse reading lists. In this I acceded to the disciplinary renewal sought by Roland Greene, who too often finds that "the categories of period and nation catch the field between them and shake out anything international . . . multicultural, or transhistorical." The British literature student's alert intertextual tracking became especially revelatory, however, when I considered it in conjunction with the "union" enabled by the earlier blog posting; that is, the two moments together made visible the consonance between my classroom pedagogy and the affordances of blogging.

This serendipitous connection only strengthened my pedagogical commitment to blogging, especially in a class like Music and Literature, which, because it is not bound by a single tradition, a single time period, or, of course, even a single art, mandates that students learn to recognize links and to create conversations between the disparate texts. The course blog serves as an important nurturer of the inter-/hypertextual sensibility and the new habit of mind students will need for the type of inquiry the course requires. As the method gains traction, the class ideally becomes capable of richly and diversely suggestive assemblages. I recall one memorable example when an almost casual discussion about street busker musicians led us, on the blog, to contemplate the idea and trope of itinerant bards from a number of angles, thus forming another "more perfect union." The posts and comments—after finding essential connections between the musical cadences of oral storytellers in Chamoiseau's *Solibo Magnificent* (which we were reading at the time) and William Blake's introduction to the *Songs of Innocence*—further riffed on the convergences by offering intriguing links to the lyrics of Bob Dylan's "Mr. Tambourine Man," a YouTube clip of a bluesman hitchhiking at the crossroads in the Coen brothers' *O Brother, Where Art Thou?* and an audio file of the dub poet Mikey Smith reading his fiery poem "Mi Cyaan Believe It."

Such moments, even when they were rarely as fulfilling and sustained as the previous example, made me wonder if I might attain even more continuity between the digital and nondigital aspects of my teaching. Marshall McLuhan proposes that "when information is brushed against information, the results are startling and effective" (77-79), which leads Jeff Rice, in *The Rhetoric of Cool*, to wonder if we can find a pedagogy that "would not just analyze but *produce* a writing comprised of juxtapositions" (84, my emphasis). In the Music and Literature class, one of the primary texts—Virginia Woolf's *The Waves*—features a narrating voice who at one point recognizes that his "philosophy, always accumulating, welling up moment by moment, runs like quicksilver a dozen ways at once" (218).

I realized that I wanted my students to bring this impression of quicksilver to their essays, to seize on as many of the available intellectual (and artistic) pathways as possible, to achieve forms of scholarly coherence that might even run counter to the types of writing typically sanctioned by the university. I'm mindful here of Robert Davis and Mark Shadle when they champion "alternative composition," or of Robert Root when he reminds us that "the best of our essayists, working in the Montaignian tradition . . . depend on a continuous thread of free association running through their essays. They let associative links of vignette, anecdote, reference, and evidence build in hopes of discovering a thesis" (79).

Could my print-based writing assignments, then, somehow nurture a comparable sort of associational thinking and scholarly emergence? Could the promotion of new arrangements and new grammars in their written work produce an antidote for the "exhaustion" Geoffrey Sirc diagnoses in student attitudes toward academic writing, and perhaps even lead students to perceive the essay's potential, in Davis and Shadle's wonderful formulation, as a "cabinet of wonder" (132)? My response to these questions, in two subsequent offerings of Music and Literature, was to retain the three short, formal (and rather conventional) reading-response papers distributed across the semester, but to replace the standard analytical research essay with the semester-long multigenre essay project. Because the latter essay is meant to be wide-angled and comprehensive, I introduce and describe the project, as I have noted, in the very first week of class, urging the students, in the process, to begin working on it from the outset, however modestly. Some of their core material gathers from stray blog posts, some from short in-class writing opportunities, some from their reading journals, and much, undoubtedly, from their typical late-semester cramming, but it ultimately creates an essay that, done well, allows its structure and its web of associative links and motifs to build incrementally and sometimes stealthily. Although it resolutely resists any sense of strict linearity, the essay, at its best, still manages to advance a reasoned argument, an issue we discuss whenever the opportunity arises, but most especially when the students turn in their preludes and we can identify their potential responsibilities for the balance of their projects.

In a course that strenuously investigates the symbolic and narrative implications of such musical structures as sonata form, theme-and-variation, and the verse-chorus-verse-chorus patterns of much popular music, I also encourage students to reflect on the formal properties of both the course texts *and* the multigenre essay. In this sense, I was excited to encounter Root's description of "the segmented essay," which he likens to an oratorio or a concerto: "The spaces are like intervals of silence between the separate elements. . . . Like musical compositions, nonfiction need not be one uninterrupted melody, one movement, but can also be the arrangement of distinct and discrete miniatures, changes of tempo, sonority, melody, separated by silences. This is what the spaces say" (86).

The journey from those initial revelatory moments to my new assignment structure has made me aware that although blogs are a technology largely dominated by written text, they nevertheless gesture toward what Paul Levinson identifies as "digital screen arts" (4); in this sense, they have the capacity to put students closer to a new relation to writing, closer to "new syntaxes for essayistic prose" (Sirc 152). Blogging in the literature classroom, then, not only produces more student investment in the inquiry of the class but also enables students to discover and create serendipitous (sometimes even magical) convergences across disparate texts. They acquire new habits of thought and new ways of perceiving coherence (i.e., in patterns, links, juxtapositions, associational logics, etc.), and thus implicitly prepare themselves for print essays that partake of a digital and hypertextual orientation. These outcomes suggest that blogging becomes a vital link between the digital elements of my classes, a prominent method of class inquiry, and a newly understood pedagogy of writing.

8. CONCLUSION

The multigenre essay has no doubt transformed my experience of the typical semester's endgame: that is, the forbidding piles of papers that gather at this time have never been more welcoming to me. There are dispiriting moments, to be sure, when I realize a percentage of the essays have not escaped the frenzied, hothouse compositional method of the typical end-of-semester essay; for the most part, however, I've found the multigenre essays to be almost unfailingly candid, self-reflective, honest, smart, and, occasionally, devastatingly poignant. The students catch the spirit of the

> "I've found the multigenre essays to be almost unfailingly candid, self-reflective, honest, smart, and, occasionally, devastatingly poignant."
>
> **Eric Reimer**

assignment and convey a rhetorical density that suggests they have, in their myriad ways, lived the material. On the course evaluations, students have

frequently expressed appreciation for the opportunity
to bring a sense of creativity into their written work, as
well as to include their own subject positions and lives
within serious academic inquiry. For my own part, the
promise of this assignment has encouraged me to seek
out other ways of bringing the realities of multiliteracy
and multimodality into my teaching, including, pres-
ently, collaboration with our Media Arts faculty and
students to try to bring a more dynamic element of literary visualizations to
my undergraduate survey courses.

> "The students catch the spirit of the assignment and convey a rhetorical density that suggests they have, in their myriad ways, lived the material."
>
> **Eric Reimer**

Being more ambitious, or simply looking ahead, whether in the context
of the Music and Literature course or other courses, I'm inclined to think
that the fullest realization of what I'm presenting here would be not a multigenre essay composed on the page, but a multimodal essay composed on the
screen. Mindful of what Levinson calls the "calculus of collaboration" actualized by the *new* new media, I'm also tempted by the possibility of pursuing
a collaborative "cabinet of wonder"—an essay in which each student contributes one section for a group oratorio that we then try to publish as a collective. The obstacles would be significant, of course, and perhaps such an
idea would be best suited for a graduate class, but especially when I find so
many of those final multigenre essays to be so probing and inventive, I find
myself tempted anew. We would do Montaigne proud, perhaps, and we
would continue to move toward an answer for Sirc when he wonders "how
[we can] get academic writing to restyle itself so as to better fit their exuberance" (200). Regardless, I am suitably gratified if, from the earliest blog
post to the final sections of the multigenre essay, students begin to sense the
power of Morrison's griot, to seek out more perfect unions, to intuit that
every story leads to another story in a garden of forking paths.

9. WORKS CITED

Arnold, Matthew. "Dover Beach." *The Poetry Foundation*, www.poetryfoundation
.org/poems-and-poets/poems/detail/435. Accessed 5 June 2012.

Blake, William. *Songs of Innocence* and *Experience: With Other Poems*. Basil, Mon-
tagu, Pickering, 1866. *Google Books*, books.goggle.com/books?id=1V8CA
AAQAJ.

Chamoiseau, Patrick. Solibo Magnificent. Pantheon, 1998.

Coen, Joel, and Ethan Coen, writers. *O Brother, Where Art Thou?* Touchstone,
2000.

Davis, Robert, and Mark Shadle. *Teaching Multiwriting: Researching and Composing with Multiple Genres, Media, Disciplines, and Cultures*. Southern Illinois
UP, 2007, p. 132.

Dylan, Bob. "Mr. Tabourine Man." 1964 *YouTube*, 11 Sept. 2012, www.youtube
.com/watch?v=DeP4FFr88SQ.

Fitzpatrick, Kathleen. "The Literary Machine: Blogging the Literature Course."
    Teaching Literature and Language Online. Edited by Ian Lancashire, MLA,
    2009, pp. 205-16.

Greene, Roland. "New World Studies and the Limits of National Literatures."
    Stanford Humanities Review vol. 6, no. 1, 1998, www.stanford.edu/group
    /SHR/6-1/html/greene.html.

Grudin, Robert. *Time and the Art of Living*. Harper, 1982.

Hornby, Nick. *High Fidelity*. Riverhead, 1995.

Jonathan Lethem. "The Beards: An Adolescence in Disguise." *The New Yorker*,
    28 Feb. 2005, pp. 62-69.

Joyce, James. "The Dead." *Dubliners*, Grant Richards Ltd., 1914.

Levinson, Paul. *New New Media*. Allyn & Bacon, 2009, p. 4.

McLuhan, Marshall. *The Medium Is the Message: An Inventory of Effects*. 196.
    Hardwired, 1996, pp. 77-79.

Morrison, Toni. "The Future of Time: Literature of Diminished Expectations."
    Nobelprize.org. 7 Dec. 1993, www.nobelprize.org/nobel_prizes/literature
    /laureates/1993/morrison-lecture.html. Lecture.

- - -. *Jazz*. 1992. Vintage, 2007.

Obama, Barack. "A More Perfect Union." *New York* Times, 18 Mar. 2008, www
    .nytimes.com/2008/03/18/us/politics/18text-obama.html?pagewanted=all.
    Transcript of speech.

Rice, Jeff. *The Rhetoric of Cool: Composition Studies and New Media*. Southern
    Illinois UP, 2007, p. 43, p. 84.

Romano, Tom. *Blending Genre, Altering Style: Writing Multigenre Papers*. Boynton/
    Cook, 2000.

Root, Robert. *The Nonfictionist's Guide: On Reading and Writing Creative Nonfic-
    tion*. Lanham, 2008, p. 79, p. 86.

Sheffield, Rob. *Love is a Mix Tape: Life and Loss, One Song at a Time*. Three Rivers,
    2007.

Showalter, Elaine. *Teaching Literature*. Blackwell, 2003, pp. 11-12.

Smith, Michael. "Mi Cyann Believe It." *Mi Cyaan Believe It*. Produced by Linton
    Kwesi Johnson and Dennis Bovell, Island Records, 1982.

Sirc, Geoffrey. *English Composition as a Happening*. Utah State UP, 2002, p. 152,
    p. 200.

Vielstimmig, Myka. "Petals on a Wet Black Bough: Textuality, Collaboration, and
    the New Essay." *Passions and Pedagogies and 21st Century Technologies*. Edited
    by Gail E. Hawisher and Cynthia Selfe, Utah State UP, 1999, pp. 89-114.

Woolf, Virginia. *The Waves*. 1931. Harvest, 1978, p. 218.

Wordsworth, William. "It is a Beauteous Evening, Calm and Free." 1807. Poetry
    Foundation, www.poetryfoundation.org/poems-and-poets/poems/detail
    /45524. Accessed 25 Aug. 2002.

6

Engaging Students with Literature in Virtual Spaces: Using Second Life to Explore Literature

Johansen Quijano
University of Texas at Arlington

Johansen Quijano is currently teaching at the University of Texas at Arlington where he is pursuing a doctoral degree in English with a focus on digital media, rhetoric, and composition. He holds a bachelor's degree in education and a master's degree in curriculum and development, both focusing on language acquisition, and a master's degree in English literature with a focus on the literatures of the Caribbean. His research in education has focused on the effects and application of digital and interactive narratives in the classroom, and his work on literature ranges from theory to digital narratives. He has published and presented on a variety of topics including video game studies, popular culture studies, education, teaching methodology, and language acquisition. His research interests include narrative, interactivity, simulation, new media in general, and literature. He also enjoys creative writing (fiction, historical fiction, and poetry) and reads poetry on his free time. Quijano has taught courses on rhetoric and composition, remedial English, ESL, introduction to English, business writing, technical communication, and media theory. He has also offered workshops on writing with Web 2.0 technologies.

1. OVERVIEW

- **Assignment:** Students explore a virtual rendition of Shakespeare's *Macbeth*, posting blog entries about the experience and writing a major paper.
- **Courses:** Shakespeare; any literature course that includes Shakespeare.
- **Literature:** Shakespeare's *Macbeth*, supplemental readings from the Renaissance period to Victorian texts.
- **Technology:** Second Life (secondlife.com).
- **Time:** Can be conducted in three 50-minute sessions or two 80-minute sessions, or extended over six 50-minute sessions or four 80-minute sessions.

> "Interactive worlds offer instructors almost endless possibilities to captivate students and make them engage with the course content through the use of participatory technologies."
>
> **Johansen Quijano**
> University of Texas at Arlington

2. GOALS OF THE ASSIGNMENT

By familiarizing students with an awareness of different adaptations of the same text and of the theories used to discuss them, this assignment provides students with additional vocabulary and tools to enhance their ability to think and read critically.

> "Instructors should be open to the possibility of teaching interactive texts side by side with traditional literature."
> **Johansen Quijano**

The focus of this assignment is on the adaptation of print texts into digital interactive texts. It incorporates elements of literary studies, digital media studies, and popular culture into its design, and allows students to think critically about literature as well as digital spaces. The assignment also emphasizes how literary modes of inquiry can help shed light on questions about digital texts.

> "The versatility provided by online platforms make them a remarkable tool to help students engage with content."
> **Johansen Quijano**

By the end of the assignment, students will learn to make connections between print texts and digital forms of literature. Students will also acquire and practice skills necessary for the analysis of literary texts.

> "The integration of interactive spaces into traditional courses helps students engage with the content at a deeper level, allows them to participate actively in the learning process, and ultimately helps them reach a better understanding of the content."
> **Johansen Quijano**

3. ASSIGNMENT SHEET

Engaging Students with Literature in Virtual Spaces: Using Second Life to Explore Literature

Course: _____

Instructor: _____

Date: _____

Procedure

You have so far in this class discussed elements of literature such as poetic genre, rhyme, repetition, and structure. You have also become acquainted with the concepts of transmedia narrative, digital storytelling, and interactivity of digital texts. We have analyzed how literature and digital texts interact, as well as discussed different ways to create digital adaptations of literature. You will now experience one of the many ways in which print texts can be adapted to digital formats by playing through a digital adaptation of *Macbeth*.

First, I will guide you through the process of opening a Second Life account and creating an avatar. You will then make your way through Tutorial Island in order to get acquainted with the controls.

I will guide you to *Macbeth* Island, where you will be able to explore the virtual rendition of Shakespeare's text. As you explore, remember to pay attention to the books scattered around the island, which include excerpts of the original text. Pay special attention to the discussion questions in these texts, as some of them will be brought up in class. Remember to think about the island's surroundings and how they symbolize elements of the original text. If you have any questions, feel free to ask me.

By the end of the class, you should have visited and read the texts located in the Throne Room, the Bloody Dream, the Labyrinth, the Path of Temptation, the Pit, and the Statue Plaza.

Evaluation

The evaluation for this activity will be holistic. You are expected to write several blog entries after you complete the activity, participate in class discussions, and write a major paper.

> **Blog Entries:** You should have a total of at least 4 blog entries — one narrating your trip through *Macbeth* Island, a second one reflecting on the experience, and two posts dedicated to the symbolism found in two of the many locations visited.

> **Class Discussions:** You will also participate in class discussions. In these discussions, you can answer the guide questions or raise issues of your own.

Major Paper: In the major paper, you will either expand on the meaning of one of the visited spaces within the context of Shakespeare's original play, or engage in a comparative reading of Shakespeare's text versus the Second Life space. You are encouraged to use the library's databases and journals of computer and game studies, like Game Studies (www.gamestudies.org) or Eludamos (www.eludamos.org).

Your paper should be in Arial size 12 font, use standard margins and MLA formatting, and be no longer than 5 pages of content.

Due Dates

The due date for the blog posts is _____

The due date for the paper is _____

4. TIME AND TECHNOLOGY

Students will need computers with Internet access; they will also need Second Life virtual world software, which is available for free online (https://secondlife.com). The installation and uninstall process is simple, and students will be able to remove the software from their personal computers after the class activity should they wish to do so. If you or your students are using institutional computers, check with your technology help desk to make sure that the software can be installed. Ideally, enlist a tech help desk or computer lab person to hold a session in which he or she guides students through the sign-up process. If this is not possible, you can demonstrate for students how to open a Second Life account. You might model the process in class, or create a video tutorial (or find one on YouTube) or a document with simple instructions explaining the procedure. However, I strongly encourage that you personally guide your students through the process of avatar creation in class.

Following is the process for creating an avatar:

1. Select an avatar. The avatar will be the virtual character that your students use to represent themselves in the Second Life virtual space. Students will have limited choices as to their avatars. They will be able to choose between several predesigned humanlike avatars (including vampires), robot, vehicle, and animal avatars. IMPORTANT: make sure to remind your students to select the free account option when they sign up.

2. The Second Life page will then ask for sign-up information, including an e-mail address and date of birth. Remind your students to set up a strong password that includes at least one lowercase character, one uppercase character, one number, and one symbol. Once they create an account, students will be able to download and install the Second Life client. To install the program, simply follow the on-screen instructions.

3. Once all students have installed Second Life, instruct them to start the program. The first time they log on they will find themselves in an introductory learning space where they can become acquainted with the Second Life controls and view the mechanics. Discussing the assignment requirements (explained further in this chapter) with students should take between fifteen and twenty minutes, and the sign-up and first log-in process (including the download and installation of the software) should take between five and ten minutes. Students can spend five to ten minutes exploring the introductory space and becoming acquainted with the controllers. Once they are all comfortable with exploring the virtual space, they will be able to move on to the core of the activity.

This activity works best when spread across three to six 50-minute sessions. If you structure the lessons into 80-minute sessions, then spread the activity across two to four sessions, depending on your needs. You will be able to select which elements to integrate into their lessons. This piece should be both critical and reflective in nature and demonstrate reflexive and critical thinking skills, as well as higher-level analysis techniques. Encourage your students to follow standard MLA (or other) format. During the first session, you will introduce them to the assignment sheet and the method of evaluation. Explain in detail Second Life's *Macbeth* virtual island and, when needed, explain briefly how the space is representative of scenes from Shakespeare's work.

During the first session, use the first 40 minutes to make sure students have signed up and selected an avatar. Then, have them spend the last 10 minutes of class in the introductory tutorial space becoming acquainted with the Second Life control schemes and navigation tools. Be sure to show students how to navigate to different places using the links available in the Second Life Web site and have them interact with the Second Life virtual space.

During the second session, have students explore *Macbeth* Island. Remind them to pay special attention to the multiple texts lying around the virtual space and encourage them to think critically about the meaning of their virtual experience when taken in the context of the entire experience of reading versus playing *Macbeth*.

The third session should involve traditional classroom discussion. You will likely have questions that you'd like to begin with, but you might also want to include some of the questions presented in the texts scattered throughout the *Macbeth* Island virtual space.

OPTIONS AND VARIATIONS. If you are teaching a survey course, you may want to have your students write a major paper from a comparative perspective. If time allows, consider asking them to participate in follow-up activities. If your course has a more active digital component, you may want to encourage students to observe and participate in virtual representations of literary texts.

If you would like to expand the assignment, you could further engage students by guiding them through one or two experiences once they've become more acquainted with Second Life. If there are plays scheduled by the Second Life Shakespeare Company, or by another group of virtual actors, you might ask students to sit in on a live performance. Alternatively, you can ask them to watch a previously recorded play.

A second option is to have students create their own Second Life rendition of a literary text. They can choose to do another Shakespeare play, or their own rendition of any poem or novel. The settings in Second Life are as diverse as human imagination itself, and finding a place to recreate their chosen text will prove simple once students have mastered the software. If you go with this option, allow students enough time to prepare the play and rehearse within the virtual environment.

This assignment should conclude with students writing a traditional paper in which they critically analyze the digital interpretation of their chosen text side by side with the original text.

The total required time for this activity is three days: this includes the installation of Second Life, exploration of *Macbeth* Island, and built-in classroom discussion. If you have time, consider expanding the assignment by adding an extra day for watching a Second Life virtual representation of a literary text, if this option is available. You can also build in an additional two to three days for preparation and presentation of students' own digital interpretations of a literary text.

ACTIVITY PROCEDURE. Even though Second Life is a great resource for teaching, it is wise to remember that, in the end, it is still a commercial virtual space. While it has spaces that are excellent for exposing students to literary and linguistic contexts, as well as virtual representations of several major university campuses and libraries, there are also less academic spaces created by users. In order to keep students on task, teach your students how to navigate using the Destinations navigation menu available in the Second Life Web site. For educational purposes, the main destinations can be found under the Arts tab (secondlife.com/destinations/arts), which includes *Macbeth* Island; the Education tab (secondlife.com/destinations/learning), which includes university campuses and virtual libraries; and the Historical Landmarks section (secondlife.com/destinations/roleplay/historical), which includes places as diverse as Chateau de Versailles and 1920s-era Berlin. For this specific activity I will use *Macbeth* Island, but you may want to explore other area-specific texts. An instructor offering a course on French literature, for example, might prefer to guide students through virtual Versailles and nineteenth-century France and have them watch a performance on the mannerisms of French royalty by those who frequent Versailles on a regular basis.

For the first guided incursion into the world of virtual literature, have your students go to *Macbeth* Island by using the Second Life's navigation feature (secondlife.com/destination/shakespeare-s-Macbeth-in-second-life). With the program open, they should click on the View in Map button, then select visit this location. They will then find their avatars in *Macbeth* Island.

The first thing you, your students, and any users should do when they are in *Macbeth* Island is to click on the Information Pedestal shaped like a fountain. This will add an item called the Macbeth User Attachment. Equipping this item will enable the player's avatar to interact and act out custom commands that heighten the immersive experience. At this point, students have the option of exploring *Macbeth* Island in an open, non-linear way or by clicking on the tablets located in front of the stones. Ask your students to start their exploration by clicking on the center rune. This will take them to the top of Macbeth's castle. From there, students can descend into Macbeth's Throne Room, where they will be able to interact with various objects representative of Macbeth's psychological state throughout various acts of the play, as well as see a virtual representation of various acts that have been programmed into various nonplaying characters. Clicking on the texts scattered around the area will allow students to read various sections of the original source text. These texts, which already have built-in questions, might provide ideas for class discussion.

Some of the more thought-provoking questions prompt players to think about the virtual *Macbeth* experience — and about Shakespeare and his writing. Furthermore, some of these questions are difficult to answer if a player is not familiar with the original *Macbeth* text. Some of the better questions and discussion prompts that you may want to use later in discussion or to prompt student writing include the following:

- How important is symbolism and metaphor in Shakespeare's verse?
- A maze is a tour puzzle in the form of a complex branching passage through which the user must find a route out. How does the virtual maze signify Macbeth's journey?

At the same time, other questions invite the reader to consider Macbeth's psychological state and the symbolism of the virtual space in relation to the original text:

- Discuss the nature of temptation and morality. What do the rotten hands in the Path of Temptation signify?
- Research and find the source quotes written on the walls as graffiti. How do these quotes represent Macbeth's mental state throughout his journey?

A full exploration of the island should take forty minutes. Students can spend the remainder of the class session reflecting on and writing about their experience. At this point, students are familiar with *Macbeth* Island and have read the source text and some of the questions to be discussed. They will be able to organize their thoughts and seriously consider how they want to contribute to class discussion. As previously stated, you should lead the discussion on the merits and accuracy of this virtual space. Because class discussions are fluid, my recommendation is to use some of the discussion prompts for *Macbeth* as a gateway into the Shakespearean text, and other literary texts, instead of as a stand-alone version. You will want to wrap this up with a conversation on how texts and genre make transitions from one form of media to another — in this case from print text to virtual space.

Depending on your course goals and time, you may or may not want to have students produce their own Second Life plays. For those who do, I recommend that you show your students the various historical and art-based destinations that have been created in Second Life. I often find myself visiting Renaissance Island (secondlife.com/destination/renaissance-island) for this purpose. Alternatively, you might prefer to have your students access one of the many archives, such as the First World War Digital Archive (secondlife.com/destination/first-world-war-poetry-digital-archive) or invite them to listen to and perform original poetry in the Second Life Poetry Club (secondlife.com/destination/the-lyrical-cafe-poetry-club). Whichever the case, you will want to become familiar with the spaces your students wish to incorporate.

Although this assignment works best when integrated into an overall course framework, the cross-analysis of Shakespeare's original *Macbeth* and the Second Life *Macbeth* Island texts is an excellent strategy for getting students to think about genre and media. In this spirit, you might ask students to write a critical analysis in which they consider the concept of adaptation as a whole, or elaborate on one of the discussion questions about how a specific section of the virtual space works as a representation of one aspect of the original text. You can give students the choice of writing a purely comparative piece that focuses only on the two primary texts and excludes outside research; however, it is always an excellent idea to encourage students to engage in outside research and incorporate their findings. If you would like your students to look for existing criticism, invite them to use databases to look for Shakespearean criticism and to read some of the major journals on video games, and virtual worlds research. Game Studies (www.game studies.org), Eludamos (www.eludamos.org), and Loading… (journals.sfu .ca/loading/) have some of the best open-access pieces on the topic.

5. ANTICIPATING STUDENT NEEDS

Most of the predictable difficulties with this assignment are of a technical nature. At smaller campuses and community colleges, or in schools located in economically challenged areas, it is possible that not all students will have laptop computers. Even if they do have their own computers, your institution might not have an open wireless connection. In either of these situations you will have to rely on institutional resources such as digital media labs. If your institution does not have a room with enough computers for all students, then carrying out this activity will be impossible. Even if your institution has enough computers with Internet access for all students, or every student has a laptop computer and access to a wireless connection, check to see if your institution has blocked the Second Life software suite. If this is the case, consider speaking with your department chair or school director and with the director of technology to allow access to Second Life during the allotted class period.

An issue that may arise in relation to this assignment is that students may find themselves distracted. Although Second Life has many educational applications, it is not an educational program in itself. Because most of the content in Second Life is user-generated, there are several spaces that serve as virtual nightclubs or other types of leisure spaces, and some students may find themselves inclined to spend time here, rather than in the assigned lesson spaces. Although there is nothing that can be done from a technical perspective—it is impossible to block these parts of the Second Life world without blocking the entire program—you may want to walk around the classroom to make sure that students are on task.

Finally, a few students may be unfamiliar with technology. In these cases, consider assigning a student who is more comfortable with technology to serve as a mentor, or provide additional one-on-one class time for students who are less proficient with technology. You could also make this a collaborative activity, having students work in pairs.

6. ASSESSMENT TOOLS

The evaluation for this assignment should be holistic. Students' overall course grades should incorporate their experiences in the virtual world, their participation in class discussions, and their written texts.

Ask your students to write four entries about *Macbeth* Island. In their first post, they will write a simple narrative of their events in the island. However, I urge you to encourage students to be thorough in their descriptions. For their second post on the island, students should engage in a short analysis of what the virtual space means and how it might change their perception of *Macbeth*. Encourage them to comment on how they experienced the virtual space. The last two entries will focus on the symbolism of space in the context of the play. Avoid using "objective quantitative" rubrics that count how many reasons or details were given and instead focus on how well students discussed the topic from an intellectual and narrative perspective. Scores received from these journal entries or blog posts should go toward a general blog or journal grade. I have found that offering fifteen points per entry or post to be an ideal number.

When I read students' posts, I allocate five points for questions of exigency and other rhetorical considerations, five points for questions of content, and five points for style and mechanics.

Following are some of the questions that I think about when reading students' entries:

Rhetorical Considerations

- Do students take into consideration that an audience beyond the instructor will read the piece (if published in a blog)?
- Do students explain why they are writing?
- Is the writing compelling and interesting?

Content

- Do students successfully get their point(s) across?
- Did students deviate and write about unrelated issues?
- Are the students' entries complete? If not, what could they have added?

Style and Mechanics

- Have students posted well-formatted entries?
- Is their paragraphing appropriate?
- Is their use of sentence structure correct?
- Are there grammatical or punctuation errors in students' entries?

The second evaluation that you can rely on is class discussion. Potential discussion questions (adapted from the texts scattered throughout *Macbeth* Island) include the following:

- Discuss examples in *Macbeth* where Shakespeare has taken poetic license with the historical sources to enhance the drama. Now discuss examples of poetic license taken by the designers of *Macbeth* Island to create an immersive world.
- What is the relationship between plot and character action in *Macbeth*? Is this relationship represented in the virtual space?
- How much is *Macbeth* a matter of choice versus a matter of fate? How is this struggle of choice versus fate represented in the Second Life virtual space?
- How does the design of the Throne Room in *Macbeth* Island lead the user to consider issues of leadership and identity?

The last assignment for this activity should be a formal paper that follows MLA (or other documentation style) standards. When evaluating students' writing, focus on content and rhetorical effectiveness, not on punctuation and grammar. For this paper, instead of using an objective quantitative rubric geared toward counting elements, I recommend that you use an open approach in which you consider how well students executed the elements of the paper and how well they fit together. Below is a list of some criteria that I tend to use:

Individual Elements — 55 Points Total

Mechanical Considerations — 15 pts total
    Grammar (5 pts)
    Punctuation (5 pts)
    Sentence Structure (5 pts)

Rhetorical Considerations — 10 pts total
    Writing Is Engaging (5 pts)
    Maintains an Academic Voice (5 pts)

Content Considerations — 30 pts total
    Thorough Introduction and Neat Conclusion (10 pts)
    Coherent and Reasonable Claim (5 pts)
    Complete Argument Defending the Claim (15 pts)

Elements of Cohesion and Content — 45 Points Total

Structure and Cohesion — 15 pts
Flow of Ideas between Sections — 15 pts
Links between Concepts within Sections — 15 pts

    I recommend that you show these evaluation criteria to students as they start to write their papers; it gives them an idea of the elements that you will be looking for without explicitly telling them what to write. It gives them a road map of the elements the paper should have, but also allows for freedom and creativity.

    I also encourage you to select which of the activities mentioned above best suits your students' needs. If you intend to ask your students to view an online play, also ask them to write a journal or blog entry and evaluate their entries as previously explained. Likewise, if you intend to ask your students to create a play, ask them to write journal or blog entries during each step of the process, including a longer entry at the end of the experience worth double the score. In terms of evaluating student plays, I have found it efficient to carry out this assessment using journal and blog entries and by having follow-up discussions in the classroom regarding their adaptations.

7. THEORETICAL BASIS FOR THE ASSIGNMENT:
Engaging Students with Literature in Virtual Spaces: Using Second Life to Explore Literature

Academic inquiry into digital media has been around for more than fifty years, with Marshall McLuhan popularizing its study in 1967 with the publication of *The Medium Is the Message*. However, inquiry into the educational potential of digital media, especially that of video games and virtual spaces, is a relatively new development, and content area–specific research on virtual spaces and the teaching of literature is all but nonexistent. There has, however, been some theorizing and research in regard to virtual spaces and literacy and language arts in general that we can draw on when creating a theoretical framework for using virtual spaces in literature classrooms. In *What Videogames Have to Teach Us About Learning and Literacy*, James P. Gee put forward a theory of education based on design principles of video game texts that explained how interactive digital narratives include certain design elements built on sound pedagogical principles. Some of these include the active, critical learning principle, the psychosocial moratorium principle, and the text principle.[1] Sadly, he noted that even though virtual spaces "have a great deal to teach us about how reading printed text actually works when people understand—again, in situated embodied active and critical ways—what they read," not many classroom instructors took advantage of these education models (100).

> "I drew heavily from various sources on the literacy, rhetoric, and narrative of digital technologies . . . but it was [James P.] Gee, once again, who provided the core inspiration."
>
> **Johansen Quijano**

Building on Gee's model, David Hutchinson and other educators developed ways of using digital technologies to enhance the teaching/learning experience in content-specific classrooms. His text *Playing to Learn* focuses on content-specific activities that involve video games and virtual spaces instructors can use in their classes. Although groundbreaking, theoretical texts like Gee's work largely explore general educational principles that are disengaged from specific disciplines, while more practical texts like Hutchinson's focus largely on school-level courses that are unrelated to literature. Furthermore, most of the studies on digital literacies that one might relate to literature pedagogies involve the rhetoric and narrative aspect of digital technologies (Bogost; Murray), and while these are the key texts one should reference when discussing the narrative and rhetoric of virtual spaces in academic discourse, they don't provide any special insight into the application of virtual spaces in education beyond pointing out that these spaces can be used for educational, narrative, and rhetorical purposes.

While designing this assignment I drew heavily from various sources on the literacy, rhetoric, and narrative of digital technologies, as well as some of the purely theoretical works on digital technologies, but it was Gee, once again, who provided the core inspiration. In his text *Situated Language and Learning*, Gee shares the story of a kid called Bryan. Gee writes that "Bryan had not been able to read when he entered Kindergarten. He had, however, gotten a Nintendo Game Boy, a hand-held video game player" (25). Gee explained how Bryan learned to read by playing Pokémon, and that "it was this experience, coupled with much interaction with the *Pokemon* universe (via cards, figures, books, and the Internet), that both motivated him to want

---

[1]See Gee's thirty-six learning principles in *What Video Games Have to Teach Us About Learning and Literacy* for a more detailed list and explanation.

to read and taught him how to read, along with a good first grade teacher" (25). In this example, Bryan used the Pokémon universe as a gateway into reading. This is the core principle behind the Second Life assignment presented in this chapter.

By using this assignment, you will be able to provide your students with a viable gateway into the world of literature from the Renaissance to the Victorian period by allowing them to experience the Second Life virtual representation of *Macbeth*—and other similar virtual spaces, if you desire—and by giving them the opportunity to both view and create their own digital version of one of Shakespeare's plays. This will allow students to experience a world and a literature that is foreign to them, and toward which they are often hostile, while allowing them to discover these texts and cultures through the familiarity of games and virtual spaces. However, it's worth noting that the Second Life engine is quite flexible, and with a bit of tweaking, you can modify this activity to have your students recreate any scene from any literary text in an appropriate Second Life setting. Further, with some practice and technical skill, you can enable your students to create their own virtual tours through the world of any given literary text.

8. CONCLUSION

As you've seen, this activity uses tools native to students as a gateway to literature. Furthermore, it allows students who are not entirely competent with technology to develop their technological literacy skills while they become engaged with literature. It also includes a research component and, if you should decide to implement it, a creative component. Because this activity shows that technology can be used in interesting and creative ways to captivate students and draw them into the world of literature, you can use it as a jumping point for future discussions regarding technology and literature. If you decide against further integration of technology in your lessons, you can still ask students to draw on the analytical and critical thinking techniques acquired in this activity for future discussions of literature. By the end of the activity, students will have experienced reading literature as an activity that transcends the pages of any given text. They will have acquired the ability to connect ideas presented in literature to trends they see online in the digital spaces they frequent, and they will have learned that the literary experience is one to be enjoyed.

In my own experience integrating this activity into the classroom, I have seen students become more engaged with their readings after they have experienced the corresponding virtual spaces. They ask questions not only about the text but also about the history, society, and general context that surround the text. This makes them more invested in the course content than they would be otherwise. I have used similar activities in composition and technical writing courses, and students are always thankful for the inclusion of a digital technologies component within the framework of the course.

In the end, this activity uses technology to engage students with literature. The activity uses tools familiar to students as a gateway to worlds, texts, and values that may seem foreign to them. This helps students view the course content as relevant to their own increasingly technocentric lives. With global trends gearing toward an increasingly digital world, engaging students by using these tools is not only smart but also the pedagogically sound thing to do.

9. WORKS CITED

Bogost, Ian. *Unit Operations*. MIT P, 2008.

Din, Feng S., and Josephine Caleo. "Playing Computer Games versus Better Learning." Paper presented at the Annual Conference of Eastern Educational Research Association, Clearwater, Florida, 20 Feb. 2000. *ERIC*, ED438905, archive.org/details/ERIC_ED438905.

Gee, James P. *What Video Games Have to Teach Us About Learning and Literacy*. Palgrave Macmillan, 2003, p. 25, p. 100.

- - -. *Situated Language and Learning: A Critique of Traditional Schooling*. Routledge, 2004.

Hansson, Thomas. "English as a Second Language on a Virtual Platform — Tradition and Innovation in a New Medium." *Computer Assisted Language Learning*, vol. 18, no. 1, 2005, pp. 69-79. *Taylor & Francis Online*, doi: 10: 1080/09588220500132332.

Hutchinson, David. *Playing to Learn*. Libraries Unlimited, 2007.

Johnson, Steven. *Everything Bad Is Good for You*. Riverhead, 2005.

Liu, Min. "An Exploratory Study of How Pre-Kindergarten Children Use the Interactive Multimedia Technology: Implications for Multimedia Software Design." *Journal of Computing in Childhood Education*, vol. 7, no. 2, 1994 pp. 71-92. *ERIC*, ED396713, archive.org/stream/ERIC_ED396713/ERIC _ED396713_djvut.txt.

McLuhan, Marshall. *The Medium Is the Message: An Inventory of Effects*. 1967. Hardwired, 1999.

Murray, Janet. *Hamlet on the Holodeck*. MIT P, 1999.

7

"Hath he not twit?": Teaching Shakespeare through Twitter

Toria Johnson

University of St. Andrews

Toria Johnson completed her PhD in Renaissance drama at the University of St. Andrews, where she teaches drama and literature courses. She has also taught at Washington State University. Toria currently works on the history of the emotions, with a particular emphasis on pity and subjectivity in sixteenth-century England. Other recent research considers the image of the female in authors' notes preceding early printed matter, and literary notions of community.

COURTESY OF TORIA JOHNSON

1. OVERVIEW

- **Assignment:** Students use Twitter to stage a Shakespeare play.
- **Courses:** Shakespeare; drama; introduction to literature (if plays are taught).
- **Literature:** Shakespeare; or other dramatic works.
- **Technology:** Twitter (twitter.com).
- **Time:** Five weeks.

2. GOALS OF THE ASSIGNMENT

This project is designed for a course that aims to give students a concentrated introduction to the Shakespearean canon and the opportunity to study multiple plays in a short span of time. By using Twitter to stage a Shakespeare play, students will gain a nuanced understanding of Shakespeare's work and a sense of the continuing development of his work over time, through adaptation and reinterpretation. By assigning a performance group to each play covered during the semester, you will expose students to multiple forms of textual analysis for every play: one directed by their instructor, in the form of lectures and classwork, and another developed by their peers.

> "This assignment is about fostering community among students, but also about using common technology to challenge literary custom."
>
> **Toria Johnson**
> University of St. Andrews

99

The intended result, therefore, is that students will discover the richness of Shakespeare's plays: how open they are to interpretation, how different layers of meaning emerge depending on individual performers, and, importantly, just how different it is to encounter a play *in performance* rather than as a text. The constraints of the technology — specifically Twitter's restriction on the length of posts and format of publication — will encourage students to consider their own interpretations of the text as they make editorial decisions about word choice and other considerations.

"Students typically find this project inventive and a nice change from what they're expecting — in my experience they respond with fresh, creative work."

Toria Johnson

3. ASSIGNMENT SHEET

"Hath he not twit?": Twitter and Shakespeare

Course: _____

Instructor: _____

Date: _____

Shakespeare's plays were written to appeal to a wide range of audiences — from the most educated viewers (royalty and the aristocracy) to the predominantly illiterate laity who made up the "groundlings" at the base of the stage. Perhaps in recognition of this, Shakespeare famously played with language, mixing highly stylized rhetoric with the colloquial. In the same spirit, and following in the footsteps of prominent theater companies such as the Royal Shakespeare Company, which staged a Twitter production of *Romeo and Juliet* entitled *Such Tweet Sorrow* in 2010, this assignment asks you to form groups, use Twitter to perform a scene from one of the course texts, reflect on the ways your use of technology informed your performance of the play, and, finally, to share your experiences and findings with the class.

Each group will be assigned one of the plays covered this semester. In your group, select a scene from your chosen play to perform; you should choose one that you find particularly interesting, problematic, or significant. Divide parts among the group, ensuring that each group member is responsible for at least one character. In cases where the characters in the scene outnumber the members of the group, you (or another of the group members) may elect to take responsibility for multiple characters.

This project requires several components, all of which will contribute to your final grade:

- **Individual Character Page(s):** Create an account (or several, if you are representing multiple characters) on Twitter (twitter.com) for the character or role you have selected to play. Twitter will allow you to personalize your profile page. Using the options available to you, create a page that you feel accurately reflects the character you're representing. This assignment is intended to encourage exploration of the characters and stories Shakespeare offers, and as such you should feel free to be creative with your representation: take advantage of options to customize your personal photo, a header image, your location, and theme (using image or color). You can also write a short biography, using 160 characters or fewer. What traits of your character will you emphasize? You will have an opportunity to explain your choices in the performance diary.

- **Performance:** As a group, decide how to perform your scene. What sort of tone and feel will your performance have? Which elements of the scene do you want to stress? What type of language will you use? The performance

(continued)

ASSIGNMENT SHEET (*continued*)

must reflect a thorough understanding of the source text (i.e., you cannot add elements that have no basis in the original text, but you may explore ideas that Shakespeare leaves undeveloped). You must preserve the integrity of the scene, considering the scene's function in the original play and preserving that function in your own performance. However, you may expand or reduce the material as you see fit. Ensure that you can justify your decisions, in both your performance diary and the group presentation.

- **Performance Diary:** The performance diary is your opportunity, as individuals, to document the progress of your project; it should begin when you join a group and choose a play, and should continue through group presentation preparations. In regular entries, discuss the considerations that influenced your interpretation of your character, and explain the decisions you made. What are you trying to achieve with your performance? Explain the work your group did in preparing and executing your performance. How does this type of work inform your knowledge of the play? What elements or characteristics are you emphasizing in your chosen character? In your chosen scene? Your performance diary can be informal in tone — it should be an accurate and personal reflection of your experience with this project — but it should be thoughtful and thorough in its construction.

- **Group Presentation:** Your group will present the results of your performance immediately after the last class lecture pertaining to your play. Your presentation should offer insight into your performance decisions (e.g., choice of scene, language, tone), it should explore the themes and ideas that became important during your performance, and it should expand on and extend beyond the analysis offered in the course lectures. You should talk about the challenges you faced as a group and how you overcame them. Consider any differences you noted between *performing* the play and *studying* the text of the play. How, if at all, did performing your scene change your ideas about the play? Your presentation should run between 10 and 15 minutes. Be aware that in addition to content, your group presentation grade will reflect the clarity, organization, and delivery of the presentation itself.

As your group presentations will immediately follow the last class on your play, your group will be partially dependent on the class schedule and will need to adjust accordingly. For example: if the first play covered in class is *Titus Andronicus*, the group responsible for *Titus* would present at the end of that unit. If your play is covered last this semester, your performance and presentation will come much later. You will be responsible for managing your own time over the course of the semester, but you should allow at least 3 weeks for your group to meet, design, and execute your performance, to maintain your performance diaries, and to prepare the group presentation.

4. TIME AND TECHNOLOGY

TIME. After the initial presentation of the ongoing class project at the start of term, and once groups are assigned plays and the schedule of performance and presentation is determined, each group should be allocated at least three weeks to design, plan, and execute their performance, and to prepare the supplemental elements of the project (performance diaries and presentations).

TECHNOLOGY. This assignment only requires access to a computer (or a Web-ready device, like a tablet or a phone) with Internet access. Twitter accounts are available, free of charge, although students who already have a Twitter account will need to set up a separate e-mail account, available free from providers like Gmail (gmail.com) or Outlook.com, in order to register a Twitter profile for their chosen character. Once the account is set up, each student will have the opportunity to customize it, according to his or her individual interpretation of the character. Twitter allows users to report their location, design a page background, post a profile picture, and write a short bio; student negotiation of these options should be considered a part of the overall performance, and as such it should be factored into the final assessment.

Students can use either personal computers or those in a school computer lab to set up their accounts, and for the performances themselves. One of the benefits of Twitter is that it facilitates long-distance communication, which means that group performances can occur without the "players" occupying the same physical space. You may wish to reserve a computer lab to assist students in creating Twitter accounts and to review basic Twitter functions (though this will depend largely on the class's familiarity with the platform). During this time, encourage students to follow their classmates' accounts; this will provide each student access to the other groups' work.

5. ANTICIPATING STUDENT NEEDS

This assignment assumes that students see Twitter as a familiar community, a space they feel comfortable navigating. The project largely relies on students' willingness to engage with nontraditional and experimental forms of learning. In my experience, the biggest potential difficulty is that the assignment might be viewed as an infringement of a nonacademic space. Requiring students to set up ghost accounts—in which they perform certain characters or figures from a first-person perspective—partially addresses this issue; it is important that students not be required to link their ghost accounts to their private accounts (and indeed, it is not vital to the assignment). Accounts can be deleted upon completion of the assignment, if desired.

Given that the parameters of the assignment already allow students to maintain a certain amount of distance, in my own classroom the majority of student resistance has stemmed from a perception of Twitter as insufficiently "serious" for an academic environment, rather than a sense that the project infringed on personal navigation of social media spaces. For me, pairing this assignment with more traditional forms of assessment—class tests and essays—helped to mitigate student worry that the course would not comprise more conventional, expected forms of learning.

> "Remind students of the difference between what David Silver calls 'thick' and 'thin' tweets—that is, the difference between trivial and insubstantial commentary and multilayered, thought-provoking content."
>
> **Toria Johnson**

Those students who persisted in complaining seemed to be responding more to an impression that Twitter is not a place for "legitimate" content; often, these students reported a prior engagement with Twitter in which most of the accessed content was perceived as trivial or entirely pointless. This type of student is often helped by a discussion (either with the entire class or on an individual basis) about the positive value of Twitter, including the growing research into its uses: developing a sense of community, cultivating a sixth sense about those we follow, and opening up the opportunity for extended or parallel discussions after class. In a literary sense, this assignment has a lot to teach students about the supporting structure of the Shakespearean canon: the significance of writing to an audience, the enduring relevance of the texts, and the importance of experimental writing.

It can also be helpful to remind students that the boundaries of the assignment will, if negotiated properly, restrict their affiliation with external writers supplying undesired content. Students can choose whom they follow, and can control access to their own content as well; it is in many respects up to them to craft a meaningful experience within the technology provided. Finally, reminding students of the difference between what David Silver calls "thick" and "thin" tweets—that is, the difference between trivial and insubstantial commentary and multilayered, thought-provoking content—may help students understand the opportunity to do important work on Twitter. In practice, many students find the composition of meaningful, course-appropriate content a challenge in itself; this is part of the aim of the project. Many students comment in their presentations about their difficulty in negotiating the space constraints, finding the right tone, and dealing with frequent posting of tweets. These are important obstacles that can (and should) be addressed by each group, and given meaningful space in both the performance diary and the presentation.

As students are aware of the public nature of their engagement with Twitter within the assignment, and as that material is later presented to the class in the group presentations, I've found that I have not experienced a problem with what Mark Sample calls a "snark valve" ("Twitter"). Sample's argument, that Twitter seemingly encouraged some of his students to feel comfortable lashing out, is still, however, a relevant concern to instructors engaging with a project reliant on Twitter: Sample suggests that this type of negative content is in fact a valuable type of composition, insofar as it leads students (some for the first time) toward articulating a clear stance. That, in many ways, is the overarching aim of the assignment: to afford students an opportunity to stretch beyond the bounds of traditional learning models, in order to fashion new and exciting content.

6. ASSESSMENT TOOLS

Because this assignment requires both group and individual work, it is appropriate to offer a grade for the group and also grades for each individual.

The *group grade* should reflect the following elements:

- **The quality of the Twitter performance.** Has the group understood the thrust of the scene they are portraying? Have they adequately covered the information, tone, and feeling of the scene as Shakespeare offers it? How innovative has the group been with their interpretation? Does the group's interpretation of the scene have a solid basis in the source material?
- **The quality of the in-class presentation.** Does the group's work reflect an understanding of the assignment? Have they expanded on the textual analysis provided in lectures and class discussion? Is the presentation clear, informative, and well organized? Has the work been divided evenly among group members?

The *individual grades* should reflect the following elements:

- **The construction of the individual Twitter profile.** Has the student taken full advantage of the opportunity to construct his/her character's identity? Has the student made thoughtful decisions about his/her character's tone, language, commentary, biographical description, and photo? Does the profile demonstrate a thoughtful engagement with the source text, and a reasonable representation of the character?
- **The quality of the performance diary.** Has the student kept a thorough diary? Does the diary clearly track the project's development? Is it reflective and thoughtful? Does it provide details of the process of constructing the student's assigned character?

Since the due date for each group depends on the progression of the course, some groups will have more time to prepare their projects (though students will not be required or expected to take advantage of this in order to achieve success). Instructors may nonetheless wish to acknowledge the different time scales while grading. They may also take into account that groups presenting at the start of the semester will be unable to benefit from first seeing other groups present.

7. THEORETICAL BASIS FOR THE ASSIGNMENT:
"Hath he not twit?": Twitter and Shakespeare

In 2008, on the literary humor Web site *McSweeney's Internet Tendency*, run by McSweeney's Publishing House, Sarah Schmelling authored an immensely popular piece entitled "*Hamlet*: Facebook Feed Edition." Originally presented as a list, and later reworked to include the visual characteristics of a Facebook home page, Schmelling rendered Shakespeare's great tragedy as a series of (often comical) status updates, such as "Hamlet thinks it's annoying when your uncle marries your mother right after your dad dies," and notifications, including "Ophelia removed 'moody princes' from her interests." Schmelling's piece translated the play—itself a network of interacting characters—according to the community principles of Facebook: a space in which family, friends, and acquaintances connect and share information. Using Facebook, Schmelling was able to present Shakespeare's play intelligently, irreverently, and, most importantly, in a familiar and accessible way. In another case, in April 2010, the Royal Shakespeare Company used Twitter as a platform for a five-week performance of *Romeo and Juliet* entitled *Such Tweet Sorrow*: characters set up profiles and worked through the story using modern language and convention, without the traditional time restraint, and in accordance to the culture of the Twitter community. During the performance, the players moved beyond the traditional format by interacting directly with other users—effectively, their audience—engaging in conversation, conducting polls, and commenting on contemporary events.

Using these social network–based performances as inspiration, this assignment asks students to use Twitter to perform a scene from one of Shakespeare's plays while engaging with performance decisions which include (but are not limited to) pace, tone, language, and delivery. The assignment includes the performance itself, which happens as group work, and also requires the construction of individual character profile pages, a performance diary, and a group presentation. Together, these elements encourage students to use a medium which is likely very familiar to them in order to more thoroughly (and perhaps more comfortably) analyze a potentially intimidating text. Studying Shakespeare's plays in this manner challenges the notion that they are either static or outdated, and will emphasize themes, questions, and ideas present in the plays that remain relevant and resonate with a modern audience (and modern students).

The value of Twitter has been explored by a number of people, with journalist Clive Thompson noting in particular that the application's high volume of often trivial information actually fosters a community in which users are able to maintain an ongoing, low-level awareness

> "Schmelling rendered Shakespeare's great tragedy as a series of (often comical) status updates, such as . . . 'Ophelia removed "moody princes" from her interests.'"
>
> **Toria Johnson**

of those they follow. The potential of this type of connectivity has been increasingly assigned a pedagogic value
by scholars such as Rick Reo and Mark Sample, whose
"Twitter Adoption Matrix" highlights the technology's capacity for enhancing the classroom community outside
of direct contact time; Sample also argues that Twitter
allows instructors to cultivate back-channel class discussion, to extend those discussions held in classes, and to
solicit feedback (Sample, "Framework"). This assignment,
however, draws more directly on what Jesse Stommel has
identified as the "certain charm, [and] playfulness in-
volved" in composition for Twitter. "The pleasure in the act of composing with
[the application's 140-character] constraints," he writes, constitutes "an intentional and curious engagement with how sentences, words, and letters make
meaning."

> "By placing the assign-
> ment within the context of
> a familiar community, the
> exercise also encourages
> students to practice writing/
> performing for their peers,
> and challenges them to
> anticipate and react to peer
> audiences."
>
> **Toria Johnson**

This type of writing has a clear academic benefit, and yet the relative informality of the medium, for many students, reduces the anxiety that
often accompanies traditional academic writing. Moreover, the potential for
a high volume of tweets, each immediately published to audience, encourages a low-risk form of experimental writing while simultaneously reminding students that their writing should speak to an audience beyond their
instructors. This model also, importantly, creates a platform for ongoing
feedback and more gradual development of composition skills. In terms
of individual involvement for students, this project envisions a short-term
initial engagement — ideally opening students, and you, up to the possibility
of Twitter's larger-scale pedagogic value without requiring an unreasonable
level of commitment at the preliminary levels.

The performance portion of the assignment, in which students actively
work through a scene of their choice from their assigned play, is supplemented with performance diaries. These documents outline the process
of preparing for and executing the performance on Twitter. In part, this
piece is also intended to prepare students for the group presentation, during
which time each group shares their experience with the rest of the class and
reflects on the interaction between technology and text. These presentations
come at the end of the unit on each play, and serve as a conclusion, a chance
to sum up the play in a meaningful and multifaceted way before moving on.
The primary goal of the assignment is to use Twitter as a comfortable space
for students to explore one of Shakespeare's plays, and the intention is that
this project will challenge students to offer new analysis in a fun, original
way, while at the same time considering the many angles one might use when
studying a literary text.

The assignment relies on the principle that the act of interpreting an academic text — in this case, a Shakespearean play — for a familiar community

(Twitter) will require a more intimate connection between the text and the student. Individually, in order to accurately represent a literary character, each student is required to consider, for example, character motivations, his/her character's role in the larger plot, and the personality traits suggested over the course of the entire play. Within their groups, students have to reconcile individual character performances with the scene they choose to recreate. All told, this work necessitates extensive engagement with the text, as well as the sort of close-knit group work required by more traditional performance projects. By placing the assignment within the context of a familiar community, the exercise also encourages students to practice writing/performing for their peers, and challenges them to anticipate and react to peer audiences. The project is intended to encourage an experimental approach, which allows students to push the boundaries of the texts covered in the course and, in so doing, to gain a deeper understanding of the richness of Shakespeare's plays.

8. CONCLUSION

This assignment challenges students to become intimate with one of the class texts, to push their understanding by transplanting it into an unconventional (but simultaneously familiar) space. On a textual level, the project demonstrates the suitability of Shakespeare's plays to adapt to new technologies, and in my experience students respond positively to a more unusual method of approaching the course texts. I have found that the assignment helps students bond to their play, and the parameters of the assignment encourage them to scrutinize the play more thoroughly. Additionally, the informality of the medium in many cases pushes students to rise to the occasion: many groups go beyond the call of the assignment to ensure that they produce quality work. Students in particular respond positively to the opportunity to focus on a specific character — the portions encouraging character development yield a huge amount of creativity, indicating to me that students certainly don't think about the characters in a passive sense.

On a more general level, applying Twitter in this way helps students to reconsider the technology in an educational setting, and many respond positively to the sense of connectivity that the application bring. Although it was not required (or even suggested), some students began interacting with later groups' performances, under the guise of their already established character from an earlier play. This provided a fantastic opportunity to discuss the ways in which Shakespeare's plays speak to one another, and it allowed students to imagine characters and themes from different plays, all interacting in one space. On the whole, I've found that this project prompts

> "I found that this project prompts my students to become more engaged, more enthusiastic members of the classroom, and this has a knock-on effect with their more traditional work."
>
> **Toria Johnson**

my students to become more engaged, more enthusiastic members of the classroom, and this has a knock-on effect with their more traditional work. Particularly in the case of the students who had already completed their project by the time of the first paper, essays were more inventive and more thorough in their analysis, and more connected to the texts they discussed.

9. WORKS CITED

Cordell, Ryan. "How to Start Tweeting (And Why You Might Want To)." *Prof-Hacker, The Chronical for Higher Education*, 11 Aug. 2010, chronicle.com /blogs/profhacker/how-to-start-tweeting-and-why-you-might-want-to/26065.

Royal Shakespeare Company. *Such Tweet Sorrow*. Feb. 2010, twitter.com/Such _Tweet.

Sample, Mark. "Twitter Is a Snark Valve." *Sample Reality*, 7 Oct. 2009, www .samplereality.com/2009/10/7/twitter-is-a-snark-valve/.

- - -. "A Framework for Teaching with Twitter." *ProfHacker, The Chronical for Higher Education*, 16 Aug. 2010, chronicle.com/blogs/profhacker/a-framework -for-teaching-with-twitter/26223.

- - -. "Practical Advice for Teaching with Twitter." *ProfHacker, The Chronical for Higher Education*, 25 Aug. 2010, chronicle.com/blogs/profhacker/practical -advice-for-teaching-with-twitter/26416.

Schmelling, Sarah. "Hamlet: Facebook Feed Edition." *McSweeney's Internet Tendency*, 30 Jul. 2008, www.mcsweeneys.net/articles/hamlet-facebook-news-feed -edition.

Silver, David. "The Difference between Thick and Thin Tweets." *Silver in SF*, 25 Feb. 2009, silverinsf.blogspot.com/2009/02/difference-between-thin-and -thick.html.

Stommel, Jesse. "The Twitter Essay." *Hybrid Pedagogy*, 6 Jan. 2012, www.digital pedagogylab.com.

Thompson, Clive. "How Twitter Creates a Social Sixth Sense." *Wired*, 26 June 2007, www.wired.com/2007/06/st-thompson-4/.

8

A Digital Approach to Teaching Postmodern Literature

Jason Parks
Ball State University and Anderson University

Jason Parks has been teaching writing and literature at the college level for the last six years. He has a master's in English from Butler University and is completing his PhD at Ball State University. He is currently an assistant professor of English at Anderson University (Indiana). He once taught an advanced undergraduate course on the works of William Shakespeare to eleven extremely bright young women and it changed his life. He has presented papers at national conferences on topics such as how to use digital audio remixes in literature classrooms and the relationship between avant-garde magazines and the popular press.

COURTESY OF JASON PARKS

1. OVERVIEW

- **Assignment:** Students use a class Twitter feed—directly related to an assigned literary work containing postmodern features—to critically think and write about literature.
- **Courses:** Postmodern literature; literature courses that incorporate postmodern works; literary theory; postcolonial literatures.
- **Literature:** Teresa Hak Kyug Cha's *Dictee*; Toni Morrison's *The Bluest Eye*; Jonathan Safran Foer's *Extremely Loud and Incredibly Close*; J.M. Coetzee's *Foe*; William Faulkner's *Absalom, Absalom*.
- **Technology:** Twitter (twitter.com), blog/discussion board (I suggest using a private Blogger account, Moodle, or Blackboard).
- **Time:** One week or three 50-minute class sessions.

2. GOALS OF THE ASSIGNMENT

After completing this assignment, students will be able to

- post a tweet with a hyperlink to a video, picture, audio file, or web page related to the assigned text;

- apply knowledge gained from tweets to their understanding of a literary text;
- use Twitter to seek out and contribute information related to a work of literature; and
- define some of the key concepts of postmodernism.

> "One of my objectives is to see students develop a passion for literary works that challenge their ideas and assumptions about narrative and the world around them."
>
> **Jason Parks**
> Ball State University and Anderson University

> "Students need to see how literature is directly relevant to their everyday experience, especially their social media experience."
>
> **Jason Parks**

> "This assignment has the potential to make visible both the inner workings of postmodern literature and new media technologies."
>
> **Jason Parks**

3. ASSIGNMENT SHEET

A Digital Approach to Learning Postmodern Literature

Course: _____

Instructor: _____

Date: _____

Postmodernism and Technology: Assignment Instructions

This assignment is intended to familiarize you with some of the conventions, or "anti-conventions," of postmodern literature and to gain a better understanding of how to thoughtfully and creatively use technology to help us analyze literature.

During the week of _____, we will be using a variety of technologies, including Twitter and the class discussion board, to help us build a collaborative interpretation of a postmodern novel. While the novel may not be classified solely as postmodern, it contains significant features that allow us to explore it through this lens.

Objectives

Over the course of 3 class sessions, we will examine and reflect on the stylistic features of postmodern texts. We will familiarize ourselves with key aspects of postmodernism to help us gain more confidence in our ability to analyze and interpret postmodern art.

The specific assignments are as follows:

- Reflection on initial reading experience of postmodern fiction
- Create and post 1 tweet with a hyperlink related to your assigned passage from the novel
- In-class activity analyzing and applying the Twitter feed to the text
- Discussion board reflection on tweets
- In-class live tweet activity on postmodern fiction
- Final reflection

Prior to the First Class Meeting

1. Read the text all the way through and spend two hours closely examining the assigned text. Do not use any online resources, including plot summaries or *Wikipedia*. You are not expected to be a master of the text. Just make some notes and annotations in the text on any stylistic or genre-related features that seem familiar, especially the genres like letters, poems, paintings, photography, or even stream-of-consciousness prose that you

recognize. *Make sure you avoid all technology or you risk failing the assignment.* If you are used to consulting Google for quick summaries, outlines, or reviews of books you are reading, please refrain from doing so with this book. It will completely spoil the activity. Many postmodern works are by nature difficult to interpret, so I do not expect you to have any definitive arguments about the book when you arrive on the first day of class.

2. Sign up for a Twitter account. If you have never used Twitter, please find someone who can give you a basic tutorial. If you need additional assistance, contact me at least 2 weeks prior to this assignment to arrange a meeting. Also, make sure you understand the concepts of hashtags and hyperlinks.

Assessment

Your grade for this weeklong activity will be based on participation in classroom discussion and writing exercises, the originality and relevance of your tweets, and the depth of critical reflection in your discussion board posts. If you miss class, you will not be able to make up the in-class work, so please plan ahead for these class sessions.

4. TIME AND TECHNOLOGY

TIME. Three 50-minute class sessions are used to introduce, explore, and then reflect on postmodernism. All week long, students collaborate through technology, including using image archives, Twitter, blogs, YouTube, and online translators. This will lead to lots of engagement inside and outside of the classroom.

Prior to the class meeting, students must read through the entire book without consulting the Internet or any other digital technologies. The three classroom sessions are as follows:

Session 1 (50 Minutes) Introduction to Postmodernism

1. Have students write a short, timed journal entry about the most bewildering aspect of the book. Ask them which image or script they found most difficult to read or interpret. Have them share their journal entries with a small group of classmates (10 minutes max).
2. Present key concepts for understanding postmodern literature that apply most directly to the text you have assigned. Discuss the following: surface features, pastiche, intertextuality, temporal distortion, multiple narrators, historiographic metafiction, and resistance to closure.
3. Hand out and explain the purpose of the assignment. Divide up the literary text and assign specific passages ahead of class for students to use as the basis of their tweets.

Task to complete prior to session 2: Each student will post a tweet with a hyperlink and a hashtag that includes the course title, such as #ENG102, as well as #postmodernism.

Session 2 (50 Minutes) Opening and Closing the Text

In this class session, students use the Twitter feed to help them analyze the book, which they should also bring to class. You may want to divide the class session into two parts: one for small group analysis of the feed for initial discussion of how the feed works as a resource, and the second for the genre itself. During the session, students should match up tweets to different parts of the book and discuss how the additional information helps them make thematic or content-related connections between sections of the book.

Task to complete prior to session 3: Each student will make a blog/discussion board post of 100–250 words. The post should answer the following questions: Which tweet or tweets (including links) had the greatest impact on your understanding of one particular section of this book? Were there any tweets/links that you think interfered or changed your interpretation of a passage?

Session 3 (50 minutes) Postmodernism without Technology

Hand out a list of the terms you discussed on the first day: surface features, pastiche, intertextuality, temporal distortion, multiple narrators, historiographic metafiction, and resistance to closure. Then give the students a new text ("Is About" by Allen Ginsberg would probably work well) and give them fifteen minutes to pick out and reflect on why the new text is postmodern. Have them tweet their observations and ideas about the text's postmodern features. Conclude with a five-minute written reflection on how they can use social media as a tool for building interpretations of postmodern literature.

TECHNOLOGY. You will need a computer with web access, an individual Twitter account, and a class blog or other course management software such as Blackboard or Moodle for students to post and respond to each other's writing. You may want to reserve one or more days for the class to meet in a computer lab. Students will need a computer, tablet, or smartphone with Internet access for viewing images and video, and a Twitter account. If students prefer not to use their personal account, have them create one solely for this assignment, or suggest that they create one to use as their academic account, since it is likely that multiple professors will require them to use Twitter from time to time.

RESOURCES

Image Archives. I highly recommend using Getty Images or the Smithsonian Image Archive first, as opposed to a broad Google image search due to the unpredictability of Google searches. However, if students want to use Google, be sure to recommend an advanced search.

- Getty Images (www.gettyimages.com/EditorialImages/Archival)
- Smithsonian Image Archive (collections.si.edu/search/)
- Google Images (images.google.com) [Safe Search Moderate]
- Online Translator/Language Sites
- Google Translate (translate.google.com/)
- Alphabet Global (www.alphabetglobal.com/korean-alphabet.php)
- Omniglot (www.omniglot.com/)

YouTube. While I prefer YouTube for video searches, students who post video links can certainly use other video hosting sites. Again, please caution your students about safe searches.

Twitter. Having each student create a Twitter account can be time-consuming and may require additional class time. A week or two before this assignment, you should survey your class to assess their level of familiarity with this platform. If they are unsure of how it works, you can set aside additional class time to help students familiarize themselves with Twitter, or designate a couple of student leaders who are familiar with Twitter to explain it to small groups outside of class.

Blog or Discussion Board. Students should have a public forum to reflect and react to the assignment at the end of the week. A course blog or discussion board enables students to dialogue with one another and you. This will also feel less formal or structured than handing in a response paper. It may also help you gather some ideas for a follow-up class discussion session.

5. ANTICIPATING STUDENT NEEDS

If students are reluctant to sign up for Twitter accounts or do not get started at least one to two weeks before the weeklong assignment, they may have trouble understanding what it means to "follow" someone, how to navigate Twitter feeds, as well as what hashtags (#) and hyperlinks are. You must build the classwide network of users before the week begins. To build this network, you might consider giving points for completing the sign-up and following of all classmates prior to the week of the assignment.

Also, if students cannot attend class, they are going to struggle to keep up with the work. While they may be able to participate in some of the activities through Twitter, missing class will undermine the purpose of the activity, which is to discuss and reflect on the relationship between the postmodern text and how a technology like Twitter can aid our understanding of a text, both because of its ability to connect us with information and because of the postmodern features of the Twitter feed itself.

6. ASSESSMENT TOOLS

PARTICIPATION. Somewhere from 50 percent to 75 percent of the grade should be based on participation and completion of the classroom and homework activities, including correctly posting to Twitter with a hyperlink that has relevance to the student's close reading of the text. For this project to work, everyone has to have a Twitter account ready by the first day of class. Also, they must have read through the text prior to the first meeting.

REFLECTION. Another 25 percent to 50 percent can be given for the blog/discussion board and in-class written reflections. A sample rubric for a 50-point assignment grade for this weeklong assignment follows.

Postmodernism and Technology Assignment	
Day 1 Class Discussion/Journal Entry Through the in-class journal entry on the "bewildering" aspects of the book, students demonstrate whether they've engaged with its content. For a book like *Dictee*, I don't expect them to have any clear argument for the overall meaning of the book, so participation can be judged mostly on the questions they come up with in their journal activity. They should also have the book with them and their Twitter accounts set up.	____/10 points
Tweet #1 (Including Working Link) The tweet needs to have a functioning hyperlink that adds to our understanding of the book in some way. However, the link should not be simply a link to a summary of the book, but should be a link to a dictionary definition, a picture of a city or map, a link that expands on a literary allusion, and so on. To get full credit, students should try to find something that clarifies or adds to their assigned passage. They can definitely push the boundaries on the connections, especially since we're talking about postmodernism.	____/10 points
Day 2 In-Class Participation Students work together to explore how the tweets and links affect their interpretation of the novel. They should get credit as long as they stay on topic by reading the tweets together and discussing both the literature and the twitter feed itself.	____/10 points
Blog/Discussion Board Reflection Assignment This assignment is mostly based on completion. They just need to write up a reflection of what they did in class based on one particular tweet.	____/5 points
Day 3 In-Class Activity Twitter Participation To earn these ten points, students must make some observations about the postmodern poem, film clip, or short story you assigned at the beginning of class. They will tweet them in a live feed during the hour.	____/10 points
Final Reflection This is mostly a "What can you take away from this activity?" reflection. Did it help the students understand something about postmodernism, technology, or something else? They can definitely express frustration here as well, to help you understand how to revise the activity. **TOTAL**	____/5 points ____/50 points

7. THEORETICAL BASIS FOR THE ASSIGNMENT:
A Digital Approach to Postmodern Literature

Robert Scholes, author of *The Rise and Fall of English*, has written extensively on the relationship between the future viability of the English department, the shifting definition of texts, and the pedagogical aims of literary studies. While his recent work focuses primarily on the integration of cultural studies into the literature classroom, he also urges teachers to consider ways in which new media and technology are revitalizing and reshaping all facets of the literature classroom. "The point we need to register," Scholes writes, "is how texts in various media, and their authors, move from one world to another, one medium to another, making a culture that is interesting — and teachable — on many levels" (235). While Scholes may be emphasizing the importance of bringing new materials into the literature classroom, such as periodicals, film, and digital texts, his article raises questions about how new media will influence the way we read and understand the literature created prior to the digital age.

> "[Robert Scholes] urges teachers to consider ways in which new media and technology are revitalizing and reshaping all facets of the literature classroom."
>
> **Jason Parks**

Ellen Cushman echoes Scholes's acknowledgment that literature teachers need to give more consideration to new media and the broader category of texts that play a role in shaping a culture (Scholes 232). Cushman's argument stems from a long-standing prejudice against new media within literary studies. She points out that "the discipline [literary studies] values the interpretation of text above the production of text, image, sound, and motion. Yet intellectual activities and media are intricately connected and mutually sustaining in what [she calls] a hierarchy of signs. This hierarchy privileges the letter, text, and their consumption over image, film, public and student writing, and their production" (Cushman 65).

Just as Yancey and others in the field of composition studies have begun to embrace the multimodal aspects of writing and learning, literature teachers must also consider the implications for their own classrooms (Williams; Juhasz). "If English studies has revised the artifacts it values for study," asks Cushman, "why have similar changes not taken place in the production of knowledge and methods of teaching English education?" (65). In other words, if we are going to redefine the text in the classroom, we must also acknowledge how these texts (including blogs, Web sites, and online videos) are not just something to be studied and critiqued but are being woven into our entire literate experience.

> "Just as Yancey and others in the field of composition studies have begun to embrace the multimodal aspects of writing and learning, literature teachers must also consider the implications for their own classrooms."
>
> **Jason Parks**

In *Writing Technology*, Christina Haas asserts that "technology is the place where culture and cognition meet—technologies are cultural artifacts imbued with history, as well as tools used by individuals for their own motives and purposes" (229). What, for a literature student, are the "motives and purposes" behind the use of emerging digital technologies as they relate to literate practice? What do they expect YouTube or Google to do for them in their pursuit of understanding a work of literature? In particular, what happens when a literature student is presented with a postmodern, multimodal text, such as Theresa Cha's *Dictee*, where "contextual understanding" may not be the pedagogical aim? If, as Scholes and Cushman argue, we are redefining the text for the literature classroom, have we given sufficient thought to how we define the role of technology in our engagement with postmodern texts?

> "Is there any better place for exploring the relationship between technology and literature than in a postmodern, multimodal text?"
>
> **Jason Parks**

Consider the conclusion to a recent article on Cha's postmodern work *Dictee*:

> This hesitation, pausing and stopping, captures Cha's fascination for that space that cleaves places together that binds and separates simultaneously; it is that liminal space where subjectivity is irreducible to a place in the ordinary sense of the word. The logic of "almost a place" recalls the "vast" textual space of the page. The "stop start" in betweenness of her writing refuses the measure of "uni formed" trajectory of arrival or departure, or the circular logic required for transparent reading. Cha puts on trial not only the status of identity as "uni formed" but also the "I" demanded by the autobiographical logic. The particularity of the references to Korea and to Korean America remains but survives as a trace, as marks on the page while the liminal subjectivity remains resistant to any "uni formed" identification: "All along, you see her without actually seeing, actually having seen her. You do not see her yet. For the moment, you see only her traces." (Kim 475)

Is there any better place for exploring the relationship between technology and literature than in a postmodern, multimodal text so rich with questions about liminal spaces, irreducible subjectivity, and "seeing without actually seeing"?

Dictee, however, is not the only or even the most definitive postmodern text. In fact, the idea for this assignment originated from a course on Asian American literature where we extensively discussed Theresa Cha's *Dictee* and the Asian American immigrant experience. While this Twitter assignment does not have to be used within the context of an Asian American or postcolonial literature course, it would, however, fit well within this setting. It can also be used in a course on literary theory or an introductory course on postmodern literature.

I have listed the following as texts that I think would all work for this assignment: Theresa Hak Kyug Cha's *Dictee*; Toni Morrison's *The Bluest Eye*; Jonathan Safran Foer's *Extremely Loud and Incredibly Close*; J. M. Coetzee's

Foe; William Faulkner's *Absalom, Absalom*. There are countless other texts that could work as well.

8. CONCLUSION

A decade ago, I would have been content if my English teacher had brought in a paper handout with a list of key terms and then asked me to apply them to the text of the day. Slower, contemplative forms of learning are still necessary. For the past six years, however, teaching and researching students in both literature and composition classrooms has changed my perspective on the value of active learning. I have also been on my own journey of reconciling my paper-based pedagogical heritage in English studies with these emerging technologies.

> "As much as these technologies are regarded as tools for invigorating the classroom, they have also invigorated my feelings about teaching."
> **Jason Parks**

One of my goals as a teacher is to constantly challenge myself to try new approaches. Every semester I try to learn and integrate one new piece of technology into one lesson plan. This approach has allowed me to build up a diverse storehouse of ideas for engaging my students. Furthermore, as much as these technologies are regarded as tools for invigorating the classroom, they have also invigorated my feelings about teaching.

Postmodern literature embodies and engages many of the same experiences our students confront, consciously or unconsciously, while using asynchronous, multigenre writing technologies like Twitter. When my students first encounter these activities, there is always a mixed response. Some have even admitted to initially criticizing my assignment. As the activities unfold, though, the students often become more receptive and show a new level of comfort with speaking up and sharing their ideas with each other. My primary teaching objective is to see students develop a passion for works of literature that challenge their ideas and assumptions about narrative and the world around them. I also believe that students need to see how this literature is directly relevant to their everyday experience, especially their social media experience. For our students, this assignment has the potential to make visible both the inner workings of postmodern literature and new media technologies. Give it a try. Modify it to work with your objectives. Your students are sure to surprise you.

9. WORKS CITED

Cha, Theresa H. K. *Dictee*. U of California P, 1982.
Coetzee, J. M. *Foe*. Viking, 23 Feb. 1987.

Cushman, Ellen. "New Media Scholarship and Teaching: Challenging the Hierarchy of Signs." *Pedagogy: Critical Approaches to Teaching Literature, Language, Composition, and Culture*, vol. 11, no. 1, 2011, pp. 63-79. *Project Muse*, muse.jhu.edu/article/409321.

Faulkner, William. *Absalom, Absalom*. 1936. Knopf Doubleday Publishing Group, 2011.

Foer, Jonathan Safran. *Extremely Loud and Incredibly Close*. Houghton Mifflin Harcourt, 4 Apr. 2005.

Haas, Christina. *Writing Technology: Studies on the Materiality of Literacy*. Erlbaum, 1996, p. 229.

Juhasz, Alexandra. "Learning the Five Lessons of YouTube: After Trying to Teach There, I Don't Believe the Hype." *Cinema Journal*, vol. 48, no. 2, 2009, pp. 145-50. *Project Muse*, muse.jhu.edu/article/258255.

Kellner, Douglas, and Gooyong Kim. "YouTube, Critical Pedagogy, and Media Activism." *Review of Education, Pedagogy & Cultural Studies*, vol. 32, no. 1, 2010, pp. 3-36. *ERIC*, EJ880583, eric.gov/?id-EJ880583.

Kim, Hyo. "Depoliticising Politics: Readings of Theresa Hak Kyung Cha's *Dictee*." *Changing English: Studies in Culture & Education*, vol.15, no. 4, 2008, pp. 467-75 *Taylor and Francis Online*, doi: 10.1080/13586840802493118.

Morrison, Toni. *The Bluest Eyes*. 1970. Vintage International, 2007.

Scholes, Robert. *The Rise and Fall of English*. Yale UP, 1998, p. 235.

- - - "The English Curriculum After the Fall." *Pedagogy*, vol. 10, no. 1, 2010, pp. 229-40. *Project Muse*, muse.jhu.edu/article/366188.pdf.

Williams, Tara. "Multimedia Learning Gets Medieval." *Pedagogy: Critical Approaches to Teaching Literature, Language, Composition, and Culture*, vol. 9, no. 1, 2009, pp. 77-95. *Project Muse*, muse.jhu.edu/article/259068/pdf.

Yancey, Kathleen Blake. "Made Not Only in Words: Composition in a New Key." *College Composition and Communication*, vol. 56, no. 2, 2004, pp. 297-328. *ERIC*. EJ728786, eric.ed.gov/?id-EJ728786.

PART TWO ASSIGNMENTS

Digital Tools

9

2B or n2B: Texting about Literature

Abigail G. Scheg
Elizabeth City State University

COURTESY OF
ABIGAIL SCHEG

Dr. Abigail Scheg is an assistant professor of English at Elizabeth City State University where she teaches first-year composition, advanced composition, and literature courses. Dr. Scheg researches, publishes, and conferences in the areas of online pedagogy, social media, and popular culture. Her book *Reforming Teacher Education with Online Pedagogy Development* was recently published with IGI Global. She hopes that this chapter provides instructors with the boost they need to embrace a social technology in their literature classes, be it text messaging, Twitter, podcasts, or anything else!

1. OVERVIEW

- **Assignment:** Students critically analyze and discuss a literary work using text messaging.
- **Courses:** Introduction to literature; literature and composition.
- **Literature:** Any texts, particularly a list that includes both brief and longer works.
- **Technology:** Cell phones, mobile devices (paper and pencil or modified technologies if necessary).
- **Time:** Varies depending on needs; can be completed during or after class periods.

2. GOALS OF THE ASSIGNMENT

The goal of this assignment is to explore a new way for students to discuss and interpret literary texts using text messaging technology.

Note: I recommend that the assignment sheet that follows be incorporated into your syllabus and/or handed out prior to requiring cell phones for discussion.

> "Technology can create opportunities for instructors and students to learn, create, and build knowledge together."
>
> **Abigail Scheg**
> Elizabeth City
> State University

3. ASSIGNMENT SHEET

2B or n2B: Texting about Literature

Course: _____

Instructor: _____

Date: _____

For this assignment, we will tap into and test your texting abilities. Although many instructors may require you to put away your cell phones or ban them entirely from their courses, I would like you to take yours out . . . and use it. Undoubtedly, you know that text messaging has become a popular tool for communication. Sometimes, at the close of class, I may ask you to text me your reflection on the class discussion. Or, if there is a time that we will not be able to formally meet as a class, I will require that you text me your response to our reading.

Some of you may be thinking, "Texts are *so* short. That is so easy! I love this teacher!" Well—you are right. Text messages *are* supposed to be short (160 characters or less). However, that does not mean that they should be vague or pointless. When I ask you to text me, you have one chance to send me a carefully crafted and thoughtful message in 160 characters or less to offer a reflection or to answer questions I might pose. You must think carefully. Choose wisely. B cr8iv.

Some of you may also be thinking, "How am I supposed to summarize or reflect on a whole story, poem, or essay in just a text message?" You must think wisely before you type. You may have a hundred separate thoughts about a single reading, but before you press Send, you'll need to find the common thread, locate the theme, or decipher a code the author has laid before you. Be succinct, and once you've thought it through: Txt me ur &ser.

If you do not have a cell phone, or have limited text messaging capabilities that you feel would hinder your ability to participate in this activity, that is no problem! Please talk to me after class about this as soon as possible and we will discuss an alternate e-mail solution. **Please do not upgrade your personal cell phone service or purchase a new phone just for this class. That is not necessary and is *not* a requirement.**

Please text me your answer to the following: After reviewing the syllabus, what piece are you most looking forward to reading in this course and why? Be thorough—in 160 characters or less.

4. TIME AND TECHNOLOGY

This assignment does not take much time to set up. You can use your course syllabus to convey your expectations of how texting will be used in the course. This will afford students the opportunity to familiarize themselves with this technological requirement at the start of the semester.

The actual assignment also takes a very short amount of time to complete. You will need to decide what you want students to text about, and whether they should text during or after class. For students, brainstorming and planning a succinct text message should be the longest, most involved part in the process. However, this should also be organic to the constraints of the genre of text messaging. Therefore, it should only take a few seconds for students to text you and, likewise, seconds for you to text back.

In terms of the time limitations of this assignment, that depends on you, your students, and their overall level of engagement with the assignment. Some students will be highly engaged, while others will not. If a group of students is highly engaged, be sure to set limits so that you are not receiving messages 24/7. Provide a schedule for responses, and let students know the parameters, for example: "I will not respond to any text messages that I receive between 9:00 P.M. and 7:00 A.M."

You will need to schedule time to review the messages that transpire outside of class. Perhaps the texting assignment went well, perhaps it didn't go as you'd envisioned it. Either way, share these realizations with your class so you can work on developing or revising the assignment to make it appropriate and applicable to your students in terms of level, demographics, or other considerations. If a first attempt at text messaging about a reading did not go well, you can modify and try it again. Each new reading and corresponding text message response can be considered a new assignment and, as such, you can use the assignment just once or twice a semester or, if successful, for every course reading.

The tools that are required for using text messaging *in* the literature classroom have two possibilities: using cell phones for actual text messaging *or* using paper/pencil, chalk/chalkboard, marker/dry-erase board for simulation of text lingo (specifically the limited characters) for various assignments.

Although it may seem like all of our students are constantly plugged in to their iPods and cell phones, not all of our students own cell phones. Or perhaps they do own a cell phone, but they do not have texting capabilities or have a limited text messaging plan. Personally, I ask students at the beginning of the semester about their access to text messaging. If there are students who do not have texting capabilities, I would use the same pedagogical concept and have them text message me with paper and pen (or e-mail) rather than ask them to pay for additional cell/texting services.

For the purposes of the assignment featured in this chapter, the texting is done outside of class to supplement (or possibly take the place of) class discussion. Therefore, students can text responses directly to your phone or they use e-mail (or a nondigital medium) with the understanding that the character limit still applies.

5. ANTICIPATING STUDENT NEEDS

One of the greatest potential difficulties with this assignment is that some students may not have a cell phone or texting capabilities. As noted above, you might adapt the assignment so that students use e-mail (or analog options) as a substitute, while still conforming to the limit of 160 (or fewer) characters.

Another potential issue is that you might not want to give your cell phone number to students. Since my years as an adjunct, I have always offered students my personal cell phone number. Because I had no office and spent the majority of my time driving around to campuses and classes, I felt that only offering students my e-mail did not afford me the opportunity to be as connected and available to them as I wanted to be. To date, students have not abused (yet) this arrangement, and I make it a point to tell them, "I will not text you over the weekend and ask what you are up to or to hang out with me; I expect you to extend the same courtesy to me." This has been successful in my experience at various institutions. However, the potential difficulties or problems of extending a faculty member's personal phone number to a large number of undergraduate students can be a cause for concern. If this is something that you are unsure about or unwilling to do, I recommend that you still explore the option of text messaging as a means of communication in your classroom, just modify it in a way that makes you comfortable. Make sure that your rules for text messaging are clear to your students and remind them that, although text messaging is a familiar technology, they are using it in this instance as part of a class assignment. When they write, they need to keep that purpose and the audience in mind.

6. ASSESSMENT TOOLS

Grading this assignment will depend on what is appropriate for your course, department, or institutional policies. The most obvious grade opportunity for this assignment would be to incorporate it into an overall class participation grade. Therefore, the inevitable student who drags his/her feet and does not willingly attempt this exercise (as can happen in any classroom with any assignment or "fun" technology) will do so at their own peril. I like to remind students that text messaging affords any who are wary of speaking out in class an opportunity to participate in a different way.

I typically base my courses on a 1,000-point scale with major assignments and participation out of 100 points. A text messaging discussion assignment would be 10 points out of the 100 possible participation points for the semester. Of course, use your discretion or current discussion rubrics to score the assignment. Because I use this as part of a participation grade, I do not have specific nuances within a rubric to assess students. Basically, they either participate or they don't. As long as they try—that is, demonstrate that they *have* read the assigned text, and send a text message to show this—they will score well. I follow these guidelines:

10 points—Students earn all 10 points for this assignment if they send at least one text message to succinctly describe or define a specified text. Text messages are limited to 160 characters and students may not use extended or a string of text messages to send a longer analysis.

Example: "repetition showed impt themes in Raven.
imagery&darkness w + suspense.Rhyme also + suspense."

5 points—Students earn 5 points for this assignment if they send at least one text message that partially describes a specified text. Major details of the text are omitted.

Example: "poem is abt darkness & death."

0 points—Students earn 0 points for this assignment if they do not send a text message about the assigned reading.

Example: No message sent.

7. THEORETICAL BASIS FOR THE ASSIGNMENT:
2B or n2B: Texting about Literature

In recent years there has been a drastic increase in the amount of and types of technology used in the classroom. There have been small steps such as transitioning from a chalkboard to a dry-erase board to SMART Board technology. Then, there have been major opportunities to rethink education in terms of new technologies including social media, which has allowed instructors to extend the walls of their classrooms to include other instructors, students, classes, and universities. Although these technologies are not yet considered mainstream in higher education, positive recognition of their utility as scholarly tools has increased dramatically. One of the technologies that still has negative connotations and is presumed to have limited educational capabilities is text messaging.

While Facebook, Twitter, LinkedIn, and Google+ (among many more) are becoming acceptable ways to communicate, text messaging still has the connotation of a mindless pastime that sucks teenagers' attention away from the rest of the world (Cheung; Girardi; Mitra; Phipps, Wise, and Amundsen).

The knee-jerk reaction to text messaging seems similar to negative reactions that many of these new technologies received in the past (and to some degree, still do), but text messaging is even less accepted (Grant, "Embracing"; Grant, "Textperts"; Mahatanankoon and O'Sullivan). However, examining the educational opportunities and positive impacts of text messaging in both college and K–12 has become a critical piece of research in highly regarded publications, as well as at conferences (Amicucci; Drouin; Jones and Schieffelin; Sweeny; Wood, Jackson, Hart, Plester, and Wilde). An NCTE September *Inbox* includes an article by Lisa Nielsen entitled "Enriching Literacy with Cellphones: 3 Ideas to Get Started" that discusses the opportunities cell phones provide (even in elementary classrooms) via transmitting text, audio, and video files.

> "I always advise that students consult the *Oxford English Dictionary* not only to find the answer they seek but also to learn about the progression of language over time."
>
> **Abigail G. Scheg**

Having personally made scholarly presentations about the use of text messaging in the classroom, I can tell you that this topic is typically met with scoffs, disbelief, and anger toward those students who refuse to participate in class and only want to spend their time texting. I advocate for the opportunity to brainstorm using technology (such as texting) in new ways. Try it in your classroom in any way that you see fit. Like any lesson (with or without technology), it has the same chance of being successful. This chapter examines the pedagogical advantages of using text messaging in your literature classrooms and provides specific examples of incorporating such a tool in your lessons, readings, or projects.

Naomi Baron's *Always On: Language in a Mobile World* examines the progression of language, which she explains as always being in a state of flux, within the realm of technological progression. She draws on extensive research to present linguistic analyses of instant messaging, Facebook, and text messaging, among other technological communication tools. Baron starts at the beginning in order to frame her investigation:

> When Samuel Johnson first set about writing his landmark *Dictionary of the English Language*, he somewhat naively believed his task to be setting down, for generations to come, the composition of the English lexicon. More than a decade later, when the long-awaited volumes appeared, Johnson acknowledged his initial folly. In the famous Preface of 1755, he explained that word meanings evolve over time and that pronunciations of these words do as well. (ix)

When my composition and literature students ask about using dictionaries for their research and writing, I always advise that they consult the *Oxford English Dictionary* not only to find the answer they seek but also to learn about the progression of language over time. Oftentimes these students report back to me about the extensive passages they found on just one word, claiming that they didn't know language had such a unique developmental pattern over time.

David Crystal's *Txting: The gr8 db8* introduces the concept of text messaging as a new dimension in language progression, a change which is inevitable with or without the addition of technology. Crystal claims that "texting has added a new dimension to language use, indeed, but its long-term impact on the already existing varieties of language is likely to be negligible. It is not a bad thing" (10). The language changes brought about by text messaging center on the character limits of typical SMS (short messaging service) programs. People have found that eliminating vowels and looking for phonetic shorthand makes it possible to write longer messages without going over the character limit. What is accomplished in this seemingly thoughtful act? According to Lily Huang in "The Death of English (LOL),"

> the language of texting is hardly as deviant as people think, and . . . texting actually makes people better communicators, not worse. Crystal spells out the first point by marshaling real linguistic evidence. He breaks down the distinctive elements of texting language — pictograms; initialisms, or acronyms; contractions; and others — and points out similar examples in linguistic practice from the ancient Egyptians to 20th-century broadcasting. Shakespeare freely used elisions, novel syntax, and several thousand made-up words (his own name was signed in six different ways). (1)

What Baron, Huang, Crystal, and others, and by extension, this research, are arguing for is not recognition of text-ese as *the* new official language of university, but rather the recognition of its place in time and its possibility — particularly its possibility with an age group that so furiously thumbs away below their desks. Rather than prohibiting the behavior, we should teach students about the pedagogical possibilities of various modes of communication. Some instructors use Twitter, whereas others don't even have an account; some instructors use straight lecture, whereas others do not believe in lecturing. Just as there are different types of instructors and instruction, there are varying levels of technological appropriateness in the business world. Preparing our students with a world of possibilities and communicative opportunities is a logical place to start.

As text messaging is a medium to share short bursts of information with one or more individuals *and* a communicative mode that can be used in the classroom without speaking, it seems an ideal vehicle for students to share literary interpretations of and questions about a text. The assignment that I offer in this chapter uses text messaging (or its paper-pen substitute) for a literature classroom discussion.

Using text messaging as a means of communication with students (and, by extension, this chapter and activity) started when I was an adjunct at several institutions. In order to be more readily available for my students, I distributed my cell phone number to them in case they had questions, comments, or concerns about the class or assignments. In the first few years that

I gave my phone number, I received a few phone calls here and there, but most students still preferred to contact me via university e-mail if they had a question.

However, in recent years, giving out my cell phone number has opened the doors for students to text me with questions about major assignments or the class in general. At first, I admit, I was horrified that a student texted me regarding a homework assignment. And then I really thought about it. Why should I be horrified? I gave them my number and said they could contact me if they needed me; the students were polite and identified themselves in their messages, and their questions were quick and easy. It was, in fact, the perfect type of correspondence to transpire via text messaging. Now, many of the instructors in my department provide students with their cell phone numbers at the beginning of the semester.

> "Students were polite and identified themselves in their messages, and their questions were quick and easy. It was, in fact, the perfect type of correspondence to transpire via text messaging."
>
> **Abigail G. Scheg**

This inspired me to conduct more research into the possibilities of text messaging as a teaching tool, or, at least, an accepted communicative mode in higher education. As I stated earlier, texting is usually met with a dismissive and pained groan from many instructors who only associate it with poorly behaved students not paying attention in class. However, more research regarding the positive impacts of text messaging is emerging, as well as more implementation opportunities.

Text messaging is a technology that is still in its experimental phase; many naysayers remain, many have sworn it off completely, and still others are seriously looking into or actually using it in their classrooms. This assignment and technology is not limited to literature or writing courses, but could be used in any type of course at any institution or at any level. The possibilities are endless, if you are willing to try texting in or for class.

8. CONCLUSION

This assignment gives students the opportunity to practice their writing in a mode with which they are familiar and comfortable. This is particularly useful with work such as literature, about which they may not be as familiar. In my experience, using text messaging as a communicative mode in classes has been successful because students are intrigued with the concept and appreciative of the quick nature of the discussion. Although I am not proposing that text messaging be the official mode of communication for a course, I do feel that its pedagogical opportunities are vast and it should be acknowledged as a valid communicative tool.

One of the other lessons to be learned through this assignment is a better recognition on the part of students of what is appropriate and what is not.

In the assignment, I state that other instructors do not allow text messaging in their classes and I make clear that I do not place judgment on that regulation. However, I state that in my class texting will be permitted and we will talk about permissible ways to use the tool. This is exactly how the real world, particularly business, operates: in some positions, it is entirely acceptable and appropriate to be on a cell phone, texting, tweeting, Facebooking, or using any other technology. In some positions, it is not appropriate. Banning a technology because we are unsure how it will work or we are concerned that it will be taken advantage of does not allow for a teachable moment; giving it a try does. Text messaging has become an acceptable and widely used mode of communication; we need to work acceptable texting behaviors and opportunities into our curriculum so that our students *are* prepared for the increasingly tech-savvy business and academic worlds.

> "Banning a technology because we are unsure how it will work or we are concerned that it will be taken advantage of does not allow for a teachable moment; giving it a try does."
>
> **Abigail G. Scheg**

When I have used text messaging in the classroom, students have reacted positively by the end of the semester. Although students are typically unsure of this medium for discussion at the start of the semester, they grow to appreciate the new opportunity to utilize a technology that they enjoy and typically find to be very accessible. Also, when I have utilized texting in introductory literature classes, my students have found solace in the familiarity of the technology that they typically couldn't find in the unfamiliar literature. Such an assignment is easy to manipulate, modify, and personalize for a specific group of students or a particular type of literature course, which makes it ideal if you are looking to make a change in your curriculum and get more involved with your students.

9. WORKS CITED

Amicucci, Ann M. "They Aren't All Digital Natives: Dismantling Myths about Students' Relationships with Technology." Paper presented at Computers and Writing, Ann Arbor, 19-22 May 2011.

Baron, Naomi S. *Always On: Language in an Online and Mobile World*. Oxford UP, 2008.

Cheung, Stephen L. "Using Mobile Phone Messaging as a Response Medium in Classroom Experiments." *Journal of Economic Education*, Winter: 2008.

Crystal, David. *Txting: The gr8 db8*. Oxford UP, 2008.

Drouin, Michelle A. "College Students' Text Messaging, Use of Textese and Literacy Skills." *Journal of Computer-Assisted Learning*, vol. 27, no. 1, 2011, pp. 67-75.

Girardi, Tamara. "Working toward Expert Status: Love to Hear Students Go Tweet, Tweet, Tweet." *Social Software and the Evolution of User Expertise: Future Trends in Knowledge Creation and Dissemination*. IGI Global, 2013.

Grant, Abigail A. "Embracing the Inevitable: Utilizing Student Text Messaging to Teach Composition." Paper presented at Computers and Writing, Ann Arbor, 19-22 May 2001.

- - -. "Textperts: Utilizing Students' Skills in the Teaching of Writing." *Social Software and the Evolution of User Expertise: Future Trends in Knowledge Creation and Dissemination*. IGI Global, 2013.

Huang, Lily. "The Death of English (LOL)." *Newsweek*, 11 Aug. 2008, www .newsweeek.com/technology-textese-may-be-death-english-87727.

Jones, Graham. M., and Bambi B. Schieffelin. "Talking Text and Talking Back: 'My BFF Jill' from Boob Tube to YouTube." *Journal of Computer-Mediated Communication*, vol. 14, no. 4, 2009. *Wiley Online Library*, doi: 10.111/j.1083 -6101.2009.01481.x.

Mahatanankoon, Pruthikrai, and Patrick O'Sullivan. "Attitude toward Mobile Text Messaging: An Expectancy-Based Perspective." *Journal of Computer-Mediated Communication*, vol. 13, no. 4, 2008, pp. 973-92.

Mitra, Ananda. "Collective Narrative Expertise and the Narbs of Social Media." *Social Software and the Evolution of User Expertise: Future Trends in Knowledge Creation and Dissemination*. IGI Global, 2013.

Nielsen, Lisa. "Enriching Literacy with Cellphones: 3 Ideas to Get Started." *SmartBlog on Education*, 10 Sept. 2012, smartblogs.com/education/2012 /09/10/enriching-literacy-cell-phones-3-ideas-get-started/.

Phipps, Laurie Craig, et al. "The University in Transition: Reconsidering Faculty Roles and Expertise in a Web 2.0 World." *Social Software and the Evolution of User Expertise: Future Trends in Knowledge Creation and Dissemination*. IGI Global, 2013.

Sweeny, Sheelah M. "Writing for the Instant Messaging and Text Messaging Generation: Using New Literacies to Support Writing Instruction." *Journal of Adolescent & Adult Literacy*, vol. 54, no. 2, 2010, pp. 121-30.

Wood, Clare, et al. "The Effect of Text Messaging on 9- and 10-Year-Old Children's Reading, Spelling, and Phonological Processing Skills." *Journal of Computer-Assisted Learning*, vol. 27, no. 1, 2011, pp. 28-36.

10

Visualizing Literary Arguments with Digital Mapping Tools

Kathryn E. Crowther
Georgia State University Perimeter College

Kathryn E. Crowther is an assistant professor of English at Georgia State University Perimeter College in Atlanta. She received her PhD from Emory University where she specialized in Victorian novels and nineteenth-century print culture. Her research focuses on nineteenth-century British literature, neo-Victorian literature and steampunk, and disability studies. Her teaching frequently incorporates digital pedagogy and she uses blogging, digital mapping, and data visualization in her writing and literature classes. Crowther has published previously on Victorian literature and print culture and has forthcoming essays on representations of disability in steampunk and using blogs in the first-year writing classroom.

COURTESY OF
KATHRYN E. CROWTHER

1. OVERVIEW

- **Assignment:** Students use data visualization and mapping to make an argument about one or more literary texts.

- **Courses:** Introduction to literature; literature and composition; upper-division literature; literature courses taught with a thematic focus.

- **Literature:** Any, though the assignment is particularly well suited to those with a thematic focus on place.

- **Technology:** Mapping tool or application (for example Google Maps, Google Earth, Web sites like Weebly, and blogs like WordPress or Blogger).

- **Time:** Four to six weeks, or approximately 8–10 class meetings. (At the beginning of the assignment, you may need to take time in class to demonstrate the different digital mapping and visualization tools, or, build time into the schedule for students to attend institutional technology workshops.)

> "Using digital tools for mapping and visualization allows students to move from a close reading of a text to a broader scrutiny of patterns and connections, making visible the process of analysis and the evolution of literary arguments."
>
> **Kathryn E. Crowther**
> Georgia State University Perimeter College

2. GOALS OF THE ASSIGNMENT

- To develop an argument about a work of literature
- To explore creative options for visualizing a literary argument
- To create a user-friendly resource in which to embed the mapping artifact
- To use visual design principles and consideration of audience to construct a visualization/mapping resource
- To practice using Web resources responsibly (i.e., fair use, copyright, citation)
- To work collaboratively with peers
- To work through the stages of a large group project including brainstorming, planning, setting deadlines, developing and producing a visualization/mapping concept, participating in peer review, revising and proofing the final product
- To reflect on the process and produce a portfolio of project documentation

> "This mapping assignment asks students to be creative, to experiment with digital spaces, and to build something collaboratively, all while practicing their literary analysis skills and deepening their engagement with literature."
>
> **Kathryn E. Crowther**

3. ASSIGNMENT SHEET

Visualizing Literary Arguments with Digital Mapping Tools

Course: _____

Instructor: _____

Date: _____

Overview

For this project, you will work as a group and choose a text, or a part of a text, to "map" in a digital format. We will discuss what this involves and I will demonstrate some different ways to map or visualize data in a meaningful way using different media. You may use any of the *literary* texts we have read so far this semester (fiction and poetry). Using a medium or technology of your choice, you will create an artifact that visualizes or maps—*and thereby makes an argument about*—some element of one of our literary texts.

Projects could include creating a hypertext, an annotated text, a Google map, or a text cloud, for example. You can choose to think of mapping in terms of geographical or geospatial mapping, or in terms of data mapping or data visualization. (See "Choosing a Topic and a Medium" below.) Either way, you should zoom in on an element of the literary text and develop a project that communicates an "argument" in a primarily visual fashion. It is okay to incorporate other methods of communication (accompanying text, voice-over, digital medium) but the central mode should be visual communication. *Think about your project as a "resource" that could be used to teach the text you are mapping—you will embed your map(s) in a larger stand-alone resource such as a Web site or a blog.*

There are several components to this project:

- Your map(s)/data visualization(s)
- The format/medium in which you embed your map/data visualization
- A formal presentation of the project in class with a visual presentation (e.g., Poster, PowerPoint, or Prezi)
- Participation in an end-of-semester display of your projects in the library

Groups

You will work together in groups of 4 or 5. To make sure that each group contains a diverse skill set, you will "apply" for a position based on your interests and skills. I will form the groups based on your preferences for working with a particular text and by your self-defined strengths to ensure that each group has members with a range of experience and expertise. However, once you are assigned to a group, you are not limited to only contributing to the project in

(*continued*)

ASSIGNMENT SHEET (*continued*)

the role you applied for; rather, you will all contribute equally and the "expert" in each skill will serve as a leader or arbitrator in the decision-making process.

Materials/Technology

You will need a laptop and access to the Internet. You may use any mapping or data visualization applications — most of them are freely available on the Web. I will give a brief overview of some of the most common applications and tools (e.g., Google Maps, Prezi, Word Cloud generators) and I will walk you through how to use them. I will also provide a list of possible mapping and visualization tools along with resources and training videos on our class Web site (CMS). For the larger resource in which you will embed your map/visualization, you may create a Web site (there are many free platforms like Weebly or Wix) or use a blog on a free site such as WordPress, Blogger, or Tumblr. You may want to attend a training session hosted by the library if you are unfamiliar with sites like this. You may, of course, use more sophisticated technologies like Dreamweaver or Flash and Java scripts to build your own Web site or application.

Tasks

In order to complete this assignment, you will follow these steps (in groups):

1. Choose a text or a selection of texts that you would like to work with and develop some topics/ideas that interest you.

2. Brainstorm about what kind of mapping you would like to do — think about the texts we have read and what information you might be interested in mapping. See "Choosing a Topic and a Medium" below for specific ideas. Consider the ways that different types of media and technology could contribute to the idea you are trying to convey. You may not know exactly what you want to argue about the text(s) yet; sometimes that will become clearer as you construct your visualization. For example, by mapping the movements of the characters in *Mrs. Dalloway* you might develop an argument about the way their physical movements work together with the narrative plotting of the novel. An important part of the process will be justifying why you chose your medium to express that particular type of information. Think about how/where you will "put" your project — will it be embedded in a web page or on a poster or in a video or narrated slide show? How will you present it as a resource?

3. Make a process plan outlining the steps you will need to take to complete your project (I will give you a handout with more details). *You will need to factor in any time needed to set up any technology or learn to use a particular tool.*

4. Develop a presentation to showcase your research. I will give you a separate assignment sheet for the presentation component.

5. Complete your project and write a one-page "project statement" explaining the rationale behind your choice of medium and the idea/argument you are making. *Don't forget to include the citation/source information for any material you use or draw from that was created by someone else.* You may include this information on your actual project (e.g., credits at the end of a video, sources on the bottom of a poster) or in a separate bibliography.

6. Present your project in class and at the end-of-semester exhibition in the library.

Choosing a Topic and a Medium

Think about the texts we have read and the types of information that they contain. Then think about the type of mapping you'd like to do. Mapping essentially means that you are laying out a set of data in a visual format that makes it easy to quickly interpret. You might think about mapping in three different ways:

1. Mapping in the sense of **visually displaying certain data sets *extracted*** from the novels/poems we have read. For example, mapping information about the plague in London from *A Journal of the Plague Year* (death statistics, districts that were infected and in what order, the different accounts of people infected) or data sets about London from *Oliver Twist* (the route Bill Sikes takes as he flees London, the specific places that are visited by different characters in the novel). Notice that the information you map doesn't have to be numbers or locations; it could be stories or historical backgrounds.

2. Mapping in the sense of **diagramming or giving information to help *interpret* a text.** So, for example, you could annotate and hyperlink a text like *Mrs. Dalloway* in a similar way to the annotated mapping of the hypertext version of *The Waste Land* that we read. Or you could take a chapter of *Oliver Twist* and map annotations of the working-class dialect and slang onto a hyperlinked version of the text.

3. Mapping in the sense of **mapping information *onto the texts we have read*.** So you could take information you have learned about Victorian England (how the poor laws affected the working class, or how many orphaned children there were and what happened to them, or the workings and layout of Newgate Prison) and map that information onto *Oliver Twist*. Or you could take information about the architecture of 1923 London, or the causes and symptoms of PTSD, and map that data onto *Mrs. Dalloway*.

As you try to choose a medium for your topic, think about what your main idea and/or argument is — what do you want your viewer to learn about the topic? What is the takeaway message of the piece? Then think about how different types of media will affect that message or influence the viewer. Also consider your proficiency in using different types of visual media, or think of something you would like to learn how to use. It's probably not practical to start learning

(continued)

ASSIGNMENT SHEET (*continued*)

how to program a Web site just for this project, but you could easily learn how to use Google Mapmaker or how to build a poster in PowerPoint in a few hours.

Here are some ideas for possible projects:

- Using Google Mapmaker, you can add text, pictures, video, and so on, to different points on a map of London in order to map out a particular scene, journey, set of landmarks, historical buildings in one of our texts.

- Pick a chapter or a section of one of the texts and annotate it in a Web site, linking to words related to a particular theme (dialect, locations, representations of the working-class living situations, prostitution, women's clothing, religion, etc.)

- Create (and print and mount) a professional poster using PowerPoint. Use the poster to visualize some of the data from one of our texts. For example, you could graph out some of the statistics from *A Journal of the Plague Year* in an interesting visual format and connect it directly to certain scenes from the novel.

- Design a document that visualizes data using word clouds or other formats. Find a creative way to present it (poster, Prezi, etc.)

This is by no means an exhaustive list — there are many more ideas so don't just copy these. Remember, you will be graded on the creativity of your project as well as your execution of the idea.

Two Important Points

1. The projects should *directly and clearly connect to the literary text you are mapping*. If you are mapping data onto the text (e.g., information about the Poor Laws) you must clearly align the data with *specific* parts of the literary text.

2. Most importantly, *there should be an implicit argument in your project* — the data that you are mapping should give us new insight into the text, or should provide us with a new way of looking at the text that broadens our interpretation of it. So, for example, simply creating a word cloud of all the words in *Mrs. Dalloway* wouldn't be sufficient — you would need to use the word cloud to show something important about the novel, or to make an argument about it. You should find a way to articulate what that argument is on the project itself; you will also explain it in more detail in your project statement.

As you work on your project you should pay attention to the following:

- **Your Audience:** Who is your audience? How much can you assume your audience knows about this topic? What is the best way to appeal to your viewer (e.g., humor, vivid examples, serious tone)? How will they be impacted by your choice of media?

- **Your Message/Argument:** What do you want the viewer to learn from your project? How can you articulate it clearly so you can be sure that they understand what the takeaway message is?
- **Your Medium:** Is it easy to read/view/interpret? Is there a logical connection between the medium and the data you are mapping? Have you taken into consideration the design principles we discussed in class?

When you submit the assignment you will include the following eight items:

1. Your final project
2. Your project statement
3. All draft copies
4. Your works-cited document
5. Your worksheets from *all* the draft workshops
6. Your process plan
7. Your brainstorming notes
8. Your progress reports

Please note: If you use text or media belonging to other people, you *must give full credit* for it either on the project itself or in an attached works-cited document.

4. TIME AND TECHNOLOGY

TIME. This assignment requires a significant time commitment, although the actual class time devoted to the project depends on the amount of out-of-class group work you can expect your students to do. In my course, we spend the first half of a sixteen-week semester reading literary texts (novels and poetry) related to the topic of London and completing two writing assignments, one with a research component. The second half of the semester is devoted to reading and discussing our final longer text (a contemporary novel) and working on the digital mapping project. In total, we spend about six weeks actively working on the assignment, though students begin thinking about the project a few weeks before that. However, because we do not devote more than one class period per week to working on the project in the classroom, we have time in other classes to continue our larger discussion of literary and communication-related issues. A more condensed version of the project could be completed in three to four weeks if each class period was devoted to working on the project. Alternatively, a mini-version of the project could be developed during one class period with the whole class working together on one visualization.

In my case, the course where I've used the digital mapping project is focused on both literature and composition, so I designed my syllabus to move students through a sequence of assignments that practice the composition skills required to meet the course objectives, which fall under the categories critical thinking, rhetoric, process, and modes and media. I scaffolded the course to incrementally build the skill set necessary to complete the large, comprehensive final assignment, our digital mapping project. Thus, the first assignment practiced close reading and literary analysis, the second introduced students to research skills and using evidence to support an argument, and the third introduced visual design principles and ways to responsibly use and remix visual media. In this way, the final project was a synthesis and application of the skills practiced throughout the course, but it also pushed the students to use their own ideas to creatively apply those skills to the creation of a loosely defined artifact. However, in an upper-level course with students experienced in composition and research, the assignment could be a stand-alone project that takes the place of a more traditional literary analysis paper.

I deliberately time our discussion of literary research tools, effective group-work strategies, citation and copyright guidelines, and oral presentation skills to coincide with the corresponding stages of the project. I recommend breaking the assignment into several stages:

1. Introduce the concept of digital mapping early in the semester in order to give students time to begin thinking about the ways visualization techniques can be used to analyze literary texts. Use their

ideas to start discussing strategies for turning literary arguments into visualizations; I also recommend introducing them to some large-scale digital humanities projects that use technology to explore and analyze texts in a visual fashion in order to demonstrate the ways that those visualizations reveal an interpretation of the text that could not be accessed with traditional straightforward close reading.[1]

2. When you begin working on the project, devote at least one class period to a demonstration and hands-on exploration of the various digital mapping and visualization tools available for students to use on the Internet. If your students do not typically bring laptops to class, it would be ideal to conduct this class in a computer lab. If you have media/technology specialists at your school, you might ask them to come and speak to the class and/or direct the students toward any classes and resources available at the library or media center. You might also use this class to have the students apply for positions in the groups.

Once you have set up the groups, give the students a clear timeline for the project, along with due dates for progress reports and deliverables. Your schedule might look like the one below:

Week 1: Learning about digital mapping/visualization. Set up groups.

Week 2: Project concept proposals and timelines for completion due (returned with instructor feedback and recommendations).

Week 3: Progress report 1 due. (Optional: group meetings with instructor.)

Week 4: Second progress report due. Rough demonstration of map/visualization in class for peer and instructor feedback.

Week 5: Peer-review workshop and user-testing of beta version of project (map/visualization embedded in larger resource).

Week 6: Final version of project due and demonstration in the library. Students submit personal reflections and peer evaluations.

TECHNOLOGY. This project allows students to determine the technology they find most appropriate for their form of mapping or visualization, so the requirements for the assignment are basic: computer access (in and outside of class) and a basic knowledge of computing skills (composing on blogs, uploading and editing images, using "what you see is what you get" [WYSIWYG] formatting tools, etc.). I designed this assignment to focus on creativity, so I did not want technical expertise to be a determining factor for successfully completing the project; essentially, I wanted all students

---

[1]Some examples of the visualizations that I demonstrated include "Mapping the Republic of Letters" project out of Stanford University (republicofletters.stanford.edu/), "Digital Harlem" (acl.arts.usyd.edu.au/harlem/), and "Wordseer" (wordseer.berkeley.edu/).

to use the technology at their comfort level and let the cogency of their argument and the creativity of their visualization form the basis of the evaluation criteria.

"I challenge students to design the project as a resource that teachers and other students could use to learn more about the texts under analysis."

Kathryn E. Crowther

In addition, students are required to embed their map in a larger resource that explains the concept behind the visualization and give detailed instructions on how to use it (most students used a blog or a basic Web site for this). I challenge them to design the project as a resource that teachers and other students could use to learn more about the texts under analysis. In this way, students are prevented from simply designing a stand-alone visualization; instead they have to think about the user's experience (important for the rhetorical consideration of audience) and provide background information, instructions, and a clear user interface to ensure that their resource meets the needs of the targeted user. Given free range to use any digital tools, most of my students chose visualization applications and platforms ranging in complexity from blogs and online word cloud and timeline applications to self-coded Web sites with Java scripts and Flash animation.

Mapping Applications. Google Maps allows users to create an account and then personalize maps with icons, text, and embedded media. As part of the introduction to the project, I show my students a YouTube video explaining how to use Google Mapmaker and then showcase some personalized maps to demonstrate the application's functionality. Students quickly adapt to the application—which has functions similar to most social networking sites (uploading images, embedding links, customizing appearance, etc.)—and they generally have no trouble using the actual mapping features to place pins on particular locations and to mark routes between pins. On the pin markers (which have customizable icons), students can add text, links, images, and even sound/video files that relate to the location they are highlighting. Students are required to embed their Google Map in a larger resource (such as a blog, Tumblr, or basic Web site—see section "Blogs and Web Sites" below) in order to provide background information and navigation guidelines. Again, these sites are often familiar to students and, if not, require only a brief overview in class because their functionality is simple and easy to learn.

Google Earth is a more robust application that provides a 3D mapping visualization, but also requires more technical knowledge. Students can download it to their local computers and then customize the map of their chosen area using accurate historical overlays. Some of my students mapped specific routes and then recorded 3D "fly-throughs" that could be saved as videos.

Visualization Software. For their visualizations, most students use tools such as maps, graphs, word clouds, timelines, and other freely available web tools. One popular application is Prezi, the dynamic presentation software that can be found online and used as a platform in which to embed a live presentation (or an active link) within a Web site. As Prezi software has zooming capabilities, students can embed maps within Prezi and then use the zooming function to highlight places on the map accompanied by related media. Other students use blogs to create hypertexts by selecting excerpts from their chosen literary work and annotating words with literary or historical significance with embedded links and images. For the most part, blogs and Web sites serve as platforms in which students can embed the actual digital visualization or map.

Blogs and Web Sites. Many students find that blogs hosted by companies like WordPress and Blogger, or microblogging sites like Tumblr, provide a customizable platform for their visualizations. Blog templates can be designed to look like Web sites and allow most kinds of embedded media. Similarly, easy-to-build Web sites with drag-and-drop functionality and WYSIWYG editing are user-friendly and free. My students have had success with sites like Weebly and Wix, but there are many more available at no cost (although some free sites do contain small advertisements). In my experience, students with only minimal experience in blogging found these sites relatively self-explanatory and easy to use. Additionally, some of my students felt comfortable building and coding their own Web sites, and some even added Flash animation and Java scripts. Many of those students were computer science majors, although others participated in a training session and then used the school-provided software (Dreamweaver) to build a site from scratch.

You need to be carve out class time to demonstrate some of these technologies, and, later in the project, to run testing and troubleshooting sessions. I have found that walking students through some examples and providing them with videos and online tutorials is sufficient to introduce them to the useful digital tools — this may vary with different student populations. Students also have the option of attending short technology workshops at the library or working individually with media specialists. Again, the flexibility of the assignment allows students to choose a technology or tool that fits their skill level and does not require them to have access to any technology beyond a computer and an Internet connection.

5. ANTICIPATING STUDENT NEEDS

There are two main potential difficulties with this project: time requirements and potential student resistance to (and anxiety about) completing a nontraditional literature assignment using digital technologies. To address the first issue, be sure to include a significant block of time in your

syllabus for work on the project. While you might not
need many in-class sessions (barring a possible session
introducing the technology), students will need several
weeks to work on the project outside of class and may
benefit from having some class periods devoted to peer
review and instructor feedback. At institutions where
group work is less common or more difficult (commuter
colleges for example), a project like this might only work
if time is carved out during several classes to give the students time to work
together. Your syllabus should clearly state that some out-of-class group
work is required in order to give students with schedule constraints advanced
warning.

> "A discussion of why we use
> different modes and media to
> present our ideas . . . is help-
> ful, as is demonstrating some
> of the large-scale digital
> humanities projects."
>
> **Kathryn E. Crowther**

Another potential problem is that students may be resistant to or anxious about a project that moves deliberately away from the traditional model
of literary analysis with which they are generally very familiar. To persuade
students on this issue, I find that a discussion of why we use different modes
and media to present our ideas (and why some are more effective than others at reaching particular audiences) is helpful, as is demonstrating some of
the large-scale digital humanities projects that can give students a sense of the
serious work digital visualization can do. Stanford University's Mapping the
Republic of Letters (republicofletters.stanford.edu/) is a great example of a
large-scale visualization project that demonstrates how Enlightenment ideas
spread across Europe and to the Americas by mapping the movement of letters exchanged by prominent writers.

Similarly, Wordseer (wordseer.berkeley.edu/) allows users to search bodies of texts for words and themes and then visualizes them in customizable formats. The site has a demonstration example that visualizes the data
derived from a search for narrative conventions in an archive of slave narratives. It also has a selection of videos that demonstrate the functionality of
the site. Projects like these can help inspire students not only by giving them
ideas about how and what to map, but also by showing how digital projects
serve a new and vital function in humanities studies. By showing them how
visualizations can reveal information and arguments that are inaccessible
through traditional close reading, students see the relevance and innovation
of such large-scale digital projects.

In order to address the possible anxiety that working with technology can inspire, I suggest having the students sketch out their ideas for
the visualization first without necessarily determining the technology they
wish to use. Then in a consultation with you (or in a peer-brainstorming
session), they can determine the technology that will work for their concept
and select the one with which they feel most comfortable working. If you
are trying this assignment in a setting with limited access to technology
or with a student population that is less comfortable working with digital
tools, I suggest narrowing the scope of the assignment to one or two options

(for example, a Google Map or a blog with embedded word clouds) and then spend time in class walking the students step-by-step through each application.

Finally, I would add that, while this could be a challenging assignment for some students, giving them the opportunity to experiment integrating literature and technology — and even fail — can be a valuable learning experience in itself. If you are concerned that students may have difficulties, I recommend building several opportunities for feedback and revision into the assignment timeline; that way, if a group finds itself with a digital tool they cannot master or an idea that is too complicated to realize, then they will have enough time to return to the drawing board and try again with a simpler tool or design. To this end, asking students to conclude the assignment by reflecting on the process of invention, experimentation, and failure they experienced can lead to some of the most valuable learning moments in their college careers.

> "I recommend building several opportunities for feedback and revision into the assignment timeline."
>
> **Kathryn E. Crowther**

> "Asking students to conclude by reflecting on the process of invention, experimentation, and failure they experienced can lead to some of the most valuable learning moments in their college careers."
>
> **Kathryn E. Crowther**

6. ASSESSMENT TOOLS

This assignment is the culmination of a course devoted to literature and communication. Consequently, the grading reflects an assessment of a variety of skill sets. I designed my grading rubric (see below) to represent the categories of the course objectives, so I evaluate projects on rhetorical awareness, stance and support, organization, design for medium, and conventions. These general categories allow me to evaluate how well the projects fulfill the specific criteria, regardless of which media the students employ or what format the final resource takes. The majority of the points are allotted for the final digital mapping artifact, although there are some points allocated for the three progress reports, a formal write-up of the project, and also for the performance of each student individually (based on their self-reflections and anonymous peer evaluations). The latter is a way to accommodate the individual performance and contributions of each student.

Because the goals for my class are focused on both literary and communication skills, my assessment rubric reflects both types of criteria. You might choose to grade the project on the completion of the smaller milestones, or on the accomplishment of goals related more specifically to your course topic. I do, however, feel that giving frequent low-stakes feedback and/or completion grades is very important in a multistage project of this type. This can be done on a weekly basis with the completion of

> "Allowing students to present their work to a larger audience at the end of the semester presents a 'real-world' or authentic user experience."
>
> **Kathryn E. Crowther**

SAMPLE RUBRIC: Digital Mapping Project: Areas and Criteria for Evaluation

Rubric	Areas	Criteria	Points
Rhetorical Awareness and Stance and Support	Central Idea/Thesis	Your project should clearly convey a central idea or argument about the work(s) of literature that can be identified by the audience.	___/25
	Audience	Consider your audience — make sure your style, tone, and message are appropriate and appealing.	___/10
	Supporting Points (Content)	Lead your audience through the argument you are presenting in your resource. Each point or step should contribute to viewers' overall understanding of your central idea. (Also, see Sequence.)	___/25
Organization	Sequence	Think about the order in which your audience will view your map/visualization resource. If there is a logical order, be sure to mark that using transition statements (written or verbal), headings/subheadings, graphics (such as arrows), or other features to make sure that your viewer can follow your ideas. If there is no specific order in which to view/experience your project, be sure that your audience will understand how to put the parts together to understand your main idea.	___/20
Design for Medium	Use of the Medium	There should be a logical connection between your choice of medium and the idea you are presenting; that is, the medium should be well suited (and fully exploited) to make your argument about your identity. You will also be graded on how well you use the medium, taking into account its capacities and your skill level. You will address your justification for your choice of media in the project statement.	___/15
	Design	Your artifact should effectively deploy design elements such as chunking, contrast, alignment, tension, color, etc.	___/15

			Points
	Accessibility	Ensure that your project is easy to read (use large, clear font), logical to navigate, and (when applicable) easy to hear.	___/5
	Consistency	Use the same style/color fonts, make sure spacing is equal, pay attention to the organization, and ensure all elements are consistent.	___/5
Conventions	Conventionality	Write and/or speak in clear, grammatically correct English (unless you are making a point about language).	___/5
	Attribution	Give full credit to any outside sources you use in your project (this includes text, images, video clips, audio) using MLA format. You can include this information on the artifact itself or you can turn in a separate works-cited list.	___/5
	Origin	The project should identify its creator/s (be sure to give credit to anyone who assists you), the course that fostered its growth, the institution that hosted the course, and the date of its release.	___/5
	Project Statement	Your project statement should be a 1- to 2-page discussion of the origin of your idea, your choice of medium, and how you expect viewers to experience your work. You might also address any problems you encountered in the execution of the project or any aspects of the final piece that didn't work as you had hoped. Your project statement should be properly formatted using MLA guidelines.	___/25
	Process work/ Progress reports	The final project should include completion of all process work including process plan, rough version(s), peer-review worksheet, and progress reports.	___/20
	Individual contribution		___/20
	COMMENTS		TOTAL

written progress reports (which you evaluate and return to the group with comments) or with an informal oral check-in at the beginning of each class period, with each group presenting their progress and soliciting feedback from the instructor and students. I also recommend meeting with students early in the process to make sure that their project will meet the criteria and to prevent a group devoting the majority of their time to an infeasible or inappropriate project. Finally, allowing students to present their work to a larger audience at the end of the semester presents a "real-world" or authentic user experience, and you could allow the feedback from their peers or visitors to the exhibition to contribute to their grade.

7. THEORETICAL BASIS FOR THE ASSIGNMENT: Visualizing Literary Arguments with Digital Mapping Tools

Most students enter the literature classroom expecting assignments that practice traditional literary analysis: writing an analytical or argumentative essay based on a close reading of one or more literary texts. However, as a teacher of both composition and literature, I was inspired by the creativity and innovation my students showed in the composition classroom when they were encouraged to move away from the rigid structure of the traditional five-paragraph essay and instead use tech-

> "I was inspired by the creativity and innovation my students showed in the composition classroom when they were encouraged . . . to develop compositions that integrated all modes of media."
> **Kathryn E. Crowther**

nology to develop compositions that integrated all modes of media (written, oral, visual, electronic). In particular, I found that students responded especially well to assignments that focused on answering a specific question or performing a task using a targeted set of skills but that left the medium, concept, and design of the final product open and undefined. With such assignments, the critical thinking and creativity of the students drove the direction of the project and forced them to consider not "what is the answer to this question?" but rather "what are the different ways I can answer this question?" and "what considerations must I address in order to find the best answer?" These questions push students away from rote learning and force them to resist basing their responses to assignments on preexisting models. When I returned to teaching literature, I decided to apply this pedagogical technique to a literary analysis assignment.

Therefore, in my Writing about Literature course, I created this assignment which is designed to bring creativity and critical thinking to the forefront. The digital mapping project combines traditional literary analysis, which deploys close reading, analysis, and argumentation, with a focus on visualization and mapping in a multimedia environment. Although I give the students broad suggestions about the possible projects (such as creating a hypertext, an annotated text, a Google map, or a text cloud), I leave the final product open to any creative interpretation of mapping using digital tools. I allow students to incorporate other methods of communication (accompanying text, voice-over, video, etc.) but I emphasize that the central communicative mode should be visual. To give the project a broader scope (and to fit the research requirement of the course), I direct students to think of the project as a resource that could be used to teach the text they are mapping, and I encourage them to embed the map/visualization(s) in a larger stand-alone resource such as a Web site or blog (I point them toward free, online options). The assignment concludes with a formal presentation of the resource to the class and to a broader audience at a library showcase.

The digital mapping project puts to work several pedagogical principles: First, assignments that build upon concepts and skills that have already been presented over the duration of a course allow students to develop mastery of the concepts and to push their skills to a more sophisticated level (Bean 225). In the digital mapping project, students work through the same initial steps of a literary analysis assignment: close reading, textual analysis, crafting an argument, and choosing sections of the text as evidence to support that argument. However, rather than stopping there and converting that argument into a standard essay narrative, the students are asked to translate that argument into a visualization that serves to explicate and elucidate the argument. In this way, the students rehearse the steps of literary analysis but are pushed to reconceptualize the way that an argument about a text can be expressed (Birdsell and Groarke 309).

Second, creativity and collaboration are highly desired skills in the professional world, yet they are rarely the explicit goals of an academic course.[2] Removing the structure of a predefined final product and giving students free rein to interpret the goals of the assignment together challenges them to think critically not only about the objectives but also the medium, the design, and the audience or user experience — all skills they will need in the workplace. Henry Jenkins writes extensively about digital literacy and the "participatory culture" that new and web-based media encourage. These new media literacies are built through "collaboration and networking" and use skills that "build on the foundation of traditional literacy, research skills, technical skills, and critical analysis skills taught in the classroom" (Jenkins et al. 4). According to Jenkins, students need to practice skills such as "play, performance, simulation, appropriation, multitasking, collective intelligence, transmedia navigation, networking and negotiation" in order to remain

---

[2]See, for example, "Creativity and Education: Why It Matters" at cdx.dexigner.com/article /23057/Creativity_and_Education.pdf.

competitive in the contemporary workplace (3). Designing assignments that allow students to engage with a
variety of media without mandating the final product
reintroduces play, improvisation, and invention to the
classroom space and gives students the chance to experience the pleasures and frustrations of experimentation
in a low-risk environment. (See also Bjork 100-02.)

> "Creativity and collaboration are highly desired skills in the professional world, yet they are rarely the explicit goals of an academic course."
> **Kathryn E. Crowther**

Finally, by asking the students to produce a resource that will be freely
available on the Internet, this assignment compels students to conceptualize their project as an authentic product with a real end user. Students
must consider the needs of their target audience, the ways that visual design
contributes to user experience, and the protocol for using web resources
responsibly (i.e., fair use, copyright, citation). As their resources could reach
a global audience, students absorb the rhetorical implications of audience
more readily, and the generally tedious issues of copyright and citation take
on greater import. In their article, "Infusing Multimodal Tools and Digital Literacies into an English Education Program," Aaron Doering, Richard Beach, and David O'Brien argue that "given this ready access to these
broader, even world-wide audiences, adolescents must then know how to go
beyond simply creating multimodal texts to knowing how to design these
texts using visual rhetoric to effectively attract, engage, and influence their
audiences" (41). Focusing on an external audience redirects the students
from focusing solely on assessment via teacher evaluation to assessment via
user experience, and they ultimately feel proud that the final outcome of the
assignment is a product that has potential for use outside of the classroom.

8. CONCLUSION

When I first assigned this project, I had no idea that it would inspire
such a variety of interpretations and design concepts. I found that the students—while anxious at first—appreciated the trust I
placed in them to find an innovative way to meet the
assignment criteria, and they enjoyed the sense of play
the focus on creativity engendered. Examples of some
of the projects I received include: word maps analyzing
the use of color imagery in *The Waste Land*, a Google
Earth fly-through of Mrs. Dalloway's walk through
London to demonstrate the distance she covered, a
Google map of the regional accents of characters in

> "Students were proud to show off their work and to answer difficult questions . . . about the ways that mapping and visualization can answer questions about literature."
> **Kathryn E. Crowther**

Oliver Twist accompanied by sound files, a hypertext of the first five chapters of *Oliver Twist* annotating the references to the Victorian workhouse

with links and images, a Prezi examining the possible outcomes of decisions made by the central characters in *Saturday*, and a comparative project that mapped the sites in London mentioned in all the texts we'd read and made the argument that there is indeed a "Literary London."

In the final presentation of the projects in our library showcase, students were proud to show off their work and to answer difficult questions (often from skeptical students and professors) about the ways that mapping and visualization can answer questions about literature. When challenged that their work didn't represent traditional literary analysis or composition, students were quick to argue the contrary: that not only did their maps translate a literary argument into a visual format, but that they often revealed patterns, trends, and, ultimately, arguments about texts that were not visible through traditional close reading. As one student wrote in the final reflection: "I learned that looking at literature from a different perspective often helps to discover new themes or motifs."

Converting data from a text format to a visual format allows both the scholar and audience to view information in a way that is easily understandable. In their evaluation of the course, most students identified this project as the most challenging but most rewarding assignment of the semester. Several of them noted that they hadn't expected a writing about literature course to challenge them to "build" something with digital tools or to consider a global web audience. Students also commented on the role invention and creativity played in the assignment and expressed surprise that they were given such freedom to determine the format and content of the final product; they were consistently proud of the results. Ultimately, as the final projects and the students' individual feedback showed, the students learned not only about literary analysis and argumentation but also about the tools they can use to combine their creativity with digital technology in order to answer traditional questions in unique and innovative ways.

9. WORKS CITED

Bean, John C. *Engaging Ideas: The Professor's Guide to Integrating Writing, Critical Thinking, and Active Learning in the Classroom*. Jossey-Bass, 2001.

Birdsell, David S., and Leo Groarke. "Toward a Theory of Visual Argument." *Visual Rhetoric in a Digital World: A Critical Sourcebook*. Edited by Carolyn Handa, Bedford St. Martin's, 2004.

Bjork, Olin. "Digital Humanities and the First-Year Writing Course." *Digital Humanities Pedagogy: Practices, Principles, and Politics*. Edited by Brett D. Hirsch, Open Book, 2012, pp. 97-119, www.openbookpublishers.com/html reader/DHP/chap04.html.

Doering, Aaron, et al. "Infusing Multimodal Tools and Digital Literacies into an
    English Education Program." *English Education*, vol. 40, no. 1, Oct. 2007,
    pp. 41-60. *JSTOR*, www.jstor.org/stable/40173267.

Jenkins, Henry, et al. "Confronting the Challenges of Participatory Culture:
    Media Education for the 21st Century." *MacArthur Foundation*, 2006, www
    .macfound.org/media/article_pdfs/JENKINS_WHITE_PAPER_PDF.

11

Mapping Literature, Cultural Artifacts, and Communities: Reveal the Living Map of Latin@ Letters

Charli G. Valdez

University of New Hampshire

Charli G. Valdez teaches Latina/o literature, American literature, and literature and the visual arts at the University of New Hampshire. Recipient of a Fulbright for his dissertation research in Spain, he received his A.M. in comparative literature at Brown University and his PhD in Literature and Creative Writing at the University of Houston. He has presented on Chicana/o culture at the MLA and other conferences and has recently published fiction in the *Saranac Review* and scholarship in *Film and Literary Modernism* and *The Great Recession in Fiction, Film, and Television: Twenty-First-Century Bust Culture*. He is from Albuquerque, New Mexico.

COURTESY OF
CHARLI G. VALDEZ

1. OVERVIEW

- **Assignment:** Students construct a digital, interactive, socially networked cartographic representation of a local Latino community and of the community of the literary text (e.g., New Mexico).
- **Courses:** Mexican American literature; Chicana/o literature; Latino literature; any literature course that includes literature by Chicana/o or Latina/o literature (introduction to literature, literature and composition, American literature, etc.).
- **Literature:** Although this assignment is constructed around the specific example of *Bless Me, Ultima*, by Rudolfo Anaya, it can be applied to any text/community in which an emphasis on locality or regionalism is especially important.
- **Technology:** Ready access to computers and the Internet, Panoramio and Google Earth, and a course Web site (e.g., WordPress) where the final projects can be published (either privately or as an open-access resource).
- **Time:** This project can readily run for three to four weeks beyond the week dedicated to the novel itself, depending on the digital literacy of the students. It helps to announce the assignment at the beginning of the

155

semester to allow for several additional weeks of flexibility for students who need to set up a plan to travel to a local community to make the images they will need for the project.

2. GOALS OF THE ASSIGNMENT

After completing this assignment, students will be able to

- demonstrate how region impacts race and ethnicity;
- bridge cultural divides in regions where there is little local and/or experienced diversity;
- develop students' digital literacy; and
- meditate on how historical, geographical, and cultural forces intersect.

3. ASSIGNMENT SHEET

Mapping Literature, Cultural Artifacts, and Communities: Reveal the Living Map of Latin@ Letters

Course: _____

Instructor: _____

Date: _____

We have already signed up for and explored some of the new technologies and open-source software, which have resulted in exciting new advances in interactive, socially networked literary cartography. Students today, including you, are uniquely positioned to learn and advance such technologically enhanced research. In Latin@ studies, literary cartography can be especially useful in locating which Latin@ community, and what aspect of it, is being aesthetically represented in a text. This geovisualization of the text will be enriched through navigable images, socially networked discussion, and links designed by you.

We have prepared for this project, having discussed how specific Latin@ communities are depicted and how particular figures, metaphors, and settings are represented in the literary texts that we've read over the course of the semester. In particular, we elaborated on this while reading Rudolfo Anaya's *Bless Me, Ultima*, which will be the primary literary text for this project. If you would like to work on a different Latin@ community vis-à-vis a different literary text, please let me know as soon as possible. It will depend on whether you and I are able to secure the right contacts.

You will now construct a digital, interactive, socially networked cartographic representation of a local Latino community and of the community of the literary text (in this case, New Mexico). This project will consist of the following steps:

1. Create an Image
In your small groups, you have researched, located, and made plans to visit a local Latin@ community. You have cleared these plans with me. Now you should visit as a group, leaving yourselves enough time to photograph, draw, paint, or otherwise make the images you will use for your cartographic representation.

Consider how you will represent the community at all levels of detail. For example: How did you frame the photograph you took? Is the subject familiar and represented widely throughout popular culture (e.g., la Virgen de Guadalupe)? Is it a cityscape?

2. Conduct Online Research
Review your technical preparation from earlier in the semester.

- You have already signed up for Google and Panoramio accounts.
- You have already signed up for our WordPress blog and our Panoramio Group.

(continued)

ASSIGNMENT SHEET (*continued*)

- You have already downloaded Google Earth.

- You have already practiced tasks and watched the tutorials for Panoramio and Google Earth.

Browse for user-generated, amateur images of this local community.

- Begin with Panoramio.

- Continue with Google searches.

- Get creative and try other approaches.

- In small groups, research (with my input and supervision) archived and curated images that have some bearing on this community. The archives that are relevant will depend on the community and subject that you've decided to work on, but ARTstor and the collections in the Library of Congress *Prints & Photographs Online Catalog* (www.loc.gov/pictures/) are a good place to start.

- Finally, supplement this research with more quantitative work such as how the community figures in the most recent census, with an eye to relative population density.

3. Construct the Cartographic Representation
Review the maps, tours, and Web sites that we previewed earlier in the semester. You will find the links at our WordPress site.

- Put your images and research together in Google Earth:
  - Use the placemark tool.
  - Attach an image URL for each placemark.
  - Consider how to strengthen your placemarks with links.
  - For each placemark, include a narrative analyzing the attached image, discussing its geolocation, and addressing its role as representation.
  - Consider how to strengthen your work using the Tour, Polygon, Path, and other tools.
  - Save your work as a single .kmz document.

- Upload your document to the class dropbox. We will workshop this draft; you will have only one final chance for revision before we publish it to the blog.

4. Construct a Cartographic Representation of the Literary Text

- Review the primary text that you are using for comparison — for example, Rudolfo Anaya's *Bless Me, Ultima*.

- Use the images acquired through research.

- In small groups, research (with my input and supervision) archived and curated images that have some bearing on this community. The archives that are relevant will depend on the community and subject that you've decided to work on, but ARTstor and the collections in the Library of Congress *Prints & Photographs Online Catalog* (www.loc.gov/pictures/) are a good place to start.

- Supplement this research with more quantitative data, such as how the community figures in the most recent census, with an eye to relative population density. Remember to pay attention to the historical moment. In the case of Anaya's *Bless Me, Ultima*, we are talking about the 1940s, not the present day. You might consider a historical overlay in such cases.

- Put this all together in Google Earth, as described above, and save it as a .kmz document. Upload this to the class dropbox. We will workshop this and you will have one final chance for revision before we publish it to the blog.

5. Prepare an Essay

Prepare a final discussion essay in which you reflect on the process of representing two distinct Latin@ communities. Specify the differences you've seen between your representation of the local community, your collage representation of the community of the literary text, and the literary text's representation itself. Some of the issues that you should take up in this essay include technical questions, the task of literary cartography itself, the meaning produced by contextualizing images through geopositioning, the visualization of literary representation, and how transborder considerations develop a more nuanced understanding of Latin@ communities.

4. TIME AND TECHNOLOGY

As we move from the technology of the slide and overhead projector, beyond digital PowerPoint presentations, the static images and mapped space previously used have rapidly evolved into a more dynamic and interactive environment with enormous pedagogical implications that can be especially useful to education majors.

In considering the potential of an assignment such as this, it can be useful for you as the instructor to start by reviewing and browsing online maps generated by scholars, university students, and high school educators. Students will benefit from a similar review of the digital humanities landscape in which they will be working and this should be covered in class. While I discuss below the tools that students will use in this assignment, namely Google Earth and Panoramio, some other Web sites that can give you an idea of the potential of literary cartography include:

- The interactive map to Luis Urrea's *The Devil's Highway* (devil.ucdavis .edu/)
- Hypercities' interactive interface with historical map overlays (hypercities .com/)
- Digital Concord, an interactive map that seeks to go beyond print-culture models for user interface and is dedicated specifically to Concord, Massachusetts (www.digitalconcord.org/maps/map)
- Shiva, a software bundle with a convenient image search (www.viseyes .org/shiva/)
- Google Lit Trips, a collection of mostly K–12 literary adventures, which is of special interest to the many education majors in my department (www.googlelittrips.org/)

Panoramio and Google Earth are user-friendly with a relatively quick learning curve. Google Earth has a discussion forum for educators and students, although it sprawls. You will want to reserve some time to watch the tutorials and familiarize yourself with the tools available in this software. Although there is a Pro version of Google Earth, the free download should be sufficient for the student project.

This assignment will require some early technical preparation. At the beginning of the semester, students should download Google Earth and sign up for a Google account, a Panoramio account, and any social networking group that you, as the instructor, have organized or deemed relevant to the project. It is worth assigning minor orientation projects at the same time so that students work out the bugs and confusion they might have with the software and user interfaces. For example, you might consider having them develop a placemarker including a short narrative, a link, and an image and have them e-mail it to you.

You will also want them to be aware from the start of the semester of the time and scope of any field trips and social networking that they will engage in. Once the students have read and discussed the literary text, a class field trip or the trips small groups make out into the community shouldn't be much of a drain on time—accounting for travel time may be the most significant element.

If you give students one and probably no more than two weeks before they have to workshop the representation that they build, that should be sufficient. A weekend will be enough for subsequent revisions before handing in the final project for publication.

Panoramio allows you to search for geolocated photos by tag, or metadata, and place. Since you can point at a region and browse for photos (e.g., by more specific place and popularity), it lends itself to a casual exploration of the borderlands. A first reading of a book like Luis Urrea's *The Devil's Highway* can benefit from a virtual field trip, allowing students to visualize not only the sheer geographical scope of the empty desert space (which can be unimaginable to those from the Northeast), but also the images of the border fence and border crossings, which are easily browsable on Panoramio. Locating useful images on a given theme or figure should be rehearsed beforehand as there are often very few images on particular Latin@ subjects and it can be instructive to illustrate and model this in class with students. However, this limitation can become an opportunity for discussion: What kinds of photos are popular (and allowed) in Panoramio, or Pinterest for that matter. Why? To what extent is this a new form of cultural erasure?

The users of Panoramio vary, but include many photography enthusiasts and professionals. The site is neither educationally nor academically oriented. It is worth noting that Panoramio doesn't impose a limit on photo descriptions, so students can upload a short essay speaking to the specific image that they posted. You can bookmark photos as favorites, and form and join groups over which the group's moderator has membership control (although anyone can still see the images and activity of the group). For example, I have organized a group, Latin@ Living Map for this assignment, which can accommodate users regardless of where they study or teach.

There is a delay of up to three weeks before Panoramio will review an image. It takes another week for it to be reviewed by Google Earth. If you want to have your students publish their images, you will have to account for that delay. I ask my students to simply save their work in a discrete file to be handed in at the end of the project and thus we bypass that problem as well as the polemic of requiring students to publish their work.

Google Earth is a powerful platform. There are a number of sources that can help you learn how it works, including Google Group educator discussion forums and Google Earth Lessons (www.gelessons.com/). Of particular relevance to this assignment is the fact that you can organize tours, make folders, and pin placemarks (filled with images, links, and text) to the map, and save your work as .kmz files, which are then easily distributed to Google Groups or e-mailed with a simple right click of the mouse. In the Google Earth interface, you can browse Panoramio images already geo-located to that site or create the placemark, find a relevant image elsewhere, and add that image's URL to the placemark.

When students capture images from their local community, they find they can most easily shoot photos from cameras on their phones, so having proper digital cameras has not been a factor. Students without access to camera phones and art students will appreciate the opportunity to draw, paint, or otherwise render images from the local community. Students who do not have phones that can record the location of the photo should make note of where on a map they took the photo for use in building their map later.

Small working groups can be organized among the students to maximize the use of resources, including vehicles and digital camera phones, as well as capitalize on discussion they will have in the particular Latino community that they depict. In that much, you can depend on students' own transportation methods, although in rural areas, it might make sense to develop a planned field trip with a van or bus to travel to a particular town or neighborhood.

In acquiring images online, students will browse for two kinds of images: user-generated amateur images, such as those on Panoramio or Flickr, and archived, curated, or institutional images. There are many relevant sites to which you might direct students for the latter, depending on the community in question, including:

- The Library of Congress *Prints & Photographs Online Catalog*, and in particular the Farm Security Administration Collection (www.loc.gov /pictures/)
- Farmworker union galleries, such as that of Pineros y Campesinos Unidos del Noroeste (www.pcun.org/gallery)
- The Web site of the Social and Public Art Resource Center and the Great Wall of Los Angeles (www.sparcmurals.org)
- Collections of public art such as Public Art in Public Places (www.public artinpublicplaces.info/)

Geolocating images that students have acquired online, but not on Panoramio or Google Earth, may take some creativity on their part. It might be as simple as conducting a Google image search for an architectural marker, such as Cordova Bridge border crossing in El Paso, Texas. The Historical Marker Database (www.hmdb.org/) can be useful for locating specific sites to connect with narratives.

Social networking can be the most difficult and rewarding aspect of this assignment. You may be best served by tapping into your own connections and contacts. However, in the absence of such contacts and, more importantly, in the interest of more fully networking conversations of this nature, list-servs, centers, and Latino studies blogs can be useful starting points. By successfully networking the assignment with another instructor in a different region of the country, the comparative impulse of this assignment and the transborder sensibility that it imparts will be most effective.

I have broken down how the project might unfold below. This is only one model, and probably that with the lightest gloss. It would be easy to extend it and increase its depth, but I would hesitate about trying to shorten the project beyond what follows.

Week One	<ul><li>Review the assignment.</li><li>Demonstrate how to sign up for Google and Panoramio accounts and how to download Google Earth.</li><li>In class, have students sign up for these accounts, download Google Earth, and watch the tutorials for Panoramio and Google Earth. Organize the students into small groups (3–4 each).</li><li>Homework: ask students to plan to make images from their local Latin@ community for presentation and discussion in week four.</li></ul>
Week Two	<ul><li>Read/discuss the novel (e.g., *Bless Me, Ultima*).</li><li>Ask students to make note of images, landscapes, symbols, and tropes relevant to the assignment and review it in discussion and response papers.</li><li>Homework: ask students to browse for user-generated, amateur images from the community of the novel. Begin with Panoramio and compare these to curated and archived images (e.g., in the Library of Congress *Prints & Photographs Online Catalog*). Students should also find 1–2 pieces of quantitative data (e.g., census) to supplement their study of the community.</li></ul>
Week Three	<ul><li>Finish the novel (e.g., *Bless Me, Ultima*).</li><li>Continue discussion of images, landscapes, symbols, and tropes relevant to the assignment.</li><li>Homework: discuss and compare images that the students found.</li></ul>
Week Four	<ul><li>Demonstrate/practice the placemark tool (including attach an image, link, and narrative).</li><li>Homework: students should bring in the images they made in their local Latin@ community along with relevant curated/professional images and quantitative data about the same community.</li></ul>
Week Five	<ul><li>Homework: students put it all together and present/workshop their maps in class. Discussion can emphasize regional differences and richness and how to improve the final project.</li></ul>
Week Six	<ul><li>Final revised project due (online). Post to the course Web site.</li></ul>

5. ANTICIPATING STUDENT NEEDS

In certain regions of the country, depending on what space the students occupy, access to the cultural artifacts necessary for this assignment may prove problematic. When transportation is an issue, you can ask students to acquire images virtually.

Students are asked to explore beyond the confines of the university setting. Field trips, photo assignments, and virtual excursions should be discussed with your department chair and you should familiarize yourself with the corresponding university policies. Students should be advised to stay on responsible and accountable platforms and a list should be provided of the platforms and Web sites that you intend to use. Even on such sites, there is the possibility students will encounter inappropriate or offensive material. Panoramio, as other advisably accountable Web sites, has options to report and flag images and users as inappropriate. If such a situation arises, this can easily be anticipated and prepped for in advance. It can provide real-world application of a discussion of, for example, sexism, homophobia, or racism. Students should be advised, in the syllabus and verbally, ahead of time to prepare themselves for the discomfort of any such possible encounter as well as the potential discomfort of the resulting discussion.

Privacy can also be an issue when students publish their work online. You can ask students to sign waivers at the beginning of the course. You can also encourage students by telling them that the technoliteracy they gain through these assignments can be reflected on their resumes and that blogging or publishing their work can reflect positively on them.

There is a distinct, and self-proclaimed, term-and-conditional bias toward landscape in Panoramio and Google Earth. Panoramio's photo policy excludes logos, mini-images, images that are not real photos, scanned documents, text documents, screen captures, collages, copyrighted images that are not yours, and photos that someone else took, even if the original photographer is credited. Panoramio does have an indoor section, which Google Earth does not. Google Earth and Google Maps exclude people posing, machines, animals, details, interiors, events, representations (such as paintings and logos), and images smaller than 100kb.

Copyright can be an issue when browsing for images online. Students will probably be relatively familiar with this concept, but it bears reinforcing. Images with a URL, when layered into placemarks in Google Earth, act as a link and, as such, a workaround of this issue. Students will not, however, be able to upload and geolocate anything other than their own images on Panoramio.

Be sure, too, to review and have your students follow your university's policy regarding photography projects, especially if it ends up involving live subjects.

6. ASSESSMENT TOOLS

Depending on the specific course and your goals, you may decide to emphasize technical competency, and thus assign a significant portion of the grade to mastering specific techniques, or you might emphasize critical analysis of representation strategies. Likewise, you might consider informing students that the creative caliber of any images that they make will not be a function of the grading, but that a thoughtful reflection on why a particular image was made, how it was framed, and how the subject related to the assignment will be. Certain decisions they make — deciding which images to use, how and where to locate them on a map — may be of larger importance in the assignment. A rubric that I've designed for this project is on page 166.

7. THEORETICAL BASIS FOR THE ASSIGNMENT:
Mapping Literature, Cultural Artifacts, and Communities: Reveal the Living Map of Latin@ Letters

Latin@ literature is only now a burgeoning discipline due to historical and academic erasure and negligence. While Latin@ visibility (in terms of culture and community) has increased in regions and barrios around the country, in other areas (such as northern New England) the Latin@ presence and contributions remain subaltern — and yet also provide an opportunity to study the nationwide invisibility of prior decades.

While a number of digital humanities projects and literary mapping assignments ask students to map multiple locations referenced in a text, the heart of this project tasks students with interrogating a community, theme, or figure by mapping multiple external representations that can be used to illuminate the primary text's representation.

Students will acquire a more nuanced, visceral, experiential, and engaged understanding of setting and place, thematic interests, tropes, and major figures from the literature being studied in the classroom, which might include la Virgen de Guadalupe, Aztlán, cityscapes, agricultural workers and urban day laborers, border fences, and more.

In this project, students begin by discussing how a specific Latin@ community is represented in a literary text. Students then construct a digital representation of a local Latin@ community; they make images of this community, research how it is represented in the most recent census, and locate archived or curated institutional images as well as socially networked user-generated images. Students then develop a similar representation of the community

> "In other areas (such as northern New England) the Latin@ presence and contributions remain subaltern — and yet also provide an opportunity to study the nationwide invisibility of prior decades."
>
> **Charli G. Valdez**
> University of New Hampshire

Rubric for Mapping Literature, Cultural Artifacts, and Communities: Reveal the Living Map of Latin@ Letters

	Excellent	Very Good	Good	Below Average
Technologies	The images are well designed. The narrative and links are formatted with an eye to ease of reading. Perfect execution and delivery of the files.	The images are well designed. The narrative and links are formatted with an eye to ease of reading.	There are no bugs; images load.	There are minor technical problems and/or images don't load properly.
Images	The images are creative, original, and add great depth to the representation.	The images are not especially creative or original, but add some depth to the representation.	The images are not especially creative or original, and add only moderate depth to the representation.	The images are not especially surprising or illustrative.
Geolocation	Geolocation is precise, accurate, and illustrative.	Geolocation is precise and accurate, but not especially illustrative.	Geolocation is accurate, but not very precise or illustrative.	Geolocation is not accurate.
Social Networking	The student has engaged in insightful, generous, and inquisitive conversation with their peers.	The student has engaged in generous and inquisitive conversation with their peers, and although he/she has fully developed their ideas, the originality and insight could improve.	The student has engaged in generous and inquisitive conversation with their peers, but has not fully developed their ideas.	The student has engaged in generous conversation with their peers, but has not been very inquisitive, nor has the student fully developed his/her ideas.
Narrative	The curated images and quantitative data are illustrative and relevant, adding depth to the representation.	The curated images and quantitative data are illustrative and relevant, but add little depth to the representation.	The curated images and quantitative data are not especially illustrative or relevant, adding no depth to the representation.	The curated images and quantitative data are not relevant.

of the text, paying attention to the historical moment. Finally, students workshop their representations and publish the final revision online.

> "This project tasks students with interrogating a community, theme, or figure by mapping multiple external representations that can be used to illuminate the primary text's representation."
>
> **Charli G. Valdez**

This assignment works well for nonmajors, gen-ed students, and majors in a variety of courses ranging from literary analysis to American literature surveys and dedicated Latino studies or Chicano studies courses. Its pedagogical power derives from a convergent understanding of regional identity, visualization, and social reinforcement. Since some of the images are amateur, user-generated texts, the specifics of this project depend greatly on the grounding literary assignment.

In a dedicated Latin@ literature class or in an American literature course, Rudolfo Anaya's *Albuquerque*, Emma Pérez's *Forgetting the Alamo, Or, Blood Memory*, and Luis Urrea's *The Devil's Highway* are texts that more obviously lend themselves to literary cartography. If taught in a post–Civil War survey, certain selections in the Norton anthology work well: Maria Amparo Ruiz de Burton's *The Squatter and the Don*, Anaya's excerpt, Anzaldúa's selections, and Lorna Dee Cervantes's poetry. The Heath anthology has selections by these same authors as well as Pat Mora's "Border Town: 1938" and selections by Gary Soto as well.

The borderlands concept figures centrally in Chican@ literature and invites historical context. The U.S.-Mexican War of 1846–1848 and the resulting Treaty of Guadalupe Hidalgo are immediately relevant to discussions of the contemporary border with Mexico, both of which work well with the cartographical approach, historical layering, and archival photography available for this project.

Geopositioning images can be especially beneficial, as a kind of virtual-experiential exercise, in locations where students don't have immediate access or funds to go on field trips to Latino barrios. Since I currently teach in New England, effectively all of my students have no real conception of what the borderlands look like: the vast empty spaces, the desert and dunes, border crossings, and the border fence itself. In developing a differentiated transborder understanding of Latin@ life, you can layer in a third spatial representation, such as a study of maps and images from places like Woodburn, Oregon, and Morganton, North Carolina—Lynn Stephen's *Transborder Lives* and Leon Fink's *Maya of Morganton* cover these spaces, respectively.

In this assignment, students begin by thinking and discussing how a particular author depicts a specific Latin@ community. In classroom discussion, that specificity should be broken down as thoroughly as possible, addressing layers of nationality, linguistic practice, gender, socioeconomic class, sexuality, and regional background. There are opportunities to focus on specific thematic interests and representations (for example, la Virgen de Guadalupe or the border with Mexico) found in each literary text.

In a poem like "Beneath the Shadow of the Free-way" by Lorna Dee Cervantes, students with no working familiarity of these regions can browse geopositioned images to better understand, in a context of freeway proliferation, what Cervantes means in shorthand by Santa Barbara as opposed to Los Altos. For that matter, students can investigate whether Los Altos and "Sal Si Puedes" are indeed literal places in order to better understand the binaries in the poem.

> "Geographically locating these images will help students develop a more nuanced sensibility of how Latino culture varies across region."
>
> **Charli G. Valdez**

Luis Urrea, in the above-mentioned *Devil's Highway*, speaks of the Wellton 26, the devastating deaths of a group of immigrants trying to cross the border near the Organ Pipe Cactus National Monument. Students could begin by reviewing the map in the book itself, compare it to the interactive map located on the University of California, Davis Web site (devil.ucdavis.edu/) and then proceed on to the assignment itself. Students could build their own Google Earth tour or map folder of the same trek. Hopefully, you're beginning to see not only the contextualizing potentials of this assignment but also the possibility, advisability even, of adjusting it specifically to the literary text you choose.

At some point, students will take pause to consider what images they should make of the local community as they engage in Latino (cultural) studies. They may raise the issue of what constitutes Latinidad and Latino culture. It can be a productive conversation to plan for. Some time in class should be dedicated to what ideas students have and, depending on the region, you may need to research in advance where the local Latino communities are.

In approaching the convergent nature of this assignment, it can be useful to break it down into its primary components.

- **Why work with digital images?** Students will visualize the metaphors, tropes, and images that constitute and define Latin@ letters. Visual correspondence will not only reinforce a working literacy with these tropes and a more nuanced understanding of them, but it will also emphasize the fact that students are reading literary and visual representations of, for example, la Virgen de Guadalupe. Students can put into practice new literacies by engaging with these found images. This can be especially beneficial to communities that don't have direct access to Latin@ neighborhoods, murals, and border walls. However, the majority of digital images we encounter lack historical and geographical context. Geolocating specific visualizations can provoke a deeper reading of the image in geohistorical context.

- **Why mapping?** Geographically locating these images will help students develop a more nuanced sensibility of how Latino culture varies across regions, strengthening a transborder sensibility rather than a merely binary transnational perspective. If we are to extend Moretti's theory of "distant readings" to regional cultures, the simplification inherent in this project (a simplification that stands in lieu of fieldwork or field trips to distinct regions of the country) can be understood not as reductive, but a gloss that allows for an overall comprehension of how culture varies regionally. Geopositioning also gives particular images a regional, national, and geographical context and a historical reality. Furthermore, students are much more likely to have had experience with digital images than with digital maps (Harley et al. 4-22) in their undergraduate education. This assignment can provide them with a unique digital experience.

- **Why social networking?** Students will gain a socially reinforced perspective by speaking to, and sharing with, other students from distinct regions who have had different experiences of Latinidad. Latin@ presence, in this construction, thereby becomes a cultural richness that can be valued and the nuances of one's regional culture and migration patterns will inform another's. Here I only discuss using Panoramio and Google Earth (with its easily organized and accessible Groups feature), but social networking tools like WordPress could easily be tied into this project. Personal contacts with colleagues in other educational settings (whether secondary or higher-ed) can be tapped before the start of the semester to bridge regions.

This assignment bridges the gap between technologically and humanities-oriented students. While students of literature repeatedly invest in critical analytical practices, this assignment asks them to improve their technical literacy as well. Digital literacy is not merely a function of having access to hardware, or having the proper software installed on a school's network, but is fundamentally a measure of knowing how to use technology (Ritzhaupt et al. 3). Such literacy is furthermore fundamental to greater pedagogical aspirations — educating good digital citizens, a responsibility realized through technological fluency (Simsek 130). To engage in digital literary cartography has become increasingly easier (Crampton 5). For majors, this can be explained in the context of the latest work in the digital humanities, while for nonmajors and gen-ed students, its practical and professional applications can be emphasized.

8. CONCLUSION

Students are eager to connect what they learn in the classroom to their lives in the real world. By asking them to acquire images from a local community, they are able to make such connections and speak to them in class in a manner that can facilitate and enhance real cultural education resulting from reading Latin@ texts. It can also present opportunities for students to lead and teach material that nobody else is familiar with. One student of mine noted how many local Latinos are working in ski areas in a wide variety of capacities. Although we dedicated class time to many of the early technological tasks of the assignment (e.g., downloading Google Earth), I might add more time to workshopping and revising the material that they've generated and include a model beforehand.

> "Part of what I want to achieve with this is based on my experience using LGBTQ+ student panels in my classrooms."
>
> **Charli G. Valdez**

In my first iteration of this assignment, I didn't emphasize the social networking aspect of the assignment, but intend to do so on my next implementation. I relied instead on my own expertise and experience regarding New Mexican culture in teaching this text to students in New England. I intend on improvising intercampus discussion via a WordPress blog by contacting a colleague at the University of New Mexico and setting up an exchange. I will supplement this with a Skype class discussion with both classes. Part of what I want to achieve with this is based on my experience using LGBTQ+ student panels in my classrooms. Students on these panels teach their peers in my class about sexuality and gender. Although I could communicate the exact same information, the result is radically different. The first time I invited these panels into my class, my mid-semester evaluations were suddenly filled with praise for a class that "opened my mind." The material content hadn't changed, but by merely changing who delivered that material, there was a radical shift in how it was received. I hope to demonstrate to my students here in New Hampshire how well-equipped their Latin@ peers are in a different part of the country. By having a not dissimilar student panel teach my students, I expect the reaction to be similarly inspired. This social networking will further demonstrate that the knowledge embodied in a diverse upbringing is precisely that—knowledge, not superfluous minutiae.

Students were readily able to handle the technological challenges, but I found myself repeatedly reflecting on how clumsy mapping software still is. Indeed, it has a way to go to be as seamless as other kinds of software. Nevertheless, students were able to move beyond that and focus on the work at hand. I furthermore discovered the limits of our building's mediocre Wi-Fi system, which made the day we tried to download Google Earth a problem. If you have access to computer clusters, it's better to move the class into a LAN-wired setup.

There is additional discussion that I didn't originally anticipate and that I will plan for in future iterations. While this assignment rewards the culturally rich landscapes of students who inhabit diverse communities, others will struggle with what constitutes a "a visual representation of the community." They might ask if the Mexican restaurant that they drive by will work for the project. This can generate interesting questions and discussion. What is culture? What defines a community? What is cultural appropriation? For this project, if students arc trying to create an enlightening publication, in particular for people not unlike them in a different part of the country, what might they find surprising about the Latin@ community there? What will surprise students in New Mexico, or Oregon, or Florida about the Latin@ community in New England?

9. WORKS CITED

Crampton, Jeremy W. *Mapping. A Critical Introduction to Cartography and GIS.* Blackwell, 2010.

Fink, Leon. *Maya of Morganton.* U of North Carolina P, 2003.

Harley, Diane, et al. *Use and Users of Digital Resources: A Focus on Undergraduate Education in the Humanities and Social Sciences.* Center for Studies in Higher Education, U of California, Berkeley. *CSHE/UCB,* 5 Apr. 2006, www.cshe .berkeley.edu.sites/default/files/shared/resources/study/report/digital/resource study_final_report_goal1pdf.

Moretti, Franco. *Graphs, Map, Trees.* Verso, 2005.

Ritzhaupt, Albert, et al. "Differences in Student Information and Communication Technology Literacy Based on Socio-Economic Status, Ethnicity, and Gender: Evidence of a Digital Divide in Florida Schools." *Journal of Research on Technology in Education,* vol. 45, no. 4, 2013, pp. 291-307.

Simsek, Eyelem. "New Literacies for Digital Citizenship." *Contemporary Educational Technology,* vol. 4, no. 2, 2013, pp. 126-37.

Stephen, Lynn. *Transborder Lives: Indigenous Oaxacans in Mexico, California, and Oregon.* Duke UP, 2007.

12

Text Meets Hypertext: An Online Approach to Teaching Poetry

Vicki Pallo
Virginia Commonwealth University

Vicki Pallo holds a PhD in English literature with an emphasis on Victorian literature and culture from Binghamton University, State University of New York. She teaches writing, communication, and Victorian literature at Virginia Commonwealth University (VCU). Her current research focuses on teaching with technology and service learning. She also regularly writes and reflects about pedagogical issues on her blog, http://teachwritelearn.com.

1. OVERVIEW

- **Assignment:** Students use an online platform such as a blog or wiki to create web-based annotations of a poem or other text, accompanied by additional contextual information, analysis, and possibly reflective writing.
- **Courses:** Any literature course or poetry course.
- **Literature:** Any, but note that the shorter the texts under examination, the more manageable the project will be for students.
- **Technology:** Web 2.0 formats (blogs, wikis, etc.), potentially access to school computer lab.
- **Time:** Can be conducted in four to six weeks, with one to four hours of class time, plus additional time at the end if you wish students to present their work to the class; or the assignment can be extended over a full semester.

2. GOALS OF THE ASSIGNMENT

Students will be exposed to, practice, and work to master

- increased knowledge of the Victorian era and the poetry of the period;
- deeper critical reading and textual analysis;

- understanding of the intertexuality of literature, specifically poetry;
- annotation skills;
- effective multimodal communication;
- information fluency;
- digital literacy;
- increased audience awareness;
- collaboration skills (if done as a group project);
- time-management/project-management skills; and
- creative engagement with the works under examination.

"My hope with this assignment is that our students will come to the literature they are studying with fresh eyes and new ways of understanding and engaging with these wonderful and inspiring works."

Vicki Pallo
Virginia Commonwealth University

3. ASSIGNMENT SHEET

Text Meets Hypertext: An Online Approach to Poetry

Course: _____

Instructor: _____

Date: _____

Wiki Project and Presentation Assignment

Wiki Project Description

This will be an ongoing, collaborative project that allows you to engage more deeply with some of the texts/ideas we are exploring in the course. It can draw from ideas and texts we have discussed, but should demonstrate original thinking and research as well. Each group will pick one of the general topics we are addressing each week as an umbrella issue (e.g., "gender and sexuality"), but should determine a narrower thesis to serve as the focal point for your project within that larger issue. During the last week of classes, each group will present their wiki projects to the class. **Keep in mind that this project will be in lieu of a final exam, and should be treated with the same preparation and depth.** *This assignment will be worth 20 percent of your course grade.*

Each member of the group is responsible for annotating/explicating at least one poem related to your thesis. Annotations should be partly your own ideas, but also should draw from scholarly research. In addition, you can use images, video, and audio to enhance your text and illustrate important ideas. You may use any combination of footnotes and hyperlinks to annotate your text, but there should be a minimum of 15–20 annotated passages/words throughout the work in question. In the explication section, you will provide a way to interpret the poem or raise some problems or questions in or about the poem. This section should only be about 2–3 paragraphs long, but should demonstrate original thinking on some aspect of the poem. (See the "Ozymandias" example on the Britlit wiki provided on Blackboard for examples of how to do this part of the assignment.)

To facilitate collaboration and the annotation part of the project, groups are expected to develop a wiki on their selected topic. Instruction for using this technology will be provided during class in the first week, and class time will be allotted each week (when possible) for collaborative work on the project. The strength of wikis for group projects is that you don't always have to meet together in person to get work done; you can work at your own pace, when it fits your schedule. As long as you are staying in touch with each other, reviewing each other's work, and all meeting your responsibilities, things should go well.

GUIDELINES

1. Create a wiki using Wikispaces (wikispaces.com) or something similar. As an alternative, there is a wiki feature in Blackboard, but you don't have as much design flexibility here. (See the Tools page if you want more info on that option.) Make sure to add all of your users, and invite me to your wiki as well so that I have the URL and can view your work.

2. As a group, select a thesis for the project and make sure that each of your individual elements ties in directly to this thesis.

3. Each person is responsible for a *minimum* of 2 pages on the wiki:

   - The first page should contain the poem you have selected with annotations and explication (a complete poem or a minimum of 100 lines if the work is longer; at least 15–20 highlighted passages/words is needed to create a thorough annotation). Each student should select a different poem for their contribution to the project.

   - The second page should be a general content area, to be determined by your group. (This should be mainly context.) For instance, one student might elect to do a page on the political climate during the writing of the poem; another might focus on relevant artistic or cultural events, and so on.

4. At minimum, your wiki should contain the following components:

   - A home page that introduces your group, the project, and especially the thesis

   - A statement indicating the fact that this is a student-generated project, including the course, instructor, and institution name

   - An annotated/explicated poem from each group member

   - Background on the author relevant to the topic/thesis

   - Relevant historical, social, and political contexts

   - Literary/artistic context (author's contemporaries, influences, etc.)

   - Images, video, or other media to enhance pages

   - A works-cited list

5. Each group member should be available to peer-review the work of your group mates (provide feedback on ideas/work) so that the entire wiki is cohesive and consistent. However, you *are not* responsible for completing the pages of a group member who does not wish to do the required work. Grades will reflect any imbalance of labor that occurs. See the folder on Blackboard for additional information on annotating poems and working with wikis.

(*continued*)

ASSIGNMENT SHEET (*continued*)

Oral Presentations

During the last week of class, each group will present its wiki. The guidelines for this portion of the assignment are as follows:

- Each person in the group should have a (roughly) equal speaking role in the presentation.

- Expect to take roughly 15–20 min. minimum to share ideas, with an additional 10–15 min. for discussion (30 min. max). Come prepared with questions for discussion.

- Don't just rehash ideas from the class — make sure you bring new information and go deeper with any ideas drawn from class materials/previous discussions.

- Make sure you have a clear thesis and make that the central point of your presentation. Don't just "show and tell" your wiki; organize your presentation to make the main point clear, and share ideas only when they are relevant.

- Each individual should also discuss his or her own poem and its relation to the main argument, demonstrating your ability to analyze the poem and sharing things you learned through the annotations that led to your interpretation.

- Make sure to post your wiki links to the discussion board on our course site so that we all have access to your info (and so that I can grade your projects!).

- After the completion of your presentations, you will have 2 additional days to polish your wiki using the feedback you received from the class.

4. TIME AND TECHNOLOGY

The only technological requirements for this assignment are a laptop or access to a computer with Internet capabilities. To facilitate the process of familiarizing students with resources, working through ideas, and building the components of the project, I recommend reserving a computer lab at least once or twice early on in the course.

You may want to experiment with web platform(s) first before sharing the assignment with students in order to troubleshoot difficulties. In addition, most platforms have online tutorials, and technology staff at your institution may also be of assistance. Sometimes, institutions also have their own versions of the platforms tailored specifically to their own student populations, and course management software such as Blackboard may also have a wiki feature (depending on the version) that can be easily accessed by students and teachers.

The course in which I use this assignment focuses on Victorian poetry, so naturally many of my Web recommendations pertain to that literary period. However, even if your course does not cover that era, some of these links might serve as useful examples for student work. For more traditional scholarly research, I typically recommend databases such as JSTOR or even Google Scholar as a starting point. Here are examples of a few of the web-based resources shared in my course:

- The Victorian Web (www.victorianweb.org/)
- Literary Resources on the Net (andromeda.rutgers.edu/~jlynch/Lit/)
- Voice of the Shuttle (vos.ucsb.edu/browse.asp?id=2751)
- Internet Library of Early Journals (www.bodley.ox.ac.uk/ilej/)
- British Literature Wiki (britlitwiki.wikispaces.com/): student-generated; used as a model, not a resource

Web platforms that work well for this assignment include the following:

- WordPress.com
- Blogger.com
- Wix.com
- Wikispaces.com
- PBworks.com/Education

Ample time and planning for this project are essential to make it a successful learning experience for your students. Factoring in all of the considerations below, I recommend introducing the assignment at minimum four to six weeks before the deadline.

When planning the timing of the assignment, the first consideration may be the need to address disparities in student experience with technology.

Despite personal use, many have little practical knowledge with using technology in academic work. As such, it is important to allow time initially to orient students to the platform you will be using. If possible, I try to arrange at minimum two computer lab sessions: one at the beginning of the assignment, and one just prior to the presentation and/or final draft due dates. This provides students with an additional meeting time (if using the group project option) and instant access to peer and instructor feedback as they wrap up their ideas.

Once this learning curve has been addressed, you will need to help students scaffold the assignment so that they can incrementally build their projects rather than having to rush at the end. As many of my students have discovered to their chagrin, a blog or wiki cannot be produced overnight, no matter how good a student is at last-minute projects. Whether it is a group or individual assignment, I require students to develop work plans that outline a schedule and indicate benchmarks for progress. With more inexperienced students, you may also want to assign deadlines for submitting sample work or progress reports to help keep them on track. For many students, organizing a project of this size can seem daunting without a little guidance and instruction.

Depending on the experience your students have with analyzing literature and annotating texts, some time and/or resources may be needed to facilitate this process. If time and resources allow, developing an in-class annotation of a short poem can be a useful exercise, as well as reviewing online examples of annotated texts and discussing choices the authors made for determining the placement and content of hyperlinks. Even a *Wikipedia* entry can be useful in this exercise.

If oral presentations are assigned, I schedule them toward the end of the term, a few days prior to the final draft deadline. As I mentioned earlier, this allows additional time for students to process their ideas through the presentation, obtain feedback from the class, and compare their efforts to those of their peers, thus making their own final projects stronger.

5. ANTICIPATING STUDENT NEEDS

Perhaps one of the greatest strengths of this assignment is also its greatest potential weakness: the use of technology. Students are often assumed to be very "net savvy"; however, this is only half of the story. Siân Bayne and Jen Ross relate some of the pitfalls of this assumption:

> While use of Internet technology, particularly for social networking, is almost ubiquitous among 16–18 year olds, this does not translate into a desire among this group for more technologically focused approaches to teaching and learning at university. On the contrary, "fundamentally, this age group suspects that if

all learning is mediated through technology, this will diminish the value of the learning." (30)

I have certainly found this to be true in my own teaching practice, and have learned to make no assumptions about technology use and familiarity among my students. When possible, I try to assess their experience level early on in my courses, and offer students a number of informal ways to try out technology for the purposes of learning prior to the assignment of a larger task.

Another common misconception is just how prevalent the use of computers and access to technology is among all students. Ronald A. Berk points to this potential for a "digital divide":

> A digital divide also exists among Net Geners based on machine vintage, connectivity, online skills, autonomy and freedom of access, computer support, and interest in using the technology (Hawkins & Oblinger, 2006; Oblinger, 2008a). For those students who are neither tech nor net savvy due to class, nationality, or other factors that limit access, special instruction or training sessions should be provided to give them opportunities to be brought up to the same level of their more proficient peers. (4)

While in many cases it is no longer the norm for students to be without a computer of their own, there are still times when this situation arises, even in an institution (like mine) where computers are required on entry. Certainly we should be sensitive to these situations; however, it is important to still hold students accountable to the same expectations for accomplishing tasks. To do less than this in an age when technology use is becoming almost a necessity would be doing a disservice to our students.

A further potential difficulty in a hyperlinking project lies in the uncertainty of sources on the Web and the potential for plagiarism. This is compounded by the fact that you may be encouraging the use of untraditional sources for academic work, such as images, videos, and other multimedia. The discernment required to do this effectively may be lacking in an inexperienced undergraduate researcher. In addition, much of the students' work will not be their own thinking; the dilemma then becomes encouraging this but also discouraging inappropriate "borrowing." This can be a source of great confusion and error for a student who is unaccustomed to appropriate citation. As Tom Franklin and Mark van Harmelen explain, "Much Web 2.0 based student work is about content sharing and repurposing. This can easily be seen by students as part of a new teenage copy-and-paste culture that runs counter to traditional notions of plagiarism, and adjustments may need to be made" (23). Specific instruction and regular feedback on the part of the instructor is therefore essential. The benefit of these challenges will hopefully be apparent here: although it certainly requires vigilance and intentionality, it provides an excellent opportunity for teaching information literacy and encouraging critical thinking.

One final concern that may need to be addressed is the issue of privacy. While this is a justifiable concern, especially for students who are thinking ahead to when they are in the job market, there are several options for alleviating this issue. One option, although in my opinion not ideal, is to move the blog or wiki into a course management site (if available). This gains privacy for the students and ease of access for you, but the students will also lose the opportunity to be creative and autonomous. In my experience, students prefer having flexibility in designing their online spaces and many wish to carry their projects with them when they leave the course. Another option to address privacy concerns is simply to help students create an alternate Web identity. This may seem slightly unorthodox, but is actually not that uncommon on the Web, and can provide many opportunities for discussing issues of identity, audience, purpose, and style.

6. ASSESSMENT TOOLS

Projects like this can often present quite a challenge to instructors, as there may not be as much "original" writing to assess. The key components of a hyperlink activity are the *choices* students make, as well as how well they can *reflect* on and *justify* those choices. By the same token, what exactly is being assessed can also be vague for students. In most cases, this might be the first time they have been required to undertake such a task, and this can be unsettling. Without specific benchmarks for progress and completion, both parties may struggle to make sense of the assignment during assessment. To avoid this, I typically itemize a minimum number of links, sources, and pages (if using a wiki); I also specify other components required to fulfill the assignment (e.g., reflection essay, explication paragraphs, context pages, etc.).

> "The key components of a hyperlink activity are the *choices* the students make, as well as how well they can *reflect* on and *justify* those choices."
>
> **Vicki Pallo**

In my course, this assignment replaces our final examination. As such, I want it to have a fairly substantial impact on the course grade. At the same time, I am sensitive to the fact that this is a new approach to learning for many students taking my course; given the fact that there are so many variables that could impact success, I try not to penalize them unduly. I want them to take the project seriously, but not give up or think that I am deliberately stacking the deck against them.

What Are Some of the Variables That Might Impact Success?

Running the assignment as a group project as I often do can certainly become a factor. This will require special measures for accountability and transparency, as well as guidelines for minimum amounts of work to be accomplished by individual students. As you see from the assignment description, I require both individual and group contributions, and will not penalize groups if one person fails to live up to his or her individual responsibilities on the project.

Familiarity with and access to technology can certainly impact a student's success, but as I have mentioned elsewhere, scheduled computer lab time can alleviate this issue to a degree. Certainly the number and quality of sources used will have a bearing on the outcome of the project, and the amount required will depend a great deal on the grade level of your students, as well as your goals for the assignment. On the assignment sheet, I indicate the minimum number of hyperlinks/notes required in order for the annotated passage to be successful, and I encourage a fairly broad assortment of material for students to use, such as video and audio files, still images, passages from other written works (if relevant), and the student's own ideas to expound on a particular word or passage (a straightforward annotation, in other words). However, I am careful to specify that the links should not be superfluous; the provided material or ideas should enhance the understanding of the poem in meaningful ways. Further, while I don't stipulate limits for any one particular form of media, if I begin to see a student leaning too heavily on one medium (e.g., videos), we will discuss redirection of the project as necessary.

Originality of ideas is paramount, but may also be hard for a student to identify. I always insist that students go beyond class discussions; this would include, for example, not simply hyperlinking to passages/words that I point out in class. The originality, then, should be evident in both the types and amount of material linked to the poem, as well as the thesis that underlies the interpretation of the text and the explanation of choices for hyperlinks. We also spend time in class discussing copyright infringement issues, and I direct them to copyright-free sources for images and videos whenever possible.

7. THEORETICAL BASIS FOR THE ASSIGNMENT:
Text Meets Hypertext: An Online Approach to Teaching Poetry

As literature instructors, one of our primary goals for our students is to develop the deep-reading and analytical skills that equip them to engage more thoughtfully and meaningfully with the literature under examination as well as the world in which we live. The traditional method for obtaining this goal is the term paper, sometimes accompanied by or replaced with a midterm and/or final examination. While these methods certainly offer opportunities to demonstrate close reading and analysis, they are often far removed from students' daily experience, thus losing relevance and even significance in their estimation. In many cases, these assignments shun the use of Internet resources (often with good reason), thus further disassociating the assignment from the students' real-world experience and methods of making meaning.

> "While these methods [the use of term papers and exams] certainly offer opportunities to demonstrate close reading and analysis, they are often far removed from students' daily experience, thus losing relevance and even significance in their estimation."
>
> **Vicki Pallo**

Today's students are certainly using technology more than ever before, and this has inevitable implications for teaching practice. Ellen Evans and Jeanne Po note that the question is no longer *whether* technology should be used in our classrooms, but *how best* to do so: "as students of the 'millennial generation' (i.e., young people born between 1982 and 1998) enter our classroom the question of whether or not to use technology becomes eclipsed by more substantial issues involved in successfully teaching a generation of young people whose lives are mediated and circumscribed by digital culture." While there is debate about just how tech savvy today's students are,[1] courses taught without any reference to technology may be missing key opportunities to connect with their students and take advantage of the additional skills many of these students now possess.

Further, as Carlin Borsheim, Kelly Merritt, and Dawn Reed observe, "technologies (including computers, cell phones, PDAs, the Internet, and Web 2.0 applications such as wikis, blogs, and other social networking sites) have impacted the nature of texts, as well as the ways people use and interact with texts" (1). It is no longer possible to discuss a text of any length or tradition without considering the potential presence of a Web version as well. Ironically, while many scholars have demonstrated that the experience of reading online texts is quite different from reading the same work in print,[2] this issue is rarely considered in teaching practice. Digital literacy thus becomes not only an option to consider but also an essential component in any course concerned with textual interpretation or expression.

The assignment outlined in this article asks students to develop a hyperlinked version of a poem (or other text) using research and analysis to inform their links and ideas (i.e., an in-depth annotation exercise meets Web 2.0).[3] The hyperlinked text can be accompanied either by supplemen-

---

[1]A key voice in this debate is Marc Prensky, who in 2001 coined the term "digital natives" to describe today's students. See his article "Digital Natives, Digital Immigrants," along with Barnes et al., and Jones-Kavalier and Flannigan for similar discussions. For a persuasive opposing view, see Bayne and Ross.

[2]A well-known discussion of this issue is Nicholas Carr's essay "Is Google Making Us Stupid? What the Internet Is Doing to Our Brains" and his book-length version, *The Shallows*. See Banerjee; Jones-Kavalier and Flannigan; Morgan; and Salmerón et al. for further discussions on this topic.

[3]Franklin and Harmelen define Web 2.0 this way: "Web 2.0 encompasses a variety of different meanings that include an increased emphasis on user generated content, data and content sharing and collaborative effort, together with the use of various kinds of social software, new ways

tal explanatory pages or by a short reflective essay in which the student is required to explain and defend her/his choices in the annotation. Students are charged with linking individual words or images in the work(s) in question to information found on the Web (definitions, visuals, audio, etc.) as well as supplying information they have gathered through scholarly research. A platform such as a blog or wiki can be used to simplify the hyperlinking process and to avoid the necessity for advanced coding knowledge on the part of either student or instructor.

By using the resources available for social media, creating, and sharing, students engage in fresh and relevant ways with texts they might otherwise have merely skimmed over or ignored altogether. The implementation of hypertext as a close reading tool encourages the kind of analysis and attention to detail typically reserved for a specialist in the field rather than the typical undergraduate student. As George Landow explains, "scholarly articles and books offer an obvious example of *explicit* hypertextuality in nonelectronic form. Conversely, any work of literature . . . offers an instance of *implicit* hypertext in nonelectronic form" (10). He points to the fact that hypertext on the web is "a fundamentally intertextual system" which "has the capacity to emphasize intertextuality in a way that page-bound text in books cannot"; utilizing this tool enables an individual "to make explicit . . . the linked materials that an educated reader perceives surrounding it" (10).[4] In effect, hypertext makes the critical reading skills of the student transparent, while providing an opportunity for the educator to encourage refinement of these skills. If used intentionally and appropriately, hypertext assignments can serve as a way to focus a student's reading experience and unleash their creativity.

In addition, by housing the hypertext assignments on a public forum such as a blog or wiki, the students are participating in the ongoing knowledge creation innate to the Web. The potential for engagement with an actual audience serves to emphasize the role of the reader that students often minimize or overlook, as they often view the teacher as the sole reader of their created text.

To further emphasize the importance of audience, I often include an oral presentation component with this assignment. While certainly not necessary to make this assignment successful, this step encourages students to consider the message and organization for the project by communicating to a live audience. It also allows them the opportunity to see what other students are doing on their projects, which in some cases challenges them to

---

of interacting with web-based applications, and the use of the web as a platform for generating, re-purposing and consuming content." Examples of Web 2.0 platforms are blogs, wikis, social bookmarking sites, and other interactive, collaborative technologies.

[4]For further discussion on the theory of hypertext, see later editions of Landow's book *Hypertext* as well his article "The Rhetoric of Hypermedia: Some Rules for Authors." See also Morgan.

polish their final versions much more than they might otherwise do. To encourage this, I allow extra time after the presentations to complete the final draft.

Finally, an additional element that can be required is a short reflective essay from each student. This essay should reflect on the overall experience of developing the project as well as justify the choices the student made in highlighting particular aspects of the work(s) under examination. Note that in the version shared here, the essay is not required. This is due to the fact that students complete an oral component and provide explications for their annotated poems on the wikis. I simply mention this option because it could be a beneficial addition to the assignment, especially if no oral component is included.

8. CONCLUSION

Hypertext has revolutionized the way in which we read and understand literature, and it certainly has the potential to impact the way we teach literature. One thing I have noticed since utilizing this assignment in the classroom is students' increased awareness of the intertextuality of poetry, and a willingness on their part to explore web resources to illuminate the text in new ways. One example of this was a class in which we were reading "The Charge of the Light Brigade" by Tennyson. I had located a few web resources to share with the students, including an actual audio recording of Tennyson reading this work, and several photographs and paintings relevant to the setting. Much to my surprise, several students in the course had already found similar resources, and were ready to share them with the class as well. I invited them to share what they had discovered, and they facilitated the rest of the discussion. This open engagement with the Web motivated them to become active readers and provided them with new ways to understand and discuss the literature under examination, thus taking works that might feel inaccessible to some and bringing them to life in refreshing and relevant ways.

An added element that I find enjoyable is the rich, varied, and creative responses to the assignment. While students might possess differing levels of technical savvy, all have their own ways of seeing and understanding the world, and diverse strengths and talents. Some students focus more on the imagery of the poem, linking images to illuminate the words and ideas; others might focus on the political or social references and link to texts or pictures that clarify the context of specific passages. Still others might elect to locate recorded readings, musical files, or even brief videos that capture the essence of a word or idea. Many students include all of these and even more. These unique offerings enrich the readings as well as the course discussions, and this assignment is often the students' favorite portion of the course as a result.

While a hyperlink project at first can seem daunting or rife with challenges, I hope I have demonstrated the potential benefits of such a project in a literature course. Each time I present the assignment to a new group of students, I am initially met with skepticism or uncertainty; however, I attribute this to the fact that this may be their first time using Web 2.0 in the classroom (or anywhere). Inevitably, once I present the stages of the assignment and provide assistance, students meet and often exceed my expectations. Ultimately, while I may have been the first instructor to ask them to examine a text in this way, I hope I will not be their last.

9. WORKS CITED

Banerjee, Parthasarathi. "Aesthetics of Navigational Performance in Hypertext." *AI & Society*, vol. 18, 2004, pp. 297-309. Philpapers, doi: 10.1007/s00146-004 -0296-z,phil, philpapers.org/rec/PARAON.

Barnes, Kassandra, et al. "Teaching and Learning with the Net Generation." *Innovate*, vol. 3, no. 4, 2007, msuworks.nova.edu/innovate/vol3/iss4/1/.

Bayne, Siân, and Jen Ross. "The 'Digital Native' and 'Digital Immigrant': A Dangerous Opposition." *Annual Conference of the Society for Research into Higher Education (SRHE)*. London, 2007.

Berk, Ronald A. "How Do You Leverage the Latest Technologies, including Web 2.0 Tools, in Your Classroom?" *International Journal of Technology in Teaching and Learning*, vol. 6, no. 1, 2010, pp. 1-13, *EbscoHost*, Accession: 52048609.

Borsheim, Carlin, et al. "Beyond Technology for Technology's Sake: Advancing Multiliteracies in the Twenty-First Century." *The Clearing House*, Nov.-Dec. 2008, pp. 87-91. *ERIC*, EJ816788, eric.edu.gov/?id=EJ816788.

Carr, Nicholas. "Is Google Making Us Stupid? What the Internet Is Doing to Our Brains." *Atlantic Magazine*. Jul./Aug. 2008, www.theatlantic.com/magazine /archive/2008/07/is-google-making-us-stupid/306868.

- - -. *The Shallows*. Norton, 2011.

Evans, Ellen, and Jeanne Po. "A Break in the Transaction: Examining Students' Responses to Digital Texts." *Computers and Composition*, vol. 24, no. 1, 2007, pp. 56-73, www2.bgsu.edu/departments/English/cconline/print/march2007 .html.

Franklin, Tom, and Mark van Harmelen. "Web 2.0 for Content for Learning and Teaching in Higher Education." Joint Information Systems Committee, 28 May 2007, www.franklin-consulting.co.uk/LinkedDocuments/Web2 -Content-learning-and-teaching.pdf.

Jones-Kavalier, Barbara R., and Suzanne L. Flannigan. "Connecting the Digital Dots: Literacy of the 21st Century." *EDUCAUSE* Quarterly, vol. 2, 2006, pp. 1-3, er.educause.edu/articles/2006/1/connecting-the-digital-dots-literacy -of-the-21st-century.

Landow, George. *Hypertext: The Convergence of Contemporary Critical Theory and Technology*. Johns Hopkins UP, 1992.

- - -. "The Rhetoric of Hypermedia: Some Rules for Authors." *Journal of Computing in Higher Education*, vol. 1, no. 1, 1989, pp. 39-64. *Springer*, doi: 10.1007/BF02942605, link.springer.com/article/10.1007%2FBF02942605.

McCombs, Barbara L. "Assessing the Role of Educational Technology in the Teaching and Learning Process: A Learner-Centered Perspective." *Ed.gov*, 30 Sept. 2003. *ERIC*, ED452830, eric.ed.gov/?id=ED452830.

Morgan, Wendy. "Heterotropes: Learning the Rhetoric of Hyperlinks." *Education, Communication & Information*, vol. 2, no. 2/3, 2002, pp. 215-33.

Prensky, Marc. "Digital Natives, Digital Immigrants." *On the Horizon*, vol. 9, no. 5, 2001, pp. 1-6, www.marcprensky.com.

Salmerón, Ladislao, et al. "Self-Regulation and Link Selection Strategies in Hypertext." *Discourse Processes*, vol. 47, 2010, pp. 175-211. Taylor and Francis Online, doi: 10.1080/01638530902728280, www.tandfonline.com/doi/abs/10.1080/01638530902728280?journalColde=hdgp20.

13

Inventing Literary Dialogues: Students as Creators and Distributors of Knowledge

Debora Stefani
Georgia State University Perimeter College

Debora Stefani was educated in Italy, where she earned an MA in English and German from Ca'Foscari University (Venice). After a gap year, she took a leap of faith and joined other doctoral students at Georgia State University. She finished her PhD in English in 2012. When she is not busy preparing classes or grading composition and literature assignments, she works on her manuscript on Asian American and diasporic literature.

COURTESY OF
DEBORA STEFANI

1. OVERVIEW

- **Assignment:** Invent a dialog between two authors covered in class, transform that dialog into a mini-movie, post it to the class Web site, and respond to at least one other classmate's movie.
- **Courses:** Any literature course and any level course.
- **Literature:** Any literature.
- **Technology:** GoAnimate (https://goanimate.com), Facebook (www.facebook.com), and a classroom with computer and projector.
- **Time:** Can be conducted in four weeks, if class meets twice a week for one hour and fifteen minutes each time (the assignment should take approximately twelve hours); or it can be extended over a full semester.

2. GOALS OF THE ASSIGNMENT

This assignment is designed to

- teach students to empathize with characters and situations presented in the texts;

- engage students in the analysis of literary texts and encourage them to read carefully;
- refine students' critical and analytical skills;
- invite students to appreciate various literary styles and genres, and to investigate historical, socioeconomic, political, and cultural contexts;
- instill confidence in students' own abilities "to make meaning" and to discover new connections between authors, themes, characters, and so on;
- prompt students to actively contribute to enrich the already existing scholarship; and
- help students understand how to use primary and secondary sources to enhance their arguments.

> "A good teacher is not afraid to try new ways to encourage students to embrace their roles as producers and disseminators of knowledge."
> **Debora Stefani**
> Georgia State University
> Perimeter College

3. ASSIGNMENT SHEET

Inventing Literary Dialogues: Students as Creators and Distributors of Knowledge

Course: _____

Instructor: _____

Date: _____

Mini-Movie Project

This assignment is intended to expand your knowledge of the characters, themes, and style of the authors we read and to increase your familiarity with the genres and the literary periods we explored together. In short, this is your chance to prove you understood why these authors are studied and to add your own contribution to the scholarship in American literature.

Procedure

This assignment is divided into four parts.

PART I.   For this first part, you will *write an imaginary dialogue* between two authors, choosing between the ones we read this semester. Have the authors talk about either option A or B.

>   A: their characters, themes, style

>   B: the genre and literary period

Pair "opposite authors" — authors who have opposite views on a theme or use different styles to achieve the same goal, and so on.

You will have a minimum of 2 and a maximum of 4 primary or secondary sources. You can use books and book chapters, as well as scholarly, newspaper, or magazine articles obtained through the online library portal of the university. Movies and Web sites are fair play, but all the sources must be reputable.

The best way to integrate information from sources in the dialogue is to paraphrase. However, if you are uncertain whether or not you are plagiarizing, do quote. Whichever technique you use, remember to cite the source that you used, using MLA style, as you would do in a regular essay.

Use no less than 1,700 words but try not to go over 2,000.

PART 2.   For this second part, you will *create a mini-movie* with the help of the Web site GoAnimate. See the "How to Set Up Facebook and GoAnimate" handout.

PART 3.   *Publish* your link to the class page on Facebook. Please also publish the text of your dialogue as your classmates, and possibly students from other

(*continued*)

ASSIGNMENT SHEET (*continued*)

sections of American Literature II, will respond to your videos, and they might want to check your works-cited list. For more specific directions, see the "How to Set Up Facebook and GoAnimate" handout.

PART 4.   Starting next week, *respond to at least one video* every other week by creating a new video. For your second and subsequent videos, follow these simple directions:

1. You can analyze the same authors you did in the first video, or you can

    • bring in a new author;

    • substitute one author with another; or

    • replace both authors.

2. While you may comment on your peers' use of props and type of characters, you need to focus on discussing the themes, characters, style, genre, and literary periods in American literature.

3. You are definitely encouraged to use primary and secondary sources, but this is not required.

4. Your new dialogue can be shorter than 1,700 words; however, it shouldn't be less than 1,250.

How to Set Up Facebook and GoAnimate

Facebook

Before you can start making your movie, you need to create a Facebook account.

1. Go to www.facebook.com. Follow the directions Facebook gives you.

2. You can complete or skip steps 1, 2, and 3, but please upload a picture of yourself.

3. On the top right corner, click on Find Friends.

4. In the box Search for Friends, write the name we decided to use for the class Facebook page. Press Enter.

5. That name should have appeared on the left. Click on Add Friend.

GoAnimate

Now you are ready to start your adventure with GoAnimate.

1. Go to goanimate.com and create an account following the Web site's directions.

2. Click on Make a Video on the right top corner.

3. Select one of the themes provided.

4. You can watch the tutorial or skip it.

5. Select two characters from the list.

6. Click on the character you want to speak first. A window will appear. Type what you want the character to say. You can select the nationality and the gender too. Click Add Voice.

7. In the same window, you can click on Actions. Here you can let your imagination run wild and choose what you want your character to do and how you want him/her to feel.

8. In the same window, you can click on Enter/Exit. This will allow you to make a character enter or exit.

9. When you want the second character to speak, you need to add a scene. Click on the plus icon next to the first scene, located on the bottom left corner.

10. Repeat steps 11–12 and eventually 13.

11. Add a new scene every time the speaker changes and repeat steps 11 and 12 until you are done with your dialogue.

12. Click on Preview and check that all the scenes are in order and that you don't have overlapping speaking parts.

13. Click Save. A new window will appear. In the first box, write the title of your movie.

14. Click Public and then Save and Share. A new window will appear. Click on the symbol for Facebook (F).

15. A Facebook window will appear. Rewrite the title of your movie and, on a separate line, the name of the authors the characters play.

16. Click Share.

Facebook: A Few More Steps ☺

1. Go to your Facebook page and find the video you just posted.

2. Click Share and then on Share drop-down menu on the top left of that window. Select "On a friend's Timeline," write the name of the class Facebook page, and click Post.

3. Please also post the text of the dialogue. In the top left box, type in the name of class Facebook page. Click on that name.

4. You are now on the class Facebook page. Cut and paste the text of the dialogue, in the box that reads Update Status, at the top of the page. You are done!

4. TIME AND TECHNOLOGY

You don't need to be in a computer classroom. Nor do you need special software. However, depending on how many technological resources you are going to need during the semester, you might want to ask to teach in a classroom with access to the Internet and a projector, so that you can demonstrate for students how to use the Web sites described below. Students don't need to carry their laptop or iPad to school, but they must have access to one of these devices outside class, and they must also have access to the Internet.

Assuming that students already have basic research skills and can navigate the library Web site, you can concentrate on explaining how literary databases such as MLA International Bibliography, JSTOR, Literature Criticism Online, Academic Search Complete, Project Muse, and others like these work. These databases could also direct students to articles in publications to which your university doesn't subscribe or to articles in books that your library doesn't hold. In that case, you may need to address how to make requests through interlibrary loan. It is true that Google Books offers previews of many books, but you should emphasize that these previews are not comprehensive. Students should understand that on Google they probably won't be able to access an entire chapter, let alone a whole book.

For the second and third part of the assignment, you will use the Web sites GoAnimate and Facebook. See the "How to Set Up Facebook and GoAnimate" handout that I give to students (pp. 190–191). You will need to first create a Facebook page for the class. I would invent a name for this page, while still using my school e-mail address. To do this, you will need to follow steps 1 and 2 of the handout mentioned above.

This project works best if you assign it toward the middle of the semester, after you have covered several authors. The first three parts of the assignment should take up to four weeks, while you could assign part 4 as many times as you deem appropriate. You should also collect and comment on the drafts of the dialogues before the students make their movies.

Approximately ten days before the drafts of the dialogues are due, you may want to devote an entire class period to reviewing the difference between primary and secondary sources and allowing students to become familiar with the databases that I listed earlier. Have them retrieve at least one article that they think might be helpful for their dialog and, if there is time, have them write a paragraph in which they explain how they are going to use that source.

Depending on how many students you have, one week before students turn in their drafts, you should dedicate one or two class periods to having students brainstorm possible connections between the authors they chose. While your students jot down notes, spend a couple of minutes with each one of them to make sure they understand what they are supposed to do.

Collect the drafts and give yourself ten days to comment on their analyses, use of sources, and citations. During this time, spend two class periods explaining how the GoAnimate Web site works and let students play with it.

After you return their drafts, students should have one week to revise them and make their movie. Once the movies have been posted, students should have a week or so before they respond to other students' dialogues. You may also require students to post at least one response per week until the end of the semester.

5. ANTICIPATING STUDENT NEEDS

Each part presents potential problems. Some are specific to the assignment, others arise from students' level of preparation, and still others may be related to the use of technology.

Early on in the semester, you will need to explain the difference between summarizing and analyzing. Each time the class meets, it might be fruitful to ask students to analyze themes and characters (and the other elements listed above) of the text you are reading that day. Generally, group work is best for these kinds of in-class activities.

Some students may not know how to start a dialogue and they will use up to a 1,000 words just to establish the setting. Concluding the dialogue may also appear difficult to them. I usually discuss a couple of beginning and concluding strategies. For example, authors may bump into each other in a museum or at a café.

Although students may have an idea, however vague, of when and how to cite, you should anticipate dedicating some time to review MLA citation style. You might also clarify how to use information found in articles, books, and such. For instance, you may point out that the sources must not become the argument but instead should be used to enhance one's ideas. Needless to say, if students are not already comfortable doing so, you will need to discuss when and how to quote from secondary sources as well as from primary texts.

To avoid issues with GoAnimate and Facebook, give students precise directions. See the "How to Set Up Facebook and GoAnimate" handout that accompanies the assignment. Both Web sites are intuitive and straightforward, and considering your students grew up with computers, they shouldn't have any problems making a movie and uploading it to the class

Facebook page. Nonetheless, you may always have a couple of students who are reticent about trying something new. So, try to reassure them by offering to help them during office hours.

If students forget their log-in information, the Web sites' customer service features will deal with these technicalities. It could happen that both Web sites might have technical difficulties; in this case, common sense is the best policy.

6. ASSESSMENT TOOLS

For any activity, it is important to explain to your students the learning goals as well as your expectations, but for this assignment it is even more so. You may need to remind students that the course you are teaching is neither a creative writing nor an art or film class — unless of course you want your course to share the goals of these other disciplines. You will find that some students think that having a fancier background would make their movie more appealing and interesting, and consequently they think they are going to receive a higher grade. Therefore, you want to clarify that you are not going to assess how creative their dialogues and movies are. Nonetheless, nothing forbids you from giving students extra points if their projects are particularly original.

As an instructor, I am moving further and further away from using detailed rubrics to evaluate students' work because I find them too rigid. I have been trying to grade more holistically, focusing on content rather than form. Consequently, I did not create a rubric for this project. However, I make sure students know that I expect the following:

- A thorough understanding of the literary and historical periods, style, genre, themes, and characters. For example, in the play *Trifles* by Susan Glaspell, students should be able to grasp the connection between the murder Mrs. Wright commits and her dead bird.
- Insightful analysis. Whether students choose option A or B, I evaluate what argument/s they are able to construct by considering the various similarities and/or differences between the two authors they analyze.
- Evidence and proper use of research. I emphasize to students that sources should be used to enhance their ideas.
- Flawless videos. Dialogues should not be cut off and should follow a clear logical order.
- Appropriate grammar. Since the audience of this project is other young scholars, students must avoid spelling and grammar errors.
- Correct parenthetical citations and works-cited list in MLA style.

You might want to grade eventual responses to other videos separately. Although responses are shorter, you should stress that you will not lower your expectations. Moreover, you will want to make sure that students indeed responded to the issues raised by the original video.

7. THEORETICAL BASIS FOR THE ASSIGNMENT:
Inventing Literary Dialogues: Students as Creators and Distributors of Knowledge

Not long ago, I attended a workshop on digital humanities sponsored by the university where I used to work. The presenter, a colleague from a nearby university, started his presentation by declaring that he had switched from teaching "simply" literature to teaching literature in "a digital way" because his students couldn't produce an original argument. What his students argued had already been argued before, or so he said. Although I could sympathize with his frustration, I found his statement inaccurate, to say the least, for two reasons. First, students can establish new connections if stimulated with the right tools. In other words, if given a more creative assignment as opposed to the usual academic essay, they are more likely to discover unique ideas to write about. Second, the complete abandonment of the "old school"—assigning students a paper—in favor of a technological approach doesn't guarantee that students will meet the learning goals of the class.

I was educated in a country where the professor is considered the ultimate authority on the subject. She could not be defied and thus it was assumed that we, as students, could not possibly have something original to say. Yet, in graduate school, I discovered Althusser's concept of ideological state apparatuses, which profoundly altered my teaching pedagogy. I tell my students that by going to school and/or church and by having a family we, too, contribute to the perpetuation of the ideology of the state, but we can decide to participate consciously or unconsciously. In order to make sure that my students understand what engaging consciously with state apparatuses means, I teach them skills and strategies that they can then apply to analyze a text—any type of text: written, oral, or visual. Once they assimilate the skills, they can recognize the agenda behind a text on their own.

In her famous book *A Critique of Postcolonial Reason*, Gayatri Spivak asserts that "in the context of colonial production, the subaltern has no history and cannot speak" (274). Yet, she also suggests that the subaltern should engage with hegemony in order to fight this condition of subalternity. Granted, students are not subalterns in a postcolonial sense, but they are too often reminded that in the academic community they have no standing. Nonetheless, they should engage in the hierarchical structure of the academy because, even though they may lack experience, they have skills that they can use to contribute to the scholarly community in significant ways.

This assignment is for a sophomore American literature survey. Although some schools treat this course as a literature appreciation class, I expect students to refine their analytical skills. At the same time, they may find the classical research and argumentative paper dull, and they will ultimately consider it another task they need to complete in order to pass the class rather than an opportunity to participate in the scholarly community. It is for this last reason and because I want to encourage students to become knowledge distributors that I designed an assignment that combines the old-school research with modern technology. Rather than write the classic essay, they invent a dialogue between two authors. While students still employ their analytical skills and discover new links between themes, characters, styles, genres, and literary periods, the dialogue format precludes students from having to write a formal essay, and ultimately, I have found, enables them to perform better.

The assignment is divided into four parts. Whereas the first two parts are carried out individually, the last two could involve at least another class, if not the whole school and possibly other schools. Moreover, during the first part, students are asked to complete a typical activity that many instructors incorporate into their syllabi — a more in-depth exploration of the themes, characters, styles, genres, and literary periods in American literature. In the second, third, and fourth parts, students use technology to enhance their learning experience.

After I finish reading their drafts, students have had the opportunity to show only me their potential as scholars. How do they become actual members of the scholarly world? They publish their mini-movie on the class Facebook page, which is accessible to anyone who has an Internet connection. Moreover, by word of mouth, other students not involved in the project may check out the page. Lastly, students will respond to their peers' mini-movies by creating new videos.

This assignment has been conceived for one class, but it could involve other sections of American literature taught at the same school or other schools. You would follow the same guidelines detailed in the Assignment Sheet section, but you do not necessarily need to cover the same authors. You may want to consider reading authors who have similar styles or present the same themes, even if they do not belong to the same literary or historical period. Students from the various classes would log on to the same Facebook page — it's easier to keep track of students' responses that way. This means that if the project involves more than one class, only one teacher would create the Facebook "class page," and all students from the different sections or schools would post to that page.

Obviously, working with a colleague from the same school may make things easier; however, if more schools are involved, students will be part of a larger community. It would be ideal to include different types of colleges — a polytechnic and a liberal arts college, or a private and a public one. Students from a polytechnic may make connections between authors, themes, and so on, that may be unlike those of their peers from a liberal arts college. Furthermore, once students learn that peers they do not know will participate in this project, they will feel more responsible toward their work, become more engaged, and realize their contribution matters.

Whether you decide to involve more classes or not, by posting their videos on a public Web site, students distribute knowledge, rather than simply absorb it, as noted by Stephen Downes. Ultimately, a community of scholars composed of students is born. Learning "is no longer an internal, individualistic activity," but a process, rather than a product, that implicates others (Simens). In his online book *Connectivism and Connective Knowledge*, Downes remarks that "knowledge is distributed across a network of connections, and therefore . . . learning consists of the ability to construct and traverse those networks" (9). According to his definition of *connectivism* — the word first coined by George Simens — learning doesn't simply comprise the acquiring of content but the ability and the practice to establish connections among the possibly infinite perspectives offered by other students. It is a collaborative, rather than individual, effort.

This assignment considers technology as instrumental, but technology does not become the subject of learning, as Downes suggests. However, teachers need to keep in mind that children of the millennium were born with advanced video games and are more than likely visual learners. Creating mini-movies will stimulate their brains in ways written texts cannot.

Why not have students impersonate the authors instead of using GoAnimate, one may ask. The pressure of performing in front of the whole Web could cause some students to concentrate on their performance, whereas GoAnimate provides enough distance and allows students to concentrate on the content of their dialogues.

> "Children of the millennium were born with advanced video games and are more than likely visual learners. Creating mini-movies will stimulate their brains in ways written texts cannot."
>
> **Debora Stefani**

Since the mini-movies are their own creations, students are likely to identify themselves with the characters or with the role of director. Either way, they tend to make sure that the characters/authors say something meaningful. Furthermore, the GoAnimate characters let students express how they themselves perceive the authors, not just their physical appearance, but their character as well. For example, one student may decide to have a man perform the role of Gertrude Stein. Highly stereotypical, true, but it becomes an occasion to explore gender stereotypes. Finally, through GoAnimate students give voice, literally, to what they've learned. While making their movies, they hear their own words played back at them. They did not only write something; they made it! It is for these reasons that I find GoAnimate beneficial.

8. CONCLUSION

When I announced in class that the last assignment wasn't the usual academic essay but something more artistic, my students felt uncomfortable and begged me to give them the option to choose. They did not want to part with what they knew how to do, but as soon as I clarified that I would not grade their creativity—though I would give extra points to the most original projects—they embraced the assignment.

As I hope I have clarified, I try to use technology to further students' learning, and I believe GoAnimate engages students in a more active way than a regular essay. As teachers, we have to recognize that visual communication is surpassing written modes, and we need to find ways to stimulate our students to learn. Making videos may be one of these strategies. Because their reputation as director and screenwriter is on the line, students tend to put more effort into writing something meaningful. Videos also allow them to see and hear what they write, and it prompts them to correct what they wrote or expand on their own ideas.

> "The idea that the teacher is not the only one to watch their videos pushes [students] to do their best."
> **Debora Stefani**

The idea that the teacher is not the only one to watch their videos pushes them to do their best. Not to mention that when a peer responds to their video, they are proud of what they have accomplished. Perhaps, not all of them may completely comprehend the significance of their contribution to the scholarship in the field, but they certainly realize they are now part of a larger community that they themselves have helped build.

9. WORKS CITED

Downes. Stephen. *Connectivism and Connective Knowledge: Essays on Meaning and Learning Networks*. 2012, self-published, www.downes.ca/files/books/Connective_Knowledge-19May2012.pdf.

Simens, George. "Connectivism: A Learning Theory for the Digital Age." *Elearn space.org*, 12 Dec. 2004, www.elearnspace.org/Article/connectivism.htm.

Spivak, Gayatri Chakravorty. *A Critique of Postcolonial Reason*. Harvard UP, 1999.

14

Witness Text Collation and Close Textual Analysis

David Large
University of Sydney

AND

Atilla Orel
University of Sydney

David Large received his MA in English from the University of Otago, New Zealand, and completed his PhD in English at the University of Sydney, Australia, where he taught undergraduate and graduate students as an arts faculty teaching fellow. His research interests include international modernist literature, the influence of tradition on modernist writers, and hypertextual methods of annotation.

Atilla Orel is a postgraduate teaching fellow at the University of Sydney, Australia, where he received a PhD in English in 2013. Orel also earned an MA in English (2010) and a master of teaching English language and literature and history (2002). In his doctoral thesis, Orel explores the "critical exploration of the vegetarian creed of Percy Bysshe Shelley, and its essential, central importance to appreciation and interpretation of his poetry."

1. OVERVIEW

- **Assignment:** Students compare two variant texts (examples are provided), and analyze the findings in an essay, using Juxta software.
- **Courses:** Literature (any); literature and composition; any course that incorporates literature and media.
- **Literature:** Any, but the assignment is particularly relevant to classes dealing with variant or frequently updated texts (e.g., manuscript, draft and editorial studies in literature classes; breaking newspaper articles or contentious *Wikipedia* entries in media classes, etc.).
- **Technology:** Juxta version 1.7 or above (www.juxtasoftware.org), or the free online workspace Juxta Commons (www.juxtacommons.org).

- **Time:** Two hours of class time (Juxta demonstration in one lecture; one hour in computer lab following lecture).

2. GOALS OF THE ASSIGNMENT

- Demonstrate student facility with scholarly research methodologies
- Encourage students to conduct original research and to analyze the importance of their discoveries
- Demonstrate student capacity for constructing and presenting analytical arguments in written form

3. ASSIGNMENT SHEET

Witness Text Collation and Close Textual Analysis

Course: _____

Instructor: _____

Date: _____

Witness Text Collation and Analytical Essay, Using Juxta (35 percent of final grade)

By this stage in the course, you will be familiar with closely reading texts, though most of us will conduct our close readings on a single text at a time. Juxta (www.juxtasoftware.org) offers researchers the capability to conduct what we would call a "distant reading" of two texts—to view the differences between a *base text* (the point of comparison, perhaps a manuscript, draft, or first edition) and a *witness text* (later drafts or republished editions) simultaneously. We can quickly generate a list of all variants to the text, and then focus our close reading of the two texts to variants we think are particularly illuminating. We move, then, from a holistic overview of the texts to an extremely close reading of both base and witness texts.

For this assignment, I'd like you to research and write an analytical essay (1,500 words in length) on the differences between a base (original) and a witness (revised) text. Choose an extract of approximately 200 words from any novel, play, or poem that we have studied in this course, provided that you can identify a significantly revised version of that extract. You might choose to compare a poem's early draft with a later published version of the text, or the quarto and folio editions of a Shakespearean play. Some suggested extracts appear below, but you should feel free to make your own selection, provided that I or your tutor approve your choice.

- Transcribe your chosen extracts into two separate, unformatted plain text files (save as .txt).

- Bring your transcriptions on a USB drive to your scheduled computer lab. During your lab, your tutor will demonstrate the process of collating texts in Juxta. You will collate your base and witness texts, and generate a critical apparatus.

- You will leave this lab with a generated critical apparatus of the differences between your base and witness texts in HTML format, and at least two screenshots: the split-frame Juxta comparison and the histogram analysis, which will display the density of any variations from the base text.

- These three files will constitute the primary sources you will draw upon, and reference, in your analytical essay. You must attach printouts of these three files to your essay as appendices.

(*continued*)

ASSIGNMENT SHEET (*continued*)

Your aim when writing the essay should be to combine your fine-grained analysis of the variance you have identified with your knowledge of the text's publication history. One way to focus your discussion would be to consider the apparent or stated intent of the publisher, editor, or author who revised the base text. Consider whether the variants you have found have changed your impression of the text.

You should also identify thematic issues that have arisen from your reading of and about your base and witness texts, and focus your discussion on those pertinent to the critical apparatus you have generated in Juxta, so far as that is possible.

Suggested Texts for Comparison

Identify a passage of roughly 200 words that has been significantly changed between the base and witness texts listed below (though not without losing its identifiable characteristics — you must be able to demonstrate that some sections of the passage have remained the same). If you choose to analyze variance between editions of a text that is not listed here, your tutor must approve your choice.

Author	Base Text	Witness Text
William Shakespeare	*The Tragicall Historie of Hamlet, Prince of Denmarke* First Quarto, 1603. www.gutenberg.org/ebooks /9077	*The Tragedie of Hamlet, Prince of Denmark* First Folio, 1623. www.gutenberg.org/ebooks /10606
John Donne	"The Sunne Rising" In *Songs and Sonnets*, 1633. www.digitaldonne.tamu .edu	"The Sunne Rising" In *Songs and Sonnets*, 1669. www.digitaldonne.tamu.edu
Walt Whitman	*Leaves of Grass* First published edition, 1855. www.whitmanarchive.org	*Leaves of Grass* "Deathbed edition," 1891–1892. www.whitmanarchive.org

T. S. Eliot	*The Waste Land* Typescript / Manuscript. *The Waste Land: A Facsimile & Transcript*. Ed. Valerie Eliot (London: Faber and Faber, 2010).	*The Waste Land* (1922) First published edition. *The Waste Land: A Facsimile & Transcript*. Ed. Valerie Eliot (London: Faber and Faber, 2010).
Malcolm Lowry	"Port Swettenham," *Experiment* No. 5, October 1930. First published edition, UK. (Full text in course reader.)	"On Board the West Hardaway," *Story* No. 3, October 1933. Revised for US publication. (Full text in course reader.)

General Tips and Questions to Consider

Pick one topic, or theme, for your analysis and try to tease out as much detail from your critical apparatus as possible in relation to that one topic; this is a short piece of writing so one topic well developed is much better than a long list of unrelated details.

Find a reliable bibliography or publication history for the text from which your extract is drawn. This will allow you to briefly contextualize your collation.

Consider the following:

- Was your base text revised by the author? A publisher? An editor? Why might this make a difference in the presentation of the witness text?
- When does the base text date from? The witness text? How might this have affected any changes between the two?
- Where, in the base text, do most of the changes occur? Are they grouped toward the beginning, the end, or spaced throughout? What might this mean?
- How do authorial, editorial, or accidental changes alter the possible readings of your extract?

Be strategic about how, why, and how much you cite secondary sources; one or two key quotations that you then elaborate on will work better than long lists of cited articles and books.

If you get stuck, go through the same process you did in the "Close Reading/ Juxta" tutorial.

You can find Juxta at www.juxtasoftware.org, and read the Juxta user manual at github.com/performant-software/juxta-desktop/wiki/UserManual.

(continued)

ASSIGNMENT SHEET (*continued*)
Aims and Criteria

This assessment is designed to test learning outcomes of this unit of study, as stated in the Unit Outline. These are that you will be able to

- demonstrate your facility with scholarly research methodologies; and
- demonstrate your capacity for constructing and presenting analytical arguments in written form.

This means that good responses to this assessment will, as a minimum expectation,

- be written in clear, precise English, and with all quotations and citations appropriately referenced;
- respond carefully, and in detail, to the texts that you have collated;
- represent *your* investigation of the differences between the base and witness texts;
- demonstrate an understanding of relevant aspects of the revision or editing process as it relates to your texts; and
- make judicious and responsible use of critical accounts of the texts you are studying. This means
  - starting with the reading material on the course reading list; and
  - not taking anything a critic says on trust, but holding it to account against the evidence in your critical apparatus.

An excellent response to this assessment will

- competently relate your understanding of the specific metaphors to a wider question, either to do with your texts, or to do with specific issues of textual materiality, editing, or revision; and
- construct a coherent argument without avoiding potential contradictions, alternative perspectives, or recalcitrant textual evidence, but will, rather, face all of these head-on.

Additional Reading

At the University of Sydney we commonly provide lists of additional reading material for interested and advanced students. The additional material listed below has some bearing on the suggested texts for comparison in this assignment, relates to many instances of variance students are likely to find, and addresses basic questions of textual history and editorial theory students might discuss in their analytical essays.

Bornstein, George. *Representing Modernist Texts: Editing as Interpretation*. U of Michigan P, 1991.

Bornstein, George, and Ralph Williams, editors *Palimpsest: Editorial Theory in the Humanities*. U of Michigan P, 1993.

Library of Congress. "Revising Himself: Walt Whitman and *Leaves of Grass*." *The Library of Congress,* www.loc.gov/exhibits/treasures/whitman-leaves ofgrass.html. Accessed 9 Jan. 2016.

McKenzie, D. F. *Bibliography and the Sociology of Texts*. Cambridge UP, 1999.

Menzer, Paul. *The Hamlets: Cues, Qs and Remembered Texts*. U of Delaware P, 2008.

Sullivan, Ernest W., and Robert Shawn Boles. "The Textual History of and Interpretively Significant Variants in Donne's 'The Sunne Rising.'" *John Donne Journal,* vol. 20, 2001, pp. 275-80.

4. TIME AND TECHNOLOGY

TIME. We have found that this assignment requires careful scaffolding over four to five weeks of teaching and learning activities, including a minimum of one demonstration of Juxta in a lecture, one tutorial class on close reading of textual variants, one hands-on class in a computer lab, and approximately two weeks for students to analyze their data and write up their findings as an analytical essay. Undergraduate students, particularly those in their first year of studies, will likely require advance warning and frequent reminders of the steps required to complete the assignment.

You should give students a copy of the assignment details as early in the semester as is practical. Students can then choose their base and witness texts, and plan ahead to fit the assignment into their workloads for other courses. If you allow students to select their own base and witness texts, ensure that you leave yourself or your teaching staff time to review and approve their choices, or to suggest alternatives. We recommend that students select their texts four to five weeks before the final assignment is due.

Once students have been made aware of the assignment details, perhaps four weeks from the assignment due date, we incorporate a lecture or tutorial exercise using Juxta to present and explore a collation. This should prepare students for interpretation and analysis of their extracts.

Three weeks before the assignment is due, we recommend that you demonstrate the process of creating a Juxta collation as a hands-on activity in a computer lab. Students should prepare for this class by transcribing unformatted versions of their base and witness texts, and saving the files separately as UTF-8 encoded plain text files (.txt). You should ensure that all students leave this class with sufficient evidence of their collation in hand, ready to analyze and discuss their findings. This evidence will normally include a critical apparatus for the comparison consisting of a lemmatized schedule of textual variants, saved in HTML format; a screenshot of Juxta's split-frame collation; and a screenshot of Juxta's histogram visualization.

While Juxta's split-frame collation only visualizes two texts side-by-side, the program allows users to add multiple witness texts. Given a frequently revised and republished text such as Walt Whitman's *Leaves of Grass*, you may wish to include in this assignment a requirement that students create and interpret a "heat map" visualization using Juxta in order to identify particular loci of revision across multiple witnesses.

Juxta version 1.7 allows users to upload comparison sets to the online workspace Juxta Commons, where they can publicly share visualizations or other elements of their work. If your course is broadly concerned with holistic overviews of textual variance, or you wish to emphasize the benefits and responsibilities of public scholarly activity, you may ask that your students display their work on Juxta Commons. (See www.juxtasoftware.org and juxtacommons.org/guide for more information.)

Usually in the same week as the computer lab, lectures introduce students to a consideration of the materiality of texts and their transmission, offering as examples one or two of the course texts; and a tutorial activity introduces students to fine-grained readings of textual variants. It is important to stage this lecture material as close to the computer lab as is possible, in order to link students' experiential learning to your teaching material.

Approximately two weeks after you have ensured that all students have generated a critical apparatus and have representative screenshots of their Juxta collation, students should submit their analytical essay. Their apparatus and screenshots should be attached to their essays as appendices.

Depending on your available classroom time (or your students' workloads), you may choose to have your students read the first draft of a peer's analytical essay. This review process is intended to provide students with formative feedback from their peers, and will emphasize to students the need to anticipate alternative interpretations of the generated critical apparatus in their finished essays.

You may decide to determine the exact edition of a text to be studied and the settings to be applied in Juxta, allowing you to assess students on the accuracy of their transcriptions via the generation of a critical apparatus in HTML format. If students submit this apparatus electronically, you can even use Juxta yourself to compare students' critical apparatuses against your model answer. Any deviations from your model will be highlighted. (We should note, however, that Juxta will read and collate the raw source text of the files, including all HTML tags and markup, which can make for a confusing comparison at first glance. Ensuring that you and your students use the same version of Juxta will help to minimize this problem.)

TECHNOLOGY. This assignment requires that students have access to a computer with the Juxta collation software installed. For desktop installations, Juxta version 1.7 or above is recommended for stability and to ensure that students are able to generate analogous outputs from their source texts. The software is freely available for download from Juxta (www.juxtasoftware .org) and is packaged for Windows, Mac OS X, and Unix systems. Students will be able to install Juxta on their own computers in a matter of minutes. Juxta also allows users to take screenshots of its window in PNG format, so your students will be able to save images of their collations or visualizations for later study.

Juxta version 1.7 requires Java 1.6 in order to run, though Juxta's Windows installer will optionally install or update Java if it is not already on the machine. Mac OS X includes Java by default, whereas Unix users should download and install Java 1.6 themselves before installing Juxta.

While Juxta can collate documents in a range of formats, the program responds best to plain text with UTF-8 encoding. We find that most students are familiar enough with their word processing software to save their transcription files as plain text (.txt) using Notepad (Windows) or TextEdit (Mac OS X), though some students may need to be shown how to do this in Microsoft Word under the Save As option.

5. ANTICIPATING STUDENT NEEDS

We have found that some students worry when faced with an assignment that is even slightly more complex than a thematic close reading or comparative literature essay question. While the majority of students very quickly realize the value of Juxta as a tool for distant reading of textual transmission and holistic comparisons of editions, it is important that this assignment is presented to your students as a consideration of the process by which a particular edition of a text was created. Of course, clearly linking the assignment to your course content, aims, and objectives will help to contextualize the assignment for your students.

Students without access to personal laptops or home computers may be disadvantaged for this assignment; anticipating this possibility, you should arrange for Juxta to be installed in campus computer labs before classes start. Further, we recommend you arrange to hold a backup class in a computer lab for any students who have problems in the first class.

Students may choose a comparison set that has only minor changes between versions. (For certain students, even analysis of punctuation or minor misspellings will lead to a fascinating analytical essay, so this may not prove a problem.) When approving a comparison set you have not recommended, however, you should consider the kinds of changes the student expects to find in his or her text collation. Consider also the availability of bibliographical information on the author or text to ensure that students will have enough primary or secondary material from which to draw.

Once students have generated a critical apparatus using Juxta, they may have problems identifying which changes are meaningful, and which they could analyze or discuss in their essay. This depends entirely on the text, of course, but you might encourage students to focus only on changes of certain parts of speech, or to focus on changes that reflect the text's known or suspected circumstantial changes (e.g., the First Quarto of *Hamlet* as an actor's "memorial reconstruction"; the First Folio version of the play as an attempt to represent Shakespeare as a more literary author).

6. ASSESSMENT TOOLS

We consider the initial processes of transcription, creating a Juxta collation, and exporting a critical apparatus primarily teaching exercises and an opportunity for us to give students formative feedback, and as such we do not grade students on these steps. If you choose to do so, think carefully about how you might assess transcription: considering the absolute importance of accuracy as a first step in this assignment, how much will you penalize students for spelling mistakes in either the base or witness texts, given that Juxta will identify these as variants? Will you allow students to be misled to interpretations from a "false positive" variant? Or will you assess the accuracy of students' transcriptions separately, and then supply the class with standardized base and witness texts?

The analytical essay can be graded according to most standard essay marking rubrics. In the context of our course, essays awarded top grades should

- display a very close analysis of both base and witness texts and their contexts;
- identify key changes between base and witness texts, developing an independent critical or theoretical argument around this evidence;
- indicate an awareness of complexities and qualifications in argumentation, allowing for alternative interpretations of textual variants; and
- demonstrate careful thought about the critical, historical, and/or theoretical context of the text and its specific revision process.

We would expect students to refer to their attached critical apparatus as broad evidence to support or illustrate their argument, though references to the text itself—as either base or witness—should be to the appropriate manuscript, draft, or published edition. In short, students should recognize the difference between editions of a text as discrete objects and their collation as a process involving two textual objects, and cite accordingly.

7. THEORETICAL BASIS FOR THE ASSIGNMENT: Witness Text Collation and Close Textual Analysis

We hope that the materials presented in this chapter provide you with some adaptable tools for teaching and learning. The aligned tutorial activity and formal assignment offered here are ideal for teachers and students with little or no familiarity with digital humanities, and have been designed to blend old and new generations of literary studies pedagogy, enabling students to develop and extend their close reading skills through the employment of digital humanities tools. The resulting resources also capitalize on the inherent compatibility of digital humanities and bibliographical and textual studies, giving students experience with and knowledge of editorial practice, textual materiality, and variation, and familiarity with the processes of establishing editions of texts on scholarly grounds.

Our assignment was developed for use in an introductory English literature survey course for students in their first year of study at the University
of Sydney. The course is considered a core (compulsory) module for an
English major, and offers pathways to further specialization in English sub-
disciplines. By the conclusion of the course, students are expected to gain a
deeper understanding of major literary periods from Chaucerian Middle English to modernism, to demonstrate their capacity for constructing and presenting analytical arguments in both oral and written form, and to have
demonstrated their facility with scholarly research methodologies.

The assignment engages with the course's objective to train students in
the application of analytical tools for the interpretation of literature; further,
it is designed to ensure that students consider the aims of their interpretation before their primary analysis begins. The assignment draws on a wide
range of representative or canonical literature studied in the course, and
encourages students to identify a single author whose work or particular
process of revision is of interest to them. The course proceeds in chronological order of texts and literary periods studied; this assignment is currently
staged toward the end of the semester in order to ensure that students are
sufficiently grounded in literature studies, and that teaching staff can effectively scaffold the assignment.

Our pedagogical intent is for students to take a step back from the typical thematic, periodic, or genre-specific approach to literary texts, and to
consider these texts not simply as static objects bound to
a page, but as authorial expressions in flux. Our students should, we feel, develop research skills early in
their university education: requiring both a technical and
traditionally text-centric analytical approach, this assignment emphasizes experiential learning, students' knowledge of methods of textual production, and close reading
skills in an entry-level digital humanities context.

> "Our pedagogical intent is
> for students . . . to consider
> [literary] texts not simply
> as static objects bound to
> a page, but as authorial
> expressions in flux."
> **David Large and Atilla Orel**
> University of Sydney

Our assignment is significantly scalable beyond in-
troductory literature courses, and we also offer a selection of changes that you
may consider making to the assignment. Your course may intersect with critical theories of textual materiality or composition, or may address the complicated publication history of a single major text, perhaps responding to
editorial influences or an author's altered intentions over time. Provided that
you and your class have access to at least one draft or revised edition of a
given text, most elements of the assignment will be easily adapted to fit the
intended learning outcomes of your course.

We have chosen an explicit skills-focused approach for several reasons.
Close reading has been emphatically identified in recent digital humanities scholarship as a fundamental component of digital literary studies
(Kirschenbaum; Ciccoricco) but we are just as committed to the importance
of close reading within our broader disciplinary context.

As constructivists, we concur with Jane Gallop, who observed in a memorable 2007 MLA address that within the literature classroom, close reading is "our most effective antiauthoritarian pedagogy" (185) and that it is this quality that renders it indispensible to our discipline, our students, and ourselves as scholars and teachers. Spontaneous close reading in a classroom setting requires students to experiment with, construct, and communicate their own knowledge, and is generally incompatible with the "regurgitation" or "parroting" of memorized data from ostensibly more authoritative sources. We consider, as does Gallop, that enhanced and intensified reading is

> "Close reading is 'our most effective antiauthoritarian pedagogy.'"
>
> **David Large and Atilla Orel,**
> quoting Jane Gallop

> a widely applicable skill, of value not just to scholars in other disciplines but also to a wide range of students with many different futures. Students trained in close reading . . . apply it to diverse sorts of texts—newspaper articles, textbooks in other disciplines, political speeches—and thus discover things they would not otherwise have noticed. (Gallop 183)

As scholars of literary studies, close reading and the related skill sets of researching and writing extended analytical arguments are our bread and butter. Our own departmental Web site, for example, welcomes new or prospective students with the promise that "undergraduate English majors learn a wide range of skills in close reading, textual interpretation, and critical argument."

Over the past two years at the University of Sydney we have both worked exclusively with courses that incorporate a significant close reading emphasis (in terms of assessment weighting), if not always an explicit, transparent emphasis. Despite this consistency across courses, in our own classes we have routinely encountered students who have somehow not been cued in effectively to the nature of close reading as an essential core skill. Most of us will be wearily familiar with the experience of writing practically identical explanatory paragraphs about the critical importance of close reading on numerous successive undergraduate essays.

Modular degree structures, two-year course cycles, lower rates of student attendance, limited opportunities for one-to-one or small-group teaching situations, along with working conceptions of close reading that vary from teacher to teacher, have all contributed to an institutional context in which many teachers "see study skills training, skilled note-taking, and trained or spontaneous use of such metacognitive strategies . . . as simply not their business" (Biggs 355). A similar disconnect has been the focus of recent digital humanities scholarship where it has been claimed that

> if there is any trouble with . . . digital-literary criticism it would be the celebration of both the practice and the very possibility of close reading digital texts while at the same time failing to adequately articulate what "close reading" means, or must come to mean, in digital environments (Ciccoricco 1).

With these different factors in mind, in the words of David Hoover, "it is time for a return to the text" (53), to the "sense that language and literature are phenomena embodied by made objects, actual things" (Kirschenbaum 155). We do so by using the multiplatform freeware Juxta collation tool in tandem with a selection of scholarly digital archives of literary texts and digital reference tools such as the Walt Whitman Archive. Our assignment is designed to encourage students to consider the materiality of text and its composition, transmission, and reception, while giving undergraduate students an insight into the professional or graduate research process.

8. CONCLUSION

We hope that you will find this assignment useful for your classes, freely adapting or changing any aspects of it in order to make it more suitable for the specific context of your courses. Further, we hope to have illustrated just how effective Juxta and its resulting visualizations of textual variance can be as teaching tools in the classroom. Undergraduate students may initially be uncertain where to start their comparisons; with Juxta you can easily model this process from collation to analysis, stimulating discussions among students through a directed close reading of your texts. In this way, you can use classroom teaching to scaffold your students' application of relevant skills with a view toward their autonomy, both in the Juxta assignment and in their future research.

We have both benefited greatly from Juxta's active development during our individual doctoral research programs, but initially each of us had to overcome a slight hesitance to the idea of using a computational research tool in the English literature classroom, at a time when our teaching timetables already seemed far too full. Starting small, we first demonstrated Juxta analyses in tutorials on *Hamlet* Q1 and F, and found that the tool actually *saved* time—the whole class could see key variant passages at a glance, and began to discuss and argue their interpretations immediately. From the success of that small experiment, we structured an exercise and a formal essay for students to interpret their findings.

Our students become more engaged in the texts that they study when they can conduct a "distant reading"—of the kind Juxta provides—to focus or provoke the close readings with which literature students are typically more comfortable. Some enthusiastic students have even compared the text(s) of entire novels—where prepublication drafts were available—as a way to focus the topics of their analytical essays to a particular chapter or scene. One student reported that this process made her feel that she "owned" the essay more because of her determined role in directing its topic. In more general terms, we can see our students' understanding of textual production and transmission becoming more enriched as they begin to consider the process by which a text was changed through editing or authorial revision. Further, our students report that this assignment, together with its associated teaching and learning activities, helps them gain insight into one aspect of the otherwise opaque and mysterious scholarly research processes of graduate students and career academics.

9. WORKS CITED

Biggs, John. "Enhancing Teaching through Constructive Alignment." *Higher Education*, vol. 32, no. 3, 1996, pp. 347-64.

Ciccoricco, David. "The Materialities of Close Reading: 1942, 1959, 2009." *Digital Humanities Quarterly*, vol. 6, no. 1, 2012, www.digitalhumanities.org/dhq/vol/6/1/000113/000113.html.

DigitalDonne: The Online Variorum. Texa A & M University, donnevariorum.tamu.edu.

Gallop, Jane. "The Historicization of Literary Studies and the Fate of Close Reading." *Profession*, 2007, pp. 181-86.

Hoover, David. "The End of the Irrelevant Text: Electronic Texts, Linguistics, and Literary Theory." *Digital Humanities Quarterly*, vol. 1, no. 2, 2007, www.digitalhumanities.org/ldhq/vol/1/2/000012/000012.html.

Juxta. Applied Research in Patacriticism, *NINES*: Nineteenth-Century Scholarship Online, www.juxtasoftware.org. Open-source collating tool.

Juxta Commons Guide. Applied Research in Patacriticism, *NINES*: Nineteenth-Century Scholarship Online, juxtacommons.org/guide.

Juxta User Manual. Applied Research in Patacriticism, *NINES*: Nineteenth-Century Scholarship Online, github.com/performant-software/juxta-desktop/wiki/UserManual.

Kirschenbaum, Matthew G. "How Things Work: Teaching the Technologies of Literature." *Teaching Bibliography, Textual Criticism and Book History*. Edited by Ann R. Hawkins. Pickering, 2006.

The University of Sydney. "Chair of Department's Welcome." Department of English, *The University of Sydney*, sydney.edu.au/arts/english/about/index.shtml. Department home page.

The Walt Whitman Archive. Edited by Ed Folsom and Kenneth M. Price, *Center for Digital Research in the Humanities, University of Nebraska–Lincoln*. www.whitmanarchive.org.

15

Textual Treasure Hunting: Using Geocaching to Teach the Art of Close Reading

Jana Mathews
Rollins College

Jana Mathews earned her PhD from Duke University and currently is assistant professor of medieval literature at Rollins College, a small liberal arts institution located in Winter Park, Florida. Her research and teaching focus on digital humanities and the intersections between the Middle Ages and contemporary culture; relevant academic essays have appeared in journals and edited collections published by Praeger, the University of Michigan, and Cornell University presses. In addition, she was coauthor of "A Royal Celebration," a ninety-minute

high-tech stage adaptation of the *One Thousand and One Nights* legends at Arabian Nights dinner theater, a multimillion-dollar Orlando attraction that hosted over 500,000 visitors per year. Mathews's passion for innovative pedagogies is reflected in several current projects including the development of a digital textbook and inter-institutional blended learning course. Currently, she holds the distinction of being the most junior recipient of the Cornell Distinguished Faculty Award at Rollins.

1. OVERVIEW

- **Assignment:** Students use global positioning system (GPS) technology to locate a hidden object and explore that experience as a metaphor for the close reading of a text.
- **Courses:** Any literature course, including upper division.
- **Literature:** Any, but particularly adaptable for more advanced courses and larger student populations.
- **Technology:** GPS technology available on cell phones and tablets with data plans.
- **Time:** Can be conducted in one 50-minute class period, or extended as you need.

2. GOALS OF THE ASSIGNMENT

- Introduce and reinforce the skill of close reading via an engaging and accessible metaphor
- Illuminate how close reading is a transferable skill with applicability in contexts beyond the walls of the college classroom

"For the technologically savvy contemporary college student, performing a close reading of a medieval literary text has the potential to feel like being stretched on the rack. While no one likes the thought of being tortured, everyone likes to hunt for hidden treasure."

Jana Mathews
Rollins College

3. ASSIGNMENT SHEET

Textual Treasure Hunting: Using Geocaching to Learn the Art of Close Reading

Course: _____

Instructor: _____

Date: _____

Introduction

It is cruel to ask you to read the most famous quest narrative in the English language (i.e., *Beowulf*) and not let you go on a quest yourself. This activity invites you to seek out fame, riches, and eternal glory via a high-tech treasure hunt. While you will not be aided in your journey by a magic sword or custom-built suit of armor, you will be guided to the location of the hidden cache by a modern-day compass: namely, the GPS tool on your smartphone.

Instructions

1. Form a small group (3–4 people). At least one person in each group must have a smartphone or handheld tablet with a data plan (i.e., you need to be able to access the GPS navigational functions on Google Maps).

2. Go to Google Maps (maps.google.com/).

3. Click on the Get Directions link located in the top left-hand corner of the screen.

4. Generate a map denoting the cache's hiding place, coupled with a route planner by plugging your current location (**Address**) into Field A. Then plug the following decimal coordinates of the hidden cache into Field B, making sure to separate the latitude and longitude coordinates with a comma like this: **28.5959408951091, -81.35108568219246**.

5. Follow the navigational directions provided by Google Maps to the pin-pointed location.

6. Search for the hidden cache. All groups are looking for the same cache at the same time, so you will want to devise a search strategy that accounts for these conditions. You are looking for a **camouflaged object about the size of a strawberry**. The object may be partially obscured within its surroundings, but it is not entirely buried, nor is it underwater. I will be on hand mostly in the capacity of an observer and enthusiastic cheerleader, but am available to assist groups that need help.

Additional Information

While I would love to claim this activity as my own invention, high-tech treasure hunting is actually an enormously popular global recreational activity known in tech circles as geocaching. The premise of the game is simple: regular people hide caches in publicly accessible places and post decimal coordinates of their hiding places on geocaching Web sites and forums as a virtual invitation for others to come find them. The thrill of geocaching lies not only in the discovery of the hidden object but also in the hunt itself.

Because our quest takes the form of a geocaching expedition, we are committed to adhering to the same basic set of rules to which all geocachers must abide:

- While it is hard for all Anglo-Saxon warriors to exercise self-control, the nature of your quest makes your challenge especially difficult. The cache you are looking for is hidden in a public place, but is surrounded by private property (storefronts, office buildings, etc.). It will be hard to restrain yourself from running through and around these structures — while whooping battle cries in Old English — in order to reach the hiding place before other teams, but I am confident that you will find a way to quell the beast inside of you.

- Remember the look on Grandma's face when you ripped her flower garden to shreds searching for Easter eggs? Don't disappoint Grandma all over again. Be gentle with the flora and fauna and aim to leave your environment in the same condition in which you found it.

As you know by now, everything we do in this course — even seemingly silly activities such as this one — has a purpose and operates in unexpected ways to illuminate course concepts and instill important literary skills. To this end, as you search for the hidden cache, please be attentive to and mindful of the process of the search itself. How are you making decisions and what factors are guiding your actions?

4. TIME AND TECHNOLOGY

This activity uses technology that is accessible to most college students and their instructors. The only device needed by students is a handheld GPS device, laptop, tablet, or GPS-enabled mobile phone with a data plan. All smartphones with iOS 4.0 (iPhone 3G or later) or Android 1.6 or higher are equipped with the requisite technology. This activity is designed for groups, so only one member of each team needs to have access to this technology. According to the 2013 Pew Internet Project Survey, 80 percent of Americans between the ages of 18 and 29 own smartphones, and 74 percent of all Americans use their cellular devices to get directions from one location to another (Brenner 18). Statistically speaking, then, it is likely that the majority of your students will both have GPS capabilities on their phones and be adept at using them for navigational purposes.

While students need only to show up to class on the day of the activity with their cell phones, there are a couple of things that you need to do in advance of the activity to ensure its success. The first and most important task involves the decision to use an existing cache or make and hide one oneself. The benefits and drawbacks to both options are discussed below.

Option A: Use an Existing Cache

As of January 2014, there are more than 2 million hidden geocaches in the world and 6 million geocachers ("Geocaching"). The locations of these caches, along with other pertinent information, are listed on several online geocache registries, the largest and most comprehensive of which is Geocaching.com. To access information about any of the 2.2 million geocaches listed on this Web site, users will need to sign up for an account. A basic membership is free and is sufficient for this activity. Becoming a registered member of Geocaching.com provides you with access to its searchable database of caches, which one can locate by zip code, address, or proximity to your campus. By clicking on the title of any specific cache, you can acquire additional information about it, including its GPS coordinates, the story behind its creation, its distance from your home coordinates, the cache type and description, and user reviews and ratings. Some listings contain additional clues or information about its location, contents, or special requirements for access.

Once you have identified the GPS coordinates of your selected cache from Geocaching.com or a similar site, the next step is to upload this information to your mobile phone. A simple option that works for both iOS and Android platforms involves a web mapping service application like Google Maps. I like Google Maps because the simplicity and accessibility of the site ensures that technology will not get in the way of learning. To generate a map denoting the cache's hiding place, coupled with a route planner, simply plug the decimal coordinates of the hidden cache into the Search bar of Google Maps, making sure to separate the latitude and longitude coordinates with a comma (i.e., 28.5959408951091, -81.35108568219246). In most cases, the map generated will pinpoint the general location of the cache, usually within several feet. The fact that Google Maps leads students to the general vicinity of the cache, but does not put them literally on top of it, is a limitation of modern technology, yet as I discuss later, one that serves a specific pedagogical advantage.

Most caches registered on Geocaching.com are ranked on a 5-star system of difficulty by users (5 being the most difficult). A good rule of thumb for first-time geocachers is to select a cache that has been rated in the 1–3 star range. That being said, as any dedicated geocacher will tell you, ratings are subjective. For this reason, it is critically important that you test run the activity ahead of time. If you select a cache more than a few days in advance of the activity, you will want to confirm that your selected cache is still in its designated hiding spot a day or so before the event, as caches hidden in heavily trafficked places like college campuses are especially vulnerable to the discovery and subsequent removal by nongeocachers or so-called muggles.

In most circumstances, you should plan to spend an hour or two prepping for this activity. This time frame includes the time it takes to register for a geocaching site, identify a cache in close proximity to the classroom, and locate it. It may not be practical for larger student populations to hunt for a single geocache at the same time. If your institution is fortunate to be located in an area populated by lots of caches, you may want to consider assigning smaller groups to find different caches. The biggest drawback to using a preexisting cache lies in the unreliability of its condition. Because most caches are hidden outdoors, their accessibility is subject to the whims of Mother Nature. As a representative case in point: last year I searched for a cache that turned out to be hidden on a limb of a large tree that was growing on the edge of an alligator-filled Florida lake. In the winter months, the waterline is low enough to allow geocachers to climb the tree and gain access to the limb. During the other three seasons, however, the entire base of the tree is fully submerged in two feet of murky swamp water.

Option B: Design and Hide Your Own Cache

There are many reasons why you might want to forgo use of a preexisting cache listed on an online geocache registry beyond encountering an alligator-infested swamp. Other possible motivations include a dearth of suitable geocaches hidden near the institution or your desire to tailor a cache to fit the theme or topic of a course. Indeed, designing your own cache has the benefit of allowing you to determine the cache's hiding place and, if you elect not to register the cache on Geocaching.com or a similar Web site, full control over who has access to it.

Regardless of whether you intend your cache to be public or private, temporary or more permanent, it is important to be mindful of the environment in which the cache will be hidden, and to design a container that is built to withstand the elements. There are no hard-and-fast rules about the form that caches should take; in fact, some of the most simple and easy containers to come by (airtight water bottles, small Tupperware containers) are the most effective because they are waterproof and durable. Enterprising geocachers have upped the ante in recent years, devising ever more creative receptacles. Among the most creative containers currently showcased on the Internet are caches that take the form of a plastic blue jay perched in a fake tree nest, a replicated fossil, a hollowed-out pinecone, and a fake rattlesnake that is coiled up and ready to strike.

While the designer's creativity dictates the limits of the cache, common sense should govern its hiding place. As the number of hidden caches continues to rise, so does the likelihood that they will be discovered by non-geocachers, and, in some cases, unfortunately be mistaken for explosive devices. In April 2013, a black box hidden at the base of a tree shut down a freeway rest stop near Eugene, Oregon (Craig). The year before, a cache hidden inside a white PVC pipe lodged into a tree at Disneyland triggered a lockdown at the amusement park (Kandel). Over the past several years, numerous colleges and universities have been temporarily shut down due to the discovery of a suspicious object that initially was presumed to be a bomb or an explosive device, but turned out to be a cleverly disguised cache. In 2009, a silver box taped to the underside of a drainage grate ignited a bomb scare at the University of California, Santa Cruz; the same year, a similar incident occurred at the branch campus of Pikes Peak Community College in Colorado (Turner; Pennington). Given the heightened security measures implemented over the past decade, it would be wise to exercise good judgment in the design and placement of your cache. While the grounds of elementary schools and government buildings are obvious no-nos, if you are planning to hide a cache on campus property, it is advisable to notify both your grounds maintenance department as well as your campus security office of your intentions.

After you create a cache and decide on a place to conceal it, you need to identify its GPS coordinates. This can be done easily using Google Maps or your cell phone or tablet's built-in GPS features. You can access this function on most devices in a few quick steps: (1) Make sure that your Location is set to ON. (2) In the list of apps under "Location services," set the Compass function to ON. (3) Press the Home button to exit Settings and open the Compass app. The GPS coordinates of your current location will display at the bottom of the screen.

If you do not wish to advertise the location of your cache to an audience beyond your class, then simply provide your students with your cache's map coordinates on the day of the assigned activity. If you wish for your students to access your cache's location via a geocaching registry such as Geocaching .com, be mindful that all caches on this site and others are peer reviewed, and therefore, depending on your location, may take a reviewer up to two months to find your cache and submit approvals necessary to authorize the listing to go live.

5. ANTICIPATING STUDENT NEEDS

Besides obstacles generated by inclement weather, another problem that you may encounter relates to glitches in technology. GPS devices need to receive signals from at least three satellites to determine the general area where a cache is hidden. Recent improvements in satellite technology have dramatically decreased the number of dead zones in populated areas; however, if your cache is hidden in a location where cell phone reception is notoriously spotty or Internet connections are unreasonably slow, students may experience difficulty using their phones to navigate to the cache's hiding place. For this reason, it is always advisable to confirm ahead of time that there is strong cell phone reception at the location of your hidden cache.

Even if the satellite gods are working in your favor, it is likely that you will have at least one student who will not own a cell phone or tablet, or whose device is out of battery, broken, or otherwise unusable. The group component of this activity should ameliorate most of the problems related to technological access, but just in case, I always bring along a few screenshot printouts of the Google Maps page that identifies the location of the cache and provides step-by-step directions of how to get there. While not nearly as fun, this nontech alternative gets the job done in a pinch.

The final area of possible concern involves student accommodations. One of the inherent challenges of creating an experiential learning activity is that there will always be students who, for a host of reasons, cannot participate in the same way in an activity as his/her classmates, or chooses not to. In the past, I have run this activity in classes that included students who had physical disabilities, were legally blind, suffered from severe pollen allergies, or had simply rolled out of the wrong side of the bed that day and were plagued with uncharacteristically bad attitudes. I try to be sensitive to student needs and thus do not require students to participate in any experiential activity that makes them feel uncomfortable. This does not, however, mean that I let them off the hook. Because I expect every student to participate in the learning process in some way, I ask students who opt out of conventional forms of participation to invent their own job functions. The list of roles that have been generated from this request include clue givers, timers, observers, recorders (note takers), and discussion leaders. Over time, I have come to see these alternative roles not as a hindrance or distraction to the activity, but a critical component of its success. Specifically, individuals who are outside of the action looking in bring to the table a valuable perspective and fascinating insights that work in important ways to create a more nuanced view of the activity and its relationship to literary analysis.

6. ASSESSMENT TOOLS

In his 1938 classic *Experience and Education*, John Dewey famously remarked that "the belief that all genuine education comes about through experience does not mean that all experiences are genuinely educative" (25). At the same time as experiential learning activities put students in situations where they are invited to see the world through a different perspective, the unconventional nature of these learning environments may leave some students unclear about what they are expected to take from the experience and how their engagement with them will be evaluated. In most cases, the clear articulation of student expectations helps keep concerns about assessment in check and prevents the fear of the unknown from overshadowing the thrill of discovery. In this case, however, the power of the activity lies in the temporary deferral of its meaning. Since I use this activity as an experiential object lesson to introduce the concept and process of close reading, the most useful types of assessment of student learning are necessarily formative in nature.

The Modern Language Association's 2009 *Report to the Teagle Foundation* notes that reading and writing are "skills contingent on a lengthy learning process in which students practice reading and writing as an interrelated, complementary pair" (3). Indeed, student mastery of the art of close reading is a process that spans the entire semester, and this activity represents the first of many steps in a scaffolded learning process that takes students from the explication of a discrete passage from a single literary text to the linking together of multiple related passage explications to, finally, the skill sets necessary to produce the standard form of literary performance-based assessment: the critical essay. Because assessment of student understanding of the concept of close reading is so integrally connected to the process of teaching the skill itself, I discuss both topics together in the conclusion section of this essay.

7. THEORETICAL BASIS FOR THE ASSIGNMENT:
Textual Treasure Hunting: Using Geocaching to Teach the Art of Close Reading

On May 2, 2000, the US government permanently disabled the Selective Availability function from GPS devices, thus dramatically increasing the accuracy of civilian GPS technology ("History of Geocaching"). Within hours, GPS enthusiasts and tech junkies around the world began testing this upgrade by hiding navigational targets in random places and posting their GPS coordinates on technology blogs and Internet forums. What started out as an insular game of hide-and-seek transformed within a decade into both a worldwide phenomenon and part of what Caren Kaplan calls a "powerful metaphor and signifier for consumer culture at the turn of the century"(707).

Although geocaching is a recent invention, its basic premise is rooted in practices that have existed for hundreds, if not thousands, of years. The high-tech heir of waymarking and letterboxing, geocaching uses GPS coordinates instead of linguistic puzzles and pictorial clues to help individuals find hidden containers stashed in outdoor and publicly accessible places.

The universal appeal of treasure hunting, coupled with the high density of technologically savvy individuals, make college campuses particularly popular hiding spots for geocaches. Some large state universities have close to fifty registered geocaches hidden around their campuses. The pervasive popularity of geocaching means that rural institutions, and those with small student populations, typically also have geocaches hidden on-site or nearby as well. According to Geocaching.com, the small liberal arts college where I currently teach (undergraduate population of 1,800), for example, has three registered caches hidden on its campus and a dozen more within walking distance. With so many caches hidden in so many places, chances are that there is at least one close to you.

Educators long have recognized the utility of geocaching to their curriculum. While it is easy to see how a geocaching activity may be useful to a college botany or environmental science course, the relevance of this activity to a course that takes something like medieval British literature as its subject may be less apparent. The pedagogical value of sending literature students of any kind on an outdoor treasure hunt is rooted in three basic assumptions.

1. Individuals Possess Multiple Intelligences.

When Harvard psychology professor Howard Gardner published his pioneering *Frames of Mind: The Theory of Multiple Intelligences* in 1983, he braced for a very public and vitriolic backlash that never came. Gardner's worries were not unfounded: his theory of multiple intelligences—which maintains that each individual possesses a combination of eight (originally seven) inherent capacities that work together to "solve problems, to yield various kinds of cultural endstates—vocations, avocations, and the like"—challenged the standard understanding of intelligence as a single capacity in which an individual is born (9).

This activity takes seriously the notion that all individuals possess some combination of the following intelligences—logical/mathematical, verbal/

linguistic, musical/rhythmic, body/kinesthetic, naturalist, interpersonal, and intrapersonal—and takes up Gardner's challenge to teachers to see themselves as "assessment specialists" whose role in the classroom is not to promote or privilege a single intelligence, but "to try to understand as sensitively and comprehensively as possible the abilities and interests of the students" (10). Specifically, this activity acknowledges that geocaching not only serves as a hook used to pique student interest, but also works to address the reality that not every student learns in the same way. Over the fifty-minute class period, I move students through a variety of distinct but related learning activities designed to appeal to different intelligences: we go on a treasure hunt (body/kinesthetic; naturalist; visual/spatial); individually reflect on the process of finding the cache (verbal/linguistic; intrapersonal); work as a class to establish the relationship between geocaching and close reading (verbal/linguistic; interpersonal); and work in small groups to conduct a provisional close reading of a passage from the assigned reading (verbal/linguistic; logical/mathematical; interpersonal). The goal is to teach and reinforce a skill or concept in enough ways that leave everyone with the ability to grasp something. In addition to engaging the broadest number of students possible, this pedagogical model also serves another important purpose. By drawing multiple and surprising connections between seemingly unrelated things, I model for my students the kind of lively and complex interpretative work that I expect them to perform in their essays later in the term.

2. Close Reading Is a Collaborative Activity.

The claim that writing is a group activity seemingly contradicts the popular assertion that writing is a solitary process. One need only count the number of names listed in the acknowledgments section of any published book to dispel this myth. Indeed, as cognitive theorists have demonstrated, human development is an inherently social activity, and thus "from a social constructivist perspective, learners should be encouraged to participate in activities which foster interaction and co-construction of knowledge" (Storch 154). As scholars and teachers, we would find it both odd and unwise to submit an academic essay for publication in a journal or edited collection that has not been vetted by colleagues in our field. Yet at the same time that we hold ourselves to the rigorous process of peer review, we sometimes deny our students the same privilege on their own assignments, essays, and exams by insisting that they do not receive "any outside help" on their assignments. While there are justifiable reasons why we do not want students in our courses to submit papers that have been filtered through the hands and minds of several other people, requiring students to analyze literary texts in isolation of others is, in some ways, contrary to what we practice in our professional lives, and counterintuitive to the kinds of analytical strategies that we model and practice in the classroom.

While long-held habits are hard to break, there are signs within the Academy that the tide is beginning to turn. In 2010, *Shakespeare Quarterly*, one of the preeminent scholarly journals in premodern studies, conducted a trailblazing experiment in which the journal posted online four essays that had not yet been accepted for publication. Experts in the field, as well as members of the general public, were invited to read the essays and make suggestions for improvement and revision. In the end, forty-one people posted more than 350 comments (Cohen).

This geocaching activity instills the value of collaboration at a critical stage in the learning process: namely, the beginning. As I describe in more detail later on, the same group members who work together to search for the hidden cache reconvene later in the classroom to try their collective hand at performing a first attempt close reading of a literary passage. Group work at this stage benefits students on both ends of the spectrum. Those who comprehend the skill are able to confirm their mastery by teaching it to others. Similarly, those who are struggling to grasp the skill are able to model the intellectual labor of their peers. In addition to learning to see knowledge and skills as things that are meant to be shared and not hoarded, this pedagogical practice has led to the unexpected but happy result of cultivating a classroom culture in which students are more likely to take intellectual risks because the weight of the burden is distributed and equally shared among many. Fostering this "go big or go home" approach to collective literary analysis pays off later in the term, when students approach individual writing projects with similar levels of confidence and enthusiasm.

> "This geocaching activity instills the value of collaboration at a critical stage in the learning process: namely, the beginning."
>
> **Jana Mathews**

3. Close Reading Is a Transferable Skill.

While the current economic climate has put all academic disciplines under increased pressure to make the case for the marketability of their curriculum, the mission and values of literary studies currently is subject to some of the most intense and public scrutiny. A 2013 report by the American Academy of Humanities and Social Sciences called on "colleges, universities, and their supporters [to] make a clear and convincing case for the value of a liberal arts education" (Commission 32). In the months that followed, an array of prominent scholars, teachers, and journalists joined forces to mount a vocal public defense of literary studies. In a *New York Times* editorial, Verlyn Klinkenborg argued that critical reading and writing skills constitute the prerequisites to "developing a rational grace and energy in your conversation with the world around you." Adam Gopnik went further, arguing that literary studies — and the academic departments in which they traditionally are housed — serve an important sociopolitical function in that they "democratize the practice of reading" by making texts available to all, not just the privileged and elite.

According to Pamela Jewett, humanities scholars have long recognized "that literacy learning does not happen separately from other aspects of our lives" (342). However, as Klinkenborg pointed out, our discipline traditionally has done "a bad job of explaining why the humanities matter." Still, as Scott Saul recently pointed out, it is not all doom and gloom. Despite declining enrollments in our discipline, the strength of our majors and wide range of career fields into which they enter after graduation testifies to the "resilience of the humanities canon" (Saul). Instead of resisting the invitation to see humanities majors as viable preprofessional programs, Robert Scholes argues that we "need to connect the development of reading and writing skills in the real world around us and to the virtual world in which that actual world becomes available to us in the form of texts" (171). For Theresa Tinkle, Daphna Atias, Ruth McAdams, and Cordelia Zukerman, close reading is a fundamental skill whose utility extends beyond the classroom. "By concentrating on close reading," they write, "we invite students to learn transferable skills: the critical analysis of texts, the presentation of evidence, the correct use of disciplinary terms, and the ability to frame questions for research and analysis" (527).

If a literary text can teach us something about how to interpret the social, cultural, and/or political milieu in which it was produced, then the opposite claim also is true: namely, that the world around us can teach us something about how to read a literary text. This activity aims to demystify literary analysis and build confidence in students' preexisting skill sets by drawing connections between the art of close reading and everyday lived experience. Identifying the overlaps between the steps and strategies that students take to "read" their surroundings and those that they use to analyze a literary text works to facilitate student engagement with literature and marks its study as both meaningful and relevant. This is particularly important as a medievalist who has both the privilege of introducing students to the earliest specimens of English language and literature and the challenge of introducing the fundamentals of critical reading and writing through texts that are produced in eras, forms, and languages that are largely unfamiliar, and thus highly intimidating to most students.

While the overwhelming majority of my students will not follow in my footsteps and analyze *Beowulf* for a living, they will be asked to generate and conduct close readings of a variety of other types of documents throughout their professional and personal lives including legal briefs, real estate contracts, office memos, and financial reports. While performing a close reading of a medieval text may feel, at times, like being stretched on the rack, students leave my class knowing that if they can analyze a poem that was written in a different language 1,000 years ago, they can analyze *anything*.

> "While performing a close reading of a medieval text may feel, at times, like being stretched on the rack, students leave my class knowing that if they can analyze a poem that was written in a different language 1,000 years ago, they can analyze *anything*."
>
> **Jana Mathews**

8. CONCLUSION

Fully embracing Gardner's theory of multiple intelligences means committing to approach the central motive of my discipline — close reading — from multiple angles and viewpoints. Geocaching represents one of many noncanonical ways that you can introduce and reinforce this skill and its underlying methodology.

This activity begins when you provide your students with the GPS coordinates for the designated hidden cache. Before sending the students enrolled in my fall 2013 course out the door, I described in deliberately vague terms what they were looking for: in this case, a camouflaged container about the size of a strawberry that contained a short note of congratulations. In the three semesters that I have conducted this activity, I have tested out several kinds of caches, but found the most effective and easy to come by to be a $2.00 cylindrical black sprinkler head that can be found in the home and garden section of any hardware store. This cache works great because it is sturdy, waterproof, and contains a built-in canister (i.e., the plastic cylinder where the irrigation tubing is designed to go) that is perfect for holding a small slip of paper. I have hidden this cache in a variety of spots in and around campus, but the location that I like best is a community park situated a few blocks away from my classroom. Because I want to make the treasure hunt challenging but not impossible, I try to leave a few subtle clues about the cache's identity and location: sometimes I stick the sprinkler head in a patch of ground that does not need watering (i.e., surrounded by cement) or in a location where it stands out from its surroundings in some other small but noticeable way (i.e., I position the sprinkler head so that it sticks out from the ground a few inches or is tilted in an odd direction).

After my 2013 students located the cache and returned to the classroom, I asked them to spend about two minutes writing down a few reflective thoughts about the process of searching for the cache. The subsequent class discussion revealed that a significant portion of these comments centered on thwarted expectations. Specifically, students expected that they would find the geocache a lot more quickly and easily than they actually did. The problem, they quickly realized, was that their GPS devices put them within five to ten feet of where the cache was hidden, but did not lead them directly to its exact hiding spot.

This revelation shifted the conversation to the challenges presented by the limitations of GPS technology. When asked how they responded to the discovery that not all of the work would be done for them, and that finding the cache required the exertion of some of their own physical and mental labor, the students reported different things. Some admitted that they refused to accept the failure of technology and spent the rest of the time plugging and replugging the cache's GPS coordinates into Google Maps, hoping for a different result. Others decided to stand on top of a nearby park bench and survey the surroundings from above in hope that the geocache would sort of "magically appear." A third group took my description of the cache literally and spent their time scouring the park in vain for a container that looked like a strawberry but was painted the same color as combat fatigues. The largest of the student groups, however, adopted a divide-and-conquer approach to the task at hand. Spacing themselves out across a small area of the park, these students conducted an inch-by-inch search of the immediate space around them. Their goal was to look for anything that blended into the surroundings but did not belong there. This search yielded a number of intriguing possibilities that did not, in the end, pan out: a brown candy wrapper that was the same color as dirt, a mound of dog excrement, and a half buried aluminum soda can. Importantly for our purposes, the same strategy that produced these dead ends ultimately produced the real cache.

Our conversation about strategies employed in search of the cache circled around the powers of observation, and the importance of looking closely at things that we see but tend to overlook and ignore. According to Bauback Yeganeh and David Kolb, "the mind often neglects the rich context available for observation that makes experience unique. Instead it often automatically labels stimuli based on limited exposure and moves on to the next stimulus to under-observe" (15). This theory of mindfulness builds on E. J. Langer's four-step guide to promoting an environment conducive to mindful reflection. "When we are mindful," Langer writes, "we implicitly or explicitly (1) view a situation from several perspectives, (2) see information presented in the situation as novel, (3) attend to the context in which we perceive the information, and eventually (4) create new categories through which information may be understood" (111).

Having already moved students through steps 1 and 2 of Langer's model, I then facilitated their transition to step 3 by inviting them to work together as a group to come up with step-by-step instructions aimed at helping other novice geocachers find the same cache. What follows is a composite of what the groups collectively generated:

1. Use GPS coordinates to navigate to the general area of the cache. Your cell phone will get you close, but won't do all of the work for you.
2. Examine your surroundings closely. Look for things that stand out (in a good or bad way) or blend into your surroundings but don't belong there.
3. Scrutinize each of these objects in detail for signs that they may be the geocache (i.e., we looked for the log book and the note).
4. With a lot of persistence and hard work, you will find the geocache!

Step 4 of Langer's model involves applying learned concepts and skills to new contexts. To this end, I then asked my students to swap out the references to geocaching on their lists and replace them with references to reading.

While my request generated a few raised eyebrows at first, the process of drafting the second set of instructions allowed the function of geocaching activity to come into clear focus. Here is what one group produced:

- Background readings, lectures, and in-class discussions will lead you to the main points of the text. All of these things will get you close to analysis, but you still have to do some work.
- Examine the text closely. Look for stylistic details that stand out (in a good or bad way) or blend into their surroundings but don't belong there.
- Study each of these things in detail (i.e., examine how these stylistic details work in the text).
- With a lot of persistence and hard work, you will find the treasure!

After students made their lists, I invited group members to share their lists with the class. This experience gave students the opportunity to amend and expand their own lists if needed; it also provided me with a vehicle by which I could assess the extent to which each group grasped the concepts being taught, and, more importantly, evaluate how well each individual was able to apply a learned skill to a new context. Although I had some clarifying points that I wanted to add to my students' lists, experience has taught me the value of withholding my own insights about the process of close reading until students have generated their own rules of textual engagement. Although such professorial emendations may be well intentioned, Harvard professor Eileen Duckworth reminds us that "contributing our own ideas and thoughts about the subject matter almost always short-circuits the students' thoughts, and decreases their interest. But when we help them to take charge of their own explorations of subject matter, they do remarkable work" (186). I certainly have found this to be true in my own classroom. Enabling students to define for themselves what a close reading is and encouraging them to develop a process for how to perform one promotes a sense of ownership over the writing process (a startling new feeling for a first-year student who has spent her high school years shackled to the formulaic dictates of the five-paragraph essay) and a genuine sense of pride in their own abilities and ideas.

After students devised their own provisional instructions for how to perform a close reading, I provided them with a secondary resource in the form of an instructional handout. In an attempt to heed Duckworth's advice, I made a concerted effort not to privilege my handout over their set of instructions, and instead presented the document as my contribution to the class conversation.

After walking students through the sample reading of the passage from *Beowulf* and modeling another close reading of a related passage from the text on the board, I invited them to reflect back on our earlier conversation

Dr. Mathews
English 201 Major English Writings I

THE CLOSE READING

Like going on a geocaching expedition, performing a close reading involves searching for a treasure that is often hidden in plain sight. By definition, a close reading is a thoughtful, detailed interpretation of a short poem or an excerpted passage from a longer text (i.e., novel, play, long poem). A successful close reading examines some striking or strange stylistic detail (vocabulary, structure, meter, style, or metaphor) in order to expose a pattern that orders the passage and informs its meaning. The most interesting and engaging close readings often are those that unravel the obvious intent of the passage or buttress it in an unusual or unexpected way.

> Meanwhile, the sword
> began to wilt into gory icicles
> to slather and thaw. It is a wonderful thing,
> the way that it all melted as ice melts
> when the Father eases the fetters off the frost
> and unravels the water-ropes, He who wields power
> over time and tide: He is the true Lord
> (*Beowulf*, ll. 1605–1611)

HOW TO CONDUCT A CLOSE READING GEOCACHING STYLE

1. **Closely examine your surroundings.** Read and annotate (i.e., circle, underline, make notations in the margins) the passage. Don't know what "fetters" are? Look up the word and its etymology in the *Oxford English Dictionary* and *Middle English Dictionary* (online).

2. **Find something that stands out or does not belong.** Identify a stylistic detail that strikes you as interesting, important, and/or weird. Example: What's going on with the sword that transforms into an icicle?

3. **Describe the effect of this stylistic detail.** Does it reinforce or undermine the stated or implied intent of the passage in which it is located? *Use concrete language* and be very specific, for example:

   > As Beowulf rises out of the murky lake, the hero's weapon transforms into an icicle. The literal melting away of the sword that kills Grendel's mother suggests Christianity's triumph over paganism: the weapon is no longer necessary because the battle is over. By conflating Beowulf's melting sword with the thawing earth of early spring, the passage naturalizes the transition from a community who worships a pantheon of deities to the one "true Lord." Just as winter gives way to spring, pagan rituals evolve organically into Christian

sacraments. At the same time as the passage argues that conversion is natural, however, it also muddies the proverbial waters by exposing a central irony: namely, that as the icicle melts, its water droplets fall into and become part of the lake that was once Grendel's mother's home.

4. **Open your cache!** The last few lines of your close reading answer the "so what" question. Specifically, they explain how your reading of the passage contributes to a new understanding of the larger text as a whole. You would never locate a geocache and then not open it to see what is inside. What a waste! The same principle applies to literary analysis. As long as you can ground your claims in the text, it's almost impossible to read too much into a literary work. Therefore, be fearless! The most compelling and intriguing readings are often those that you instinctively repress (i.e., "I may be totally wrong about this, but . . .").

Example of finding a cache but not opening it: This suggests lingering tensions between Christianity and paganism in the medieval world.

The above answer to the "so what" question is super wimpy in that it makes a broad generalizing claim that more or less states the obvious. Put some muscle into your response!

Example of opening the cache: It is through this image of absorption — Christian and pagan symbols are mixed together to the point of being indistinguishable — that the poem redefines conversion as a blending of belief systems instead of a simple substitution of them.

This answer to the above "so what" question hits all the marks: it weaves all of the author's points together into a provocative conclusion that contains a claim about the significance of this passage within its larger poetic context.

in order to draw additional connections between geocaching and the art of close reading. The following are some of the students' reflections:

- You can't analyze your surroundings/text when you are too far away from it. You have to be willing to get "down and dirty."
- You can't rush through the search/analysis of a literary text. If you do, you will overlook important details that might lead you to the geocache/ treasure.
- Finding a cache/conducting a close reading takes longer than you think.
- Finding a cache/performing a close reading is a process of trial and error.
- If you read your surroundings/text too literally, you will miss what is hiding in plain sight.

I concluded this activity by inviting my students to try their hand at performing a close reading of a related passage from *Beowulf* in small groups.

Like any analogy, this one operates through layers of sophistication. On the most basic level, geocaching serves as a fun, engaging way for students to gain exposure to an important mode of literary interpretation. On a deeper level, the activity serves as an accessible and concrete guide to the interpretative process itself. Even with this learning aid, many of my students still struggled for several weeks to conduct sustained close readings. Yet despite their challenges, they were quick to embrace this mode of analysis—in large part because they helped to define it.

Although the analogy at the heart of this activity—that searching for a geocache is similar to performing a close reading of a literary text—is mobilized in my lower-division English courses as an extended metaphor that teaches students how to think about literary analysis, geocaching has the potential, however, to be expanded into a variety of different kinds of graded assignments. Students in introductory-level literature courses could use this analogy as a template for creating their own extended metaphor based on individual lived experiences. Such papers might explore how different activities (e.g., attending a rock concert, going on a blind date, or ordering off a menu) are rhetorically congruent with performing a close reading. Similarly, students in upper-division literature courses might devise and hide their own mystery caches (a special breed of cache that combines GPS technology with a series of riddles and/or pictorial clues), using course readings as inspiration and close readings of specific texts as clues.

Many students who are introduced to the concept of close reading through geocaching or similar activities do not see literary analysis as a skill they learned in the literature classroom, but as a life skill that they brought to bear on the study of literature. For the academic, it may be a chicken-and-egg kind of question. But for the twenty-first-century college student who is trying to muddle her way through Chaucer's Middle English or figure out the relevance of an Old English epic poem to her life after graduation, this distinction makes all the difference.

9. WORKS CITED

Commission on the Humanities and Social Sciences. *The Heart of the Matter: The Humanities and Social Sciences for a Vibrant and Healthy Nation.* American Academy of Humanities and Social Sciences, 2013, www.humanities commission.org/_pdf/hss_report.pdf.

Brenner, Joanna. "Pew Internet: Mobile." *Pew Research Center*, 18 Sept. 2013, pewinternet.org.

Cohen, Patricia. "Scholars Test Web Alternative to Peer Review." *The New York Times*, 23 Aug. 2010, www.newyorktimes.com/2010/08/24/arts/24peer.html?partner.

Craig, Paul. "Geocache Container Leads to Bomb Scare at I-5 Rest Stop." *KPTV*, 20 Apr. 2013, www.kptv.com/story/22111505/geocache-container-leads-to-bomb-scare-at-i-5-rest-stop.

Dewey, John. *Experience and Education*. Simon, 1938. Print.

Duckworth, Eleanor. "Helping Students Get to Where Ideas Can Find Them." *The New Educator*, vol. 5, no. 3, 2009, pp. 185-88. Taylor and Francis Online, doi: 10.1080/1547688x.2009.10399573, www.tandfonline.com/doi/full/10.1080/1547688x.2009.10399573.

Gardner, Howard. *Multiple Intelligences: A Theory in Practice*. Basic, 1993.

Geocaching. *Geocaching.com*, Groundspeak, Inc., www.geocaching.com. Treasure hunt game application.

Gopnik, Adam. "Why Teach English?" *The New Yorker*, 27 Aug. 2013, www.newyorker.com/books/pate-turner/why-teach-english.

"The History of Geocaching." *Geocaching.com*, Groundspeak, Inc. www.geocaching.com/about/history.aspx.

Jewett, Pamela. "Multiple Literacies Gone Wild." *Reading Teacher*, vol. 64, no. 5, 2011, pp. 341-44. Wiley Online Library, doi: 10.1598/RT.64.5.4, onlinelibrary.wiley.com/doi/10.1598/RT.64.5.4/.

Kandel, Jason. "Geocaching Game Triggers Disneyland Lockdown." NBC San Diego, 4 Mar. 2012, www.nbcsandiego.com/news/local/SSDisneyland-shut-down-due-to-suspicious-item-141296953.html.

Kaplan, Caren. "Precision Targets: GPS and the Militarization of U.S. Consumer Identity." *Rewiring the "Nation": The Place of Technology in American Studies*. Edited by Carolyn de la Peña and Siva Vaidhyanathan, *American Quarterly*, vol. 58, no. 3, 2006, pp. 693-714. *Project Muse*, muse.jhu.edu/article/203950.

Klinkenborg, Verlyn. "The Decline and Fall of the English Major." *The New York Times*, 22 June 2013, www.nytimes.com/2013/06/23/opinion/sunday/the-decline-and-fall-of-the-english-major.html?_r=o. Editorial.

Langer, E. J. *The Power of Mindful Learning*. Perseus, 1997.

Modern Language Association. *Report to the Teagle Foundation on the Undergraduate Major in Language and Literature*. MLA, 2009.

Pennington, Art. "Geocaching Scare—Cache Mistaken for Explosive Device." *Examiner.com*, 30 Sept. 2009, www.examiner.com/article/geocaching-com-adds-new-cache-atributes.

Saul, Scott. "The Humanities in Crisis? Not at Most Schools." *The New York Times*, 3 July 2013. www.nytimes.com/2013/07/04/opinion/the-humanities-in-crisis-not-at-most-schools.html. Editorial.

Scholes, Robert. "The Transition to College Reading." *Pedagogy*, vol. 2, no. 2, 2002, pp. 165-72. *Project Muse*, muse.jhu.edu/article/26398.

Storch, Neomy. "Collaborative Writing: Product, Process, and Students' Reflections." *Journal of Second Language Writing*, vol. 14, 2005, pp. 153-73. *ERIC*, ET724392, eric.ed.gov/?id=EJ724392.

Tinkle, Theresa, Daphna Atias, Ruth M. McAdams, and Cordelia Zukerman. "Teaching Close Reading Skills in a Large Lecture Course." Pedagogy, vol. 13, no. 3, 2013, pp. 505-35. *Project Muse*, muse.jhu.edu/jounals/pedagogy/v013/13.3.

Turner, Ramona. "Bomb Scare Closes Down Main Entrance to UCSC." *Santa Cruz Sentinel*, 22 May 2009.

Yeganeh, Bauback, and David Kolb. "Mindfulness and Experiential Learning." *Organizational Development Practitioner*, vol. 41 no. 3, 2009, pp. 13-18.

PART THREE ASSIGNMENTS

Podcasts

16

"We Hoyd the Author Died Somewhere Around Here, See": Repurposing Radio Genres as Digital Literary Criticism Podcasts

Liberty Kohn
Winona State University

Liberty Kohn is an assistant professor of English at Winona State University, where he serves as writing center director and WAC coordinator. He teaches courses in public, digital, and technical writing as well as literature, poetics, and teacher practicum courses. His scholarship has appeared in *Composition Forum*, the *Journal of Language and Literacy Education*, the *Journal of Literacy and Technology*, *Technoculture*, and other journals. In addition to writing studies, Liberty is interested in Buddhist rhetoric and poetics. He is also a musician who performs live and has composed for dance, theater, and national commercial radio.

1. OVERVIEW

- **Assignment:** Students use podcasting to contrast and/or synthesize various critical or interpretive views, or multiple works of literature, in the form of a podcast or radio play.
- **Courses:** Any literature course; nonfiction courses; literature and composition; argument courses that incorporate literature; upper-level courses including literary criticism.
- **Literature:** Any genre of fiction, nonfiction, or literary criticism; as well as theoretical, critical, or argumentative lenses.
- **Technology:** Podcast or similar audio recording technology (e.g., Audacity or GarageBand); a projector and screen are preferred for a project-ending presentation and analysis.
- **Time:** Three to four weeks, with two to three 50-minute class meetings a week.

2. GOALS OF THE ASSIGNMENT

After completing this assignment, students will be able to:

- summarize, analyze, critique, synthesize, and/or apply multiple viewpoints of a single text or issue;
- analyze and reproduce a speaking-listening genre;
- write in a new style for a new audience and purpose; and
- rhetorically analyze and reflect upon the project's written and spoken performance.

3. ASSIGNMENT SHEET

Repurposing Radio Genres as Digital Literary Criticism Podcasts

Course: _____

Instructor: _____

Date: _____

Goals

This assignment will allow you to:

- transfer our course ideas from academic, print-based genres to an aural genre;
- experiment with popular genres and their codes;
- use technology related to digital audio recording; and
- build a review of literature and gain mastery over an academic "conversation."

Task

You'll be partnering up with 1–2 classmates for this assignment, which asks you to borrow the format of a popular radio genre to put multiple theories or readings from our course into dialogue with each other (as in a literature review). You and your partner(s) will create an approximately 5- to 8-minute podcast based on a radio genre of your choice (radio drama, talk show, etc.). You will need to do a rhetorical analysis of the radio genre you choose. You should keep in mind that some genres may not work well for this assignment, which demands a decently elaborate explanation of literary and rhetorical theories. Most likely, the theories you choose will be voiced as characters of some sort.

Member Roles

Each member of your group must have a significant speaking role. Members can have more than one speaking role. Your script will be written, at least in part, in dialogue format, although expository passages are a possibility, depending on the genre you are appropriating. Writing, research, performance, and digital recording and editing must be shared by all members so that each member increases his or her skills and literacies in each area.

Hard Copy

This collaborative assignment requires a written script that takes 5–8 minutes to perform. The script must be handed in free of grammatical errors and in conventional dramatic dialogue typography. Groups must also burn a CD or send me an audio file of their final audio production. I prefer a CD.

(continued)

ASSIGNMENT SHEET (*continued*)
Grading

The assignment will be graded according to how well you:

- accurately explain and compare our course theories;
- adhere to or expand on the radio play genre conventions;
- incorporate quantitative and qualitative measures noted above (grammar and mechanics, division of labor, timely completion, etc.); and
- apply rhetorical analysis and reflective writing to answer the questions below.

Postproduction: Rhetorical Analysis And Reflection

Your group must also create a 500- to 700-word rhetorical analysis of your ideas merged into a single document with a 500- to 700-word reflection on the writing and technical production of your text. The former will analyze your basic intellectual pursuits. You may wish to include the following:

- How and why you and your partner(s) chose particular theories or theorists
- The challenges of putting these ideas into contact with each other and finding a center where they can be compared and contrasted meaningfully

The latter reflective writing should discuss technology choices; genre conventions of the radio play you chose or departed from; challenges and victories you had writing, recording, or editing the piece; and similar writing and production values. You may wish to discuss the argument, language choices, and organization you made when writing and recording the podcast (block expository script, dialogue, music, deliberate use of silence, etc.), and why you made these choices based on: (1) the experience of a listener listening, not reading; (2) argument and persuasion; and (3) the literary quality and conventions of your radio genre.

You will finish this assignment with a group presentation in which you summarize your rhetorical analysis and reflection in 2–3 minutes. You will then play your podcast for the class. Groups should gently, but audibly, point us toward the important points of their rhetorical analysis and reflection as their audio artistry plays.

Lastly, we will be working through a number of collaborative reading and writing exercises during class time to get you started. Please arrive to class with homework finished and with questions as well!

4. TIME AND TECHNOLOGY

The minimal technological requirement for this assignment is the ability to record the human voice. Any audio recording device will suffice. A built-in laptop microphone and audio capture will allow students to complete this aural/oral assignment. However, podcast software works best because of the ability to record dialogue in small chunks, to edit or rerecord sections of dialogue, to add sound effects or music, to layer voices, to record on multiple tracks, and to give students facility with podcast technology. Dozens of varieties of free podcast recorders/players exist online. One can search online for "free podcast software" to locate them. In the past, after my students have done much sorting and experimenting, they almost unanimously chose the free online software Audacity, which provides for sound effects, music, editing capability, an easy learning curve, and easy downloading from the Web.

My favorite podcast technology is the audio software GarageBand, which comes with a powerful podcast preset. My university, a laptop university, provides this program free of charge to students and faculty, but I imagine this is the exception, not the rule. Even on highly technologized campuses, difficulties of technology and access always exist. For instance, my PC students cannot install GarageBand; only my Mac students can. Students must be separated into groups in which at least one member has a Mac, or students must be willing to explore other podcast technologies. You should plan on and for such access issues. Collaborative assignments offer the greatest maneuverability in terms of both technological availability and student skill sets. If you poll students for technology, then organize collaborative groups around the diversity of technology, you will have made a wise early decision, as groups will typically have at least one member who can meet the technology requirements.

Free online technologies such as Audacity do have advantages over GarageBand. These technologies provide all students complete technological access, which allows for students to collaborate without being in the same room and to record on any computer, anywhere. Depending on how dialogic the radio play script is, students can record their own parts and e-mail or burn to disc their own contributions, then pass the audio file to the next partner, allowing collaboration to happen via the Web. However, this can be a drawback as well, as you most likely want students to collaborate in the same place and time so as to share ideas and editing procedures, to ensure an equal division of labor, and to learn new literacies and skill sets from each other.

Although I am in no way an authority on podcast technologies, the majority I've seen are fairly intuitive and function much like any basic audio recording device in existence since the heyday of the boom box and cassette player. Record, Stop, Play, and Fast Forward/Rewind buttons are the basics of all podcast software. YouTube typically contains dozens of free tutorials on any software or technology. You can recommend students watch tutorials as an introductory step to recording.

I model only one podcast technology in my class. I do this by gathering my students around my laptop. I then record a brief podcast track with my students by clicking Record while I speak and explain the process. I then stop the recording to record a second track of the students making noise. (Whooping and snapping keep the mood light.) Afterward, I may briefly add or demonstrate canned sound effects. The entire process takes about five to ten minutes of class time, and I've never had students struggle with the function of podcast technology after this demonstration. Podcasts are fairly common K–12 language arts assignments. Thus, a fair number of students will have worked with podcast technology previously for education or recreation. If you wish, students can be polled for podcast experience and those with expertise distributed evenly among groups. Beyond the technological requirements, students must be at a point in their intellectual and research abilities to put the course or disciplinary ideas into dialogue with each other.

For this reason, I've found the assignment works better after at least five to six weeks of class, if not more. This allows students time to develop their conceptual knowledge before personifying it in the form of speaking characters. Based on my experience, I suggest that this assignment be developed deliberately in class over a period of two, if not three to four, weeks. However, the length of time depends on the inclusion of in-class staging and variable documents that support student learning and prewriting during the writing process. The length of time also depends on other projects or tasks you are covering outside of the podcast. If the course is focusing on only the podcast, then stages may be slightly more compressed than I offer here. I suggest that minimal staging and scaffolding should follow the standard sequence of genre pedagogy, which "moves students from looking at models of a genre, through working collaboratively as a class to produce a text in that genre, to producing such a text in the genre individually" with the option of a reflective component as well (Devitt 192).

Early Stages

Course readings will provide the requisite content to begin the assignment. The assignment can be completed over a series of classes in three weeks in courses meeting two to three times a week. However, a fourth week may help to develop the final script, develop vocal performance of the script, and provide adequate class time to present and reflect on the podcasts. The assignment can be used at any time in a course, so long as the students have read, discussed, and come to adequate conclusions or comprehension of the texts to be used for the project. Depending on your desired pace and time frames, I suggest utilizing pedagogy similar to that of genre modeling or "me-we-they" modeling.

The basic genre of the podcast is explored by first listening to one or more podcasts, preferably while reading an accompanying script. (NPR podcasts often provide transcripts of their podcasts online. Some NPR podcasts are informational. Others are interview dialogues.) You will likely want to include a short "radio play" script with accompanying audio in your modeled examples. This genre will introduce a narrative-context and dialogue format to the assignment, which broadens the possible modes and genres students may use. Next, you lead students through an in-depth analysis of the podcast for audience, purpose, and unique rhetorical and linguistic moves that mark the relationship between the external social usage (e.g., relevant discourse communities) and the internal communication codes. This is the modeling and "norming the genre" phase.

After this initial instructor-led rhetorical analysis, you can have students analyze a second podcast in small groups under their own authority based on step 1 criteria. You should circulate and keep tabs on student progress. Time permitting, one, several, or all groups can take ownership of their analysis through a brief, informal presentation derived from their in-class collaborative analysis.

If you wish to skip step 2's small group analysis, you will certainly want to have students write short "practice" podcasts collaboratively in small groups. The practice needn't be long, but it should allow students to rehearse writing the rhetorical moves they have previously analyzed. This will complete the analytical reading-to-scaffolded writing assignment sequence. Next, students should begin the brainstorming and prewriting process for their final podcast or radio play. The listening-to-reading, analysis-to-modeling phase can be accomplished in one class meeting. The group writing practice session may require a second class meeting. You should have groups practice turning texts into speaking voices by using texts familiar to students. Students may be able to begin prewriting toward their final project by the end of a second class meeting, although this would decrease time for you to respond to and norm the group "practice" broadcasts.

Once the prewriting for the radio play has begun, class time can provide intermittent opportunities for short writing-to-learn prompts that help students decide their broadcast's content and theory, the aural genre, and the technology they would like to work with. Writing prompts can probe students' comprehension of course content or use of rhetorical strategies. The writing-to-learn prompts can be used to begin and/or end class or class time dedicated to the podcast. I would suggest at least one week for this stage. You should provide intentional, well-controlled activities to help students generate summaries and contact points between texts or ideas. Classroom activities should also help students turn expository or argumentative statements into the prose forms required for their chosen radio genre. Naturally, class time can focus on other ongoing concerns. Generally, the prewriting and writing phases require ample time for thinking, writing, and student-teacher interaction.

The period of time required to write a complete draft will vary by depth of assignment, student level, and students' familiarity with the podcast or radio genre they have chosen.

I suggest forming groups early. Groups may remain together after the initial modeling and collaborative analysis, or groups may be switched after the modeling and analysis just before prewriting begins. I favor the former—long-term collaboration—to help students develop a working relationship during the analytical stage, which is a week or more before their prewriting stage. I typically give my five- to ten-minute demonstration of GarageBand to end class after a long prewriting session as the early stage becomes the middle stage.

Middle Stages

With approximately two weeks until the due date, students should be selecting a podcast or radio play genre. I advise you to have short two- to five-minute conferences with students during class lab time reserved for collaborative prewriting. These short conferences should focus not only on students' content but also on their choice of a radio genre. As mentioned previously, some genres work better than others. You should ask students to sketch out basic sections of dialogue appropriate to the radio genre to see how much it allows for critical conversation.

Naturally, students will also need to meet outside of class time. The time requirement to perform and record the script is never extensive. Students typically complete the act of recording in 30 to 120 minutes outside of class. Writing and revising the script, however, is time-consuming and requires both out-of-class time and in-class instructor intervention and feedback for revision before students record.

In both the early and middle stages, you can pair the assignment with more traditional documents and assignments. I require an outline and rough draft of a script for even short versions of this assignment. In the past, I've also required a collaborative annotated bibliography to enhance both the research process and the critical conversation through a more traditional academic, linear, direct, paragraphic communication. You can certainly ask for other documents as part of the assignment's prewriting or portfolio, such as abstracts, summaries, a play synopsis, or a short expository or argumentative paper in a more traditional print format. Depending on the genre assigned, you can boost critical and creative prewriting as well as traditional formal writing in accordance to your goals.

Late Stages

With approximately one week to the due date, students should be going through a drafting and peer-review process. Scripts can be posted online or distributed for critique before class, if desired. I typically have my groups read their five- to seven-minute podcasts live to another group to garner instant responses on how listenable and recursive the ideas of the podcast are. I have a final short conference with each group during the final week. Time can be provided during class to revise and record, although I find students need class lab time one to two weeks before the due date to build momentum. Depending on students' availability to meet outside of class time, a day of class may need to be dedicated to performing and recording the podcast. I have my own students record outside of class time to preserve class time for writing, revision, and teacher-student conferencing. You may not have this option. The final assignment portfolio always includes an audio file or CD of the radio play as well as the script and any additional documents I request.

5. ANTICIPATING STUDENT NEEDS

As mentioned previously, technological access can be a problem, and you should poll and form groups based on a variety of technological access and experience. This best ensures students can, as a group, work around access issues. You may wish to have traditional academic genres as either prewriting or parallel writing assignments. You will want to retain the typical prewriting-writing-rewriting process. I suggest the modeling sequence of instructor-led analysis to group analysis to group rehearsal to final assignment that I outlined earlier. During the middle and late stages, you can certainly continue with other readings and projects; for best results, I suggest that new continuing assignments can be integrated by having students reflect on how new readings may inform their aural project. Writing-to-learn prompts can also help students reassess their approach during any stage of writing. Finally, keep the mood light during the late stages. Short, consistent in-class conferencing will keep students on task and revising, even as the classroom becomes aurally dynamic with students prewriting, writing, and practicing their dialogue.

6. ASSESSMENT TOOLS

Although the final product is the audio file itself, I anchor my grading around a more traditional text, the students' script. Before the radio play is recorded, the students collaborate, conference with me multiple times, and have the script reviewed by peers. Thus, the script is still the central document containing critical analysis; it bears the intellectual load proving course goals and student outcomes. A script is revisable and, therefore, best able to receive commentary and grading on the group's depth of critical analysis. It is also open to typographic critique as well as sentence-level mechanics.

Other grading factors include any early documents (outline, annotated bibliography, etc.), the rhetorical analysis and/or reflection on product and process, the oral performance and editing (listenability, technical detail) of the radio play, and, potentially, the group's live presentation of their rhetorical analysis or reflection (the *Inside the Actors Studio* component). Because I see this assignment as a potential genre-bending assignment, I do not grade for coherence to any particular audio genre. Experimentation and revision should be rewarded, not punished. Such genre bending is easily rewarded by allowing students to analyze and defend their decisions in their rhetorical analysis and reflection component. I'd also suggest that our students are not professional technicians, and rewarding proper rhetorical usage of media aimed toward social expectations (i.e., genre convention, audience, etc.) is more important than heavily critiquing small technological glitches, silences, or amateur editing phenomena.

The following basic rubrics list features of both the script and the performance of the script in a most-to-least-important order. I've included basic percentages totaling 100% for the "script" and "performance," respectively. I find that treating each separately allows for the inclusion of more features of each and thus improved response and grading. However, instructors may merge, separate, add, or delete features as they see fit.

Script

- Critical Engagement — 30 Percent: Students have performed the relevant critical goals of the assignment (summary, analysis, critique, synthesis, ideas in dialogue, implied thesis, etc.).

- Support and Organization — 30 Percent: Ideas and necessary background information are clearly explained.

- Style — 20 Percent: The prose style, modes (dialogue, exposition, etc.), and conventions of the genre are appropriately used or modified.

- Grammar/Usage/Sentence-Level Writing/Format — 20 Percent: Page layout and sentences are free of error and enhance a reader's or listener's ability to understand ideas.

Performance

- Vocal Delivery — 30 Percent: The reading is free of errors and spoken in an audible voice.

- 20 Percent: The readers' tone is not monotone and varies to enhance the meaning of the information.

- 20 Percent: The tone is professional and similar to other broadcasts of the same genre; the reader has appropriate energy to engage the listener.
- 20 Percent: The reading is at a pace neither too fast nor too slow for the reader's attention and comprehension.
- Use of Technology — 20 Percent: The volume of voices, sound effects, and other sound is evenly mixed. Genre-based sounds or voices are used to help a listener recognize the genre they are listening to.

The above rubrics do not consider early drafts, workshops, collaboration, and so on, in the grading process. You may wish to do so, or you may have alternative methods of grading participation built into the course. Collaboration, for instance, always offers problematic grading. I'd suggest a group grade be given if all participants feel the contribution was fairly distributed. You may wish to partake in one suggested schema for collaborative grading, in which collaborators grade each other based on their perception of a partner's effort and contribution to the group. This grading procedure allows students to voice their concerns, and you can intervene if necessary. However, strong early and middle stages should allow you to see and address any potential contribution problems early in the process.

Responding to content can be challenging without a depth of linear, paragraphic writing and thinking. This more linear, "paragraphic" thinking can be captured through early documents such as an outline or annotated bibliography, either of which allows students to write in a more traditional, direct linear structure. Also, the middle stage and student-teacher conferences present an opportunity for you to intervene and challenge students to increase their analysis, critique, or synthesis of course content. In short, I have found that if I ask students to explain aloud the dialogic meeting point of two theories, and they do so satisfactorily, then I can ask them to capture this in their dialogue as well.

7. THEORETICAL BASIS FOR THE ASSIGNMENT: "We Hoyd the Author Died Somewhere Around Here, See": Repurposing Radio Genres as Digital Literary Criticism Podcasts

Literature classrooms increasingly reflect the texts of daily life in the twenty-first century: digital archives, nonlinear Web text, social media, and various forms of e-reading constitute our students' educational and recreational reading diets. However, English as a discipline has often framed digital technology as an instrument (Selber 11), as opposed to a component of rhetoric and cognition. When digital technology has been defined as rhetorical and distributed, much digital theory and pedagogy has focused on visual rhetoric or traditional linear alphabetic writing transferred to the Web, leaving much of our theory and classroom activities text-centered to the exclusion of aurality (Comstock and Hocks). This exclusion "deprive[s] students of valuable semiotic resources" (Selfe 617) required for contemporary meaning making, and our classrooms are slow to incorporate assignments involving multimodal uses of print, visual, and aural texts.

Yet our students' lives are filled with sound. Their citizen and consumer identities are fully loaded with iPods, YouTube shorts, web page jingles, speaking advertisements, podcasts, and a host of other commercial and informational aural rhetoric and genres. From a pedagogical perspective, we can ask whether aurality functions on its own or in conjunction with text-based and visual rhetoric. Analyzing and critiquing aural rhetoric are useful first steps to provide an understanding of sound's use for rhetorical reasons of persuasion, identification, and a litany of related rhetorical concerns. However, to enhance any analysis of aural rhetoric, students should also be asked to create, to write with sound.

> "To enhance any analysis of aural rhetoric, students should also be asked to create, to write with sound."
>
> **Liberty Kohn**
> Winona State University

A variety of concepts are available to encourage students writing with sound. Students can simply record a webcam video of themselves responding or performing expressively, narratively, or critically to a reading or topic; students can perform and record their paper aloud; students can add a photo montage or photo narrative and add uncopyrighted sound or music track to their critical and creative writings; students can use iMovie or a similar program to make short documentaries, which can include text and graphics; or students can select from among a variety of popular informational or entertainment genres, literary or otherwise, and transform the course content for a variety of audiences and purposes.

I have used each of the above assignments at various times in the writing and literature courses I teach. Even if devoid of audio, most of the above assignments involve traditional text-to-image relationships in which written text and image restate each other, text and image do not illustrate but elaborate on each other in one direction, or text and image elaborate on or redefine each other in both directions (Stroupe 620-26). Analyses of these relationships remain important in projects utilizing sound.

I also suggest that each assignment works best when students must complete a rhetorical analysis of their own product and process. Rhetorical analyses of and reflection on one's writing and reading strategies offer metacognitive analysis similar to critical thinking (Salomon and Perkins 124), and critical thinking of this type, students' metacognitive reflection on their own process and production guided by an instructor, is the best guarantee of transference of reading and writing strategies to future projects (Reiff and Bawarshi 318; Baker and Beall 384; Birnbaum 33).

> "Each assignment works best when students must complete a rhetorical analysis of their own product and process."
>
> **Liberty Kohn**

I often use these rhetorical analyses to shift into a discussion that involves the students' creative process as well as their choice of technology, content, and genre. Through an analysis of their product and a reflection on their process, such assignments ask students to blend the creative writing, literary critical (poetic), and rhetorical analytic (rhetoric/argument) areas of English studies. The analysis and reflection components allow students to talk about both their critical and creative processes, respectively.

I have slowly developed a unique twist to the above assignments. I have found that having students adapt the rhetorical "moves" (see Swales; Graff and Birkenstein) of traditional critical papers through a repurposed radio genre is challenging, entertaining, and enjoyable for both writer and listener. Although a variety of literary critical rhetorical moves may work in this assignment, I have found through experience that this assignment works best when students select rhetorical moves that put ideas into dialogue with each other. For instance, an aural radio play genre may substitute for or scaffold for a review of literature, wherein each character in the radio play represents a different critical view of a text, author, or theory. The assignment allows these critical views constructed as characters to dialogically "talk to each other." That is, the dialogue allows students to critique and compare theoretical standpoints, albeit as characters with radio-based dialogue conventions. Such dialogue is simpler than academic or critical language, but it does allow for academic or critical conceptual vocabulary. Moreover, students are forced to state the ideas in simpler, easier to compare language. They cannot hide behind critical vocabulary. The radio play contains another benefit: its dialogue format is a form of two-way communication that results in dialogism. This back-and-forth response of ideas isn't automatically provoked by the writing codes of an academic paper, which offers students the opportunity to write a paper without self-provided counterarguments, antitheses, and critiques of their thesis. In selecting a radio genre based in dialogism, the genre's required contact or conversation between ideas may help students overcome tendencies noticed by Penrose and Geisler to ignore differences in viewpoint on the same topic so as to preserve a single, unproblematized definition of a topic (506).

The assignment also encourages students to engage in critical thinking while allowing them creative license to write dramatic dialogue and script. Because the radio genres are oftentimes multimodal, involving dialogue, exposition, and, indirectly, a moral argument or thesis, students cannot easily shift to the new genre and keep their "academic" organization and prose unchanged. Instead, students must reformulate and transform the style and delivery. One could easily argue that the process of invention is renewed in such a multimodal assignment. Comparatively, a well-known informational genre such as a news podcast doesn't require students to transform or translate to a great degree their academic papers or their everyday expository speech. Expository or argumentative writing is an easy transfer to an informative podcast. Essentially, the transfer is only a "ratcheting down" of sentence length or information load for a listening audience. Writing for new audiences is itself beneficial. However, transferring exposition and argument into a radio genre requires students to address new styles of writing in their creative process. The poetic (i.e., aesthetic or literary) patterns and prose are no longer purely informational, linear, logical, direct, and/or syllogistic, as with the rhetoric of expository or argumentative writing. Students must then invent or revise their prose to deliver the radio genre appropriately.

The radio play assignment developed out of a desire in my poetics and digital writing courses to add aural rhetoric and oral performance. Students write enough in writing and literature courses, but they don't often have to read aloud or deal with the nuance and complexity of casting words with vocal inflections and a variety of appropriate intonations, be the vocal inflections theatrical, informational, recreational, or professional. Such oral performance follows the dictates of imitation (*imitatio*), an ancient form of rehearsal for speech making that has modern roots in imitation and modeling exercises. Although imitation is frowned on because of its errant connection to rote copying, T. R. Johnson, among others, argues in favor of imitation because "writers must learn techniques and principles that, rather than arrest the play of critical thought, stimulate it, and structures that liberate rather than merely limit the composing imagination" (40). Kathleen Blake Yancey posits a similar viewpoint, but offers imitation as only the beginning of learning. She suggests that assignments can focus on student analysis and production of genres for varying audiences, which will "invite students to work both within the constraints of genre and beyond them" (91), with multiple genres anchoring a pedagogy that asks students to "work in context with others, then review, reflect, and theorize. Such a methodology, located in specifics of a particular situation, makes for good practice" (92).

I developed this assignment through two courses. The first was a literary theory course, English 472/572: Poetics of the Text, Poetics of the Mind. The course explored historical and contemporary theories of poetics in literary and cultural theory, in rhetoric, and in linguistics and cognitive linguistics. The goal of the course was to have students become fluent not only in theories, but in three basic methodological divisions of English studies (literary theory, rhetoric, linguistics). I found the podcast's dialogic nature of great use in capturing this goal.

The goals and expectations of the 400-/500-level theories of poetics course were advanced, as were the students. The course contained both undergraduate and graduate students who were expected to select a text (e.g., a poem) and read it through a variety of lenses constructed from our course readings. The radio play assignment worked well because the radio genre allowed for my students' ability to have Aristotle, T. S. Eliot, Roland Barthes, Eavan Boland, or other theorists debate back and forth over the chosen text's interpretation and the means to derive a theory of poetics in general. For this early instantiation of the assignment, most students chose a *Meet the Press* or *MacNeil/Lehrer NewsHour* format, most likely because of the debate format the "news hour" genre offered, or perhaps because advanced students gravitate less toward playful assignments. Regardless, the assignment allowed for a dialogic discussion of poetic theory applied to or through a common text, which is essentially a review of literature without the student's own thesis. Naturally, the assignment can require students to add their own theory or concepts to the dialogue as well, which means that students find themselves debating Aristotle and company in their radio play.

I have also used the assignment in English 324: Digital Writing, a course based on theories of digital texts and digital literacies. The course is primarily for education majors, but typically includes a variety of English and communication majors. The goals of the course are twofold: first, to have students understand a variety of text-based and reader/writer-based theories of digital literacy; second, to have students rewrite similar content across different genres, including digital genres. This latter is a requirement of Minnesota's teacher education curriculum, but it is also a staple of the genre-based writing classroom.

The "playfulness" of the radio play assignment arises more often in my Digital Writing course, perhaps because most students are future teachers working through an assignment that can be modified for the K-12 levels, or perhaps because I now encourage more experimentation because of my comfort and past success with the assignment. Former students have used radio dramas, game shows, *All Things Considered* NPR-style broadcasts, and similar pop culture genres in the assignment. One challenge for instructors is to offer guidance on selecting a genre that allows students maximal critical voice and dialogic interplay of ideas. The aforementioned game show genre works less well (or breaks down) because it is based on a question-and-brief-response format. Students must either abandon or modify the genre to make it sufficiently dialogic and elaborative. Still, this is part of the students' learning curve and experimentation with genre, and they can incorporate these struggles and modifications into their closing reflective writing and rhetorical analysis on their own text. Often, students find that their original genre becomes a hybrid or new genre, which is also directly relevant to their education in how content and form mutually inform and alter each other.

8. CONCLUSION

One genre that works well is the murder-mystery, or whodunit radio genre, from which this chapter takes its title. A trio of former students wrote and performed a clever and appropriately in-depth exploration of the "death" of the author. The script and performance were based on a hard-boiled detective probing dark alleys and gin joints to find out who killed the author. The students blended literary criticism and genre theory into their assignment. By the end of the play, the detective had shaken down and roughed up a variety of theorists and schools, including Roland Barthes, Julia Kristeva, an anonymous New Critic, and a nineteenth-century historical critic, in the detective's search to discover who killed the author, how, and why the author was killed. The detective had also asked tough questions about how some genres are perceived as authored, and others are not, and who or what was responsible for this.

I enjoyed this instance of the assignment deeply, and the trio of students who wrote and performed this whodunit taught me much about the power of the assignment. In particular, the dramatic narrative underlying a true "radio play" created characters out of ideas, a complex cognitive and rhetorical task. On the opposite end of the spectrum, the trio of creators and the other students in class greatly enjoyed listening to the radio play and analyzing how the authors had managed to transform abstract ideas into characters.

I've found that less imaginative forms of the assignment work well. A basic interview format or news report asks students to revoice, reorganize, and reprioritize for a new purpose our major course ideas. One student group in my Digital Writing course provided a background mashup reading of texts from across the ages to show how literacy has changed in content and form over the last several thousand years. Although only a chronological history, this mashup background, mixed below a primary voice discussing the history of changes in literacy, exemplified with ease a history that would have taken much longer in written form.

Students in my Digital Writing course who are future K-12 instructors often compare and contrast various digital literacy theories in an interview format, and students include expository sections on changes in education, in assessment and testing, and in reading behaviors in the digital age. While some student texts resemble a serious broadcast, some groups have chosen to create humorous personas for the various demographic attitudes toward reading, technology, and government testing in K-12 education. Several projects have satirized citizens and leaders of all ages and walks of life who are zealously resistant to change or a middle ground. One student group ended each of these incorrigible persona's statements with the sound of a slamming door, itself a commentary on people's unwillingness to change or listen to other viewpoints in the public sphere.

But all is not comedy. One must push students beyond stereotypes toward the effect of leaders enacting zealous preferences on society. This places students (and in my case, future teachers) in public conversations related to literacy and other social issues. As a teacher, I enjoy watching students progress through what the government, teachers, parents, students, and other interested parties each want from education. Much like the literary critical whodunit, these assignments creating personas let students present the multiple views of a public issue, yet deliver the material in a new, and sometimes humorous, way.

Do students enjoy the assignment? It would seem so. Some groups have recruited friends from outside of class to help read character roles. Many have dedicated time to editing and technological knowledge to enhance production, which are value-added skills that arise from the assignment.

For me, the greatest sign of success is hearing a group's explanation of their critical insights from the synthesis of course texts while their peers intently listen to and/or chuckle about the radio play's rendering of these insights. I've found that the all-class discussion following the presentation spills forth fairly easily. The students' ideas seem more memorable in this form, perhaps because they are less academic, and students seem to remember each other's projects and reference them during our all-class discussion. This memorable quality of the assignments helps the course as we move forward into new theories or ideas while easily referencing older ideas by recalling each other's projects.

In terms of performance, the radio play is typically five to seven minutes long. Scripts can range from four to eight pages, depending on the genre. The aforementioned whodunit employed the voices of the three students and two extra friends. The radio play also utilized a number of genre conventions including the brisk tough talk, the "dame" seeking justice, and appropriate timing and sound effects, all of which were needed to sustain both the genre conventions and the critical task. During their class presentation, the trio of students explained their process and rhetorical critique to the class as they played the podcast, which created a forum similar to, I suppose, *Inside the Actor Studio*, except that my students presented the podcast as they talked about its creation as a technological production and an intellectual critique.

9. WORKS CITED

Baker, Linda, and Lisa Carter Beall. "Metacognitive Processes and Reading Comprehension." *Handbook of Research on Reading Comprehension*. Edited by Susan E. Israel and Gerald D. Duffy. Routledge, 2009, pp. 373-88.

Birnbaum, J. C. "Reflective Thought: The Connection Between Reading and Writing." *Convergences: Transactions in Reading and Writing*. Edited by B. Petersen. NCTE, 1986, pp. 30-45.

Comstock, Michelle, and Mary E. Hocks. "Voice in the Cultural Soundscape: Sonic Literacy in Composition Studies." *Computers and Composition Online*, 2006, www.bgsu.edu/cconline/comstock_hocks/index.htm.

Devitt, Amy. *Writing Genres*. Southern Illinois UP, 2004.

Graff, Gerald, and Cathy Birkenstein. *They Say, I Say: The Moves That Matter in Academic Writing*. Norton, 2010.

Johnson, T. R. *A Rhetoric of Pleasure: Prose Style and Today's Composition Classroom*. Boynton/Cook, 2003.

Penrose, Ann M., and Cheryl Geisler. "Reading and Writing without Authority." *College Composition and Communication*, vol. 45, no. 4, 1994, pp. 505-20.

Reiff, Mary Jo, and Anis Bawarshi. "Tracing Discursive Resources: How Students Use Prior Genre Knowledge to Negotiate New Writing Contexts in First-Year Composition." *Written Communication*, vol. 28, no. 3, 2011, 312-37.

Salomon, Gavriel, and David N. Perkins. "Rocky Roads to Transfer: Rethinking Mechanisms of a Neglected Phenomenon." *Educational Psychologist*, vol. 24, no. 2, 1989, pp. 113-42.

Selber, Stuart. *Multiliteracies for a Digital Age*. Southern Illinois UP, 2004.

Selfe, Cynthia L. "The Movement of Air, the Breath of Meaning: Aurality and Multimodal Composing." *College Composition and Communication*, vol. 60, no. 4, 2009, pp. 616-63.

Stroupe, Craig. "Visualizing English: Recognizing the Hybrid Literacy of Visual and Verbal Authorship on the Web." *College English*, vol. 62, no. 5, May 2000, pp. 607-32.

Swales, John. *Genre Analysis*. U of Cambridge P, 1990.

Yancey, Kathleen Blake. "More Than a Matter of Form." *Coming of Age: The Advanced Writing Curriculum*. Edited by Linda K. Shamoon, et al. Boynton/Cook, 2000, pp. 87-93.

17

Podcasts, Rebellion, and *Into the Wild*—Engaging Students in the Tale of Chris McCandless via the Podcast News and Talk Show

Christina Braid
University of Toronto

Christina Braid of Toronto, Canada, is a writer, educator, and researcher. Collaborating with authors, educators, scholars, and artistic organizations worldwide, Braid designs curriculum on the fundamentals of language and literature through creative writing, technology, and other contemporary forms of expression. She teaches a course for English educators titled Unleashing Creativity in Your Students Through Innovative 21st-Century Writing & Thinking Methods, which was well received at the University of Toronto's Ontario Institute for Studies in Education (OISE) in 2013. Braid holds an MA in English literature and a certificate in creative writing; she serves on the Teaching Committees for the Society for Utopian Studies and Poetry in Voice, and teaches English at Crescent School, a prestigious Canadian independent school for boys (e-mail: cbraid@crescentschool.org).

COURTESY OF
CHRISTINA BRAID

1. OVERVIEW

- **Assignment:** Write and produce an original radio or talk news podcast on Jon Krakauer's *Into the Wild*.
- **Courses:** Any literature course.
- **Literature:** Jon Krakauer's *Into the Wild*, or any nonfiction short story or novel.
- **Technology:** Note-taking software or apps (Google Docs, MS Word, Pages, Blog Web site, Evernote); scriptwriting software (Final Draft 9); audio software (iTunes); collaboration software (Google Docs, Google Drive, Edublog, Facebook, etc.); and Recording software (Audacity, GarageBand).
- **Time:** Eight to ten 60- to 80-minute classes.

2. GOALS OF THE ASSIGNMENT

- Creative investigation of *Into the Wild*
- Exploration of scriptwriting for radio
- Production of original podcast
- Explore essential questions, such as:
  - What elements, skills, tools, and techniques are required to produce an effective radio news/talk show?
  - What kind of content/material should be discussed in a podcast about Krakauer's book? How might that content be created and produced to appeal to mainstream audiences?

> "The process of editing a recording assists students in enhancing their voices with technology, through music, sound effects, and repetition. In so doing, students produce material for a variety of listeners and develop a keen awareness of audience. They want to leave an impression about their intellectual, creative, and emotional responses to narrative."
>
> **Christina Braid**
> University of Toronto

Prompted by a desire to offer students a variety of creative outlets for communication that might render memorable and unique their collective reading experiences of a biographical, teenage coming-of-age story, I developed this assignment for a senior-level English course with a desire to capture highly imaginative student responses to Jon Krakauer's story *Into the Wild*. With alternative criteria and descriptors, I've used this traditional podcast approach to reader response with units for other novels and poems for different literature courses and encourage you to do the same.

The following structure for this podcast project draws on Grant Wiggins and Jay McTighe's *Understanding by Design*, which encourages backward design aimed at helping students arrive at multiple understandings through a GRASP task or performance tasks that present students with "a real-world goal, set within a realistic context of challenges and possibilities" (157). In preparing lessons leading up to this project, you may ask the following action research questions to assess the success of this project in your own course-specific contexts:

- How might the use of technology enhance either the individual or group response to a piece of literature?
- Does the creation of a podcast help students better unravel the key themes emerging from a narrative text like Krakauer's *Into the Wild*?
- How might a student-created radio show help to illuminate how contemporary readers experience Chris McCandless's story? Does the project enhance a student's reaction and/or emotional connection to Krakauer's text?
- In what ways might analytical explorations of a true story produced through creative scriptwriting for a podcast audience heighten an English

student's analytical approach to studying, appreciating, and commenting upon a piece of literature?

While the answers to each of these questions might invite interesting action research projects unto themselves, they are important questions for you to pose in approaching this kind of classroom project and assessing the relevance and effectiveness of the exercise itself.

3. ASSIGNMENT SHEET

Podcasts, Rebellion, and *Into the Wild* — Engaging in the Tale of Chris McCandless via the Podcast News and Talk Show

Course: _____

Instructor: _____

Date: _____

LEARNING SKILLS: responsibility, collaboration, independent learning, critical thinking

ASSESSMENT STRANDS: communication, media literacy, reading, scriptwriting

LEARNING TOOLS: *Into the Wild,* by Jon Krakauer

GRASP TASK: podcast news show/talk show episode

GOAL: In this assignment, your task is to read Jon Krakauer's *Into the Wild*. Your goal is to design an original radio news show or talk show on Krakauer's book.

ROLE: You are an intern, studying journalism at a university. You just received an invitation to work at a radio station (i.e., CBC Radio 1/NPR/alternative radio). You have been asked by the show producers to be part of a team that will create an original radio news show or talk show on Krakauer's book. With your expertise as a writer, your job is to ensure the show appeals to the station's already wide audience following.

Your research, focus, professionalism, fresh ideas, and engaged reading of this true story must appeal to our sponsors by the time we air. As a group, you must ensure the team's deadline is met and that your podcast research, writing, recording, and editing is completed by the agreed-upon date.

AUDIENCE: Your listeners are readers of Jon Krakauer's nonfiction and/or those interested in reading biographies. Your target audience: 4 million listeners who will tune in to the live show and rebroadcasts of your podcast via National Radio Audience (Canada)/Northern USA (Buffalo, Seattle, San Francisco, Boston) and XM Satellite Radio (Canadian/US citizens around the globe); ABC Radio Australia; and BBC Radio.

As a skilled journalist, you need also to contribute to a team that will cowrite and coproduce an entertaining episode that sponsors will want to support.

SITUATION: One day, the show producer calls a production meeting at your posh downtown podcast studio. The station will receive an anonymous, $1 million donation if a show can be created to increase in the audience a love for reading books and produce increased listenership for the radio station.

The show producers have asked the station's staff to dedicate airtime to Jon Krakauer's popular book *Into the Wild*. Worried that reading might not appeal to all contemporary listeners, the CEO has mandated that all members of the writing team have a strong knowledge of Krakauer's book. They must also be prepared to contribute engaging ideas that will produce exceptional radio news show/talk show podcast material to inspire listeners to participate in the important activity of reading, prompt conversation, and increase general radio listenership.

PRODUCT: For this assignment you will:

1. Develop a podcast (radio news show/talk show style episode) using audio editing software such as Audacity or GarageBand of 3–5 minutes per group member.
2. Create a typed transcript of your entire radio news show or talk show.

ASSESSMENT OF LEARNING SKILLS: Learning skills developed through this project include responsibility, initiative, collaboration, self-regulation, organization, and independent work. You will evolve your skills in summary writing, critical thinking, oral communication, media literacy, and independent reading, and reflective response practices through the use of technology.

ASSESSMENT OF KNOWLEDGE, INQUIRY, COMMUNICATION, AND APPLICATION: By using role-play, you will imagine new ways to discuss, respond to, invent, and emulate a professional-sounding radio news show/talk show. You will be assessed in the following ways for a grade out of 100 points or percent.

Knowledge: The published podcast must demonstrate a deep understanding of the story *Into the Wild* and defend specific choices made for inventing the show's content. I will check for facts to prove authenticity of radio comments. All groups must provide page references, quotes, and accurate research to the instructor via the final transcript. Marks will be allotted according to the accuracy and quality of the research submitted; the final broadcast will present a good opportunity to discuss how well groups approached the reading comprehension goals of this project. (25 points)

Inquiry: A podcast transcript (with page references; specific passages/quotations in MLA format) should be submitted as the written analysis portion of this project. As well, the depth of analysis should be apparent in the content of the radio news show/talk show podcast and reveal how well you explored the theme, character, relationship, roles, and elements of the story in your creative segments. (25 points)

Communication: Be sure to employ proper English grammar and usage throughout the transcript as a way to sustain listener attention and produce a professional-looking document. We will to create a peer evaluation rubric in KICA format to evaluate the quality of podcast and its content by classes #7 or 8. The radio news show/talk show should communicate interesting,

(continued)

ASSIGNMENT SHEET *(continued)*

thought-provoking discussion through interviews, musical choices, and expressive performances (i.e., poetry or a rant), and should incorporate spontaneous improvisation and effective scriptwriting. The podcast should also engage the listener from the beginning to the end of the created episode. (25 points)

Application (The Podcast in iTunes/Blog/Web site): For a group mark, the team must demonstrate an effective use of technology to create the podcast. The final product can be published through the iTunes store, our class blog, or shared on the school Web site for listeners to download.

Finally, to reflect on learning skills acquired, you will answer a metacognitive self-evaluation of the process in the form of a typed-up response to questions relevant to this project. (25 points)

TOTAL: ____/**100 points**

4. TIME AND TECHNOLOGY

TIME. For this project, you could use eight to ten 60- to 80-minute classes for setup, brainstorming, production, editing, and presentation. Instructional time leading up to the presentation will vary depending on student skill set and grade level.

TECHNOLOGY.

- Note-taking software or apps (Google Docs, MS Word, Pages, blog Web site, Evernote)
- Scriptwriting software (Final Draft 9)
- Audio software (iTunes)
- Collaboration software (Google Docs, Google Drive, Edublog, Facebook, etc.)
- Recording software (Audacity, GarageBand)

5. ANTICIPATING STUDENT NEEDS

The setup for this project arises from a course focus on an academic method of literary analysis, while also assisting students in presenting ideas in original ways through creative writing and creative thinking.

Understanding Narrative Texts

In the lead-up to this project, I take time to model how students should share their chapter-by-chapter investigations of a literary text via a Google Doc or class blog. As well, during the previous unit on mythology, for instance, students were already introduced to various methods of commentary on narratives texts using technology, and they were given reading comprehension tests in which they applied their knowledge of the story. For the BYOD (bring your own device) classroom, tests and notes on the text are taken from the beginning of the year using a laptop or other device (iPad, iPhone, Google Phone, tablet, etc).

When presenting narrative analysis, students are encouraged to use MLA citations and references, with secondary sources documented using the free Web site Noodle Tools. It is helpful to establish earlier in the term online research skills with the help of the school librarian, with a focus on gathering evidence and exploring the relevance of research in light of a project's focus.

Technical requirements for the podcast assessment include scriptwriting software (i.e., Final Draft 9 or online freeware like Celtx, www.celtx.com); audio editing software (i.e., GarageBand or Audacity); and collaborative software (i.e., Google chat, Google Docs, Facebook, Edublog). To achieve a successful podcast project, it is important that students already have some grasp of producing creative responses to the various stories read by using word processing software like Pages, Google Docs, or MS Word for note taking.

Understanding Basic Podcast Methodology

Prior to creating this assignment, I found it useful to develop my own basic training in applications like GarageBand and Audacity. After learning how to record multiple voices, edit sound, and add music, interviews, ads, jingles, and sound effects, I created podcast exemplars for my English classes and played them for each group to demonstrate to students how easy the tools are to manipulate and master. This intermediary step is crucial to providing students with the confidence to create a podcast. It was helpful to be piloting a BYOD curriculum that year, as many students already owned laptops.

While students can easily create through trial and error their own podcasts via recording software, it is useful to invite IT specialists to visit each class and assist students in understanding some basic methods for creating podcasts. It is also helpful to post how-to videos and/or how-to instructions on the class blog or Web site.

Instructors with little knowledge of podcast creation or Google Docs can find online tutorials (e.g., www.lynda.com) to support student software training for this type of project. Depending on school policy, you might ask students to upload polished podcasts to a school Web site. With parent, teacher, and administrator permission, students might also choose to share project work free on iTunes or a podcast Web catcher.

Understanding Historical Context

Finally, online research databases provided by a local public library or the school library can potentially assist you in looking to deepen the classroom approach to understanding the context of Chris McCandless's personal history. The Web site of Carine McCandless (www.carinemccandless.com/) provides some helpful starting points for student research and reflection.

5. ANTICIPATING STUDENT NEEDS

Technology might prove to be a problem in this assignment, simply because it requires students to have knowledge of file sharing of recorded content without corrupting the data. By using a USB stick, Dropbox, or Google Drive, students can easily store, back up, and share files.

In some cases, certain students insist that they take on full ownership of the editing process. This skill set application can make sense, so long as the group tasks are evenly divided. While students can be fair in self-regulating, it is important that in setting up this kind of assignment, you ensure students have the resources they require to create a successful podcast. For this reason, this project should be geared to students fourteen and older to ensure reading level, independence, and problem-solving strategies around technology do not impede the learning outcomes of this kind of project.

I noticed that some students with PCs (not MacBooks) struggled with the use of the program Audacity at first; for schools considering podcast projects in many grades, administrators might consider having laptops and desktops with GarageBand for iPad or Mac or PC. This program can be more versatile and fun for students to manipulate, especially with the variety of preprogrammed sound effects, music, jingles, and the versatility of iTunes.

Still, every group member should be able to partake in the process of podcast creation using freeware or some kind of online audio software. Students with a strong grasp of how to string together sound bytes, weave in music, insert voice audio files, and edit segments to balance volume or manage the cross fade (fade in/fade out) should finish the assignment to their satisfaction by the eighth class.

Regarding iTunes, parents should be made aware that students might need to download music through iTunes for fair educational usage. A simple parent letter at the beginning of the Krakauer unit discussing the guidelines of the project would be helpful, especially if students do not have access to copyrighted music.

6. ASSESSMENT TOOLS

For this project, I ask students to generate their own evaluation rubrics, which I help edit. The purpose of this exercise is to allow students to reflect on the learning goals they wish to accomplish and to inquire about their success in reaching these goals with their peer group.

One student generated the rubric that follows. I edited and approved it to address the learning guidelines for the course itself. The students requested that their peers evaluate their podcasts on these criteria within the knowledge, inquiry, communication, and application areas; their choices reflect one set of student perspectives on what are important assessment outcomes of this podcast project. During the peer evaluation period, I asked guest evaluators and students to use this rubric to assess the student podcast project. Rich conversations arose from having students create their own rubrics to help establish what success looks like at the end of this project. Even with creative segments, evaluation of the podcast transcript content would be a fair and easy way for you to evaluate student understanding of Krakauer's book.

Student-Generated Rubric for Peer Evaluation

	Level 5	Level 4	Level 3	Level 2	Level 1
Knowledge	Clear understanding of story *Into the Wild*	Solid understanding of the story	Some understanding of the story	Little understanding of the story	No understanding of the story
	Evidence of research that complements the podcast and informs the story	Evidence of research	Some evidence of research	Little evidence of research	No evidence of research
	Gives a fresh and unique angle on *Into the Wild* that hadn't been seen/observed/discussed as a class	Gives a different outlook on *Into the Wild*	Gives a basic outlook on *Into the Wild*	Somewhat bland outlook on *Into the Wild*	Very bland outlook on *Into the Wild*
Inquiry	Written transcript of podcast is fully provided to turnitin.com	Written transcript of podcast is mostly provided	Written transcript of podcast is sort of provided	Little written transcript of podcast is provided	Written transcript is not provided
	Page references and two specific quotes are evident in the transcript	Some page references and two specific quotes are evident in the transcript	No page references and one specific quote is evident in the transcript	No page references and no specific quotes are evident in the transcript	No page references or quotes are provided in the transcript
	Google document is provided that includes rough notes and thought process	Google document is provided that includes most rough notes and thought process	Google document is provided that includes some rough notes and thought process	Google document is provided that includes few rough notes and thought process	No Google document or rough notes that show the thought process are provided

Communication	All students' voices are clearly heard, each having a relevant role Responsibility, collaborative effort, and initiative clearly shown in the podcast's success Lots of relevant effort from every member; solid participation is evident	Most of the students' voices are clearly heard, with a relevant role Responsibility, collaborative effort, and initiative are mostly shown in the podcast's success Effort relevant	Some of the students' voices are somewhat heard, with a relevant role Responsibility, collaborative effort, and initiative is somewhat shown in the podcast's mediocrity Some relevant effort	Only a select few of the students' voices are barely heard, with a relevant role Responsibility, collaborative effort, and initiative not shown in the podcast's failure Little effort relevant	Students' voices are not clearly heard, without a relevant role No responsibility, collaborative effort, and initiative are not demonstrated in any way No effort shown
Application	Editing clearly shown, and the effort of editing relevant Every student had a distinct role in the process of making the podcast Plethora of engaging music intros and sound effects Three or more guests, and two commercials included Performance evaluations completed Student rubric provided	Editing shown, and the effort of editing relevant Most students had a distinct role in the process of making the podcast A lot of interesting music intros and sound effects Two guests and two commercials included	Editing sort of shown, and some effort of editing relevant Some students had a distinct role in the process of making the podcast Some interesting music intros and sound effects One guest, and one commercial included	Little editing shown, and little effort of editing relevant Few students had a distinct role in the process of making the podcast Little music intros and sound effects One guest, and no commercials included	Editing *not* shown, and the effort of editing not relevant No student had a distinct role in the process of making the podcast No music intros and sound effects No guests, and no commercials are included No student rubric provided

7. THEORETICAL BASIS FOR THE ASSIGNMENT:
Podcasts, Rebellion, and *Into the Wild* — Engaging Students in the Tale of Chris McCandless via the Podcast News and Talk Show

Using Podcasts in the Classroom

The case for incorporating podcasts into classroom curriculum has not gone unnoticed in contemporary discussions on the benefits of adding technology to the English classroom (Riddle). In fact, the invention of the iPod in 2001 revolutionized possibilities for student-teacher and student-text interaction, moving students closer to those types of meaningful and collective sharing exercises when reading literature into new territories, that is, to encourage creative discovery and response to texts (Saine).

The chance to conduct such learning initiatives, which investigate reasons for why interactive technologies might benefit student learning, presents important starting points to assess student engagement as readers, with an emphasis on understanding the literature they read.

The use of modern technology in the English classroom proposes inventive ways of engaging students as self-directed learners and active readers. Traditional classroom models present student-made discoveries about the literature read via writing academic essays, personal responses, and opinion-driven papers, all of which provide important modes of exploring a story and its elements. The traditional response method creates an audience of one (the teacher) or many (the class). The use of podcast technology, however, seems to incorporate another more creative dimension to the literature response and the research needed to wield it for a wider audience for which students invent their own response.

Students exploring literature through technology might use the end goal of a creative media product like a podcast to imagine relevant and timely responses to issues addressed by writers, like Jon Krakauer. In responding to a studied text for this podcast project, students might engage with the main character, Christopher McCandless, his sense of rebellion, longing for the unknown, as well as his extreme search for adventure. Krakauer's *Into the Wild* provides an excellent philosophical study of post-transcendentalist thinking in a consumer-driven culture.

In this story, students also recognize the ironies of using technology to comment on McCandless's desire to live outside the contemporary world. Helping students to appreciate a way of being or a culture they do not have direct access to or understand situates one key purpose behind including such narrative discussions in an English curriculum. These conversations remind students of Daniel Kahneman's rule: WYSIATI (what you see is all there is), which seeks to address the contemporary dilemma in thinking. The process of developing a podcast project about a piece of literature assists students with slowing down their thinking beyond merely intuitive thought; rather, it forces them to dig for answers that will inform experience—through "more deliberate and effortful form of thinking" (Kahneman 21)—an essential skill set for the twenty-first-century learner. McCandless's story engages many points of departure for podcast-worthy material.

Further, a podcast project assists students in reflecting on the notion of empathy, while examining creative approaches through technology that will promote meaningful cross-cultural and/or countercultural classroom discourses on a narrative text. In so doing, students might approach literature more mindfully through this exercise of creative writing for radio. The addition of podcasts as an assessment tool for investigating literature not only leads students toward producing highly creative and empathetic responses to literature, but also develops skills that encourage more ways of seeking, evaluating, considering, researching, and expressing information.

Understanding the Podcast Assignment Context

This assignment appeared in a literature course for a grade 10, advanced senior-level English class. The course content included a broad study of poetry, Greek mythology, Arthur Miller's and Shakespeare's plays, the war stories of Tim O'Brien, and Jon Krakauer's *Into the Wild*. The thematic exploration of hubris and the nature of storytelling permeated the course agenda throughout the year.

Understanding Krakauer

For the Krakauer unit, students were asked to watch on their own (via DVD, iTunes, or Netflix) Sean Penn's film *Into the Wild* and to listen to the music of Pearl Jam so as to examine the relationship between grunge and McCandless's personal quest for self-discovery. As a class, we took time to discuss some of the key themes of the story; we also reflected on the philosophical resonance of Thomas Merton's thematically relevant comment in *No Man Is an Island*: "The Deep Secrecy of my own being is often hidden from me by my own estimate of what I am. My idea of what I am is falsified by my admiration for what I do. And my illusions about myself are bred by contagion from the illusions of other men. We all seek to imitate one another's imagined greatness." Students were then instructed to read Krakauer's book independently prior to the podcast project start date. Students took group notes as they read using Google Docs.

After reading Krakauer's book, I was struck by the author's personal obsession with Chris McCandless and felt intuitively that this unit would demand from students a close reading of Krakauer's text in an equally personal way. While their emotional and empathetic responses to the text represented important data found in earlier personal paragraph responses I asked students to conduct prior to introducing this project, I was also inclined and committed toward ensuring all students would participate in class discussion on Krakauer's text. I was excited to provide for them a project that might yield much deeper sharing of personal responses to McCandless's life story.

When responding to Krakauer's autobiography, students develop so many creative points of departure for their podcasts, especially regarding hubris, a person's dislocation from society, teenage angst, teenage rebellion, relationships between sons and fathers, Thoreau's and Tolstoy's philosophical reflections cited by McCandless before he died, the power of nature, the role of the supernatural, the inevitable meeting between man and death, the role of fate, and so on. Also, sharing podcasts with one another emancipated students from the obstacles often faced when addressing these big thematic questions.

The pedagogical end goal of studying a true story together challenges students to investigate McCandless's story with the broader sense of understanding that investigative journalistic authority inspires. Thus, it was easy for me to decide against the use of digital presentation tools like PowerPoint or even video to produce the unit's culminating task. Rather, like many stories of its caliber, the tale of Chris McCandless as told by Jon Krakauer is one with great potential for discussion, clever observations, and reflective abandon provided by the space of a radio broadcast. Numerous students chose a hybrid of news show and talk show to sketch their interpretation of the story.

While this project did not at the time include specific data collection or data analysis methods that action researchers might analyze to determine, in quantitative or qualitative ways, the actual effectiveness of this kind of media literacy assignment, I was happily surprised to observe how student learners with mobile devices and access to programs like GarageBand or Audacity freeware expressed their views on Krakauer's text.

When composing this assignment for students in the senior English classroom, I wanted their learning experience to help them discover, understand, and appreciate the components of a successful podcast. I also wanted them to take ownership of their project as an extension of authentic personal voice, rather than recycling preprogrammed ideas that might characterize the English class presentation.

Preparing for the Podcast Radio/Talk Show

In approaching this project, students must first have the knowledge to observe the key aspects of plot, character, setting, theme, suspense, imagery, style, narrative point of view, and so on, in order to appreciate the content and structure of Jon Krakauer's text. Depending on your school's curriculum goals, you should provide a quick review. Secondly, the process of podcast creation helps students to discover how technology, as a mode of vocal expression, can encourage an original understanding of the complex issues, opinions, and questions raised by books like *Into the Wild*. Through both an understanding of the elements of fiction and presenting a medium for interactive, personal, and innovative responses to a true story, student writing can be applied effectively using audio editing/podcast programs geared to mass audiences. Thus, as much as possible for this project, you should encourage students to imagine and construct their own radio programming decisions for the news show/talk show content. This creative freedom will allow students to present relevant and meaningful critical perspectives on McCandless's story, while making the experience of listening to the final broadcast a valuable one for the class, especially as they engage with one another's authentic voices.

Creative writing for radio draws on open-ended learning that invites students to investigate with effective scrutiny a piece of literature in a real-world context. The podcast invites research that satisfies a student's personal passions. The assignment models exemplars from real-world radio shows that you might introduce before the project is assigned. This media study should thus encourage students to explore playful and dramatic meditations on the thematic and symbolic relevance of Chris McCandless's story. At the same time, the act of creative writing develops imaginative terminologies by students who not only seek to entertain potential audiences through their original podcast, but also to showcase personal discoveries made in small groups while reading Krakauer's *Into the Wild*. Not unlike literature circles, the podcast presents students with access to the Internet, research databases, and models for news entertainment (television, YouTube, Vimeo, Podcast Channels, and FM/AM radio, etc.) with unlimited options for inspired dramatic dialogue. I am always impressed by how adaptable students are to the nontraditional parameters of the project: they easily sketch conversations using scriptwriting programs and enjoy the process of organic construction of creative content.

In their podcasts, students have a variety of creative options to show their responses to Krakauer's *Into the Wild*, including aspects of various genres such as fantasy, comedy, melodrama, satire, irony, poetry, rap, and reality shows. With so many artistic options, students might examine dimensions of Krakauer's text that would not otherwise be explored by an academic essay. Finally, the project supports creative responses both collaboratively and individually, with students benefiting from reflective self-explorations and class dialogue about the story after the podcasts are presented to the class.

From a research perspective in an age of information overload, this assignment invites students to heighten the process of journalistic fact checking, while also contemplating the reasoning behind and powerful purposes for effective research on any primary and secondary texts used to derive creative content for the podcast. I encourage you to work with the school librarian and/or IT team to increase students' research skill base in preparing their podcasts for final broadcast to an imagined audience.

As a way to assist students in discovering the power of their own authentic voices in the English classroom, this assignment provides an outlet for deepening personal awareness of one's voice. Students role-play as real members of a radio station news show/talk show, and they are expected to experiment with many types of self-expression by investigating different kinds of tone, pitch, and melody as they interpret and record their scripts for specific audiences.

Podcast Lesson Plan for *Into the Wild*

The following process was used for students in Year 10 (age fifteen to sixteen). The process might be tweaked accordingly, depending on the learning standards in your English program.

CLASS #1: MEDIA LITERACY—UNDERSTANDING "THE RADIO/TALK SHOW"

Raise the essential question: What elements, skills, tools, and techniques are required to produce an effective radio news/talk show?

Ask students to download podcasts of interest from one of the following exemplary stations:

- Jian Ghomeshi's *Q* (Canadian Broadcasting Corporation)
- Steve Paikin's *The Agenda* (TVOntario)
- NPR (National Public Radio)
- BBC Radio (British Broadcasting Corporation)
- Amy Goodwin's *Democracy Now* (Alternative Radio)
- ABC Australia

Next steps:

1. Discuss the essential question in relation to radio, an entertainment medium that markets creative content in real time and through later rebroadcasts. Have students explore the history and purpose of a radio talk show/news show.
2. Distribute the podcast episode assignment sheet and summary writing notes to assist with the style of writing for radio.
3. Divide students into groups based on the type of radio station they'd like to produce, or use some other means of division.

4. Have students democratically nominate show producers who will be team leaders that might assist with encouraging group members to meet the deadline completion requirements of the project.

5. Have students divide into pods. They should be engaging in student-directed conversations using a Google Document, student blog, or a nominated "conversation recorder" using Pages or MS Word. Alternatively, students can use flip charts and markers or a whiteboard.

6. Ask teams to brainstorm to create ideas on show content; show producers might help the group to discuss the "market feel" of the show (hip, traditional, etc.). Prior to this class, you might ask students to think about their group goals as a team and to limit the content to manageable tasks that can be completed by the deadline.

7. Ask students to assign to each group member a talk show/news show segment; students can work toward scriptwriting assigned creative writing jobs/roles by the upcoming deadline.

8. Tell students to choose a radio station name (either a real station or an imaginary one) and to keep a Team Meeting Progress Log every class.

In Ontario, the Ministry of Education requires teachers to track the following learning skills to guide student success at their learning: responsibility, initiative, collaboration, self-regulation, organization, and independent work. For this project, students can check in with you on a regular basis to reflect on their work ethic and learning skills development.

At the end of the unit, you might provide a metacognitive online reflection on the project process.

CLASS #2: READING *INTO THE WILD* (Initiative/Responsibility)
Provide students with the project evaluation guidelines to evaluate their work according to your assessment descriptors. (See Assessment Tools.)

With a strong group of readers, give students about one week to finish reading Krakauer's book and watching Sean Penn's film; give students some class time to read, but encourage them to read as literature circle groups to address the essential elements of the text. Students might parse the text for the elements of fiction (plot, character, setting, theme, symbol, narrative point of view, etc.), with or without you, depending on timing.

Have students role-play throughout the duration of this project. Explain that they are members of a radio station prepared to work and to share with the producers. The students can demonstrate this by:

- underlining key passages;
- bookmarking key pages;
- asking questions that might interest their audience;
- bringing ideas to the table that will produce an effective show;

- preparing a list of the top three characters that *need* to be on the show; and

- preparing to argue the case for their story to the producer (i.e., how their original ideas will contribute to a successful, entertaining, and engaging podcast).

CLASS #3: SHOW OUTLINE (Collaboration/Organization)

As a group, students will create a Google Document that is shared with you; they should title the document "Show Proposal." The proposal should provide most of the following elements:

- *Show Outline*: a clear, easy-to-read outline of the proposed show.

- *Marketing Plan*: a clear plan summarizing and defending the purposes, outcomes, target market, and projected audience rating. Remind students that the show should appeal to sponsors and take time to examine and discuss the role of advertising in episodes. Students can read Jason Van Orden's book or his Web site regarding promotion of a podcast.

- *Show Needs*: a basic summary of ideas accounting for every section of the show that will need to be produced:
  - Music: What music will the podcast play?
  - Show Intro: How will your host introduce the show?
  - Guest Intro: How will you introduce guests on the show?
  - Show Segments: How should the show be divided? What segments are needed to represent a thoughtful understanding of McCandless's story?
  - Interviews: Who should be interviewed on the show? Should those people be real? How about interviewing McCandless?
  - Host: What will the host's personality be like?
  - Commercials: What kinds of commercials might you include for a radio show on Jon Krakauer's *Into the Wild*?

- *Research*: a list of page-referenced, MLA-style quotes that inspired elements of the show transcript and its content; in other words, the team must demonstrate where in Krakauer's text ideas for the show came from. The team must be ready to defend the connections between the podcast and the book.

- *Audience Appeal*: the show producers and team must justify how the podcast will appeal to fans of Krakauer's book; the show needs to invite listeners to have a genuine interest in Krakauer's book and McCandless's story. Ask students to reflect on the question: "How will you grab listeners and retain potential sponsors with your show as outlined?"

- *Additional Research*: producers may require all members of their team to conduct some research on aspects of Krakauer's book. This research should uncover interesting angles on the book; the school librarian might assist any students looking for help. Students might also access books at a local public library or request help from the instructor to contact on behalf of students a professional or expert in an authentic and respectful way.

CLASS #4: INTERVIEW QUESTIONS & SCRIPTWRITING

Have students in pairs or as individuals produce a draft of their creative show segments, taking time to defend the relevance of the segment to their novel response. By class #4, prior to recording, students can begin to explore how they will perform their show segments (i.e., interview scenarios/conversations).

To incorporate media literacy initiatives, also have students create relevant commercials to appear throughout the podcast, helping them to understand the relationship between show content and sponsorship interests. Many students create their own commercials; however, some prefer to incorporate the audio of contemporary commercials from YouTube or the radio.

Teachers might instruct students to get together to record their show segments in quiet spaces within the school; students might also use programs like Skype to record materials at home. Give students the option of importing all vocal recordings as MP3 audio files to be edited on one computer by the show producer and/or with the assistance of the instructor or IT help desk at your school.

CLASS #5: TRANSCRIPT (Initiative/Self-Regulation/Collaboration)

If desired, ask the student teams to create a show transcript to record any spontaneous content and observe a text for radio. Students can see Amy Goodman's *Democracy Now* for an online exemplar from her video podcast. While editing, students should include lots of catch phrases used in radio shows/podcasts: "Now, if you've just tuned in . . ." or "Later on our show" or "Welcome back," and so on.

Remind students that parts of the show can be easily rerecorded; if you have the time, talk to them about acting, enunciation, and clear articulation for radio.

CLASS #6: PEER EDITING (Collaboration/Perseverance/Initiative)

Ask students to listen together to their rough version of the podcast as a group. Take class time to have them critically question whether their podcast content draws out the important and interesting thematic aspects of Krakauer's book. Have the students create their own peer assessment rubric for the presentation class and ensure key quotes and page references have been properly inserted throughout the transcript to demonstrate the podcast's interaction with Krakauer's text.

CLASS #7: PRE-AIR (Peer Evaluation)

After editing the podcast and inserting music, jingles, and sound effects, ask students to consider the originality of their shows. (See the sample student-generated rubric on pp. 264-65.) Some key aspects to consider include:

- The order of materials
- Feel of spontaneity and freshness in presentation
- Projected audience responses to the show
- Projected sponsor responses to the show
- Projected national responses to the show
- Projected response of other readers to Krakauer's story

CLASS #8: ON THE AIR (Publication/Collaboration)

Have students submit the WAV or MP4 file to you for broadcast, then gather students together to listen to the final shows. Depending on class time, students can play their podcasts for one another in class or stream the podcasts at home. Regardless, students evaluate the podcasts using the student-generated peer evaluation sheet.

CLASS #9: DEBRIEF (Metacognition)

Provide time for class discussion, which might include discussion about the rubric and success of the podcast itself. Did the final product generate answers to the essential question of the unit? How did students learn about team work? Group work?

OPTIONAL: JUDGES

To extend the adult audience, you might also consider asking some colleagues in the English department or school to listen to the podcasts over a period of time, for example, on the drive to and from campus. You might request the judges to evaluate the radio shows based on this same student-generated evaluation. Be sure to let students know other adults will be providing feedback and/or invite those adults to comment on the podcasts at the end of the unit.

8. CONCLUSION

There is a need to encourage new contributions to current theories on the role of podcasts in the classroom, while also deepening thematic approaches to literacy based learning in the English classroom. The use of podcasts might recognize the relevance of technology in providing to students "discipline-based research, reading, and writing" (Riddle). Such learning experiences, especially when discussing complex issues to do with teenage rebellion, coming of age, and countercultural thought in the classroom, allow students to discover the deep literary themes within narrative with more clarity and imaginative thought. At the same time, incorporating this kind of learning project into the curriculum has encouraged many twenty-first-century educators to address student skill sets developed in the English classroom, such as oral reading, presentation skills, problem solving, creative thinking, collaboration, responsibility, public speaking, and dramatic performance.

Personally, this podcast assignment was one of the most rewarding collaborative projects I've completed with students in my short sixteen-year teaching career. The students embraced the challenge of responding to narrative with technology, with each group demonstrating a greater appreciation of the work required to produce a powerful script for a radio talk show.

Students felt a great connection to the work, with the final product producing a satisfactory approach to sharing ideas on a novel. I enjoyed watching the collaborative efforts expressed through the medium of technology.

The project also provided a great learning experience for students who struggled to produce their best work. They were able to reflect on the aspects of teamwork that prevented them from achieving the assessment goals.

Rather than regurgitating information, students began to realize that their success at scriptwriting a unique radio podcast news/talk show spotlighting Krakauer's *Into the Wild* might come about as a direct result of (1) how well they conversed about the book after reading it; (2) how effectively they worked in groups as they brainstormed show ideas, cowrote sketches, and scripted conversation points or ads; (3) how well they experimented with tone and dramatic oral expression; (4) how willing they were to invest in authentic independent and critical reading of Jon Krakauer's *Into the Wild*; (5) how many risks in imaginative creative writing they were willing to take and I was willing to model or discuss during the process; and (6) how much they embraced experimenting with applying certain fundamental principles of strongly produced podcasts.

To bring together these skills sets was experimental, as I hadn't honestly put together groups of six or even ten before. Still, I was keen to observe how students might collaborate and divide responsibilities in order to produce a solid show.

Finally, students benefitted from listening to and reflecting on the most effective radio shows produced by their classmates, many of whom were students who did not always share their ideas in class. This type of podcast project provides students of many backgrounds with the opportunity to engage in an art form that exercises the power of voice and demands oral sharing of thought. The process of editing a recording assists students in enhancing their voices with technology, through music, sound effects, and repetition. In so doing, students use technology to produce material for a variety of listeners and develop a keen awareness of audience, as well as a desire to leave an impression about their intellectual, creative, and emotional responses to narrative.

I wish to thank the boys in three of my 2011–2012 senior English classes at Crescent School in Toronto, Ontario, Canada (graduating class of 2014). Their enthusiastic conversations during the creation of this assignment, amazing commitment to this project, and creative energy produced memorable reflections on Krakauer's book for the study unit as well as the conceptual skeleton for designing this creative podcast project and this lesson plan.

9. WORKS CITED

Cressey, Donald R., and James W. Coleman. *Social Problems*. Longman, 1999.

Creanor, Linda, and Janet MacDonald. *Learning with Online and Mobile Technologies*. Gower, 2010.

Goleman, Daniel. *Emotional Intelligence*. Bantam, 1995.

Hicks, Troy. *Crafting Digital Writing: Composing Texts Across Media and Genres*. Heinemann, 2013.

Johannsen, David H. *Meaningful Learning with Technology*. Pearson, 2008.

Kahneman, Daniel. *Thinking Fast and Slow*. Doubleday, 2011.

Krakauer, Jon. *Into the Wild*. Anchor-Doubleday, 1997.

McCandless, Carine. *Carine McCandless*. www.carinemccandless.com. Accessed 1 Apr. 2014.

Orden, Jason Van. *Promoting Your Podcast: The Ultimate Guide to Building an Audience of Raving Fans*. Larson, 2006.

- - -. "Podcasting Resources." *Promoting Your Podcast*, 1 Apr. 2014, www.promoting yourpodcast.com/jason-van-orden.htm.

Riddle, Johanna. "Podcasting in the Classroom: The Tech Effect." *Multimedia & Internet@Schools*, vol. 17, no. 1, 2010, pp. 23-26.

Saine, Paula. "iPods, iPads, and the SMARTBoard: Transforming Literacy Instruction and Student Learning." *New England Reading Association Journal*, vol. 47, no. 2, 2012, pp. 74-81.

Wiggins, Grant, and Jay McTighe. *Understanding by Design*. Expanded second edition. Association for Supervision and Curriculum Development, 2005.

Wittkower, D. E., editor. *iPod and Philosophy: iCon of an ePoch*. Open Court, 2008.

18

Reviving an Oral Tradition: Using Podcasting to Teach Ancient Literature

Christine Tulley
The University of Findlay

Christine Tulley is associate professor of English and director of the Master of Arts in Rhetoric and Writing program at the University of Findlay. She teaches undergraduate and graduate classical rhetoric courses in addition to courses in writing pedagogy and digital rhetorics. She is coeditor of *Webbing Cyberfeminist Practice* (Hampton, 2008) and author of several articles appearing in *Computers and Composition, Pedagogy,* and *Teaching/Writing: Journal of Writing Teacher Education*.

COURTESY OF
CHRISTINE TULLEY

1. OVERVIEW

- **Assignment:** Create podcasts of ancient literary passages with interpretation.
- **Courses:** Any literature course, especially those that incorporate classical authors, such as western literature and world literature; composition and literature; composition; and classical rhetoric.
- **Literature:** Classical works from Plato, Aristotle, or others.
- **Technology:** Microphone (external or internal on computer), audio editing software such as Audacity (PC or Mac) or GarageBand (Mac).
- **Time:** Three to four 50-minute class periods, depending on what technology resources are available outside of class.

2. GOALS OF THE ASSIGNMENT

After completing this assignment this assignment, students will be able to:

- read aloud an excerpt from classical literature to understand the impact of the oral tradition;

- interpret and analyze classical rhetorical passages for a contemporary audience to demonstrate understanding of key concepts and recognize the relevance of classical rhetoric;
- practice effective rhetorical skills of classical oratory when reading the passage;
- edit the recording using digital audio editing software; and
- publish the audio recording in an accessible venue (campus radio station, Podcast Alley, etc.).

"Creating ancient literature podcasts with contemporary interpretations allows students to demonstrate the relevance and accessibility of the material, and to see how classical literature is applicable in the twenty-first century."

Christine Tulley
The University of Findlay

3. ASSIGNMENT SHEET

Reviving an Oral Tradition: Using Podcasting to Learn about Ancient Literature

Course: _____

Instructor: _____

Date: _____

"Today's Classical Rhetoric Moment" Podcast Assignment

Introduction

At this point, you have read works by Gorgias, Plato, Aristotle, Isocrates, and Cicero, in addition to classical fragments by Sappho, Diotima, and Hortensia. You will now choose one "passage" (generally 100–200 words) from one larger work to read aloud for a podcast.

After introducing the work and reading the passage, you will conclude with an interpretation of the classical work for the modern-day college student. The entire segment of 2 minutes to 2 minutes and 30 seconds is recorded and edited using the podcast technology described below and podcasts will be played on our college radio station in a series titled "Classical Rhetoric Moment of the Day." This assignment will take place over three of our class sessions.

Similar to early tape recorder technology, making a podcast requires recording sound with a microphone, now either built into the computer or as a stand-alone auxiliary device. Free programs such as Audacity (audacity.sourceforge .net/about/) or programs such as GarageBand (www.apple.com/ilife/garage band/) recognize the presence of the microphone and open up a viewing pane for watching sound record on a frequency chart. Such software typically has familiar, iconic buttons such as a red square for "record" and forward and backward arrows representing play head directions. This simple technology allows you to click Record, speak into the microphone, and create an audio text that can be edited.

There are several parts to this assignment. Before we start our first podcasting class session, you will choose one short excerpt from Plato, Isocrates, Aristotle, Cicero, or Quintilian to read aloud. You will want to find a selection from *Readings in Classical Rhetoric* that you understand and find interesting. Try not to pick something that anyone else is using and choose something short . . . no more than a few lines/paragraph.

After reading your short selection, you will take a few seconds to analyze and interpret what your selection might mean for today's university student. In other words, attempt to encourage your peers to care about what Cicero or Plato says. Why do you find the passage interesting? Is it still relevant? Does

(continued)

ASSIGNMENT SHEET *(continued)*

it remind you of something about our campus? Does it relate to any classes many students take? Bring both your passage and written interpretation to our first podcasting class session.

In our first podcasting class session, we will share passages aloud and discuss interpretations, as well as listen to samples of previous podcasts for this assignment. After hearing feedback from your peers in class, you will draft a transcript to record both the passage and your interpretation prior to the second class session. Your transcript/whole audio recording should include (**bolded areas are worth the majority of points**):

> The opening statement/jingle that introduces our podcast series (developed as a class)
>
> A comment on who you are, using just your first name ("I'm Christine and today I'll be reading . . .")
>
> A sentence introducing what you are reading ("This selection comes from Aristotle's *Rhetoric*" or "Today's fascinating selection comes from Cicero's *De Oratore*")
>
> The short selection you have chosen, read aloud (Cicero writes, "XYZ")
>
> **Your interpretation** ("Cicero's words are relevant to university students because . . ." or "I find this passage interesting for university students because . . ." or "It is easy to see parallels between this selection and XYZ on campus because . . .")
>
> **Your analysis/critique** (What works for you in this passage? What rhetorical techniques does the author use to make it appealing for today's students?)

In the second class session we will meet in the computer lab and record the podcasts using external microphones hooked up to computers. If you like, and are familiar with audio recording, you can also record the podcast on your own laptop using the internal microphone prior to this class session. Podcasts will be recorded using either Audacity or GarageBand software, and should be saved as MP3s. A tutorial for recording using both of these software types (including testing the microphone to make sure you are actually recording something!) will be provided at the start of the second class and then we will take turns recording our podcasts and saving them as .mp3 files. Do not worry if you make an error in recording — just start over and we will delete the error in session 3.

Bring the MP3 recording of your podcast to our third podcasting class session, as we will focus on editing your podcast for volume and clarity (including deleting rough starts and unwanted background sounds) and learn how to add sounds and background music. Podcasts can be edited using either Audacity or GarageBand, depending on whether you recorded the podcast on a PC or Mac.

When your podcast is fully edited and saved as an MP3, please post it to the discussion board on Blackboard for peer feedback. You will listen to five other podcasts by your classmates and provide feedback and they will do the same for you. You may need to revise your podcast by opening it up for editing again in Audacity or GarageBand if you have peer suggestions you want to address. Once these second edits are complete, you will "turn in" your final podcast on the discussion board for grading. I will share these final MP3 files with our campus radio station.

4. TIME AND TECHNOLOGY

This assignment can be completed in a series of two to four course sessions, depending on how and where the podcasts are recorded. The actual podcast project is composed of four separate phases: (1) recording the podcast, (2) editing the podcast, (3) posting the podcast for peer feedback, and (4) publishing the final podcast (on the radio or via Podcast Alley or iTunes).

Before starting the podcast assignment as it is described here, I ask students to review the reading for class so far, choose a meaningful passage, and write a paragraph or two of interpretation of why this excerpt stands out as something "worthy" of retelling. In the first podcasting class session we then read aloud passages and interpretations in groups or in a whole class session depending on the number of students. Because the passages are short, I typically build this activity into a brief discussion of the literary canon and why and how works might be selected as part of it. To conclude this first class session, I play some samples and introduce the podcast project using the Assignment Sheet and grading rubric in Assessment Tools. (A sample is available at ufonline.findlay.edu/bbcswebdav/users/tulley/Austin %20Searfoss%20Cicero%20De%20Oratore%20Why%20Gen%20Ed%20 Courses%20Are%20Relevant.mp3).

Podcasts can be recorded through many venues including the computer (via a built-in microphone or a microphone plugged into the audio jack), smartphone, iPad, or other tablet device. It is best for first-time podcasters to record the podcast through podcasting software that will walk students through the process; software like this is available for all of these devices. I also recommend that you record a sample podcast to understand the steps, which are very similar across programs. Free software such as Audacity, but also paid programs for Mac users such as GarageBand and Mixcraft (www .acoustica.com/mixcraft/) for Windows users offer easy-to-use tutorials. Upon opening, these programs detect audio recording devices and set up a familiar interface with a red Record button and Forward, Backward, Pause, and Stop buttons; students can click Record on screen and speak into the microphone to begin making the podcast. If labs are at a premium, this step and subsequent editing and publishing steps can be completed out of class with a tutorial onscreen in class. Many of these programs have links to free tutorial videos.

If lab space is available for recording, and a few snowball microphones can be purchased (see www.bluemic.com/snowball/), students can take turns recording with the microphones and then unplug the microphone and pass the microphone to another student at another station. Because each podcast runs less than two minutes, these can be recorded quickly, and mistakes can be left in since they can be cleaned out during editing. For a class of twenty-five students, it takes roughly one to two 50-minute sessions to get everyone's podcast recorded depending on how many microphones are available. If a student technology center is available on campus, some students may prefer to record in another location or using the microphones built into their own laptops.

Editing the Podcast

Unlike earlier audio technologies, podcasting allows students to alter "emphasis, tone, pace, delivery, and content" with ease (Selfe 638): students can add additional sounds by adding another recorded "track" on top of the audio, and can move and delete segments of the podcast easily. Because the podcasts are short, editing can usually be completed in fifteen to thirty minutes within a class period. Once audio texts are fully edited, students can compress them into MP3 formats and download them to portable devices and post them on Blackboard. They can also post them on sites such as Podcast Alley (www.podcastalley.com/) or on iTunes.

Like the recording sessions, editing sessions can be completed out of class. However, students often need a tutorial in editing that shows how to remove sections of the podcast, add sound effects, change the pitch, and raise or lower the volume in specific sections. Often editing and recording can be done in tandem if a lab is used. After students record and have passed on their microphones, they can edit at the same station where they completed their recordings. To keep the noise level low in the room, I often have students bring their headphones so they can listen to their podcasts as they work. After students have completed the editing process, both programs allow students to compress their working podcast file into an MP3 file for playback and distribution.

Publishing the Podcast

Our campus radio station (WLFC 88.3) plays public service announcements and other student projects between music sets. Once students have completed their podcasts, I have them complete an "internal" and "external" publishing step. For the internal step, students post their MP3 files in a discussion board thread in Blackboard (which could be accomplished using other course management software such as Moodle or free blogging software such as WordPress). All of the students can listen to all of the podcasts and comment individually on them and I have the students complete this step out of class as a homework assignment. Students must open and comment on five podcasts and no more than five comments can be made on a single podcast, which helps to distribute the comments evenly. Specifically, students comment on each other's interpretation of the literature to determine if it works as an interpretation for "today's college student." Having students post the podcasts in one place also helps make sure the podcasts are easily accessible for grading, and I can read the comments to gauge effectiveness of the podcast for a college audience.

After the class has read and commented on the podcasts, students are able to reopen their MP3 files and do any final edits or fixes that are deemed necessary in the audio editing software. After fixes are complete, podcasts are reposted. I download all of the final podcast files to a USB flash drive to deliver to the radio station for playing on air sporadically throughout the semester. I also allow several students who are finished early or are enthusiastic about the project to record an additional podcast used as an opening to our series. They develop a file called "Today's Classical Rhetoric Moment"— a jingle that is roughly ten seconds and is played before each of the student podcasts as an introduction. At least once each semester, the jingle is played with each student's podcast and the class typically receives a schedule to know when podcasts will be played. For faculty working on campus without a radio station venue, podcasts can easily be published on Podcast Alley, a free place to hear or publish podcasts (www.podcastalley .com/) or on iTunes (see www.apple.com/itunes/podcasts/specs.html for directions).

5. ANTICIPATING STUDENT NEEDS

Most students tend to be enthusiastic about the project, particularly when it is given in lieu of a textual interpretation or some sort of analytical writing assignment. That said, there are potential pitfalls to assigning this type of project that stem from minor technology issues. The biggest pitfall is a lack of a clean, audible recording to start. If students record too far away from the microphone, the recording will be too quiet and/or pick up background noise. Therefore I encourage all students to record a ten-second reading and to play it back to make sure they can hear it clearly before recording the full podcast. To avoid background noise, I make sure that two students are not recording next to each other at the same time if the recording process is done in lab. Snowball microphones are very good at detecting just the speaker and there are settings on the back of the microphone that students should experiment with to make sure that background noise can be muted. If a class has many students who prefer to record out of class, this in-class recording session can be reserved for just the students who need help, which helps eliminate a lot of background noise.

Another pitfall in recording occurs when students fail to leave time for dead air at the beginning: occasionally the first few words of the reading might be left off if the Record button is engaged after the student speaks. It is best to have the students hit Record and wait five seconds before speaking. Students must also be encouraged to speak slowly and thoughtfully and to work out difficult pronunciations ahead of time (audio pronunciations are available at many online dictionary sites). I usually play at least one podcast (with identifying information edited out) of a student rushing through the podcast with background noise and then a clean, clear recording of the same podcast so they can hear the difference in delivery. This modeling is helpful in illustrating why it is best not to rush this part of the assignment.

6. ASSESSMENT TOOLS

Because the podcast assignment meets several objectives, it serves as a larger assignment in this class as one of three multimodal projects that make up 60 percent of the course grade total. In my own class, the podcast is worth 10 percent of the final grade. Remaining points in the course are used for print-based projects, quizzes, and participation.

Grading Rubric			
ENGL 318 Classical Rhetoric Podcast Grading Rubric 100 points You will receive a mark in each range for each category.			
Category	Developing (below C range)	Acceptable (C–B range)	Exceeds Expectations (A range)
Presence of all parts of the assignment including (10 pts): — An opening comment introducing yourself—just first name ("I'm Christine and today I'll be reading . . .") — A sentence introducing what you are reading ("This selection comes from Aristotle's *Rhetoric*" or "Today's fascinating selection comes from Cicero's *De Oratore*.") — The short selection you have chosen, read aloud ("Cicero writes, 'XYZ'") — Your interpretation ("This is relevant to university students because . . ." or "I find this interesting for university students because . . ." or "It is easy to see parallels between this selection and XYZ on campus because . . .")			

(continued)

Grading Rubric *(continued)*			
Understanding of Passage Chosen (30 pts) — Podcast demonstrates a basic understanding of concepts in chosen passage — Podcast demonstrates a basic understanding of why the classical orator may have spoken/ written this text (What is the philosophy behind it? How do you know?)			
Quality of Interpretation (30 pts) — Student has interpreted the passage logically, with a rational explanation for why the passage still applies to today's university student.			
Quality of Delivery (20 pts) — Reading was clear, slow, and audible — No background noise — Correct pronunciations			
Comments:			

Because the audio essay retains many features of the print essay, common evaluation areas such as interpretation, clarity, depth of analysis, and so on, can be worked into the final grade. In addition, because delivery is an important (and now public) aspect of the audio essay, features of classical principles are worked into the above rubric. I carefully describe each of these categories during our introductory session prior to podcast recordings so students can see that they will lose points for an unclear recording, an inaccurate recording (a passage from Cicero attributed to Aristotle), and/or a vague interpretation that lacks a guiding thesis. As a result, most grades are fairly easy to assign using the rubric. However, one important caveat is that it is occasionally difficult to determine what a worthy (and "correct") interpretation is and what isn't. This is why the peer-review "internal" publishing step is in place. Students are able to make comments on classmates' podcasts in the Blackboard discussion board (both using names and also anonymously so they can feel free to make remarks) and I can also comment anonymously if it seems that the speaker is not making an effective case for his or her interpretation or the relevance of the passage to college students.

7. THEORETICAL BASIS FOR THE ASSIGNMENT:
Reviving an Oral Tradition: Using Podcasting to Teach Ancient Literature

In 1989, Richard Lanham argued that "we cannot preserve Western culture in a pickle. It must be recreated in the technologies of the present, especially if these technologies prove more condign to that preprint part of it which is oral and rhetorical" (279). Yet classical literature courses often are slow to change and adapt to new technologies, in part because ancient literature and modern multimodal technologies such as podcasting and web page design seem incompatible. English and classics departments teaching classical texts from Gorgias through Augustine use technologies such as video and slide-ware for lecture enhancement, online dictionaries for looking up and pronouncing Greek and Latin phrases, and even virtual tours (Lister). However, these activities tend to emphasize consumption of texts versus interaction with the material. William Magrath recognizes that integration of technology enhances teaching, but potentially at a cost of hindering student interaction with the material (284-85). Therefore, he argues, many courses are static in nature when they adopt digital and/or multimodal technologies. Rather than using technologies such as videos, online tours, or multimodal artifacts such as graffiti or images to merely deliver the material, I argue students should be encouraged to produce texts that foster critical engagement.

As one example of the difference between existing technology-enhanced courses and the more dynamic, interactive classics courses Magrath calls for, this essay offers the specific, practical example of how classical literary texts by Gorgias, Aristotle, Cicero, and others might be read, experienced, and interpreted through today's technology of podcasting. Podcasts are initially performed live and often streamed in real time. Accordingly, they offer immediacy of communication and reinscribe human physicality, through the performer's voice, in a way that previous audio recordings did not. At the same time, podcasts remain coherent artifacts of the performance because they are recorded from an initial spoken act and can be downloaded at a later date (Tulley 259).

Podcasting increases student engagement because students are required to (re)produce a classical text using modern technology and in doing so, they experience the emphasis on public oration present in many early classical texts. As a result, podcast assignments have the possibility of making ancient literature more "authentic" for students in a way that has not been previously possible. This is particularly true when using podcasts to explore

fragments of ancient literary texts, such as those from
Diotima, Hortensia, and others embedded in canonized works — oral technologies enable these figures to
come to life. Though this assignment was used in a
classical rhetoric survey course, it could easily be used
in any of the literature survey courses, and especially
those with an oral emphasis such as African American,
and so on. I typically assign the podcasting assignment in the second half
of the semester as a textual interpretation exercise in a required junior-/
senior-level classical rhetoric survey course taken by all English majors at
the University of Findlay.

> "Podcast assignments have
> the possibility of making
> ancient literature more
> 'authentic' for students."
> **Christine Tulley**

Background

The cornerstone of this podcasting assignment is a recognition that students
must experience classical texts multimodally, that is, through other modes
beyond print. In *Multimodality: A Social Semiotic Approach to Contemporary
Communication*, Gunther Kress argues that many disciplines are exploring
multimodal theory ranging from architecture to urban planning because
multimodal communication is the "normal state of human communication" (1). Extending research by the New London Group (1996) on multiliteracies (or multiple ways of making literacy beyond print), Pamela Takayoshi
and Cynthia Selfe define multimodal texts as those that
"exceed the alphabetic and may include still and moving
images, animations, color, words, music and sound" (1).
Though discussions of multimodal texts typically center on digital technologies, Jody Shipka also argues that
multimodality refers to a broader range of nontechno-
logical "texts" that include paintings, sculptures, graffiti, and so on (300). In
short, multimodality assumes audio and visual texts are as valuable as print. .

> "Multimodality assumes
> audio and visual texts are as
> valuable as print."
> **Christine Tulley**

Within English studies, interest and development of multimodal theory
has primarily taken place in rhetoric and composition; however, the classical literature survey course is an excellent fit for multimodality. As I have
made the case elsewhere (Tulley and Blair), embracing multimodality is a
useful pedagogical method to immerse students in producing/experiencing
canonical texts and interpretations of them. Many early classical texts were
initially oral and social media tools, using gesture, setting, and emotion to
convey and distribute messages to a nonliterate society. Because students can
demonstrate classical rhetorical techniques from Greek and Roman oratory
learned in class as part of reading classical works, the podcast genre is effective in getting students to call on noted effective rhetorical strategies for live
performance that have been used for thousands of years, such as repetition,
emotion, segmentation, and narrative (Perelman and Olbrechts-Tyteca). As
an added benefit, this may be a more authentic way to study these texts.

Second, as Lister argues, if the teaching of classical literature tends to be somewhat static even when technologies are used, requiring students make their own podcasts allows them to become "curators" of artifacts within the classroom community (Lee, et al. 292) and to generate knowledge with the potential to decentralize hierarchies between the instructor as "active lecturer" and the student as "passive listener" (Tulley 262). Finally, there is some early evidence that students are receptive to putting other classics tools such as flashcards on portable devices such as iPods and other MP3 players (Reinhard). My experience with this assignment shows students are willing to create and distribute audio texts as another method to learn the material.

8. CONCLUSION

As the above interpretation assignment illustrates, the podcast assignment works well with the oral tradition of classical literature as it returns texts to "their native rhetorical orality" versus continuing to "mistranslate them according to the coordinates of philosophical print" (Lanham 270). By re-"creating" a classical passage orally, editing it for effective delivery, and interpreting the message of the passage for an authentic audience, students tend to better understand classical pieces. They have not only "read" the literature in print but also read it orally, while practicing effective oral techniques such as narration and segmentation, and repackaged it for a modern-day audience. In addition to increased audience awareness and critical attention to their own audio texts, because they also listen to each other's podcasts, students tend to remember those pieces as well, leading to a more engaged understanding of classical literature as a field.

As an added bonus, podcasting does appear to increase student interest in the classical rhetoric survey. Though this course has the reputation of being difficult and perhaps irrelevant, when students compose audio texts for the campus radio station, I have found they often encourage friends and relatives to tune in, call in to the radio station to make repeat "requests" for classmates' podcasts, and post links to the podcasts on Facebook and other social media venues. In the past four years I've taught this assignment, I've noticed that students are more adept at using the built-in microphones on laptops and are more likely to experiment with enhancing their podcasts with sound effects found on free sound archive sites. Early podcasts strictly consisted of students reading with background music; today's podcasts often have subtle sound effects layered over music, with both serving as secondary texts to the student voices. Podcasting allows students to sell the course to others by providing an opportunity for students to demonstrate the relevance and accessibility of the material, as well as to see how classical literature is applicable in the twenty-first century.

9. WORKS CITED

Kress, Gunther. *Multimodality: A Social Semiotic Approach to Contemporary Communication.* Routledge, 2010.

Lanham, Richard A. "The Electronic Word: Literary Study and the Digital Revolution." *New Literary History*, vol. 20, no. 2, 1989, pp. 265-90.

Lee, Mark J. W., et al. "Learning to Collaborate, Collaboratively: An Online Community Building and Knowledge Construction Approach to Teaching Computer-Supported Collaborative Work at an Australian University." *Proceedings of the 2005 Association for Educational Communications and Technology International Convention.* Edited by Michael R. Simonson and Margaret Crawford. Nova Southeastern U, 2005, pp. 286-306.

Lister, Robert. "Integrating ICT into the Classics Classroom." *Journal of Classics Teaching,* 2007, www.classicsteaching.com/research_pdfs/RP9_Lister _2007_F.pdf.

Lynne A. Kvapil, "Teaching Archaeological Pragmatism through Problem-Based Learning." *The Classical Journal*, vol. 105, no. 1, 2009, pp. 45-52.

Magrath, William. "A Return to Interactivity: The Third Wave in Educational Uses of Information Technology." *CALICO Journal*, vol. 18, no. 2, 2001, pp. 283-94.

New London Group. "A Pedagogy of Multiliteracies: Designing Social Futures." *Harvard Educational Review*, vol. 66, 1996, pp. 60-92.

Perelman, Chaim, and Lucie Olbrechts-Tyteca. *The New Rhetoric: A Treatise on Argumentation.* U of Notre Dame P, 1969.

Reinhard, Andrew. "Latin for Handheld Technologies." 1 May 2008. *eLatin eGreek eLearn.* Web. 15 June 2012.

Shipka, Jody. "A Multimodal Task-Based Framework for Composing." *College Composition and Communication*, vol 57, no. 2, 2005, pp. 277-306.

Selfe, Cynthia L. "The Movement of Air, the Breath of Meaning: Aurality and Multimodal Composing." *College Composition and Communication*, vol. 60, no. 4, 2009, pp. 616-63.

Takayoshi, Pamela, and Cynthia L. Selfe. "Thinking about Multimodality." *Multimodal Composition: Resources for Teachers.* Edited by Cynthia L. Selfe. Hampton, 2007.

Tulley, Christine. "IText Reconfigured: The Rise of the Podcast." *Journal of Business and Technical Communication*, vol. 25, no. 3, 2011, pp. 256-75.

Tulley, Christine, and Kristine Blair. "Remediating the Book Review." *Pedagogy*, vol. 9, no. 3, 2009, pp. 441-89.

19

Dialogism in the Classroom: Creating Digital Audiobooks to Teach Literary Theory

Jenne Powers
Wheelock College

Jenne Powers teaches writing and literature courses at Wheelock College in Boston. Her regular course offerings include Critical Writing and Reading and Writing as Social Action as well as courses in Russian literature. After completing a dissertation on fictional treatments of Soviet historiography, her research interests shifted to the pedagogy of literature and representations of pedagogy and education in classic Russian fiction.

COURTESY OF JENNE POWERS

1. OVERVIEW

- **Assignment:** Record an audiobook version of a narratively complex novel—in this case, *Notes from Underground* by Fyodor Dostoevsky. Upon completion of audio recording, students use the experience of articulating and listening to literary language to better understand M. M. Bakhtin's theory of dialogic discourse.

- **Courses:** Literature courses that incorporate novels or other long works (introductory and upper division); literary theory.

- **Literature:** First-person confessional narrative. To facilitate audio recording, the literary work should be of moderate length. The theoretical essays I use deal with *Notes from Underground* explicitly; however each is sufficiently broad to apply to many first-person narratives. Alternative works by Bakhtin, such as excerpts from his "Discourse in the Novel," would apply to novels with multiple narrative levels.

- **Technology:** Computers or tablets with microphones that can record sound as well as a software program or application that can produce audio files to be shared digitally. Classroom technology that allows for playing audio files may also be required.

- **Time:** Eight hours, or a little more than two weeks, of class time. The audiobook project is well suited for the beginning of the semester as it helps build community in the classroom and reinforces effective reading habits.

2. GOALS OF THE ASSIGNMENT

- To reinforce active reading habits
- To promote rereading of difficult texts
- To understand the nature and purpose of literary theory

"Asking undergraduate students to create digital audiobooks together encourages them to reread complex texts and improves the quality and depth of their analyses."

Jenne Powers
Wheelock College

3. ASSIGNMENT SHEET

Dialogism in the Classroom: Creating Digital Audiobooks to Teach Literary Theory

Course: _____

Instructor: _____

Date: _____

Notes from Underground: Monologue, Dialogue, or Both?

Guidelines for Audio Recording

As a class, we will record an audiobook version of *Notes from Underground* by Fyodor Dostoevsky. Each of you will be assigned about five pages to prepare to read aloud, and you will schedule a time to record yourself reading in the library near my office.

I will use the attached rubric to evaluate you based on the pace, clarity, and expressiveness of your reading. In order to prepare, you should become very familiar with your excerpt of the novel! Check the meaning and pronunciation of unfamiliar words. Look at the structure of your excerpt. Decide when you should read quickly to convey the narrator's rush of words or slowly to convey his thought process. Vary your pace according to variations in the text. Decide when you should pause and for how long. Consider how your section of text relates to the meaning of the work as a whole. Ask yourself how the narrator feels, what he is trying to convey, and why he uses the words and images that he does. Make sure that your tone of voice conveys your answers to these questions.

I will edit your recordings and post them in order on our learning management system, Moodle. If you would like to burn a CD or to copy the files onto a flash drive, you are welcome to make arrangements to come to my office to do so if you are not able to download the files on your own computer. Listen to the book while preparing to write your critical debate essay.

Guidelines for Critical Debate Essay

After reflecting on the experience of reading the underground man's words aloud, take a position on the debate that emerges from the critical essays we have read and discussed by M. M. Bakhtin and Victor Erlich. Is this literary work essentially dialogic or monologic? Is it something in between? Support your position by analyzing examples from the text.

Begin your essay with an introduction. Your introduction should include background information necessary for an educated general audience to understand the topic. Your introduction should also contain your thesis statement: your position on the debate. Introductions in academic writing predict the content

(*continued*)

ASSIGNMENT SHEET (*continued*)

of the essay that follows. While you should have a thesis statement before you begin writing, it is often a good idea to write the introduction last.

Next, summarize the position of each critic. Use the key terms and definitions discussed in class. You may include representative quotations to illustrate each critic's ideas, or you may convey their ideas in your own words.

After that, provide examples from *Notes from Underground* to illustrate your point of view and support your position. You will choose examples from the book that you find to be essentially dialogic or essentially monologic. Organize these examples. Use transitions to link them. Remember that any quotation should be accompanied by your commentary. As a general rule, your commentary should be longer than the quotation. For example, if you quote three lines from the book, include five lines of interpretation and analysis in your words.

Finally, include a conclusion. Your conclusion may sum up your essay. While it is true that conclusions should not bring up new ideas related to your thesis, you might raise questions for further discussion, recognizing that your paper was necessarily brief. While I am not requiring a certain number of pages, I do expect that most successful essays will be 4–5 pages long.

4. TIME AND TECHNOLOGY

Preparing for this assignment requires some work on the part of the instructor. The novel should be divided into approximately equal sections, one for each student in the class; however, each section should have some internal coherence—a logical beginning and end point. *Notes from Underground* is divided into fairly short chapters, and the narrator's abrupt shifts in tone provide opportunities to subdivide the longer chapters. To assign sections to students, I use alphabetical order. I do believe that allowing students to sign up for a preferred section of the novel could work, depending on class dynamics and size.

Reading, discussion, and explication of both *Notes from Underground* and the accompanying critical essays requires, in my experience, about eight hours of class time. I spend two hours on each part of the novel, two hours on the excerpt from Bakhtin, and one hour discussing Erlich's essay and the nature of a critical debate. Finally, we spend one hour of class discussing the novel again in terms of the theoretical perspectives. During this time, students are completing their audio recordings outside of class. After these class discussions and audio recordings are complete, I find that students need at least a week to draft their critical debate essay. I strongly recommend scheduling one-on-one conferences about this essay owing to the difficulty of the subject matter, especially for students enrolled in courses taught at an introductory level for nonliterature majors. At the same time, these one-on-one conferences allow students to talk through their ideas and reformulate their argument with an interested listener, reinforcing, in a sense, the dialogic nature of their own writing.

This assignment requires that you and your students have access to a computer or tablet with a microphone capable of recording sound, as well as software or an application that can edit sound recordings and combine or collect multiple recordings. Students can generate their own audio recordings on their own computers; however, I find it easier to manage the recordings myself to ensure that they are all in the same usable format. I have used an Apple IMac desktop computer located near my office that had GarageBand installed and had the students come to my office area to do their recordings. Most of the activities described could also be completed by reserving a computer lab. I used GarageBand to edit the sound recordings. I did not attempt to create one large file; rather, I simply edited to eliminate long pauses and interruptions and to equalize the volume. Then I exported each separate file to iTunes, where I made a playlist, titling each recording according to its place in the novel and listing the reader as the artist. I used the iTunes format based on student input. Other sound editing programs would certainly work as well as GarageBand.

I have also used a tablet with an audio memo application installed. This method has the advantage of allowing for more student involvement in the file management process. Once students record their chapter of the audiobook, they can e-mail the file to themselves and upload it on Moodle, with their names and chapter segments as titles. In theory, students could also complete this task on their own devices; however, most audio memo applications that allow sending large files as e-mails are not free, so students prefer to use my tablet. The use of an audio memo application also does not allow for editing, so the files may include long pauses and unstandardized volume.

I used my institution's learning management system, Moodle, to share the audio recordings with the students. Uploading each file onto the learning management system allows students to access them on their own, at their own pace. Some students preferred to copy the files onto disk so that they could listen to them on personal audio devices, and I allowed them to come to my office to do so if they could not complete the task with their own computers.

After the recording was complete, we also listened to portions of the book in class using classroom computer technology.

5. ANTICIPATING STUDENT NEEDS

Difficulties with this assignment arise in two areas. The first is student anxiety. Many students will find this assignment intimidating because of either the technology or the act of reading aloud. Students should be connected with resources on campus—librarians, IT support, public speaking coaches—who can help them prepare for the assignment. Our campus has a well-received program run by theater faculty providing coaching in oral presentations. I brought an oral presentation coach in to do a workshop with my class prior to the assignment. Offering the students time to practice in class or in office hours may also reduce anxiety.

The second area of difficulty is more challenging to address. Students with physical or learning disabilities may find this activity very challenging. Many students with language-based learning disabilities find reading printed material out loud difficult, and they may require extra time and practice to complete their audio recordings. Additionally, students with vision or hearing impairments may find the task nearly impossible to complete. In such cases, disability services staff should be able to help determine appropriate accommodations for the student, and the student him- or herself may have ideas for participating in a way that is both comfortable and productive.

6. ASSESSMENT TOOLS

I evaluate both the audio recording and the subsequent research paper. Evaluating audio recordings poses serious difficulties, as most of us trained to teach literature are not trained to evaluate what might be considered a performance. Students tend to express apprehension about the subjective nature of grading in general, and that apprehension is magnified with an assignment like this one. To address this difficulty, I developed the rubric on page 298 that situates the audio recording within the evaluative standards of literary analysis, and I reference the rubric on the assignment sheet and distribute it along with the assignment guidelines. I evaluate students' recordings in three categories: clarity, pace, and expressiveness. The clarity with which they read reveals their understanding of the subject matter and the assignment. The pace at which they read reveals their understanding of the work's structure. The expressiveness of their tone reveals the extent to which they have developed an interpretation of the passage.

Many considerations remain up to the individual instructor. The audio recording and the critical debate essay may be evaluated separately or together. Feedback may be given in written or oral form. The actual extent to which one assignment influences the other might be evaluated through a reflection piece. My preference is to evaluate the audio recording and the essay separately. I have found that some students who struggle with writing are able to express their understanding of the text by reading aloud with clear and appropriate dramatic inflections. Similarly, some students who write exceptionally well may fumble with oral language. Providing separate feedback allows students to understand and reflect on their strengths. Finally, in an intermediate or advanced literature class, the goals, objectives, and evaluative standards may appear quite differently, and I would expect that students would express an understanding of how reading aloud and listening to audio recordings affects their understanding of audience as an actual and theoretical construct.

Audio Recording Rubric

	1	2	3	4
Pace	The pace of the reading interferes with communication, rendering the audio recording too difficult to listen to.	Student reads too quickly or too slowly. The pace of the reading interferes with communication of the novel's meaning at many points and suggests that the student does not understand the reading.	Student reads at a measured pace and makes an attempt to vary his/her tempo; however, the significance of variations is unclear, suggesting that the student might not fully understand the reading.	Student reads at a measured pace yet varies his/her tempo according to changes in the novel's structure, using his/her voice to communicate shifts in the organization of the plot.
Clarity	Student stumbles so frequently that the recording is difficult to understand. The student appears to be questioning what she/he is reading.	Student stumbles occasionally and frequently mispronounces or misses words or phrases. Student occasionally reveals that he/she does not understand what is being read.	Student reads with generally clear enunciation and pronunciation, revealing that she/he has prepared the excerpt and rehearsed the reading and that she/he has a basic understanding of the text.	Student reads with clear enunciation and pronunciation, revealing that she/he has prepared the excerpt and rehearsed the reading and that she/he clearly understands the meaning and import of each word.
Tone	The tone is inappropriate for the subject matter. Student may laugh, groan, or otherwise indicate that he/she has not interpreted the text's meaning.	Student occasionally reads with expression and emotion, but the emotions conveyed do not always connect to the words read.	Student generally reads with expression and emotion, though some moments may be unclear or disconnected from the overall interpretation of the passage's meaning.	Student reads with expression and emotion, when appropriate, conveying not only an understanding of the text but also an interpretation of its meaning.

7. THEORETICAL BASIS FOR THE ASSIGNMENT:
Dialogism in the Classroom: Creating Digital Audiobooks to Teach Literary Theory

Teaching sophisticated works of literature in an introductory general education course offers opportunities to present students with their first taste of literary theory, potentially enriching their reading experience for years to come. Yet literary theory can also alienate students, especially those who do not consider themselves strong readers or, conversely, those wedded to the romantic idea of delving into a novel without intellectualizing the experience.

The assignment presented in this chapter is based on the premise that one of the most important theoretical approaches to the novel, M. M. Bakhtin's concept of dialogization, can be taught through digital pedagogy in a way that engages students creatively, overcoming both insecurities about and resistance to theory. This assignment was developed in the context of an introductory literature course focusing on Dostoyevsky and taught as a first-year seminar at a small liberal arts school with a commitment to preparing students for education, social work, and other human services professions. The first-year seminar program offers students a chance to take their first general education course in a subject of interest to them with a group of like-minded first-year students. This particular course introduces students to Dostoevsky's works through close reading and analysis of two major novels and several shorter works. Throughout the course, students access course material and express their developing understanding of literary analysis through multiple media: several short reflections (written and oral), two oral presentations, two critical essays, and three creative projects (visual, performed, and/or written).

The first creative project requires students to produce digital audio recordings of assigned segments of the novel outside of class, while in class we read and discuss an excerpt from Bakhtin's *Problems of Dostoevsky's Poetics* and an essay by Victor Erlich, "Notes on the Uses of Monologue in Artistic Prose." Students are then asked to listen to the group audiobook and, using their experience as narrators and listeners, compose an essay on the question of whether this extended first-person narrative is essentially dialogic or monologic. In other words, does the narrator's discourse presume the presence of another and alter itself based on this awareness of competing worldviews? Or is the narration a fundamental expression of alienation? Although Dostoyevsky's works lend themselves particularly well to this activity, any novel, whether or not written in the first person, might be analyzed in terms of its dialogic qualities, some with greater success than others.

The actual recording of their section of the audiobook promotes an understanding of the nature of literary theory. Theories arise to propose answers to problems. Often for students, the problems inherent in the nature of literary works are unclear, so the very existence of literary theory makes little sense. By embodying the voice of the narrator and listening to others do the same, students gain a true insight into a theoretical problem of literary narrative: Who is the narrator speaking to? Is the audience present in the text or not?

This activity makes literary theory into a real communicative situation. Fields such as psychology and human development regularly teach theory through observation, but literary communication is nearly impossible to observe, based as it is in human consciousness and our relationship to texts and stories. This assignment attempts to bridge that gap of possibility through technology. By becoming the narrators, in the sense that they embody the voice that communicates the novel's content, students get to feel what motivates the words. They put themselves on both sides of the communication act. Reading the novel, they imagine themselves in the position of the audience; recording the audiobook, they imagine themselves in the position of the narrator. Having experienced both roles prepares students to better understand Bakhtin and to better debate the nature of the narrator-narratee relationship. They may choose to share Bakhtin's view that all discourse is oriented toward and affected by the inevitable presence of another consciousness whose worldview shapes the language as much as that of the speaker. Alternatively, they may choose to agree with Erlich that monologue as a literary form underscores the theme of alienation from society and that the language of monologue is artistically designed to reflect the consciousness of the speaking character alone.

> "This activity makes literary theory into a real communicative situation."
>
> **Jenne Powers**

This assignment was created in accordance with the principles of Universal Design for Learning (UDL). Universal Design began as an approach to architecture: rather than retrofit buildings to accommodate people with physical disabilities, architects began to design buildings that could be accessed by anyone, arguing that such design actually benefits all users. Educators quickly picked up on the concept, finding that accommodating students with learning disabilities did not benefit the entire classroom as much as designing lessons and assessments with all learning styles and abilities in mind (Pliner and Johnson 107).

> "This assignment was created in accordance with the principles of Universal Design for Learning (UDL)."
>
> **Jenne Powers**

As an approach to curriculum development, UDL proposes that all students benefit from accessing course material through multiple media, expressing their understanding through multiple media, and engaging actively in their own learning (National Center on Universal Design for Learning). This activity allows students to engage the novel in multiple ways, through reading the text of the book, discussing the content and style in class, reading a segment out loud, and listening to the entire text. Additionally, students are able to express their understanding of the novel in two ways: reading and recording their segment and writing a critical essay. Finally, the project engages students in their own learning by providing an authentic experience with literary theory that is challenging yet has clear objectives and outcomes.

Students read *Notes from Underground* early in the semester, so this assignment sequence takes place within the first month of the course and works toward several introductory goals. First and foremost, it reinforces good reading habits. One specific objective I have is to teach the necessity of rereading for literary analysis. One time through is most often not enough to gain an understanding of how a piece of literature works. In *Notes from Underground*, this rereading is particularly crucial, as information presented in part one of the novel takes on new meaning after the reading of part two.

My second objective is to promote active reading. Preparing to read a text aloud makes explicit the rationale behind annotating a text. Students have a real need to define unfamiliar words and to think about their meaning in a specific context. Likewise, when students mark in their texts where they will pause, they are thinking about the structure of a passage. To prepare for their recording, they slow down their reading and consider each element comprising a passage. As they identify important images and interactions in their passages, they will be relating these moments to their overall interpretation of the novel. At the same time, the careful reading of literary theoretical debate helps students to understand that genuine problems often offer no single correct answer. While reading Dostoevsky, Bakhtin, and Erlich, students must begin to consider viewpoints that might differ from their own and the assumptions that underlie both arguments and works of fiction. In doing so, students engage in what Richard Paul calls, in a nod to Bakhtin, "dialogic thinking," a practice that promotes the development of critical thinking skills essential for students' development as scholars and professionals.

8. CONCLUSION

Using audio recordings offers both reluctant and avid readers an opportunity to read academically in a new way that promotes a sense of community in the classroom as well as opportunities for individual expression. Students have responded very enthusiastically to this assignment. They take pride in their own recordings, and they report that they share these recordings with friends and family, connecting their experiences in the classroom with their lives outside of the classroom. Students also express great interest in their classmates' recordings, and by listening to other interpretations of voice, inflection, and intention, they begin to see themselves as part of a community of engaged learners. As they listen to one another's recordings (often multiple times) at home, they begin to see their classmates' contributions as valuable to their own learning, and they develop greater respect for their peers.

> "By listening to other interpretations of voice, inflection, and intention, they begin to see themselves as part of a community of engaged learners."
>
> **Jenne Powers**

The written essay that accompanies the audio recordings provides evidence of student learning. I have found these essays to be written at a level considerably higher than that of comparable first-year students. The audiobook project makes the theoretical dilemma a real and vital problem for the students, so their thesis statements are specific and arguable. They have become more familiar with the novel, so their use of textual evidence is creative and purposeful. The students have experienced the rewards of reading texts closely and reading texts more than once, so their engagement with subsequent texts is greater.

While this assignment complements study of Dostoyevsky's narrative style exceptionally well, I believe that, as Bakhtin's theories have been applied far beyond the texts he used to formulate them, so can this assignment be utilized in a wide range of literature courses. Using the critical essays described here, an audiobook assignment exploring the variations among first-person narrators in William Faulkner's *As I Lay Dying* would certainly deepen students' engagement with that text. Ralph Ellison's *Invisible Man*, influenced as it is by Dostoyevsky's work, would also make a good case (although because of its length it could not be recorded in its entirety). Alternative theoretical essays, such as excerpts from Bakhtin's "Discourse in the Novel," would apply to novels with multiple narrative levels, such as Emily Brontë's *Wuthering Heights*. To provide a context of theoretical debate for novels not written in the first person, students could compare and contrast Bakhtin's concept of heteroglossia with Seymour Chatman's more structured treatment of overt and covert narration in *Story and Discourse*.

9. WORKS CITED

Bakhtin, M. M. *The Dialogic Imagination: Four Essays.* Edited by Michael Holquist. U of Texas P, 1981.

Chatman, Seymour. *Story and Discourse: Narrative Structure in Fiction and Film.* Cornell UP, 1978.

Dostoyevsky, Fyodor, and Michael R. Katz. *Notes from Underground: An Authoritative Translation, Backgrounds and Sources, Responses, Criticism.* Norton, 2001.

National Center on Universal Design for Learning. "What Is UDL?" *CAST*, www.udlcenter.org/aboutudl/whatisudl. Accessed 10 Sept. 2012.

Paul, Richard W. "Dialogical Thinking: Critical Thought Essential to the Acquisition of Rational Knowledge and Passions." *Teaching Thinking Skills: Theory and Practice.* Edited by Joan Baron and Robert Sternberg. Freeman, 127-48.

Pliner, Susan M., and Julia R. Johnson. "Historical, Theoretical, and Foundational Principles of Universal Instructional Design in Higher Education." *Equity and Excellence in Education*, vol. 37, no. 2, 2004, pp. 105-13.

PART FOUR ASSIGNMENTS

Multimodalities

20

Lit Recipes: Creating Recipes for Literary Characters

Amanda Hill
University of Central Florida

Amanda Hill is an artist, scholar, educator, and PhD student in text and technology at the University of Central Florida. She holds a BA in theater performance from Susquehanna University and an MFA in theater for young audiences from the University of Central Florida. Her articles have been published in *Incite/ Insight* and on TYA/USA's NEXTBlog. She has presented at NEMLA, SWPACA, the Florida Theatre Conference, the Georgia Theatre Conference, and the University of South Florida.

COURTESY OF AMANDA HILL

1. OVERVIEW

- **Assignment:** Deconstruct a literary text in order to create a recipe for a character using the character's personality traits.
- **Courses:** Any literature course; any composition course that incorporates literature.
- **Literature:** Any.
- **Technology:** Computer lab with video and audio editing software; Internet access; microphones for audio recording; headphones for each student; DVD burner, flash drive, and or cloud storage; digital camera and a scanner are optional.
- **Time:** For a forty-five-minute class that meets three times a week, this lesson will take roughly three weeks. This time frame can be extended or shortened depending on class time and out-of-class assignments.

2. GOALS OF THE ASSIGNMENT

After completing this assignment, students will be able to:

- use clues from a text to gain an understanding of a literary character;
- implement a process for creating a digital story;

- identify character traits;
- organize character traits in an abstract but meaningful way;
- appreciate the importance of character development in literature; and
- appreciate their ability to create a digital, multimodal final product.

The lists of guiding questions included in the assignment that follows are an amalgamation of abstract and concrete character analysis questions which I have culled over the years from various acting and writing programs around the country. These were highly effective with the original residency, where I aimed to cultivate an artistic voice within the writing.

"This 'literary recipe' asks students to deconstruct a literary text in order to create a recipe for a character using his or her personality traits."

Amanda Hill
University of Central Florida

3. ASSIGNMENT SHEET

Lit Recipes: Creating Recipes for Literary Characters

Course: _____

Instructor: _____

Date: _____

Introduction

If someone wanted to create a copy of you, what recipe would they use? "Lit Recipes" ask you to deconstruct a literary text in order to create a recipe for a character using the character's personality traits.

For this assignment, you will imagine a literary character is the final product of a recipe. Just as a cookie recipe involves certain ingredients, each character should be thought of as being made up of ingredients. The recipes are accompanied by a set of specific cooking instructions. The ingredients and instructions, as you see them, would be needed to re-create your chosen literary character. The assignment also requires you to defend your choices.

Prewriting

Begin choosing a character from a book of your choice, or I can assign a character for you. In general, you will want to choose a character who plays a major role in moving the story forward, as authors tend to flesh out these characters the most.

Brainstorm answers to the following three questions:

1. What does the character say about him- or herself?
2. What do others say about the character?
3. What actions does the character perform? (What does the character do?)

This last question is especially important. Remember, actions can speak louder than words. Often, a character's actions define what kind of person he or she is. Ingredients can be abstract, like love or jealousy, or concrete, like a guitar or a box of chocolates, and do not necessarily need to be plausible for cooking purposes. I encourage you to think outside the box! You will engage in a character analysis in which you envision your character as different objects or sensations. To get started, consider some of these questions:

- If your character were an animal, what would he or she be?
- If your character were a color, what would he or she be?
- If your character were a spice, what would he or she be?
- If your character were a mode of transportation, what would he or she be?

(continued)

ASSIGNMENT SHEET (*continued*)

- If your character were an element (earth, wind, water, fire) what would he or she be? In what ways are the two similar?

- If your character were a texture, what would he or she feel like?

- If your character were a musical instrument what would he or she look like? What would he or she sound like? Are these instruments different? Why or why not? Close your eyes and envision the sound. What colors are the sounds?

You will also analyze the type of person your character is by focusing on his/her actions and words as guidance. Use some or all of the following prompts to help you brainstorm.

- What are the turning points of your character's situation? What qualities does he or she exhibit here that he or she didn't exhibit before?

- Who do you know that reminds you of your character? Try rereading the book, or sections of the book, and imagine this person speaking your character's lines and performing his or her actions. How does this change your interpretation of the character? What can you now infer about your character?

- Is your character weak or strong? Emotionally? Physically? What factors contribute to your conclusion?

- What are the most notable personality traits of your character?

- What does your character look like? Think about his or her age, ethnicity, gender, height, and weight. Is your character able-bodied? Does he or she have any physical differences? How do these physical qualities affect his or her daily life and actions?

- What are your character's favorite pastimes? Does he or she play any sports? Create art? Make music?

- What happened to your character before the start of the book? What characteristics developed from these situations?

- How does he or she relate to others? Is he or she bossy? Meek?

- What is your character's main goal? What tactics does he or she employ to achieve it? What characteristics can you infer from his or her determination or lack thereof?

- What does your character think about him- or herself? Is it different from what he or she says?

- Describe your character in three words.

- Describe your character in a metaphor or figure of speech.

- Make lists of your character's positive and negative traits.

- As you read the book, how did you feel about the character? At what parts did you hate him or her? Love him or her? Feel sorry for him or her? Can you identify at what points in sharing your story you felt certain emotions?
- How do you want your audience to feel about and relate to your character? Do you want them to commiserate with him or her? To hate him or her? To love him or her? What is the overall tone you want to convey? When the piece is done how do you want the audience to feel about your character?

Writing

Choose your character's ingredients from the list you generated during your brainstorming session. Then, narrow your list to include only your character's most essential ingredients — with a minimum of 3 ingredients to a maximum of 10. Keep in mind that sometimes the most necessary ingredients in a recipe come in small quantities. A cinnamon bun without the cinnamon would just be a bun, even though the amount of cinnamon is less in quantity than, say, the flour. (However, it is important to note that in the case of cinnamon buns, flour is also a necessary ingredient.)

For each ingredient, be sure to provide information on measurement — how many tons, quarts, cups, tablespoons, drams, and so on, of the specific ingredient that the recipe requires. It might help to take a look around your kitchen or a grocery store to get an idea of possible measurements. Keep in mind that different units of measurement can enhance the rhythm of your recipe. Don't be afraid to be bold in your word choices.

Once you finalize your list of ingredients (and the measurements of each), think about how these ingredients are prepared. Do they get mixed together at one time or separately? Or maybe, the ingredient is layered or folded in? Don't forget that your recipe can be split into multiple parts. Maybe some of the ingredients make a topping for the main dish, like icing on a cookie. Next, think about how the mixture of ingredients would need to be cooked (baked, broiled, steamed, grilled, etc.) and served (on a bed of something? with a side dish of something else?). Be specific (and bold) in your instructions.

Reviewing and Revising

Now it's time to peer-review your recipe and the recipes of others in your class. Then, make any necessary adjustments and edits to your recipe. Even though this assignment is a poetic one, be sure to review your grammar and spelling. Once your recipe is finalized, create a clean, typed copy of the recipe.

Storyboarding

Next, break up your recipe into segments. Each segment should have its own image and voice-over, and can include one or more ingredients or instructions. The segments should be prepared in accordance with your vision of your final

(continued)

ASSIGNMENT SHEET (*continued*)

digital story. Your story should have a minimum of 3 segments and a maximum of 10. You will use the following storyboard template to plan the flow of your digital story.

The 4 components that make up a single frame of the digital story are as follows:

1. Image box: Use to write or draw the picture you want to find or take and use for that frame. The images designated should only be used for the Recipe Text directly below the image.

2. Transition box: Envision the type of transition you would like to use to move from one frame to the next.

3. Recipe Text lines: Write the words from the recipe that go with the image; no more, no less. The Recipe Text should move in order across the storyboard.

4. Special Effects line: This is optional and does not need to be used for all — or any — of the frames. However, if you desire, Special Effects are available with most movie editing software. Be careful not to overdo it! Remember, the content is more important than the effect!

As you envision the images you want to use in your project, you will also draw or write an explanation of these images and add the appropriate text to the storyboard. Make sure the frames stay in the order of your recipe. When your images and text are all designated in the storyboard, you will add transitions and special effects, if desired. Feel free to use as many storyboard sheets as needed to complete your recipe. Remember, the storyboard is your friend! A well-detailed storyboard will save a great deal of time in the computer lab and makes the recording process simpler because it limits the editing time.

Creating a Voice-Over

A voice-over is simply a digital recording of you reading your recipe. To begin working on your voice-over, it might help to think of someone you know who has a very animated voice. Consider what this person does to make his or her voice sound animated and exciting.

Review your recipe and highlight the operative — or most important — words, the ones you will want to emphasize when recording. Imagine that the words in your recipe — especially the nouns and the verbs — are onomatopoeias, meaning, the words *sound* like what they mean. A good example of this might be the difference in the vocal quality of a *dash* versus a *gallon*. If you try to vocalize the difference between a "dash" and a "gallon," it becomes possible to hear the difference in size. Be sure to take time practicing before you record your voice-over. A dull voice-over can ruin a listener's experience of a digital story. Remember that it is crucial to keep your audience engaged and excited. Be sure to enunciate your words, and speak slowly so the words have time to reach their full effect and be understood. The sound of your voice can greatly enhance the meaning of your words and affect the entire meaning of your digital story.

When you are satisfied with the way your recipe sounds as you read it, find a quiet room where you can make a digital recording. The best way to do this is to record each segment separately. This way you can redo certain parts with ease. Be sure to number the order of your files to make editing easier. Your next step will be to load your segment recordings into the video editing software available to you.

Finding Images

Here, you have one of two options. You can stage your envisioned pictures and capture them with a digital camera or you can use royalty-free images from the Internet. For example, you may want to use royalty-free images from the US government available at www.usa.gov/Topics/Graphics.shtml. You may also choose to find pictures using Creative Commons, a site that provides access to images and media, many of which are available for public use (creativecommons.org). Remember: images have the power to say things words can't. Choose your images wisely and creatively. Ask yourself: How does the image enhance my recipe? Does the image complement or work against the text/spoken words of my recipe? Once you have collected the images you'd like to use, put them into the video editing software you are using and arrange them chronologically.

Constructing Your Digital Story

When your images and voice-over that are attached to your project are in the editing software, you are ready to begin the construction process. One good judge of quality is how well timed a digital story is, so be sure to align your voice-over and images accurately in accordance with your storyboards. Also, use care when adding transitions and special effects to your story. Think about how these elements can enhance your final story, rather than overpower it. As you use transitions and effects, think about your audience. You want the flow of your story to engage (not distract) your audience. Have some fun, but don't overdo it.

Peer-Reviewing, Publishing, and Showcasing

If time allows, you will peer-review your digital story before you finalize it. Use helpful feedback from peers to revise and clarify your story as needed. When you are satisfied that your digital story is complete, you will publish it as a movie file. We will host a public showcase/art opening featuring of all student Lit Recipes and digital stories.

4. TIME AND TECHNOLOGY

This assignment immerses students in contemporary communication tools, allowing them to learn the invaluable skills associated with computer literacy. Therefore it requires a lot of technology, but have no fear! Indispensable tutorials can be easily found as part of the programs, online, and in print in many bookstores and libraries.

To complete this assignment, students will need access to computers equipped with video editing software such as Window's Movie Maker, iMovie, or Final Cut. Both Window's Movie Maker and iMovie come installed on all new computers. Final Cut is an advanced video editor that is available from most software retailers. Students will also need access to electronic microphones, which are installed on many new computers—especially laptops—but can also be purchased as an accessory that can be attached to most computers by USB. For best sound quality, have students record their voice-over in a room free of ambient sound and other voices. If students are also responsible for editing their voice-over, they will need access to sound editing software such as Nero, Audacity, or GarageBand, which comes installed on most Mac computers. If students are working in a computer lab or other communal place, it is important for them to have headphones with which they can listen to their projects while creating them. If desired and available, students can use digital cameras to capture the images for their digital stories instead of using images from Internet archives. Digital cameras may also provide an opportunity for students to capture sound and video to incorporate into their digital stories. Existing photos can also be digitized with the use of a scanner. To save completed projects, students will need access to a computer with a DVD burner or access to a flash drive or cloud storage on which these can be stored.

The time frame of this project depends on the class meeting schedule as well as the amount of work to be done in class rather than outside of class. Many students, middle school through college, may be unfamiliar with the technology utilized in this assignment, and for this reason, it would be valuable to spend time working with students to understand the technology before the start of this project. In addition, before the project begins, students should have identified a literary character they would like to analyze, to avoid delays in the time frame of the project's core. The body of the assignment works best when divided into the following sections: writing (including prewriting and revisions), storyboarding, collecting assets (including vocal recording and image collection), construction, and showcase.

Phase 1: Writing

Allow at least two to three class periods for students to brainstorm ingredients for their characters, and then write and revise their recipes. To help students brainstorm, ask them to think of their favorite recipes. What ingredients go into these dishes? How does the end product differ from the original ingredients? Ask students to think about what ingredients might be needed to create a person. Encourage more creative answers, such as grit and confidence, over scientific answers, like blood and bones. Ten ingredients will yield a recipe between thirty and forty seconds. Determine the desired length of the final digital story and give students the number of ingredients they should strive to have in their recipes. If desired, schedule times for peer review.

Phase 2: Storyboarding

Allow another one to two class periods for the creation of the storyboard. However, if students struggle with this phase, allow more time for the storyboards to be completed. This step is invaluable to keeping students on track for the remainder of the project. To help ensure the timely completion of storyboards, use class time to go over the storyboard template with the students. First, locate the four components of the board: (1) Image box; (2) Transition box; (3) Recipe Text lines; and (4) Special Effects line. In the Image box, students can write or draw the image they want to find. The images designated should only be used for the Recipe Text directly below the image. In the Transition box, students can envision the type of transition they would like to use to move from one image to the next. On the Recipe Text lines, students should write one line from their recipe. Each section should contain only one line, and the Recipe Text should move in order across the storyboard. The Special Effects line is optional and does not need to be used for all—or any—of the frames. However, if a student so desires, the option for Special Effects is available. Students can use as many storyboard sheets as needed to complete the recipe.

Phase 3: Collecting Assets

Give students no more than three days to find the images they desire and create a strong vocal recording. Since these are going to be the assets used in the creation of their final digital stories, it is important that students have time to contemplate the combination of words, sound, and image. This step may also be time sensitive if you are using a communal computer lab in order to complete this phase.

Phase 4: Constructing Digital Stories

Give students at least one week to construct their digital stories. This is the most time-consuming step. Here, the students are tasked with importing all of their assets into the editing software and arranging the material to create their digital story. This phase is highly dependent on the availability of and access to technology. As this is the meat of the project, use your judgment during the process to assess any adjustments to the time frame which need to be made based on student progress. At the end of this phase, students should have a completed copy of their digital story saved on a DVD or flash drive.

Phase 5: Showcasing

Depending on the number of students in your class, it should take only one class to showcase students' completed digital stories for other members of the class and community (if desired). Before this day, you will need to collect all the completed assignments and put them onto one DVD (again, depending on the number of students) to play during class.

This assignment can also be elongated or shortened if needed. Elongation of the project allows students more time for the writing process and in the computer lab to perfect their projects. An elongated time frame can also allow time for students to take their own photos, if cameras are available. Shortened time frames would require more work done by the students outside of the classroom.

Regarding the digital aspects of the assignment, you will need to determine which file type students need to use. Macs and PCs differ here, so be sure you know what kind of computer you will be using to create the DVD. Save the students' digital stories to a DVD and have them turn in any required paperwork (perhaps you ask students to write a reflective essay on their process and product). And for more information about how to use specific movie editors, you can locate user manuals, which are available online through most software companies.

5. ANTICIPATING STUDENT NEEDS

One of the greatest advantages of working in multiple literacies is that doing so gives students a broader range of expression. However, this does not mean that all students are familiar or comfortable with all the literacies addressed in this assignment. Some students may struggle to express themselves in one or more of the literacy forms. It may be effective to help students envision how each literacy mode works together to form the whole. For instance, a student might hesitate because of the performance aspect of this project; however, there is not a live performance component. To get students comfortable with performing and expressing themselves, this project makes use of a prerecorded vocal performance, which is done well before the presentation of the final event.

In my experience the majority of the students' challenges arise while working at the computer. They might not be familiar or experienced with the programs used to create their digital stories. If this assignment is completed in class, it may be beneficial to walk students through the programs and technology they will use before they begin their work on computers.

Another challenge that may arise, if this project relies on class time, would be student absences. Since this project is time sensitive and requires prerequisites to move on to future phases, it is vital to have students attend the class to further their work. If possible build extra time into the schedule to allow for absences. You can always use any extra time for peer review. Should a student miss more than one or two class periods, additional actions will need to be considered to ensure the student finishes. During the writing and storyboarding phases, it is possible to assign work outside of class time. In some cases students can make up the process of collecting assets and constructing the digital story at home, but only if they have reliable access to the necessary technology. If students need to make up these tech-based projects at school, speak with the computer lab supervisor and the student's parents and teachers to find an appropriate time.

6. ASSESSMENT TOOLS

As this assignment culls from an after-school residency and not a classroom, I do not have a formulated grading rubric that I use. However, I have provided some points below, which I hope you find helpful in determining grading structures.

- I would encourage the grading to incorporate the prework, including prewriting and the storyboard. This ensures thought over the course of the project and discourages students from completing the project just before it is due.

- Furthermore, students can be encouraged to adhere to length requirements of your choosing. For this project, length could mean the number of ingredients and/or the temporal length of the completed story. It is important to note, however, that longer recipes are not necessarily better recipes. The recipe should be concise and should adequately describe the character.

- Overall effort and neatness of the digital stories' construction should be a major component, bearing in mind that students may be unfamiliar with the technology. The content and construction of the digital story is more import than flashy effects. Does the digital story adequately convey the character, or is it muddied by effects?

- Does the recipe include well-thought-out ingredients, cooking instructions, and serving instructions?

As this project has the possibility of looking drastically different from student to student, it is hard to pinpoint a grading scheme that addresses both the quality of the final piece and the creativity of the writing, performance, and uses of literacy modes. I might invite the students to review the desired goals and outcomes for the project with me, to help keep expectations clear. Another option is to ask students to keep reflection journals as they create, or to have them write a final reflective essay to accompany their creative work—an essay in which they discuss their choices, how they considered their audiences, and other such matters.

7. THEORETICAL BASIS FOR THE ASSIGNMENT:
Lit Recipes: Creating Recipes for Literary Characters

This assignment developed from an exploratory residency I created and facilitated entitled "The Recipe of Me," in which middle school and high school youth designed digital narrative recipes of themselves. The residency was jointly produced by a professional theater company and a homeless services provider, and its initial development came about as a way to identify unique ways to promote autonomy and authority in disenfranchised youth, through a means of digital performance. The process and results of "The Recipe of Me" (Hill) led me to believe in the potential for this assignment to be used in classroom settings to create an autonomous learning structure in which students are empowered to coauthor the learned material by engaging in a critical analysis of a literary character, and "Lit Recipes" was born. The original assignment has been reconsidered here as a lesson in character analysis, using digital storytelling, which can be used in literature classrooms in middle and upper grades as well as higher education.

While digital storytelling is often associated with the creation of short, personal narratives, it has a wide range of applications, and can be especially useful for the classroom. Digital storytelling can establish a creative learning experience for students, which promotes innovation and respect for creativity among participants. Using multimodal forms of communication, including written, oral, and visual literacies, students share their own interpretations of literary characters, allowing them deeper insight into the characters and thus, the story.

> "Using multimodal forms of communication, including written, oral, and visual literacies, students share their own interpretations of literary characters."
>
> **Amanda Hill**

In this assignment, students create a single recipe for a chosen literary character, which is presented as a digital story. The first stage of the assignment involves writing the recipe and planning the combination of literacy modalities through the use of a storyboard. This process focuses on analysis of the material. Students should be able to argue why they chose their ingredients, the recipe instructions, and the images they selected. This will help inform their interpretation of the literary text. The second stage of the assignment involves the creation of the digital recipe, in which students identify and construct a short, cohesive digital story. This section involves the actual use of technology to create a meaningful text that explains the students' interpretation of their literary character in an artistic and abstract way.

A relatively new practice, digital storytelling, as it most commonly is understood, originated approximately twenty years ago. Christopher Fletcher and Carolina Cambre elaborate on its origins:

> In recent years, the "digital story" genre has become associated with a specific style of popular media work developed in California in the early 1990s. A small group of visual artists, designers, performers, and videographers became interested in fostering the production and dissemination of personal stories, marginal histories and counternarratives in the emerging social space of the World Wide Web. Members of this group ultimately formed the Center for Digital Storytelling (CDS). (113)

At the helm of the Story Center (formerly CDS) is Joe Lambert, whose definitive *Cookbook* offers those interested in creating a digital story a wealth of valuable knowledge and tips.

Digital Storytelling has gained considerable speed in recent years, due to an increased awareness of and theoretical research on non-text-based modes of literacy and the resulting combinations of multiple literacies in order

> to create digital artifacts that do not necessarily privilege linguistic forms of signification, but rather that draw on a variety of modalities—speech, writing, image, gesture, and sound—to create different forms of meaning. (Hull and Nelson 1-2)

> "Within a single digital story, numerous ligaments connect layers of semiotic and contextual meaning."
> **Amanda Hill**

While this assignment may not take advantage of all of the above modalities, it is indebted to the research of Hull and her compatriots, whose continued writings offer research and case studies showing the ways in which "a multimodal text can create a different system of signification, one that transcends the collective contribution of its constituent parts" (Hull and Nelson 2).

Within a single digital story, numerous ligaments connect layers of semiotic and contextual meaning, juxtaposing literacy modes and creating new meaning in the process. Lambert defines the multiple visual and audio layers that are used to create a single story:

Visual Layers

- The composition of a single image
- Multiple images within a single frame, combined either through collage or fading over time

- Juxtaposition of a series of images over time
- Movement applied to a single image, either by panning or zooming or the juxtaposition of a series of cropped details from the whole image
- Use of text on screen in relation to visuals, spoken narration, or sound

Audio Layers

- Recorded voice-over
- Recorded voice-over in relation to sound, either music or ambient sound
- Music alone or in contrast to another piece of music (44)

In this assignment, students shape their digital stories with written text, images, and speech, thus revealing their unique understandings of literary characters through multiple modalities. The layering process becomes a period of "construction" (Lundby 5), where students create visual and verbal representations of literary characters.

The layering process is a formulation of participants' representations of their characters. This is where they begin to see how their interpretation fits together over multiple modalities. Speech, text, and image build upon one another to fashion quasi-tangible collages of characters, delving into the inner depths of multifaceted characters. This assignment thus involves an in-depth study of a literary character, which is then used by the students to construct knowledge and communication. In this way, the creation process of the digital stories has the potential to engage students as coauthors of their subjects, allowing them to engage in deeper meaning making and analysis of their chosen characters by reviewing the words of the character, the character's actions, and what the author and the other characters say about him or her. This textual analysis is key to defining the characteristics and personality traits of a chosen character.

By "decentering" the character from his or her literary work and "recontextualizing" the character within the student's digital storytelling analysis, a student gains agency as a coauthor, developing the character through his or her own unique vision with the implication that the resulting video will be displayed and seen (Bauman and Briggs). This "act of control" enables the creation of "an authoritative voice by the performer, which is grounded at least in part in the knowledge, ability, and right to control the recentering of valued texts" (Bauman and Briggs 76-77). Thus the assignment in this chapter becomes a way for students to creatively construct a character analysis that grants the student the position of coauthor and gives him or her authorial standing within the classroom.

8. CONCLUSION

"Lit Recipes" is one of my favorite lesson plans. It is intriguing to see how creative students can be when describing people abstractly. I have had students incorporate all sorts of objects into their analyses, such as "red, gold, and ruby-colored pencils," "a pinch of procrastination," "4-5 books, as needed," and "one cup of awkwardness." The combination of abstract and concrete possibilities that define a person are numerous and inspiring to explore. The details one can infer about a character from the snippets of text found in a student's recipe (the ingredients and instructions) are an exciting way for the student to create an informative and artistic analysis. One student made sure to emphasize the instructions, "Caution! Do not heat!" as a means of letting the audience know this character was not someone to mess with. This lesson encourages students to be creative and have fun while creating a work that has the ability to teach and engage the classroom audience. Using digital technology to finalize this project is a unique and intriguing way to further students' involvement and encourage them to author texts in multiple modalities. This becomes more important as we consider the increase of technology and visual modalities in our society. "Lit Recipes" provides a way for students to craft an artistic voice while engaging in a critical analysis of literature.

9. WORKS CITED

Alrutz, Megan. "Digital Storytelling: Sites of Possibility." Lecture at U of Central Florida, 23 Feb. 2012.

Bauman, Richard, and Charles Briggs. "Poetics and Performance as Critical Perspectives on Language and Social Life." *Annual Review of Anthropology*, vol. 19, 1990, pp. 59-88.

Fletcher, Christopher, and Carolina Cambre. "Digital Storytelling and Implicated Scholarship in the Classroom." *Journal of Canadian Studies*, vol. 43, no. 1, 2009, pp. 109-30.

Hill, Amanda. "The Recipe of a Digital Story: An Analysis of the Residency, 'The Recipe of Me.'" MFA thesis, at U of Central Florida, 2013.

Hull, Glynda A. "At Last: Youth Culture and Digital Media: New Literacies for New Times." *Research in the Teaching of English*, vol. 38, 2003, pp. 229-33.

Hull, Glynda A., and Mark Evan Nelson. "Locating the Semiotic Power of Multimodality." *Written Communication*, vol. 22, 2005, pp. 1-38.

Hull, Glynda A., and Mira-Lisa Katz. "Crafting an Agentive Self: Case Studies of Digital Storytelling." *Research in the Teaching of English*, vol. 41, no. 1, 2006, pp. 43-81.

Lambert, Joe. *Digital Storytelling: Capturing Lives, Creating Community*. Digital Diner, 2006.

Lambert, Joe, and Nina Mullen. *Memory's Voices: A Guide to Digital Storytelling: Cookbook and Travelling Companion*. Center for Digital Storytelling, 2000.

Lundby, Knut. *Digital Storytelling, Mediatized Stories: Self-representations in New Media*. P. Lang, 2009.

Ohler, Jason. *Digital Storytelling in the Classroom: New Media Pathways to Literacy, Learning, and Creativity*. Corwin, 2008.

21

Multimodal Anthology Foreword

Lisa Whalen
North Hennepin Community College

Lisa Whalen has a PhD in postsecondary and adult education from Capella University, and an MA in creative and critical writing from Hamline University. She teaches writing and literature at North Hennepin Community College in Brooklyn Park, Minnesota, and has mentored graduate students preparing to teach college composition. Her published work includes book reviews and articles on teaching writing, directing writing centers, and examining correlations between empathy and reading narratives. Her creative nonfiction essays have been published in peer-reviewed journals, and her short fiction has been accepted for presentation at the National Creative Writing Conference.

COURTESY OF LISA WHALEN

1. OVERVIEW

- **Assignment:** Students create a mini-anthology by selecting four texts from the course anthology, analyzing them, supporting the analysis with research, and integrating what was learned by writing a foreword for the anthology that incorporates electronic media.

- **Courses:** Introduction to literature and any literature course, especially those with reading lists that include multiple genres; composition and literature.

- **Literature:** Any, but it is most effective when students have access to multiple genres.

- **Technology:** Research sources (e.g., databases, Google Scholar, library Web sites, etc.) and a wiki platform, some of which are available on the Internet for no charge (e.g., DokuWiki).

- **Time:** Can be conducted over four weeks of two 75-minute class periods a week, or extended over eight weeks of two 75-minute class periods a week.

2. GOALS OF THE ASSIGNMENT

After completing this assignment, students will be able to:

- apply steps of the writing process to a college essay;
- shape content and writing style to meet audience needs;
- evaluate research sources for relevance and credibility;
- incorporate research effectively into a college essay;
- cite research sources correctly in MLA style; and
- demonstrate ability to analyze literature according to genre, theme, character, or other literary elements covered in class.

"Using electronic media to research and write about literature provides students with unique opportunities to connect what they learn in the classroom to their lives outside of the classroom."

Lisa Whalen
North Hennepin Community College

3. ASSIGNMENT SHEET

Multimodal Anthology Foreword

Course: _____

Instructor: _____

Date: _____

Imagine that the chair of the English department has asked you to create a new anthology for next semester's ENGL 1112 students. Your job is to select four texts (poems, short stories, dramas, or essays) from our textbook, *Literature and the Writing Process*, that you think "go" together, meaning they address the same theme, represent or comment on the same culture, have similar characters, represent a particular writing style or time period, juxtapose different cultures, and so on. Two of the texts you choose should be from among those assigned this semester. The other two should be texts in our anthology that have not been assigned.

As the person assembling this anthology, it's your job to provide supplementary information to accompany the texts you've chosen by writing a foreword for your anthology. That's where your research comes in. Here are some ways you might think about designing your research:

- Tell readers about the authors and text you've chosen, explaining how literary critics or movements interpret them.
- Explain how each text reflects the culture or era in which it was written. What was happening in the world, the United States, the author's neighborhood that seems to have influenced his/her writing? What comment on society does the author seem to be making?
- Create a study guide for students to use as they read the texts.
- Create a teaching guide for the instructor that explains what to emphasize and how to teach each text.

Although you will include research sources in your foreword, *your* ideas about the texts are most important. The research sources should simply support your ideas.

Your foreword will be multimedia, meaning you'll include other forms of information (explained below) in addition to your own written words.

(*continued*)

ASSIGNMENT SHEET (*continued*)

Research Requirements

You must have a total of *five outside sources* (not counting our textbook) that comply with the following:

- At least *three* of your sources must be *scholarly*.

- You may include *one Web site*, though you are not required to have any Web sites at all.

- You should include at least *two different types of media* (e.g., links to Web sites, images, audio clips, video clips, PowerPoint slides, etc.) in your foreword. The media should be relevant and help convey or support your ideas about the texts.

NOTE: I may ask you to turn in your actual research sources or photocopies of the pages you used from each source with the final draft of your project, so keep all of your sources until I grade your project.

Tips for a Successful Project

- *Begin early!* I cannot emphasize this enough. Writing an analysis supported by research isn't like writing a reader-response essay. Research takes longer than you may think. If you need to request sources through interlibrary loan, it may take a week or more for them to arrive, so plan ahead.

- Read some prefaces, forewords, or introductions to anthologies to get an idea of what they are like. Study how the writers put together their ideas about the texts they have chosen.

- Ask librarians for help. Their expertise can save you a lot of time and frustration.

- Come up with a note-taking strategy and stick with it. Many cases of plagiarism begin with students who unintentionally write down a quote in their notes, then think it's a paraphrase and copy it into their essays. That is plagiarism.

- Visit the Writing Center. Tutors can help you organize your ideas and avoid procrastinating.

Length: 2,400 words minimum (not including works-cited page), 3,000 maximum

Due Date: _____

4. TIME AND TECHNOLOGY

Like the research source requirements, the timeline for this project is flex-ible and easily adapted to meet course goals. For example, when I assigned this project in a composition course, I stretched the project over eight weeks to accommodate library orientation, discussion of scholarly versus popu-lar sources, and peer review. However, when I assigned it in introduction to literature, where most students have already completed the composition course, I shortened the timeline to four weeks and required fewer research resources.

A breakdown of the eight-week timeline follows:

- *Week 9 (of our 18-week semester): Introduction to the assignment.* I allow two class periods (approximately one hour each) for introducing the assign-ment, discussing scholarly versus popular sources, and completing library research orientation.

- *Week 11: Research proposals due.* If the schedule allows, I set aside class time and/or office hours to meet individually with students to discuss their research plans and alert them to any potential challenges. I've found that even five minutes spent with each student leads to improved writing processes and final products.

- *Week 13: Outlines due.* I spend two class periods teaching students how to incorporate quotes and paraphrases from research sources. I also cover citing sources in MLA style. Ideally, students bring one of their sources to class and practice quoting, paraphrasing, and citing that source, but I also provide a sample journal article for those who don't bring a source.

- *Week 16: Rough drafts due.* I use one class period to demonstrate uploading essays to the wiki and to facilitate peer review. For peer review, students form groups of three, read their essays aloud, and talk through the ques-tions I provide. Depending on how much time is available and whether I think it's necessary to keep students focused, I ask them to write down their peer-review feedback and submit a copy for grading. If possible, you may want to schedule this class period in a computer lab so that students can get the full multimedia experience of one another's forewords.

- *Week 17: Essay final drafts due.* Essays are written and uploaded to wiki.

- *Week 18: Peer responses.* Students' responses to classmates' essay final drafts due (on wiki).

A four-week timeline is as follows:

- *Week 1: Research proposals due.* At the start of the week, I introduce the assignment and discuss scholarly versus popular sources. Students submit their proposals at the end of the week.

- *Week 2: Outlines due.* As students are working on their outlines, we discuss quoting, paraphrasing, and MLA style to prepare them for writing a rough draft of the foreword.
- *Week 3: Rough drafts due.* Students submit a copy of their rough draft to me, which I comment on and return to them. They also bring a copy to class, where they conduct peer-review workshops.
- *Week 4: Final drafts and peer responses due.* Students submit a final draft to me and then upload a copy to the wiki where they comment on one another's forewords.

A wiki is a Web site created by an administrator, such as a classroom instructor, that others can not only visit but also contribute to. The most widely known wiki is *Wikipedia*, an encyclopedia to which anyone with Internet access can add, change, or delete content.

To complete and post their Multimodal Anthology Foreword (MAF) assignment on a class wiki, students need access to a computer, Internet access, and an e-mail address. They can complete the MAF in a school computer lab or at home. Students who have experience navigating the Internet and using a word processing program should have no problem using the wiki, as the menus and functions are very similar.

Students will also need access to college or public library electronic databases, such as JSTOR or Academic Search Premier, to conduct research. Most colleges subscribe to such databases and make them available to students on- and sometimes off-campus, so students shouldn't incur any extra costs or require additional computer software to access these sources. If the college doesn't provide access to databases, most public libraries do.

To create the wiki, you will need access to a computer, the Internet, an e-mail address, and a wiki software platform. Depending on class size, you may also require funds to subscribe to a wiki software platform; however, a simple Google search yields many free wiki software platforms adequate for this assignment. The software I used is available at no cost from PBworks (www.pbworks.com). Experience editing or creating wikis is helpful but not necessary. PBworks is similar to but simpler than most online teaching software (e.g., Desire2Learn, Blackboard, WebCT, etc.), so instructors familiar with such software will have no trouble creating a wiki. Simply create an account at PBworks, name the wiki, and select "create a new page" each time you want to add a new area for content. Two tabs at the top of each new page enable you to move back and forth between editing, which allows you to add, change, or delete content, and viewing, which allows you to see each page as it will appear to students. The editing menu is nearly identical to most word processing programs, such as Microsoft Word, so modifying text, adding links, and inserting objects (tables, shapes, video, audio, etc.) will be familiar to most computer users.

I suggest creating a home page that welcomes students, explains the purpose of the wiki, provides a link to the assignment sheet, and gives directions for uploading completed essays. Instructors who want to use the wiki for more than just this assignment may also choose to upload additional readings, handouts, and other resources.

You can designate each wiki page as public or private in addition to designating students' level of involvement. If a page is designated private, only individuals that you invite through e-mail can view that page. To invite students, select "invite more people" from the menu at the right side of the screen and enter students' e-mail addresses. Students will receive an e-mail inviting them to join the wiki by creating a free account. Once they've created an account, students can access the wiki anytime.

You can also designate invited students' level of involvement in the wiki on a page-by-page basis by selecting "control access to this page," which makes each page visible to or hidden from students. Among students who are invited to view the wiki, designate their level of involvement by choosing the "custom security" option and selecting one of three options: *readers*, which allows students to view but not edit pages; *writers*, which allows students to view and edit pages; and *editors*, which allows students to view, edit, move, and delete pages. I designated my students as writers so they could upload their own projects and view each other's but could not accidentally delete content from the site.

The last step is to create a page where students submit their completed assignments. When viewing that page, students click on "upload files" at the right side of the screen and then select their project from the list of available files on their computer.

5. ANTICIPATING STUDENT NEEDS

Time constraints may be a challenge. Students need ample time to research and write between stages, but you may also need to continue covering new literary texts as students are working on their forewords. If you have the opportunity, it's helpful to schedule one or more class periods in a computer lab and allow students to work independently as you check in with each of them. This can reduce the amount of time you need to spend meeting with individuals outside of class, improve the quality of the final products, and maintain a reasonable pace for covering curriculum.

It doesn't come up in every class, but occasionally, one or two students express discomfort at having their work posted in a public setting and/or having to comment publicly on their peers' writing. When these concerns arise, I address them by explaining that the wiki is visible only to members of the class, not the general public, and that they will probably have to do similar writing, commenting, and editing in their careers. I also suggest viewing their final drafts as another stage of the ongoing writing process rather than as a judgment of final products. Most students have participated in some form of peer review by the time they enroll in my class, so these explanations have been enough to assuage their anxiety. No students have reported negative experiences, such as overly critical or mean-spirited comments, as a result of posting their writing in the wiki.

6. ASSESSMENT TOOLS

Depending on whether you use this assignment for a composition or literature class, you may choose to vary the emphasis you place on process versus product. You may also want to consider whether to provide individual grades for each stage or one grade for the entire assignment. I prefer giving grades for each stage so students know how they are doing throughout the process; however, while I attach a point value to each stage, I make the research proposal, outline, and rough draft pass/fail and provide multiple

Grading Criteria for Final Draft

Skill Demonstrated	Proficient (A/B)	Adequate (B/C)	Needs Improvement (D or lower)
Analysis of texts is insightful and clearly explained; avoids summary.			
Introduction grabs readers' attention, introduces important background/context information, establishes the topic's significance.			
Research sources are diverse, timely, credible, reliable, and meet the requirements for the assignment.			
Synthesis of sources effectively blends research with writer's own words and ideas.			
Purpose of the foreword is clear and easy to identify.			
Thesis is clear and easy to identify; reflects the central focus of the foreword.			

Organization is apparent, logical, and appropriate to the topic.			
Paragraphs include sufficient support for the main idea(s).			
Paragraphs are unified.			
Transitions are used to connect ideas; are elegant and effective.			
Section headings (optional) are clear and appropriate; aid in focusing and organizing the foreword.			
Quotes are "sandwiched" effectively.			
In-text citations adhere to MLA 2009 style.			
Works-cited page adheres to MLA 2009 style.			
Formatting follows MLA 2009 style.			
Grammar and mechanics are correct.			
Other: _____			
Extra Points for Tutoring (optional): Writer provides evidence of having been tutored by a Writing Center tutor and revising based on the tutor's suggestions (see syllabus for information).			
Total Points Possible: 100	**Your Points:**		

opportunities for revision. I want students to understand that research and writing are messy, recursive processes. If their first proposal isn't complete, or if there are problems with the sources they've selected, they receive a zero but have the opportunity to revise and resubmit as many times as necessary. Once they have revised to a satisfactory extent, they receive the full points for that stage of the assignment. The final draft of the foreword is worth significantly more points than the earlier stages because even though process is important, in the real world students will ultimately be evaluated on their finished product. I want to prepare them for that reality.

Although this assignment makes some forms of plagiarism difficult, you may want to require students to submit their research sources (or photocopies of them) along with the final drafts of their forewords so that you can refer to them if something looks like it might be plagiarized.

Another consideration is how much you want to emphasize content versus style. When I use this in a composition course, content, style, and correctness (e.g., grammar and mechanics) are each one-third of the score. When I use this in a literature course where we emphasize understanding the texts and spend less time talking about the writing process, content is worth three-quarters, and style and correctness together are worth one-quarter of the score.

7. THEORETICAL BASIS FOR THE ASSIGNMENT: Multimodal Anthology Foreword

As technology advances and educational budgets shrink, teachers are being asked to do more with less, to cover more material—including introducing students to new technology—in the same amount of time. This challenge creates frustrations but also opportunities for innovation. I learned firsthand how challenging circumstances can lead to innovation when I discovered I would be teaching a three-credit, literature-based composition class with course goals that included critical analysis of novels, poetry, drama, and/ or nonfiction; a research paper that exhibited mastery of MLA style documentation; and twenty total pages per student, per semester of polished writing. I was used to teaching composition and literature separately, each in a four-credit course. These new course goals encompassed much more than I was accustomed to covering in a single class, and I had one less credit in which to accomplish them. After thinking carefully about how to meet these goals and introduce students to the technology they would likely be asked to use in future careers, I created the Multimodal Anthology Foreword (MAF) assignment. The assignment was so effective that I have since used it in introduction to literature classes as well.

> "Challenging circumstances can lead to innovation."
> **Lisa Whalen**

According to L. Dee Fink, assignments designed to accomplish specific goals are more likely to result in deep learning (29-32). He suggests instructors ask: "What is it I want students to be able to do when they have completed this course?" and develop assignments based on the answer(s) to that question (34-35, 75). I want students to be able to analyze and synthesize literary texts, to conduct research, and to convey their ideas in clear prose. I also want them to practice asking and answering what is arguably the most important question writers must consider: What is the best way to convey this information to my audience? I settled on assigning a multimodal project because it pushes students to consider more often and more deeply than a traditional essay how they can best convey information to an audience. Multimodal essays can include links, images, audio and video clips, voice-over narration, PowerPoint slides and more; therefore, rather than simply finding the right written phrase, students much choose from among a wide range of tools and decide which will best convey a particular idea. In considering which tools to use, students interact with many different forms of technology.

MAF uses technology to promote active learning, an important part of constructivist learning theory. Active learning places each student "in charge of his or her own learning experience" (Whelan 14). According to Robert Whelan, students who shape their learning experiences "build on prior knowledge and create their own understanding of ideas and concepts," which enables them to recall and apply those ideas and concepts more effectively later on (14). David Jonassen, Kyle Peck, and Brent Wilson also emphasize the importance of active learning. They explain that "students learn by doing—that is, by engaging in meaningful projects that require them to explore, experiment, converse, and reflect on what they are learning" (194). MAF includes each of these processes in that students select the texts they'll analyze, conduct research (explore), develop a theory about the texts (experiment), participate in peer review (converse), and revise their essays based on feedback (reflect). Lastly, students are introduced to using a form of technology that is likely new to them, a wiki, as a means of presenting their work.

I developed MAF for a literature-based composition course and have since used it in introduction to literature. Since the composition course encompasses course goals from introduction to literature as well as additional goals, I'll discuss the assignment in terms of the composition course, College Writing II (CW2). CW2 is the second class in a two-part sequence that fulfills the standard first-year composition requirement at a medium-sized community college. It is a prerequisite for some upper-level literature courses, and students are encouraged to complete it before registering for any literature course. CW2 introduces students to works from literary genres and asks them to write essays analyzing those works as well as essays that support a thesis with evidence from sources. It also requires them to document their sources in MLA style.

MAF is an end-of-term project students complete in stages. Before students begin working on it, they have read, discussed, and practiced analyzing poems, short fiction, and nonfiction essays. They have also been oriented during class by the college's librarian to available research resources. Instructors may vary the number and types of research sources they require students to include as support for their analyses of the texts. I require a minimum of five sources (not counting the anthology textbook students are selecting texts from), three of which must be scholarly sources and only one of which may be a Web site. Regardless of a source's format, it must conform to the criteria for a credible, reliable source, which we've discussed in class. They must also include in their foreword at least two forms of media other than written words, such as audio clips, images, or links to Web sites.

The first stage of the assignment is a one-page research proposal, in which students explain the following:

- which texts they've selected;
- why they selected those texts;
- which purpose their foreword will serve;
- which types of research sources they anticipate using (e.g., author biographies, news stories, articles in scholarly journals, etc.); and
- what tools they'll use to conduct their research (e.g., JSTOR, ProQuest Newspapers, library books, etc.).

The second stage of the assignment is a detailed outline. Their outlines must indicate which two or more types of media they'll include in their forewords and a brief explanation of why they have chosen those two particular media. The outline is designed to reinforce the writing process, which should unfold over a period of time rather than in a single sitting.

The third stage of the assignment is a rough draft of the foreword, which students peer-review during class. I provide them with questions to consider as they read one another's forewords. The questions help ensure they provide constructive feedback on clarity, organization, purpose, and use of research and media.

The fourth stage of the assignment is a final draft of the foreword, which students post on the class wiki.

The last stage of the assignment is a requirement that each student read and respond (on the wiki) to at least two classmates' essays. I ask students to note in their responses what they found most interesting and how the multimedia component enhanced the content and style of the foreword.

8. CONCLUSION

This assignment enabled students to meet a collection of learning goals I initially thought impossible to fit into a three-credit course. In their completed forewords, students employed electronic media, a tool required in many careers, to demonstrate what they learned about analyzing literature and supporting analysis with research from credible sources.

Students enjoyed having the freedom to choose which texts and elements of literary analysis they focused on. Although some initially resisted outlining, nearly every student reported finding the step-by-step process of proposing, outlining, drafting, receiving feedback, and revising helpful. They also appreciated being required to read and comment on classmates' forewords because, while they admitted they wouldn't have done so voluntarily, they learned from one another and liked having a wider audience for projects in which they'd invested significant time and effort. Finally, students enjoyed the creativity inherent in producing multimodal texts.

I enjoyed commenting on rough drafts and grading final drafts more than usual for this assignment because instead of reading twenty-five to thirty versions of the same essay, I encountered a variety of approaches to many different texts. Despite the freedom students had to select texts and approaches to the assignment, grading was fairly easy due to consistent requirements for analyzing the literature, evaluating sources, and synthesizing research. The assignment also significantly reduced the amount of policing for plagiarism. Although thousands of essays are available on the Internet for some of the texts students wrote about, virtually no essays exist that examine similarities and differences among any three or more of the assigned texts from which students could create their anthologies. Perhaps best of all, discussing one another's forewords meant the course ended with an emphasis on students learning from one another rather than solely from the instructor.

9. WORKS CITED

Fink, L. Dee. *Creating Significant Learning Experiences: An Integrated Approach to Designing College Courses.* Jossey-Bass, 2003.

Jonassen, David H., et al. *Learning with Technology: A Constructivist Perspective.* Merrill. 1999.

Whelan, Robert. "Instructional Technology and Theory: A Look at Past, Present, and Future Trends." *Connect: Information Technology at NYU*, 2005, pp. 13-17, www.slideshare.net/glassbox/instructionaltechnology-and-theory-by-robert -whelan.

22

Exploring Multimodality through Film and Textual Analysis

Andrew Bourelle
University of New Mexico

AND

Tiffany Bourelle
University of New Mexico

Andrew Bourelle is an assistant professor of English at the University of New Mexico. His research interests include multimodal and online learning. His work is published or forthcoming in *Computers and Composition; Journal of Teaching Writing; Kairos: A Journal of Rhetoric, Technology, and Pedagogy*; and the anthology *Digital Writing Assessment & Evaluation* (from Computers and Composition Digital Press, 2013).

Tiffany Bourelle is an assistant professor of English at the University of New Mexico where she teaches courses in multimodal and online pedagogies. Her research includes examining the intersections between online learning and multimodality, specifically focusing on how distance education students can successfully benefit from completing multimodal projects. Her work is published or forthcoming in *Computers and Composition, Technical Communication Quarterly,* and *Kairos: A Journal of Rhetoric, Technology, and Pedagogy.*

1. OVERVIEW

- **Assignment:** An analysis of a film adapted from a work of literature, composed in two formats: a written paper and a short multimodal video.
- **Courses:** Any literature course including literature and film; writing about literature; literature and composition. The authors originally created this assignment for English 218: Writing about Literature.
- **Literature:** Literary works (novels, stories, etc.) that have been adapted into movies.

- **Technology:** Windows Movie Maker, iMovie, or a similar video creation program.
- **Time:** Five weeks or ten class sessions.

2. GOALS OF THE ASSIGNMENT

By completing this assignment, students will:

- practice skills of critical analysis;
- practice skills of evaluation;
- recognize the effects, limitations, and rhetorical medium can have on communication; and
- develop skills of multimodal communication.

"When asking students to analyze films adapted from written works of literature, it also makes sense for them to create their own video adaptations of their written papers. This way, they're not only analyzing film adaptation but also experiencing it for themselves."

Andrew Bourelle
University of New Mexico

"Multimodal projects give students the freedom to think beyond the traditional parameters of alphabetic text. Students must consider how their audience will receive or interact with their multimodal composition and if their piece conveys their intended purpose."

Tiffany Bourelle
University of New Mexico

3. ASSIGNMENT SHEET

Exploring Multimodality through Film and Textual Analysis

Course: _____

Instructor: _____

Date: _____

Format for Written Portion

Typed, double-spaced, 12-point font (preferably Times New Roman)

MLA style and format

1,200 words minimum (about 4 pages)

Format for Multimodal Portion

Video presentation that uses text, audio, and visual elements

Length: 2 to 5 minutes

Imaginative Context

You've just seen a job advertisement for one of the coolest jobs you can imagine, and you plan to apply. The open position is for a movie critic for an online magazine, but it's more than that: it's a movie critic who analyzes movies based on literary works. Movies are made all the time based on source material; however, movie critics rarely take the original works into account when critiquing the films. And if they do, the book or story is merely mentioned, not a significant part of the evaluation. The online magazine that is hiring wants to provide readers with an analytical comparison between the movie and source material.

Furthermore, because the magazine is online, the editors want both a written version of your analysis (in the form of an academic essay) as well as a multimodal version (meaning, one that is in a multimedia format).

ASSIGNMENT

The word *analysis* literally means separating something into parts to better understand the whole. In a generic sense, to analyze something is to think critically about it. To analyze something—a movie, a song, a politician's speech—is to try to better understand it. For this assignment, I am asking you to analyze a literary work. However, I am going to complicate the assignment: you must choose a literary work and a movie based on it, and you must analyze both. Therefore, not only are you analyzing a text, you are also analyzing a film based on that text. You're analyzing both and analyzing the differences between the two and what effects those differences have on the individual works of art.

Your paper should contain a summary of the literary work and movie, an analysis of both, and finally, an evaluation of both. Therefore, you're doing a lot in this paper, and yet you have to write it in such a way that you want to keep readers' attention. You need to be articulate and analytical, while at the same time engaging and clearly communicating with your readers.

MULTIMODAL COMPONENT

In contemporary society, communication is happening more and more through multimedia. At one time, if someone wanted to read a news article, they would open a newspaper and read the story. As the Internet was developed, those stories were simply transferred online without change. Today, however, when you want to read a news article, you are often given the printed text as well as an accompanying video or some other multimedia component. This is just one example of how multimedia is changing and influencing society.

Technology is also changing the way we view literature. One of the reasons for this assignment is to get you to think of literature more broadly. Literature, some would argue, can take more forms than simply printed, alphabetic texts. Can comic books or graphic novels be considered literature? Illustrated books? What about films? Even those who would argue that these media are not "literary" still recognize that they are forms of art that intersect with genres of literature. These genres/media/formats can be used to tell stories and communicate literary meaning. An analysis of a film and its literary source text — comparing and contrasting the two, looking at differences and similarities that arise from the different media — can help people begin to understand these complicated relationships.

I want you to go a step further than analysis alone. Along with your written paper, you must create a multimodal project to accompany this assignment, wherein you give an abbreviated version of your analytical argument in video form.

To create a video, you may use iMovie, Movie Maker, or another program. Think of the video as a shortened version of your paper created for a different purpose and audience. In creating the video, please think about what your audience needs.

Please note: I do not expect the work of expert graphic designers or videographers. What I'm looking for is that you're able to consider how medium affects what you write. I will be looking for whether you understand the needs of different audiences and how to fulfill those needs in different media.

(*continued*)

ASSIGNMENT SHEET (*continued*)

Here is a partial list of movies adapted from books and stories (you are not limited to these options):

Based on Novels

> *Atonement*
>
> *Blade Runner*
>
> *A Clockwork Orange*
>
> *The Cider House Rules*
>
> *Cold Mountain*
>
> *Dracula*
>
> *The English Patient*
>
> *The Girl with the Dragon Tattoo*
>
> *The Hobbit* or *The Lord of the Rings* movies
>
> *Fear and Loathing in Las Vegas*
>
> *Fight Club*
>
> *The Godfather*
>
> *LA Confidential*
>
> *The Last of the Mohicans*
>
> *Little Women*
>
> *The Lovely Bones*
>
> *Mystic River*
>
> *No Country for Old Men*
>
> *Of Mice and Men*
>
> *The Perks of Being a Wallflower*
>
> *Pride and Prejudice*
>
> *Schindler's List*
>
> *The Shipping News*
>
> *To Kill a Mockingbird*
>
> *The Wizard of Oz*

Based on Short Stories/Novellas

> *3:10 to Yuma*
>
> *The Adjustment Bureau*
>
> *Brokeback Mountain*
>
> *It's a Wonderful Life*

The Killers

Legends of the Fall

Lifeboat

Minority Report

The Man Who Would Be King

Rear Window

A River Runs Through It

The Shawshank Redemption

Sleepy Hollow

Stand by Me

The Secret Life of Walter Mitty

4. TIME AND TECHNOLOGY

Because this assignment asks students to create their own videos, a portion of the lesson must focus on the creation of the multimodal project. Students' comfort level with technology will fall in a broad range; there will likely be students who have never attempted something like this and others who are proficient in programs and have created videos before. Therefore, it is important to emphasize to students that you are not asking them to do the work of expert graphic designers or videographers. Technological expertise is not necessary for you or your students. Developing expertise in the technological programs is not the goal of the project; instead, the goal is to learn about how genre and medium shape how we communicate. Technology affects how we communicate, but technology changes rapidly. Rather than emphasize expertise in programs that might soon be outdated, we would rather students learn the rhetorical concepts about communication that can then be applied to future technologies.

We recommend giving students options of what programs to use to make their videos, such as iMovie, Windows Movie Maker, PowerPoint, Jing, and others (some of these programs are free to download, so there should be no cost to students), focusing a lesson or two of instruction on one particular program (whichever you are most familiar with) and allowing students to choose one of the others if they want. Volunteers from the class with specific expertise can also explain programs to peers and can be grouped to brainstorm and troubleshoot. If your class is online, tutorial videos are available on YouTube that you can provide to students to help them get started; these videos are also beneficial to give to students who wish to improve their projects and try new tools. It is not essential that you be an expert in every program students are allowed to choose from. We recommend being upfront with students, explaining that the assignment is not focused on daily instruction using technology, but rather is a lesson regarding the goals of the course and the assignment. Students will likely run into questions that you might not be able to answer, but classmates and online tutorials should provide access to resources they need to solve whatever technological problems might arise.

As this assignment has multiple components, students should start the project well in advance of the due date. To begin with, students will need to select and read a work of literature that has been turned into a movie. While there are plenty of stories that have been adapted to the screen, many students will choose novels and will therefore need some time to do the assigned reading—and movie watching—before even embarking on the print and video forms of the project. Then the work itself—analyzing the two versions of the story, writing the paper, and completing the multimodal component—can be time-consuming as well.

The following is a recommended time frame that could be adjusted to meet different instructors' needs:

- *Beginning of semester.* Whether the project is the first major assignment or the last, it's a good idea to inform students about it at the very beginning of the semester. They don't have to see the assignment sheet at this time or know all of the details, but instructors should inform them of the basic premise of the project—analyzing a literary work and movie based on that text—so that they have plenty of time to select the book or story. Even if students have read the book and seen the movie before, they will need to reread and re-watch them.

- *Week 1.* A few weeks—or even a month—before the assignment is due, instructors should show students the assignment and give them a thorough explanation of it. At this point, students should be comfortable with analyzing literary works. We recommend making this assignment the final project of the semester, or close to the last assignment, so that students have been practicing their skills of analysis throughout the term. If they have already analyzed stories or poems, then this project seems like a logical next step, a more complicated and more challenging assignment that can act as the culmination of their work. During the assignment unit, we have found that students benefit from time spent discussing analysis beyond alphabetic texts. The assignment must be placed in the context of discussions of multimodality, multiliteracies, and the effect of media on literature, rhetoric, and communication.

- *Week 2.* It's also important to allow time to model analysis of a film based on a work of literature. Set aside class time to show a movie based on a short story or novel that students have read, and then lead students in a discussion about the differences. Instructors are welcome to use a feature-length film, but if they feel like that would take up too much time, there are shorter movies available on the Web. Or, if a movie is a relatively new release and would be easy for students to rent and watch outside of class, then both the reading and viewing can be done as homework, and class time can remain reserved for discussing the literature.

- *Week 3.* There must also be time set aside to address the technological aspect of the lesson. The lesson should not become dominated with teaching technology; however, you should address the fact that some students will have difficulty making the videos. This can be handled, as stated previously, with presentations by you, presentations by students, group work in class, and other ways. We recommend, if you have the requisite access, to provide a workday or two in a computer lab or a classroom with desktop computer stations. While you should not let "teaching technology" dominate the project, you must also not simply leave students to do the work on their own without guidance and expect them to create quality projects.

- *Week 4.* As the deadline approaches for the project, we recommend providing time for peer workshops, perhaps even two: one for the written project and another for the video. Students can benefit by seeing what their classmates are working on, as well as from giving and receiving advice about how to improve their written and video projects. When it comes to the videos, a peer workshop in the middle of the composing process is likely more beneficial, and matching students with less knowledge about the technology with others who are proficient can be helpful to both. Those who need to learn more about the programs can do so from their peers; those who are knowledgeable about the necessary technology can themselves learn by being teachers.

- *Week 5.* When the projects are due, students should reflect on what they've learned. Moreover, it can be an enjoyable, celebratory experience for the class if students are able to display their video projects once they are finished. Students can stand before the class and explain what they did, putting their own level of knowledge about video creation into context. Also, as they talk about the project, students have a chance to reflect on what they've learned, not only about multimodality but also about literary and film analysis. Such reflection can help them better understand and retain what they've learned from the project. Therefore, when presenting, students should not simply say, "Here's my video. It speaks for itself." They should spend at least some time addressing what the learning experience was like. You can tell them that this introduction and reflection is similar to what film directors do when they screen a movie at its premiere, where they often introduce the film to the audience, talking about the experience of making it. We recommend that students also be asked to write reflective narratives about the project, which will give students agency in their own learning and help instructors evaluate how well students learned the goals of the assignment.

5. ANTICIPATING STUDENT NEEDS

We suggest giving students freedom in choosing what to write about; however, you must have oversight or approval of the book-movie pairs that they choose. For example, we recommend that students not be allowed to choose movies that were made from original screenplays. We also recommend that students be free to interpret "literary" somewhat broadly here. Often books that aren't necessarily regarded as literary produce highly respected, artful movies (*The Silence of the Lambs* and *The Shawshank Redemption*, for example). On the other hand, even great books can be adapted into terrible movies (such as practically every film adaptation of *Frankenstein*). In either case, interesting papers can be written. However, we advise that students refrain from writing about certain titles, such as *Twilight* or adaptations of Nicholas Sparks's books. With no disrespect to such authors, it's best if students choose a comparison with more analytical potential. Students should choose a book-movie pair that has interpretive depth so that the analyses can go beyond simply describing nuances of plot differences. We recommend that you endorse your students' decisions on a case-by-case basis to determine whether their idea for the project is acceptable. It's up to you whether you want to accept, say, a *Harry Potter* installment or a graphic novel/comic book adaptation such as *Watchmen* or *The Walking Dead*. Students might want a list of potential books/movies that are acceptable, and providing such a list shouldn't be difficult (comprehensive lists of movies based on novels and short stories can be found on *Wikipedia*).

Additionally, it can be helpful to provide an analysis model that students can discuss in class: choose a book/story and its accompanying film that all students read and watch, and then facilitate discussions about the adaptation. Without providing a model for analysis, students will likely focus on the plot of the movie and book/story, considering only the ways in which the movie adaptation was altered from the book. Students often overlook other aspects: character representations, depictions of the setting, issues of tone (as it's defined respectively in the mediums), and so on. Often students will say that they don't see much difference between the book and movie without realizing that the act of translating it from one medium to the other changes it significantly. There are sometimes several (more or less) faithful adaptations of a particular novel that are still quite different. Students need help to see beyond the obvious changes in plot and look at movies and books/stories more deeply. For instance, there are many questions you can pose to help them in their analyses, including the following:

- What is the effect of leaving out a particular scene or changing an aspect of a particular character?
- How have the filmmakers compressed, expanded, or otherwise changed the narrative told in the story or novel?
- Were the filmmakers attempting to be faithful to the source material or did they deliberately deviate for apparent cinematic purposes?
- What was the effect of these decisions?

Ultimately, as students consider these types of questions and more, they learn not only about literary analysis but also about the importance of genre, medium, and audience awareness in communication.

We have found that the assignment works best as part of a unit on multimodality. Students shouldn't feel as if they are spending time creating videos simply because it's a neat exercise. Most students will likely enjoy the project, but there might also be students who object, saying that the project isn't "writing." It's essential, therefore, to link the assignment to the pedagogical goals of the unit. Discussions about multimodality, adapting texts to new formats, effects of adapting texts to new mediums, effects of technology on communications, and so on, will help make it clear to students *why* they are being asked to create videos instead of simply writing another academic essay. In the end, even the students who were resistant at first will likely enjoy the project and cite in their reflections how much they learned from it.

Finally, a note about technology: PowerPoint allows students to create presentations and then use voice-over narration, and students need to understand that a slideshow without narration does not make use of multiple modes. Providing PowerPoint as an option (in addition to iMovie, Movie Maker, etc.) without emphasizing that the project must play as a video could result in basic PowerPoint presentations, which is not the assignment. The assignment is for students to create videos (or short movies, if you will) that use text, images, and sound to make their argument. A PowerPoint presentation that the instructor must actively navigate is not what they are being asked to do; therefore, lessons surrounding technology must be prefaced by a discussion of what makes a multimodal video successful.

6. ASSESSMENT TOOLS

In preparing to grade this assignment, it's important to have a clear understanding of what the written portion of the project and the video portion should be worth. Are they each 50 percent of the project grade? Should the multimodal portion be worth less than the written portion? We recommend making it clear to students—in discussion and in a rubric—that aesthetics of the video are of secondary importance. It's quite possible that a well-designed video might still fail to meet important requirements for the assignment. Conversely, a student who is new to the technology necessary for the project might do everything she is supposed to, but her presentation simply appears amateurish. We recommend that the latter, rather than the former, be rewarded in the rubric. Because this is a literature class, not a graphic design or video production class, the focus of the lesson is directed toward helping students learn the *concepts* within the assignment: multimodality, medium, audience awareness, literary analysis, rhetorical communication, and so on.

It may be beneficial for students' composing processes to invent and discuss rubric criteria as a class, deciding which factors are most relevant to include. By discussing these elements and allowing students to take part in designing the assessment tool, students learn what rhetorical choices are most important when creating a multimodal text. Furthermore, the collaborative nature of the rubric will ensure that students ask questions if they are confused about the criteria; this should also eliminate any surprises that can occur if rubrics are introduced at the end of production instead of the beginning. As students may be unfamiliar with multimodal projects, this type of collaborative assessment tool may be beneficial in explaining the potentially new elements of multimodal design; thus, the rubric can be used as an instructional tool, not simply an evaluative one (Borton and Huot 2).

The rubric and the lesson need to focus on the course goals. What should students learn and take away from the course? Perhaps it is just as important that students learn to analyze literary elements as it is to learn to create texts for specific purposes and audiences. First and foremost, you should decide how the assignment fits the course outcomes, discussing with students how the assignment furthers their learning of the specified goals.

In general, the assessment of multimodal texts is not always an easy task. As Pamela Takayoshi indicates, "there are no correct or easy answers for writing. Instead, there are rhetorically informed decisions writers make about text" (249). To this end, we suggest asking students to write a self-reflection throughout the project that accounts for the choices they make as writer and creator of the multimodal text. Using reflection provides insight into the conscious decisions made by the students when designing their projects, and it also asks students to become agents of their own learning (Yancey 8). While creating their multimodal projects, students can write reflections-in-action (Schön 8), learning to think about their choices and improve their projects as they progress through the composing process. This reflection should help the instructor give facilitative feedback that will guide revision of the project and the final assessment as well.

7. THEORETICAL BASIS FOR THE ASSIGNMENT: Exploring Multimodality through Film and Textual Analysis

This assignment asks students to analyze a literary text and a corresponding film based on the text, creating both written and multimodal projects that showcase their analysis. The dual components of the lesson emphasize multimodal literacy in two ways: by prompting students to think critically about a multimodal text and asking students to create a multimodal project of their own. For the assignment, students write an analysis of a literary work (most likely a novel or short story) and an accompanying film based on that text. The goal of the assignment is for students to not only practice their analytical skills but also learn about how medium shapes communication, whether academic or creative. Therefore, to go along with the written portion of the assignment, students are expected to also create a short video of their analysis. Their video should use text, images, and sound to make the same argument their written analysis does. In other words, just as they are analyzing the adaptation of a work from text to video, they are also creating an adaptation from text to video.

This assignment can benefit the literature classroom in numerous ways. Alison Gibbons claims that showing students creative versions from different media "exposes the reader to multiple forms working in synchronicity to communicate narrative meaning" (114). Specifically, she argues that multimodal printed literature, or texts that make use of verbal and visual modes of communicating, can engage readers with text in new ways and enhance the learning process. Expanding on Gibbons's argument, we suggest that viewing multiple forms of a novel (i.e., written form and a film representation) can open up the possibility for greater understanding of the literary work. Considering how meaning varies between works that use different modes of communication, this assignment asks students to perform literary analyses of a film and the text from which the film was based. In doing so, students are learning to "negotiate and make sense of not only a multiplicity of meanings, but also of modes which in turn expand and add to those meanings" (114). While what we describe is intended for sophomore-level introductory literature courses, variations of the assignment might work for other literature courses, including survey courses, literary theory classes, or genre-based literature classes.

> "Viewing multiple forms of a novel can open up the possibility for greater understanding of the literary work."
>
> **Andrew Bourelle** and **Tiffany Bourelle**

Using two versions of the same story can encourage new approaches to literary deconstruction. Asking students to read and view multiple representations of a literary work can bring to light the variances in interpretation between the original author and the director of the film. In addition, because the medium of print and the medium of film have different properties, there may be differences in the interpretations of the viewer or reader and the director of the film or the author of the text. For instance, the way a director chooses to place elements in the film (i.e., an interactive scene with characters) can allow a potential difference in meaning for the audience (Jewitt 8). Likewise, a character may be represented differently than the author's representation. Or simply the spoken dialogue can produce nuances undiscovered in the original text. These variations between film and text can alter the way an audience interacts with the piece, which can lead to a discussion of rhetorical choices as well, including audience and purpose of the original text and the film. Opportunities for multilayered analysis abound, from loose adaptations such as *Apocalypse Now* (from Joseph Conrad's *Heart of Darkness*) to more faithful adaptations such as *Brokeback Mountain*. The literary works could range from classics (*Pride and Prejudice*, for example) to popular entertainment (*The Hunger Games*) and can include short stories that have been expanded greatly for the screen (such as Elmore Leonard's "3:10 to Yuma"); novels that have been adapted faithfully in spirit but not necessarily in plot (such as Stephen King's *The Shining*); adaptations that resemble the plot of their source material but differ greatly in other ways (such as *One Flew Over the Cuckoo's Nest*); or nonfiction (such as Tobias Wolff's *This Boy's*

Life or Jon Krakauer's *Into the Wild*). In all of these cases, there are differences—both subtle and overt—that provide rich analytical opportunities.

Upon deconstruction and discussion of the two texts, students can create multimodal representations of their own analyses, using multiple modes to communicate their message. This aspect of the assignment can enhance the students' literacy skills necessary for success in the twenty-first century. Maxine Wright argues that "multimodal transaction with literature can be a pathway for English educators and students to cultivate multiple ways of knowing while entering the medium of the digital world" (104). Now more than ever, the concept of literacy is expanding to include multiliteracies, or the movement beyond the written and spoken word to encompass interaction and production of multimodal texts (Jewitt 245). Pamela Takayoshi and Cynthia Selfe remind us that within various professions, graduates will be expected "to read and be asked to compose multimodal texts of various kinds, texts designed to communicate on multiple semiotic channels, using all available means of creating and conveying meaning" (3). We suggest that multimodality in literature courses can be a way to invigorate our practices and students' interaction with texts while at the same time prepare them to become literate citizens in the digital world.

8. CONCLUSION

We thought of the idea for this assignment in our own discussions of film adaptations. To really consider the subtle and not-so-subtle changes a work undergoes when it is adapted to a new medium is a rich analytical endeavor, and our students benefited from the assignment. We began by simply asking students to write analytical essays. And, from this, we worked out many of the challenges with the analysis part of the assignment, such as students focusing too closely on plot or writing about works that lack interpretive depth—problems that often go hand in hand. For example, the first time the assignment was taught, several students wrote analyses of Nicholas Sparks's novels, and while we mean no disrespect to that author, those books are often plot driven and lack the indeterminacies and layers of meaning that can lead to rich analysis of literature. The analyses tended to only address surface differences within the plot. In contrast, other students wrote interesting, thorough analyses. For example, one student wrote about *Brokeback Mountain*, and although the movie follows the plot of the story very closely, there are fascinating differences because of the change in medium, such as the way author Annie Proulx provides the story in a less linear format or how secondary characters from the story are given more attention in the movie. The student explored such differences in depth (and won an end-of-the year award from the university's writing program for the paper). Therefore, while some of the essays failed to fully accomplish our expectations, we could see the potential because others were just what we were looking for: rich analyses showcasing critical thinking.

Having worked the problems out of the written portion of the project, we decided to add a multimodal component. If students were writing about adaptations, they would benefit from attempting adaptations themselves. Such projects, with written and multimodal components, help students understand the effect their choice of medium has on the delivery of their message to an intended audience. Working with multimodal projects, we have discovered through research and trial and error what works best for such projects: emphasizing the rhetorical concepts of multimodality, not the technological; asking students to write reflections on what they learned and basing the project evaluation at least partly on those reflections; and making sure students see the connections between the assignment and the course goals of multimodality. Through the course of developing this assignment, we have held class discussions or read/viewed projects about a variety of movie adaptations: *3:10 to Yuma*, *Apocalypse Now*, *Frankenstein*, *Freaks*, *The Scarlet Letter*, *The Shawshank Redemption*, *Watchmen*, *Whale Rider*, and others.

Asking students to analyze a work of literature and a film based on that work is a challenging and compelling exercise in critical thinking. The assignment doesn't simply trick students into being interested in the project because they get to watch a movie — it has important pedagogical benefits as well. With this assignment, students gain valuable practice in analyzing literature, but they also learn rhetorical considerations that go into creating a work of textual or visual art. When comparing a book to its movie, a reader/ viewer must think about what effect the differences of medium have on their respective audiences. Further, students must think about what choices the films' directors and production teams made when adapting the works of literature.

Furthermore, a written analysis assignment that asks students to compare a movie and its source material has validity on its own. However, because students are analyzing two mediums, we suggest there is additional value in requiring the students to work in two mediums as well. When this assignment is introduced, we recommend you begin discussing analysis beyond alphabetic texts, talking about multimodality. Class discussions can focus on ways in which text-based literature has blurred boundaries with other media. You might start with the example of William Blake's illuminated prints, which brought together literary writing and visual art. You can lead students in discussions about graphic novels or illustrated novels wherein the artwork is integral to the overall effect. You can have students listen to podcasts of stories or dramatic audio performances. No matter what multimodal works are introduced, the assignment should be addressed in the context of multimodality and multimodal literacy in order to maximize the pedagogical benefit of the project. The point of the project — analyzing two mediums and composing in two mediums—is to stretch students' analytical skills to understand how media and technology are used to shape literature and communication.

9. WORKS CITED

Borton, Sonya C., and Brian Huot. "Responding and Assessing." *Multimodal Composition: Resources for Teachers.* Edited by Cynthia L. Selfe. Hampton, 2007, pp. 99-111.

Gibbons, Alison. "Multimodal Literature 'Moves' Us: Dynamic Movement and Embodiment in *VAS: An Opera in Flatland.*" *Hermes—Journal of Language and Communication Studies*, vol. 41, 2008, pp. 107-24.

Jewitt, Casey. "Multimodality and Literacy in School Classrooms." *Review of Research and Education*, vol. 32, 2008, pp. 241-67.

Schön, Donald A. *Educating the Reflective Practitioner: Toward a New Design for Teaching and Learning in the Professions.* Jossey-Bass, 1983.

Takayoshi, Pamela. "The Shape of Electronic Writing: Evaluating and Assessing Computer-Assisted Writing Processes and Products." *Computers and Composition*, vol. 13, no. 2, 1996, pp. 245-57.

Takayoshi, Pamela, and Cynthia Selfe. "Thinking about Multimodality." *Multimodal Composition: Resources for Teachers.* Edited by Cynthia Selfe. Hampton, 2007, pp. 1-12.

Wright, Mary F. "Multimodal Trans(ACT)ions with Literature through the Creation of a Zine." *Minnesota English Journal*, 2005, pp. 89-108.

Yancey, Kathleen B. *Reflection in the Writing Classroom.* Utah State UP, 1998.

23

From Page to Stage: Using Technology to Demonstrate an Understanding of Literature

Melissa Vosen Callens
North Dakota State University

Dr. Melissa Vosen Callens is an assistant professor of practice in instructional design at North Dakota State University in Fargo. She teaches introductory literature courses and advanced composition courses in business and professional writing and visual communication. Her research interests include distance education, collaborative writing, and a wide variety of pop culture topics.*

COURTESY OF
MELISSA VOSEN CALLENS

1. OVERVIEW

- **Assignment:** Students choose a short story studied earlier in the semester, transform it into a play, and collaborate to create a video of one scene in the play. Students are asked to think about the similarities and differences among literary genres and show their understanding of a work of literature through a traditional academic format (an analysis paper) and a multimedia format (a video).

- **Courses:** Introduction to literature and any literature course or literary genre course; literature and composition.

- **Literature:** Short stories, poetry, and drama. For this course and assignment, any reader of your choosing will do.

- **Technology:** Video camera (most students have access to a camera via their smartphone, but in case they don't, your school may also have cameras available for students to rent for free); video editing software (e.g., Windows Movie Maker).

*Thank you to Dr. Kevin Brooks and Jo Cavins for inspiring this project. This assignment is a hybrid of two assignments they created—a video essay assignment and a drama assignment.

- **Time:** Four weeks to write, shoot, and edit the video. Some in-class time is given, but much of the work is to be completed outside of class.

2. GOALS OF THE ASSIGNMENT

After completing this assignment, students will be able to:

- read—analyze, interpret, critique, evaluate—written and visual texts; and
- write and speak effectively for a variety of purposes and audiences in a variety of genres and media.

This assignment requires students to not only analyze and interpret a short story of their choosing, but also demonstrate their dramatic interpretation of that story by writing a script and creating a video.

"In a literature classroom, the use of digital technologies can provide students the opportunity to demonstrate understanding of course texts with interactivity—making the students instant publishers and distributors."

Melissa Vosen Callens
North Dakota State University

3. ASSIGNMENT SHEET

From Page to Stage: Using Technology to Demonstrate an Understanding of Literature

Course: _____

Instructor: _____

Date: _____

For this assignment you will write a critical analysis paper and create a video.

> **Paper:** Story Analysis and Script for Scene
> Length: 3–4 pages, double-spaced

> **Video:** Performance of Scene
> Length: 2–3 minutes

> **Paper** Due Date: _____ (50 pts)

> **Conference and Rough-Cut Video** Due Date: _____ (25 pts)

> **Final Video** Due Date (with Script): _____ (100 pts)

Working with your assigned group, I would like you to take one of the short stories we read this semester and turn it into a play. For the paper portion of this assignment, you will outline the acts and scenes you envision for your play. For the video portion of this project, you will stage and film one scene. See below for step-by-step instructions.

Paper Steps: Story Analysis and Script for Scene

1. Choose one of the short stories we read together this semester that would translate well to the stage/video. I don't want more than one group to work on a story, so I've set up a special Discussion Board where your group can claim a story — first come, first served.

2. What about this story makes you believe it could be a successful play? This answer should take 1–2 paragraphs. You need to show that you understand the particular needs and characteristics of this genre (as opposed to fiction or poetry).

3. If you were to transform the story into a play, what kind of play would it be? Comedy or tragedy? Modern drama? Feel free to play around with this. This should take 2–4 paragraphs to answer.

4. Create an outline of the acts and scenes you envision.

5. Describe the action of one scene in some detail — write dialogue. Choose this scene carefully because you will be asked to film and edit it.

6. In 1–2 good paragraphs, describe the stage set you think would be necessary for this scene.

7. Cast at least three characters with contemporary actors. Who would be your ideal choices and why? You should provide 1–2 paragraphs per character. What qualities do these actors have that might have made them good choices?

8. Note: Work together please. Don't just delegate tasks.

Video Steps: Performance of Scene

1. For this part of the assignment, I would like you to record and edit the one scene you developed in detail for the paper portion of this project. The final product only needs to be 2 or 3 minutes long.

2. As part of the above paper, you will be required to brainstorm and write a 2- to 3-minute scene.

3. In class, we will discuss the importance of storyboards. Before you shoot your video, you not only need to have the scene written, you should also have a rough sketch of a storyboard. A storyboard shows what you plan to do in each frame in terms of content, set, costumes, and so on. You will be expected to meet with me, before your video short, to discuss your script and storyboard. A storyboard is a first draft of an essay.

4. Shoot all video to prepare for editing process.

5. Edit video.

6. Final video completed, screen for class.

Practical goals for this assignment are to introduce you to using a digital video camera to extend a scholarly conversation and using digital video editing software.

The content goal for this assignment is to demonstrate your understanding of your chosen short story as well as the genre conventions for drama.

4. TIME AND TECHNOLOGY

For this assignment, it's best to give students four or more weeks for completion. I recommend devoting part of your class time to introducing the assignment, and another portion to covering assigned literature. I typically continue to assign different plays for students to read during this four-week time period; I call this part of the semester our drama unit. Part of our class time is spent discussing and working on the project, and part of our class time is spent discussing newly assigned readings.

Because this is the final project in my course and it replaces a final exam, students also have the last week of the semester to finish. During final exam time, students screen their videos. I tell them that the screening is not an exam, but rather a celebration of their knowledge and work. It is also fun to bring popcorn and soda to the screening and invite others to attend.

First and foremost, in groups of two or three, students must choose one of the short stories they read earlier in the semester that they believe will translate well to the stage. Students are required to share which story they will be using in order to avoid duplicate productions in the class.

As a group, they will need to create an outline of the acts and scenes they envision for their chosen short story as well as make decisions about costumes, stage direction, and sets. Because this could easily become an overwhelming project, I ask students to develop (dialogue, costumes, set, etc.) *one* scene in detail. A scene, for the purpose of this assignment, is two to three minutes, and it is what they will film and edit. This may seem like an extremely short scene, but it is important to consider the time commitment involved when writing, shooting, and editing a video — particularly for students who are unfamiliar with video editing software. I have found that while many students regularly capture video on their phone, very few edit what they capture. Often students share their videos in raw form via text messaging or social networking sites.

After the students write their scene, they are required to record and edit it. As the instructor, I typically meet with groups after they have a rough draft, but before they shoot their video. It is important to allow adequate time for students to complete this project. It is also important to set smaller deadlines for students for two reasons. First, most of the students in the course are first-year or second-year students; they may or may not be good at setting deadlines and managing large projects. Second, it is easy, even as an experienced videographer, to devote copious amounts of time to an editing project. Typically, students are enthused about this project. While this makes me happy, I also am careful that students do not devote too much time to the project.

For this assignment, as mentioned in the overview, students will need to have access to a digital video camera as well as video editing software. At

North Dakota State University (NDSU), students may check out cameras for free through our Information Technology Services Department. In addition, in recent years, I have noticed that more and more students have smartphones that have the ability to shoot high-quality video. Every year there seems to be a smaller number of students who need to check out a video camera, but the option to do so remains available.

Students must also have access to video editing software. All computers on campus have Windows Movie Maker. Additional editing software programs, such as Adobe Premiere Elements 10, are available on select computers on campus. I have also had students use their own personal copies of iMovie, which is preferable to most Mac users. Windows Movie Maker, however, is the most accessible software for students because it is on all PC campus computers. It is also an easy program to use for students who have had no prior experience editing video.

As an instructor, if you are inexperienced with a video camera and/or with Windows Movie Maker, you may wish to have someone demonstrate the technology and/or software for your class. I typically invite a student who is employed by our school's Technology Learning and Media Center (TLMC) to do a workshop on the software. The TLMC helps students with technology-related coursework and multimedia projects and are willing to conduct workshops for classes. I have found that most students have a basic understanding of how to operate a video camera and at least half in each class are familiar with Windows Movie Maker.

Finally, I make sure to reserve a computer cluster twice during the unit. On the first day in the cluster, students work with the TLMC student staff member to upload their video and practice using Movie Maker. On the second day in the cluster, I allow students to work in small groups editing their project. Depending on the skill level of your students and your own personal preferences, you may wish to give them additional time in a cluster. While most students have their own desktop or laptop computer, some do not have video editing software. Because of this, it is important to give students some class time working on campus computers. In addition, campus computers are available at NDSU for student use in certain buildings 24 hours a day, if they need to work on the project outside of class.

5. ANTICIPATING STUDENT NEEDS

In my experience, the biggest difficulty with this assignment is the range of student ability and experience with video and video editing software. Admittedly, some students looked bored during the Window Movie Maker training while others are in need of constant help. Typically, if students do not need the training, I ask them to go to an adjacent cluster if available or one area of the room to work on editing their projects. I still believe, however, that it is important to have training available to students during class time because there are still a good number of students with little experience.

Finally, as we all know, many students procrastinate. This assignment, however, is impossible to finish if started one or two nights before the due date. If your class is populated with mostly first-year and second-year students, it is important that you walk students through the process. I would recommend setting benchmarks—include a paper/script due date, raw video due date, and first edit due date on your course schedule.

On my schedule, the first due date is a paper rough draft and storyboard due date. Students are required to turn in a "rough sketch" of the scene they plan to shoot and conference with me. After the storyboard due date, students are given a week or so to provide raw video (video that does not have to contain any editing). At this point, I offer the editing workshop. From there, students have one additional due date where they are expected to turn in a draft of their video with some edits. The final due date, the screen date, is the week of finals.

6. ASSESSMENT TOOLS

Undoubtedly, grading creative work can be difficult. There are, however, several items I look for when grading this assignment. First and foremost, I want students to be able to demonstrate their understanding of their chosen short story.

Second, I want students to demonstrate their understanding of common literary terms in regard to drama. The paper and script I ask them to write, before shooting their video, allow students to demonstrate their understanding. In addition, students also have to understand these terms in order to shoot their video.

Finally, I want to introduce students to using a digital video camera and using digital video editing software before sharing their work. I am more lenient in this area, but do expect students to produce a two- to three-minute video employing at least two or three of the editing techniques discussed in class. I have included a rubric for both the paper and video on page 357.

Paper and Video Grading Rubric	
Key Elements of the Paper	**Comments**
Rationale for project (why your group believes this short story could be a successful play)	
Outline of acts and scenes provided	
One scene described in detail Dialogue Set Costumes	
Cast for play outlined (3 or more contemporary actors cast)	
Key Elements of the Video	**Comments**
Scene outlined in your paper filmed	
Good, appropriate transitions and editing techniques are used	
Video shows knowledge of other aspects of visual language effectively (set, costumes, etc.) and your understanding of the needs and characteristics of the genre	
+ _____ / 100 pts (Paper) + _____ / 100 pts (Video)	

7. THEORETICAL BASIS FOR THE ASSIGNMENT:
From Page to Stage: Using Technology to Demonstrate an Understanding of Literature

As instructors, at one time or another, we have all faced a class of glassy-eyed undergraduates. When this happens, most of us seek solace in colleagues as we carefully revise future lesson plans, hoping our revisions spark some interest in the content we feel so passionately about. Stephanie Vie argues that one way to increase student engagement in the classroom is to incorporate technologies that students are familiar with, but have not thought critically about (10).

Hani Morgan, associate professor of curriculum, instruction, and special education, believes "student-created video projects can enhance motivation,

multimodal literacy, problem-solving skills, and content
knowledge" in the classroom (52). In an introductory literature course, a course where many of the students are
enrolled only to fulfill a general education requirement,
it can be difficult to motivate and encourage students to
think critically and evaluate course texts. By asking students to create videos interpreting short stories of their
choosing, students are able to use technology creatively
to demonstrate their understanding and extend a scholarly conversation on the subject.

> "Stephanie Vie argues that one way to increase student engagement in the classroom is to incorporate technologies that students are familiar with, but have not thought critically about."
> **Melissa Vosen Callens**

Video production, because it is something many students have already
experimented with in their personal lives, is also likely to spark their interest. In their study, Mary Lea and Sylvia Jones observed forty-five undergraduates' literacy practices, specifically how they read and produced digital
texts, and discovered that their participants engaged in a "range of modes,
integrating written, visual and multimodal texts as part of the process of
meaning-making" like viewing and posting videos on YouTube (383).

In my introduction to literature class, as mentioned in the overview, I ask
students to create a two- to three-minute video. In groups of three or four,
students take a short story studied earlier in the semester and turn it into a
play. Their video is one scene in their play. I like this assignment because it
requires students to think about and demonstrate their understanding of the
similarities and differences of all the genres typically studied in an introductory course: short story fiction, poetry, and drama. It also requires students
to think critically about meaning-making in video production. The course
is split up into three major units like many introductory literature courses:
short story, poetry, and drama. The video project is a culminating project
for the course and is a substitute for the final exam. The purpose of the
assignment is to have students demonstrate their understanding. Students
also show their understanding of the particular needs and characteristics
of drama (as opposed to the other genres studied this semester: fiction
and poetry) in addition to developing and/or honing their video production skills. According to Anita Brooks Kirkland, asking students to create
a video of a dramatization of a literary work helps them to not only gain a
better understanding of the material but also improve their media literacy
skills (19).

This assignment is designed for a general education, introduction to
literature course—although I think it could be used, with some modifica-
tion, in upper-level literature courses. My course, English 220: Introduction to Literature, typically consists of freshmen and sophomores from a
variety of different majors who are looking to fulfill a general education
requirement in the humanities. Occasionally, an English education or
English major will take the course; it is not, however, required for either
major. One of the primary objectives of the course is to help students improve

their understanding and appreciation of writing as well as their ability to think, speak, and write intelligently about literature. Students also learn common literary terminology and are asked to read and discuss representative examples of poetry, drama, and fiction.

While technology is important, it is essential to remember it is more than a tool. In a literature classroom, the use of digital technologies like video can provide students with interactivity—making the students instant publishers and distributors. Jeffery Grabill and Troy Hicks argue that instructors must move beyond viewing technology as a tool; they need to view technology, specifically information communication technologies (ICTs), as a way to open spaces for socially situated rhetorical practice.

These technologies can provide authentic audiences for students and can transform the traditional academic essay. These technologies also give students a chance to extend the conversation and receive instant, or near instant, feedback by using a platform they have already used, but perhaps had not used in a learning setting or thought critically about. Upon conclusion of their study, Lea and Jones urge universities to "redefine what is meant by literacy in the university, paying much more attention to the mutability of digital texts, and more specifically, the ways in which students are accessing, reading and integrating these in their study and assessed work" (391).

Technology can provide these opportunities for students to engage critically with course content as well as with digital tools they access and use every day; it can lay the groundwork for a teachable moment. While technology can provide students with opportunities to demonstrate their knowledge, join a greater community of learners, and enter and extend the conversation, it can only do so if the instructor supports the students and platform. Technology is not a substitute teacher. Grabill and Hicks argue that "using ICTs isn't enough; critically understanding how these writing technologies enable new literacies and meaningful communication should also be a core curricular and pedagogical function of English education" (307). In other words, students are able to learn about course content *and* new literacies in tandem; it should not, and does not, replace your primary course content and objectives. Priscilla Norton and Dawn Hathaway write,

> One way to combat concerns about video production as decontextualized or without a focused content is to link it with the ongoing curricular requirements of particular learning contexts. Video production then becomes an instructional strategy for teaching content, not a set of tools and processes to be mastered as isolated skills. (147)

As Grabill and Hicks argue, "Our students, those we have called 'digital writers,' rely on a rhetorically sophisticated combination of words, motion, interactivity, and visuals to make meaning" (308). This assignment also allows students to demonstrate their understanding of course material in a manner familiar to them. The video format allows for this process to be collaborative and provides students with an authentic audience, the class and anyone else they wish to share the video with.

In addition to the objectives outlined above, practical goals for this assignment are to introduce students to using a digital video camera and video editing software. Even if students have used a video camera before, it is likely they are inexperienced with the editing process. In her study, Penny Thompson found that "students may be using a narrower range of technology tools than the popular press authors claim, and they may not be exploiting the full benefits of these technology tools when using them in a learning context" (23). By learning how to use editing software as well as the steps to produce a video for a specific purpose and audience, students are able to apply this in future courses as well as their daily lives. When many students create videos on a personal level, they now will be able to think more critically about the components of their videos and how these components contribute to the meaning-making process. It helps them think about visual communication, a currently dominant mode of communication, in a more analytical light. Morgan believes when teachers implement video production, it helps students "stay connected to their world and promote motivation, acquisition of content knowledge, critical-thinking skills, and multimodal literacy" (53).

8. CONCLUSION

I like this assignment because it allows students to demonstrate their understanding of course material, and it allows them to be creative. I also like this assignment because it is extremely difficult to plagiarize. Students seem to enjoy screening their videos, and it is a nice way to celebrate their hard work at the end of the semester. When groups are done screening, it is common for other students to ask questions about the video and their filmmaking process, which, I believe, is a good indicator of their interest in the projects. There are chuckles during funny parts and gasps at shocking ones. Students also enjoy that it is a substitute for the final exam.

> "I like this assignment because it is extremely difficult to plagiarize."
>
> **Melissa Vosen Callens**

As I mentioned above, our students, by nature, are digital writers. By asking them to complete this project, I am allowing them to demonstrate their understanding in a way that is familiar to them and allows them to "access and participate more seamlessly and instantaneously within web spaces and to distribute writing to large and widely dispersed audiences" (Grabill and Hicks 304). It also gives students a chance to think analytically about a medium that many already use on a regular basis. Despite this use, however, many students mention to me that they are surprised at the work involved in editing a video. Finally, most students are kinesthetic learners, and this project gives them a chance to work hands-on with material.

9. WORKS CITED

Grabill, Jeffery T., and Troy Hicks. "Multiliteracies Meet Methods: The Case for Digital Writing in English Education." *English Education*, vol. 37, no. 4, 2005, pp. 301-11.

Kirkland, Anita Brooks. "Making Movies: Digital Video Production in the School Library Program." *School Libraries of Canada Online*, vol. 25, no. 3, 2004, pp. 16-21. EbscoHost, Accession number 19812874, connection, ebscohost .com/articles/19812874/4-making-movies-digital-video-productions-school -library-program.

Lea, Mary R., and Sylvia Jones. "Digital Literacies in Higher Education: Exploring Textual and Technological Practice." *Studies in Higher Education*, vol. 36, no. 4, 2011, pp. 377-93.

Morgan, Hani. "Technology in the Classroom: Creating Videos Can Lead Students to Many Academic Benefits." *Childhood Education* 89.1 (2012): 51-53. Print.

Thompson, Penny. "The Digital Natives as Learners: Technology Use Patterns and Approaches to Learning." *Computers and Education*, vol. 65, 2013, pp. 12-33.

Vie, Stephanie. "Digital Divide 2.0: 'Generation M' and Online Social Networking Sites in the Composition Classroom." *Computers and Composition*, vol. 25, 2008, 9-23.

24

Restaging Shakespeare through Multimodal Composition

Jacob Hughes
Washington State University

AND

Tim Hetland
*North Seattle Community College and
Washington State University*

COURTESY OF JACOB HUGHES

Jacob Hughes is finishing his PhD in English literature at Washington State University. He teaches early English literature, Shakespeare, and composition courses at Washington State University's campus in Richland. He has also taught courses on medieval and Renaissance humanities, and digital diversity. Hughes's dissertation, titled "Shakespeare's Chaucerian Entertainers," focuses on how Chaucer not only informed some of Shakespeare's key characters, such as Falstaff, but also influenced the playwright's views on dramaturgy. He has published articles on English pedagogy, digital humanities, and several book reviews. Between 2009 and 2013, he was the managing editor of *The Rocky Mountain Review*.

COURTESY OF TIM HETLAND

Timothy Hetland, the editor of this collection, describes himself as a humanist and technologist. Hetland earned his PhD in contemporary English literature and film at Washington State University. In his dissertation, he examined the parallel development of the contemporary horror film genre and molecular biology. Hetland has taught English at Washington State and North Seattle Community College. He is a contributor to Bedford's *LitBits*, where he blogs about teaching literature in general and fiction in particular. Hetland is currently director of marketing at Black Pixel (@blackpixel) and cofounder of @showqase and @orto.

1. OVERVIEW

- **Assignment:** Digitally produce a key or ambiguous scene from one of Shakespeare's plays.
- **Courses:** Drama; Shakespeare; any literature course that incorporates plays.
- **Literature:** Shakespeare, the works of any playwright, and even authors of different genres and media, such as novelists, memoirists, graphic composers, and so on.

- **Technology:** Any digital medium including, but not limited to, digitally captured films, computer animation, any web-based text, photographs, or a combination of these. Students can complete this project with most any computer, tablet device, or smartphone.

- **Time:** Can be conducted with a fifteen- to thirty-minute assignment introduction and one fifty-minute period devoted to academic research and presentation strategies. If time within the term allows, students should showcase their works at a venue either inside or outside class. Can also be extended over a full semester.

> "Just as reading and watching are distinct interpretive experiences, writing and performing arguments open the way to rich learning opportunities."
>
> **Jacob Hughes**
> Washington State University

2. GOALS OF THE ASSIGNMENT

By completing this assignment, students will:

- develop critical thinking skills additional to and outside the essay format, most notably multimodal argumentation and composition;

- employ an integrative and multidisciplinary approach to understanding and interacting with literature;

- consider the rhetorical (i.e., persuasive) impacts visual and aural aesthetics have on our understanding and interpretation of literature and art in general; and

- explore how and why humans compose in different mediums through participant observation and practicing different acts of composition.

3. ASSIGNMENT SHEET

Restaging Shakespeare through Multimodal Composition

Course: _____

Instructor: _____

Date: _____

Preparing to Perform Digital Shakespeare

Begin by knowing your objective: Your goal is to digitally perform, produce, direct, perhaps costume, stage, and edit — and most importantly — interpret some key scene from a Shakespeare play we've read this semester. Using the hard-earned knowledge and skills you've developed throughout the term, augmented by your access and use of digital technology, strain your creative and critical thinking skills in crafting a performance modeling (not rebooting) of the Bard's words. Make no mistake: this assignment is not to be trifled with as a cheesy and quick path to an "easy A," but rather serves as a monumental and immortalizing academic and artistic achievement that puts your readings into practice, both Shakespearean and scholarly. Here are the depressing logistics:

You, as an individual or in a tightly knit alliance with a few colleagues, will be responsible for every aspect of this digital production. When working in a group, you will be accountable for some significant slice of the performance and scholarship in action. Furthermore, group projects should scale with appropriate ambition: the larger the group, the more content (both scholarly and performance) I'll expect turned in.

At a minimum, you'll need to consider the following before executing your project.

Choose a scene: You probably won't have time to stage a whole play, but you could consider a longer scene or a series of shorter ones. Or, develop an abridged version of an entire play (like Lego Macbeth). However, your analysis will be well served by razor-sharp focus, so don't get too carried away with the storytelling aspects. Choosing to interpret an ambiguous or otherwise difficult scene will increase your chances of reaping great analytic rewards. As with all aspects of this project, you must justify your decisions using acute scholarly acumen.

Select a digital medium and venue: If all the world's a stage, you are responsible for making sure we know it. Besides, the Globe is booked. Choosing your medium can be a hefty task: there are many potential ways of digitally interpreting Shakespeare's drama. It's very important to consider how your chosen medium and creative process affects your perspective on the Shakespearean text. Remember: your project will need to be performed in some regard, though that "performance" might simply be uploading the finalized project to YouTube.

The transmission of your final project is entirely up to you, though I will need to have access to it. For further suggestions on potential digital mediums, see below.

Consider stagecraft/composition: While you won't necessarily be undertaking a film project, you'll nevertheless need to consider the significance of real or implied spatial relationships in your work. In other words, why and how did you place "things" (speakers, actors, text, props, etc.) to forward your work's message/argument/goal? Why is Juliet ten feet above Romeo for the window scene rather than at eye level? Why did you dress Puck up like Dame Edna? Why did your hypertext performance link to Hamlet's last speech when the setting is in the graveyard? Your rationale should be symbolically significant and at the very least pragmatically justifiable, once again supported by specific references from the Shakespearean texts and guided by scholarly perspectives.

Research: Some form of detailed analysis — minimally accompanied by an annotated bibliography of no fewer than five scholarly academic sources, preferably from peer-reviewed journal articles or well-focused book chapters — must serve to highlight not just your erudition, but the educated rationale for your performance. You may wish to experiment via performance with a particular scholar's perspective on a key scene. Or, more likely, you'll use scholarly perspectives to guide how you go about setting up your performance. Ultimately, you are still undertaking an academic conversation; you'll just be using a different mode.

Composing the Written Work

We will require some written work turned in prior to seeing your performance. Here's the breakdown:

Part One: Develop a 3- to 5-page analytic argument on some aspect of staging/interpreting a particular Shakespeare play with focus on a key scene to illustrate your examples. We don't want an outline; we want analysis. The final page(s) should be devoted to fleshing out the beginnings of an annotated bibliography with at least two relevant scholarly sources at this point. This part of the project is due _____ [sometime during the first half of the semester].

Part Two: This portion of the project will be turned in at the same time as your digital performance. Essentially, your task here is to compose a minimum 3- to 5-page production journal replete with annotated bibliography of additional relevant sources. Employing an academic and analytic tone, explain the process of remodeling Shakespeare from a digital perspective. What critical perspectives were most valuable to how you interpreted your scene? Why did you choose your particular medium(s), and how did working with them shape (or reshape) your understanding of the scene? Ultimately, all of this material should be packaged with a succinct thesis regarding the significance of your

(continued)

ASSIGNMENT SHEET (*continued*)

interpretation. Setting images of a *Twelfth Night* performance to Pink Floyd's *Dark Side of the Moon* is peachy, but how does this mode expand your perspective of the scenes in question? Your production journal should include an annotated bibliography with at least five relevant scholarly secondary sources.

Performing

Length: Take care not to bite off more you can chew. A well-focused project composed of 10 to 15 minutes' worth of performance content is a good approximation. In some cases, 7 to 10 minutes will be more appropriate. Think "quality" instead of "quantity." While this duration might not seem like much, many hours can go into preparing only 10 minutes. For projects that don't have duration per se, consider carefully how many hours of labor you will have to put into executing the final performance. If you invest too little, your project will seem shallow; if it's too much, you won't have time to finish.

Turning your project in/venue: Consider how you want your performance viewed. Will you be using YouTube, a DVD, a Web site or some other mode? How does the venue affect your readers'/viewers' interpretation of the Shakespearean text? Regardless of what method you choose, make sure that I can readily access a copy for grading purposes.

Suggestions for digital mediums: This list is in no way exhaustive, nor should you consider yourself limited to the options below. There are vast arrays of digital technologies that can be used creatively to perform your scene. Also, they can potentially be used in combination.

- **Prezi:** found at prezi.com
  Prezi is a cloud-based presentation/storytelling tool that allows users to upload images and videos to form collages. Eschewing the traditional slideshow, Prezi lets users trace a path through a storyboard. This site would work best for multimedia Shakespeare projects and/or nonlinear storytelling.

- **Digital video editing:** found on most Windows- and Mac-enabled machines, free programs abound. Check out Bryan Axelson's "Lego Macbeth" for a stop-motion example of an abridged play here: http://www.youtube.com/watch?v=uRohPxQQRiY. Many students may find that equipping themselves with a digital camera and performing Shakespeare will be the best and most direct route to interpreting a key scene. However, you need not limit yourself to any single medium in this case, nor do you have to create a static scene. If you film portions of your project, consider your digital venue carefully. Will you showcase your performance on YouTube, or will it serve as a piece in a multimedia Prezi storyboard?

- **Hypertext:** an example project can be found at www.eastgate.com/TwelveBlue/.

While you're probably familiar with the idea of hyperlinks, the notion of hypertext as an art may have passed you by if you weren't using the Internet in the '90s. Though perhaps out of fashion, works remodeled in hypertext will necessarily change the reader's experience. Should you use this technique, you will be able to explore how.

- **Wix:** found at wix.com
  A free flash-based Web service, Wix is typically used for personal site creation. There are undoubtedly better flash animation programs available, but this site can help you experiment.

- **Paint.net:** found, unsurprisingly, at www.getpaint.net
  This is probably the best free image editing software available online. Though it might not serve as your only medium, it may prove useful.

- **Audacity:** found at audacity.sourceforge.net
  This free audio recording and editing platform would be useful for audio-based projects. Visual performances can be stunning, but don't underestimate Shakespeare's aural power.

- **PowerPoint and other Office programs:** free alternates of these programs are available via the OpenOffice project, www.openoffice.org
  As we mentioned before, any digital medium can work for your performance, and those mediums undoubtedly have creative potential beyond what they're traditionally used for. PowerPoint, for example, can be used to create stop-motion films!

4. TIME AND TECHNOLOGY

While we wrote this assignment with the time frame of a full semester in mind, you could easily adapt it as a shorter exercise. We recommend that you introduce the overall project early on — ideally well before midterms — and use the first assignment as an intellectual springboard into the digital mode. You can assign more than one traditional paper assignment conjoined with the digital project; the idea in this case would be to lay the critical framework before moving on to the project's more creative aspects. The Assignment Sheet (see p. 364) discusses the project in terms of a semester-long arc: a written assignment with annotated bibliography precedes the digital performance.

Though this assignment has only been tested within the time frame of a semester, so long as its key concepts are addressed beforehand there shouldn't be any problem shortening its scope. The following concepts/lessons should precede or closely accompany the assignment sheet:

- Prior to assigning this project, students should be familiar with researching peer-reviewed journal articles and have some exposure to a few arguments in Shakespeare studies. The first assignment and/or a few homework tasks can be useful in establishing this knowledge.

- Some discussion of an "argument in action" should take place through showing some portion of a staged Shakespeare play or film. Why maybe did the director and/or actors choose to approach a play or characters in such a way? These discussions can be easily scattered throughout the semester and are useful regardless.

- Some time should be spent discussing ways to access and utilize digital technology. Though they frequently already have access to some form of digital technology, students can benefit from lists of available campus resources (i.e., computer labs, equipment rental, etc.). It might be most helpful to discuss this aspect shortly after assigning the project.

While timing this project outside of a semester system during the regular school year might seem difficult, minor adjustments can be made to accommodate more compressed schedules. Our recommendation is to adjust the scope of the performance and/or the written portions, aiming for greater focus. For example, a project that undertakes a whole scene, or series of short scenes, can be adjusted to focus on one or two key conversations. Depending on the nature of the project, this strategy might be appropriate for projects in a semester system. Essentially, the whole project could dominate an entire semester's worth of work, but in no way should this assignment be viewed from an all-or-nothing perspective.

In terms of technology, both you and your students need access to personal computers or some other machine capable of rendering digital media.

While the assignment requires students to remodel a Shakespeare drama in some sense digitally, this task can be completed in any number of ways. For example, a student might eschew working on a desktop computer in favor of a tablet. Or, students could sample Shakespearean dialogue using an appropriately equipped synthesizer workstation. Relatively simple digital recording devices—or even cell phones—could also be useful. When we've given this assignment in the past, most students used their own devices to complete this project. However, more than a few either supplemented or completed their entire projects at campus computer labs. Additionally, having regular Internet access will significantly empower students with greater access to digital creation tools. We have listed several potential digital mediums in the Assignment Sheet.

For the research component of the course, no Internet or computer is technically required, though these tools have become relatively ubiquitous in most college environments.

5. ANTICIPATING STUDENT NEEDS

It is possible that students might balk, at least to some degree, at the potentially numerous interpretations that the term *digital performance* could invite. In some respects, this assignment could benefit from a focused approach to a particular digital medium (the limitations and benefits of short, user-generated YouTube content comes to mind). For a specialized course on Shakespeare in the digital era, that degree of focus would work especially well. However, it's reasonable to assume that most of us teaching Shakespeare won't be in the position to offer that kind of course; any Shakespearean digital manifestation will largely depend on time and pedagogical and technological constraints. A broad-based approach to digital technology will hopefully open the playing field to a wide variety of possible interpretations. As has been the case with our own students, their knowledge of available technology surpasses ours.

Despite this oft-uttered trope, we can't cast aspersions on our students' digital literacy too widely. Simply having access to school lab computers and the like doesn't ensure operator knowledge. It will help for you to have some level of comfort with at least one digital medium to demo the program in class and be prepared to answer questions. Referring students to better-qualified tech tutors can help, but there's always the potential for disconnect: teacher and tutor expectations aren't always easy to disentangle. Therefore, the project's focus should remain primarily scholastic.

The learning goals of this assignment should reflect those of your overall course. If you're teaching a Shakespeare course, you probably won't be able to devote much time to the discourses surrounding new media. For this assignment, new media multimodality is being employed as a pedagogical technique, not as a theoretical paradigm students will adopt for reading Shakespeare throughout a semester. Ideally, the different modes and digital media options will mix with the literature students have already been learning, and ultimately help them process the course's critical and literary materials from a new perspective.

6. ASSESSMENT TOOLS

The primary grading consideration for this assignment should be on its scholastic merits rather than on the technical execution of the project itself. Presentation quality will vary widely among students, as will their access to and literacy of digital technology. While you might view the performance aspect of the project subjectively, you might first consider the objective learning goals. Namely, did the student (1) interpret some key Shakespearean scene through a digital lens, (2) provide thoughtful analysis on how that scene's performance in some way expands our understanding of the text, and (3) use scholarly research to support her/his decisions? In many respects, you may grade this assignment as you would a more traditional essay. The idea is to convey and achieve the same learning goals through a different mode. Whatever rubric or grading standard you choose to adopt, its measurement standard (or unit) should not be arbitrary to the assignment's learning goals in totality. For literature courses, we use a critical thinking rubric slightly adapted from Michael Delahoyde's "Thinking about Shakespeare" web page. We generally include this rubric, along with the specific grading expectations, with the Assignment Sheet. Here is our own breakdown of this assignment's grading priorities:

- **Project "thesis" or position:** In effect, going beyond presenting the basic elements of a scene, recognizing its nuances and ambiguities. These can be revealed through intentional and clever performance choices. Performances make arguments; they contain their own rhetoric. This aspect of the project should be based on these choices, the rationale students provide for them, and least of all their execution. For example, if a student wants to argue that Henry V is a war criminal in a LEGO production, she or he could use a Darth Vader figure to represent him at certain points through the production. Additionally, that particular figure can highlight complexity of character (after all, Darth Vader can be seen as a redemptive figure). Ultimately, the performance should tell us something about the text being performed and realize a particular argument *about* it.
- **Project perspective or focus:** This aspect might regard a scholarly point of view, our literal vantage point of viewing the performance, or a combination of both. Regardless, perspective should be an intentionally realized standpoint on what and where a student chooses to focus her or his

interpretive lens. For example, does the project comprise an entire play, or a carefully selected group of scenes; or maybe even better, a single scene? Further, what types of conclusions does this standpoint yield? Perspective should help highlight the project's overall argument and thinking process.

- **Recognizing other perspectives:** This aspect might be generally relegated to the analytic portion of the project or even the annotated bibliography, though not necessarily so. Regardless of approach, students should read what others are arguing and recognize salient viewpoints contrary to their own.

- **Identify and assess key assumptions:** In other words, reading between the lines. A good example question: Is Shylock really bloodthirsty? Students shouldn't wholesale adopt someone else's view on Shakespeare.

- **Identify and assess the quality of supporting evidence and provide additional evidence to support their own assertions:** Students should view other scholars' work as a part of a larger academic conversation, not simply texts we should read and revere. Simply regurgitating what others have argued misses the point of the project. Rather, students should closely examine the relevance, completeness, accuracy, and precision of the evidence provided by other scholars and themselves.

- **Identify and consider the influence of context on the issue:** These of course include social, political, and historical aspects, but should be much more specific to the project in particular. Certain aspects of Elizabethan stage practice, for example, might serve as essential context for Rosalind's epilogue in *As You Like It*.

- **Identify and assess conclusions, implications, and consequences:** In essence, so what? What is the significance of what we have seen or read? Students can address these issues both in the performance and in the analysis sections of their project. For example, we saw one heavy-handed performance of *Titus Andronicus* strongly imply — through a giggling, knife-wielding Lucius at the end of the play — that the violence we just witnessed was cyclical.

Generally, we grade these elements holistically with a focus on argumentation and perspective. Since these elements are closely interconnected, the quality of one tends to affect the quality of others. For example, a focused and original thesis will not serve an essay well if supporting evidence is not considered. But of using this type of rubric, Michael Delahoyde cautions students:

> Not every assignment demands your success in demonstrating all the above skills with anything like equal emphasis. Rather, the Critical Thinking Rubric is designed to lend us some framework and/or some language with which to help pinpoint some ways to evaluate not writing strictly, but thinking. Texts and

materials in the humanities exist not to be "appreciated" reverentially, but rather to encourage critical thinking themselves. I think Shakespeare would agree. ("Thinking of Shakespeare")

Therefore, this rubric should be adapted to each assignment's needs, depending on its own context, whether it's semester-long or much shorter. Our own interpretation of this rubric fits well with a longer project in mind, where all of its elements can and should be addressed.

7. THEORETICAL BASIS FOR THE ASSIGNMENT: Restaging Shakespeare through Multimodal Composition

The idea for this assignment grew out of conversations between us and Michael Delahoyde at Washington State University. While at first the conversations were not in the spirit of digital technology per se, they evolved as we progressed through a digital rhetoric course as part of our PhD studies. We used Dr. Delahoyde's specific concerns about Shakespeare pedagogy as a springboard for developing a series of assignments that asked students to develop a hypertext version of a Shakespeare play. While particulars of those assignments have changed over the years, the spirit of casting Shakespeare in a digital mode remained.

In the fall of 2010, Dr. Delahoyde was considering revamping his long-standing essay assignment for his introductory Shakespeare course. The assignment, in short, was to focus on a single line, or small selection of related lines, hopefully selected from a potentially confusing or highly ambiguous portion of a Shakespearean text. Naturally, the assignment aimed to discourage students from simply adopting the perspective of one of their academic sources and mirroring that author's own argument. Moreover, targeting ambiguity generally increased the propensity for thoughtful, original responses students could feel invested in, even if this course were to be their last Shakespeare outing.

However, as with any long-standing academic discourse with a well-established student paper tradition, plagiarism—both accidental and intentional—became an increasing problem over the years for Delahoyde. Since following the essay prompts required a high degree of creative effort and focus, demanding a firm understanding of the works in question, an increasing number of students were following their secondary sources' arguments too closely. A common cant reverberated across semesters: "I can't find any sources on my topic." A gnawing irritation for teachers everywhere, this complaint has dangerous implications. Students have been conditioned, on one hand, to accept what teachers say at face value—we're the experts, not them. As such, students very often find themselves tempted to support (or "prove") their analysis with exactly coinciding points from published experts. The implication being, student voices are inherently inferior to those experts. In this manner, both students and teachers potentially are unwittingly fostering a culture of academic nihilism. Though the vast minority of students who cross our paths will become literary scholars, does this mean their perspectives are without value?

Certainly, there's a reason why these experts earn PhDs before going on to work at universities and publish articles and books in the academic community, but undergraduates are capable of participating in these conversations regardless. Another related complaint we often hear, and have since the earliest days of high school—"When will I ever use this information?"—partially explains this (potential) phenomenon. The term *use* implies, in more than one aspect, profit acquisition. While this notion may seem a stretch, the use or misuse of skills acquired in schools are what presumably lead to employment. And what, specifically, indicates the great critical thinking skills any given student may employ on a Shakespeare essay when she or he gets the coveted "piece of paper"? Naturally, the logic behind these questions is flawed. No single class provides the skills necessary to undertake a career in any given field. Regardless, students still want something to take with them, whether it's a greater appreciation for the text or a well-composed essay for a portfolio. In other words, many students see even humanities courses as investments.

If students don't feel valid in developing their own perspectives, however, they won't "get" anything out of the humanities. Really, literature teachers will not have the time to comprehensively instruct students on essay construction, regardless of the context. In most cases, students will have only their past experiences with composition to help them understand how effective essays and assignments are composed. And on the other hand, those expectations are ultimately a crapshoot across disciplines and instructors. Thus, once again, the safest route is to closely model what other scholars have argued, which doesn't necessarily precisely count as "engaging" secondary perspectives and authorial voices.

> "Digitizing a Shakespeare performance requires students to think critically about what a scene means, and how this meaning changes based on different potential mediums."
> **Jacob Hughes and Tim Hetland**

Designed with an introductory Shakespeare course in mind, this assignment calls on students to prepare a digital performance of a key scene. Rather than emphasizing only the traditional essay format, students are required to incorporate multimodal compositional and interpretive strategies. Acts of performing—or playing—encourage students to personally engage with a long-dead author in analytically meaningful ways. The work presented here will be best paired with ambiguous or difficult scenes. Overall, the chief learning goal is to help students uncover, construct, recognize, and convey meaning. Digitizing a Shakespeare performance requires students to think critically about what a scene means, and how this meaning changes based on different potential mediums.

As digital technologies have become arguably ubiquitous, rhetoric and composition scholars have begun to ask necessary and important questions about the changing nature of the composition classroom. In those discussions, scholars like Cynthia Selfe, Richard Selfe, Kathleen Blake Yancey, and Doug Hesse have confronted more traditional and Eurocentric academic discourses by suggesting that the academy widen its understanding of "writing" and "literacy" by looking at how computers and digital technology can be used in the classroom by students. Though at times some have tempered the argument of compositional expansion by saying that changing definitions of literacy and composition will not necessarily work with many university programmatic writing goals, the conversation's power is truly in its suggestions. Whether or not practical, pragmatic, or even possible, discussing how composition might change opens up the possibility for a more democratized classroom. Additionally, however, the conversation also opens up how composing in new mediums, specifically digital mediums, makes way for new ways of argumentation and ultimately, scholarship.

This assignment was developed in the underlying yet fundamental implication of the compositionists' conversation, but in a different context. Building on the work of composition scholars, we asked what happens when multimodal composition is used in a college Shakespeare literature classroom. More specifically, when students engage in multimodal projects, what potentially happens to their understanding, interpretation, and engagement of the literature of study?

The goal of this assignment is for students to compose a kind of performance-inspired digital text, interpreting complex meanings from Shakespeare's plays and incorporating their arguments into a practiced theory. Much scholarly ado has been made of how new media—or even more specifically digital media—changes the way we read and understand texts in those contexts (i.e., outside of traditional print culture). For example, George Landow asserts that hypertexts are read in a "multilinear" or "multisequential" manner, stating that "new rules" and "new experiences" apply versus how print texts are read (3). However, we must ask, will these factors necessarily distinguish student critical thinking efforts in different ways than they have been previously used to when composing and analyzing print texts? What really happens when students interpret, translate, and otherwise electronically stage their interpretations of a particular Shakespearean scene and character?

Landow argues that something is "lost" when a "new information regime" overtakes a prior form—such as the movement from print to electronic lit (29)—and that some scholars seriously doubt the validity of print in an electronic information age (67). While decontextualizing writing will certainly serve to exacerbate some tangible loss of understanding—the material conditions of reading are important to processing them cognitively—the process of recontextualizing (or remediating) can serve to illuminate understandings of a text that may have heretofore been unrealized. However, there is the question of print media's relevance in a burgeoning age of electronic reading and writing. While it is beyond our purview in this piece to fully discuss the implications new media has and will have on the future of print, this question sometimes manifests as "what will new media do to literature?" Janet Murray provides insight: "Just as there is no reason to think of mystery novels or role-playing games as merely versions of chess, there is no reason to think of the new forms of storytelling as extensions of filmmaking or board games, though they may include elements of all of these" (8). In other words, new media will not do anything to literature—anything much more than it has already done to itself. Writers, including and especially those from the medieval and early modern periods, tend to build upon the forms left by their exemplars, but those forms never usurp and replace, instead they reinterpret. Murray continues,

> I would argue that we stop trying to assimilate the new artifacts to the old categories of print- or cinema-based story. . . . We should instead think of the characteristics of stories and games and how these separable characteristics are being recombined and reinvented within the astonishingly plastic world of cyberspace. (10)

In other words, print narratives or stories in movies can become something else altogether when remediated. They may contain the "separable characteristics" Murray refers to, such as narrative structures, filmed scenes, or even text, but they ultimately recombine into something else that might defy a reading that would otherwise work for a book or movie. Modern readers in general are acculturated to reading books and films according to their respective modes, so the same sensitivity to medium should apply to digitally rendered art. Thus, as students approach this assignment, they will not be expected to arbitrarily preserve the integrity of a text that they do not yet understand very well, or in the least have something potentially new to learn from. They'll be building from their exemplars while moving elsewhere with a hopefully unique interpretation of a rather well picked over text.

> "Print narratives or stories in movies can become something else altogether when remediated."
>
> **Jacob Hughes and Tim Hetland**

Using digital media for teaching literature, as Landow points out in his discussion of hypertext, is far from radical. His own students at Brown collaborated using Intermedia and Storyspace to provide annotated versions of stories by authors such as Kipling and Laurence (69). Moreover, the project grew to include still more collaborators, and survived beyond one semester. Essentially, these students were contributing their perspectives to a lasting and usable corpus of information. Even if they never returned to literature studies, their intellectual and creative investment remained. A particularly interesting and important case brought up by Landow regards Phil Gyfford's collaborative conversion of Samuel Pepys's diary into a blog (79, cf. 143). He quotes Gyfford's explanation of the project:

> "I thought Pepys' diary could make a great Weblog. The published diary takes the form of nine hefty volumes—a daunting prospect. Reading it day by day on a website would be far more manageable, with the real-time aspect making it a more involving experience." (qtd. in Landow 79).

The blog, supported by a base of contributors, includes annotations, links to pertinent materials including maps, and is all packaged in the form of a twenty-first-century weblog. Not only has Gyfford's group collaborated as Landow's students at Brown have done, but they've importantly changed the fundamental ways in which Pepys can be read and understood.

The ultimate goal of this assignment is to get students thinking about Shakespeare in a similar manner to how Gyfford cast Pepys, and with an accompanying critical perspective of their own construction. We want them to understand the cultural, social, and artistic implications (among other factors) of their creative choices. We are not aiming for this assignment to manifest as a willy-nilly free-for-all. Instead, students are to construct an argument that's augmented by a thesis supported by pertinent secondary critical perspective. Really, in many respects this assignment's origins are deeply rooted in those kinds of essays we found so often plagiarized. The key difference here, however, is to get students to actually apply their own original theses—work that cannot easily be plagiarized, nor undertaken flippantly.

Yancey's idea of interconnectivity between texts composed in an academic setting and real-world genres essentially coincides with what we're attempting (311). She poses that students aren't being asked—at least not habitually—to draw real-world connections with academic writing. While it's not difficult to mount threats ("you will fail out of school and therefore fail to get a degree that will lead to you never being employed if you don't pass this class") to make our material applicable, it doesn't really ensure its survival beyond a single classroom moment (as Yancey puts it) or moments. This assignment not only calls for a movement between mediums, but also a series of justifications for why those movements make sense within a critical framework.

8. CONCLUSION

While this assignment potentially offers many exciting opportunities for both students and teachers, its incarnation here won't fit every pedagogical context well. Regardless, many of the general principles forwarded here can be pared down into smaller assignments (such as written analyses of preexisting digital interpretations of Shakespeare), or even as a topic for class discussion. While this assignment might even work well in a course that focuses primarily on new media, not many Shakespeare teachers will have the time or inclination to set aside a large block of time to discuss the principles of how medium affects the way we read. However, if regarded as a different "mode" of research project—one that doesn't completely eschew the traditional essay—this assignment could open interpretive doors that might otherwise be closed to students in a more traditional setting. The essay is a creative format in its own right, but sometimes it is difficult to get students to see it as such. "Essay" to them very frequently translates into "verbose misery."

For Shakespeare teachers, this assignment's chief draw should be its multimodality. There is very little time in the space of a semester or quarter to experience Shakespeare onstage, or to watch an entire play on video in class. There is simply too much to talk about and read. However, if we just read Shakespeare in one way—essentially as "closet drama"—we are missing important interpretive opportunities. Essays offer one good way of talking about Shakespeare. Digital performances, however, offer many other ways. Instead of just hearing a soloist or small ensemble, we get to hear an integrated orchestra. Multimodal reading adds dimension, so it really doesn't eschew essays at all.

But the essay isn't all that's at stake here. We and many other Shakespeare teachers have heard the collective groans of countless students over the years bemoaning the prospects of rereading *Romeo and Juliet*. When we ask, there are many different answers: "I hate that the characters are all so *stupid*"; "The language is alien to me"; "I can't stand the idea of reading in front of class"; the list goes on. Most of these answers regard some lack of agency or point of engagement. And while the aim isn't to relocate ownership of Shakespeare, creatively actualizing an argument is both exhilarating and relevant for students. Several have told me that they appreciated the opportunity to *choose* their mode of expression. We do get some effusive remarks about how much a student now loves Shakespeare, which while nice isn't really the point. The point is to encourage critical thinking both within and outside the texts. Students can, in principle if not practice in our experience, despise this project and still make observations about a particular character or scene we have not otherwise heard. For example, one person very convincingly played Sir Toby Belch in *Twelfth Night*—who is almost universally played as a drunk—as completely sober. The core question here is what about Sir Toby's text is inherently intoxicated? Should we take what others say about him for granted?

Generally, in practice we have found that this assignment, if completed in good faith, yields good results both from a critical thinking standpoint and a student engagement perspective. It's frequently more effective in getting students to think about multiple perspectives and potential arguments when they have to work in groups together. They see better how their voices interact with others. Essays can exercise some of these intellectual muscles as well, but too frequently essays are seen as both a means of *and* an end to argumentation. In popular culture we hear the residuals of this effect when anyone says, "It's just a movie, don't overthink it" (just a movie compared to what?). Text is a paragon of ethos. Maybe the best way to exercise evaluating authority or efficacy—a cornerstone to good critical thinking and essay writing—is to practice writing in modes that are, at least in Western culture, not traditionally viewed as authoritative themselves.

9. WORKS CITED

Cougar Scholars' 306 Final. Directed by Katherine Culbertson, et al. *YouTube.* Accessed 2 Sept. 2012.

Delahoyde, Michael. "The Major Shakespeare Project." *Washington State U,* 16 Apr. 2012, www.wsu.edu/~delahoyd/shakespeare/assignment2.html. Assignment.

- - -. "Thinking About Shakespeare." *Washington State U.,* public.wsu.edu /~delahoyd/shakespeare/crit.html. Accessed 2 Jan. 2014.

Hesse, Doug. "Response to Cynthia L. Selfe's 'The Movement of Air, the Breath of Meaning: Aurality and Multimodal Composing.'" *College Composition and Communication,* vol. 61, no. 3, 2010, pp. 602-05.

Joyce, Michael. "Twelve Blue." *Eastgate Systems,* 1996, www.eastgate.com /TwelveBlue/.

Landow, George P. *Hypertext 3.0.* Johns Hopkins UP, 1997.

"Lego Macbeth." Directed by Bryan Axelson, *YouTube,* 30 Apr. 2012. www .youtube.com/watch?v=uRohPxQQRiY.

Murray, Janet. "From Game-Story to Cyberdrama." *First Person.* Edited by Noah Wardrip-Fruin and Pat Harrigan, MIT P, 2004, pp. 2-11.

Selfe, Cynthia L. "The Movement of Air, the Breath of Meaning: Aurality and Multimodal Composing." *College Composition and Communication,* vol. 60, no. 4, 2009, pp. 616-63.

Selfe, Cynthia, and Richard Selfe. "The Politics of the Interface." *Computers in the Composition Classroom: A Critical Sourcebook.* Edited by Michelle Sidler, et al., Bedford/St. Martin's, pp. 64-86.

Sorapure, Madeleine, et al. "Web Literacy: Challenges and Opportunities for Research in a New Medium." *Computers in the Composition Classroom: A Critical Sourcebook.* Edited by Michelle Sidler, et al., Bedford/St. Martin's, pp. 333-49.

Wysocki, Anne Frances. "Opening New Media to Writing: Openings and Justifications." *Writing New Media.* Edited by Anne Frances Wysocki, et al., Utah State UP, pp. 1-44.

Yancey, Kathleen Blake. "Made Not Only in Words: Composition in a New Key." *College Composition and Communication,* vol. 56, no. 2, 2004, pp. 297-328.

25

Remapping World Literature through Multimodality

Clay Kinchen Smith
Santa Fe College

1. OVERVIEW

- **Assignment:** A researched, multimodal project on aspects of world literature chosen and designed to communicate that information to general, online audiences.
- **Courses:** Created for an upper-division world literature course, but can be adapted for any literature course.
- **Literature:** Any literature.
- **Technology:** Computer with basic word processing and presentation software, Internet access, and technology of the student's choice (i.e., video, podcast, or animation software).
- **Time:** Four weeks.

2. GOALS OF THE ASSIGNMENT

This assignment meets several goals:

- **Institutional Goals:** Given its heavy emphasis on communication, this project meets Santa Fe College's General Education Learning Outcome (GELO) for this course; the additional emphasis on research aligns with other learning outcomes for our courses.
- **Individual Goals:** In addition to meeting those goals, this project meets Santa Fe College's class goals of fostering:
  - enhanced compositional skills (traditional and multimodal);
  - increased awareness of canonicity;

- promotion of world literature (in general as well as the specific subjects of the projects);
- multimodality through widely disseminated examples; and
- realization of students' goals as active participants in global communications.

3. ASSIGNMENT SHEET

Remapping World Literature through Multimodality

Course: _____

Instructor: _____

Date: _____

Overview

As you know from our work this semester, this final project is designed to enable you to (re)articulate your relationships to canonicity and the world's literatures. To do so, you will:

- **Create a researched project that engages those areas in ways that are meaningful to you and to your audiences.** In most cases, you will be introducing general audiences to aspects of world literature. In doing so, you will need to define relevant aspects of your subject in ways that engage and empower your audience. For audiences familiar with your subject and/ or world lit, you will be providing additional information and perspectives; for those unfamiliar, you will be introducing them to new information and perspectives. Regardless, you will be engaging your audiences in a dialogue that can and should continue after they have seen your project. Moreover, I hope that you communicate enthusiasm for your subject to your audience; your enthusiasm can be very persuasive.

- **Publish that project through an appropriate online venue.** This aspect of your assignment increases audience access to your subject specifically and promotes world lit generally. Easily accessible online venues (e.g., Facebook pages, radio programs, Web sites, wikis, YouTube videos) increase the likelihood of reaching the broadest possible audiences, thereby affecting positive change by promoting world lit and multimodality.

- **Directly engage the forces of canonicity.** By featuring your subject (again, I encourage you to choose a noncanonical subject), you will demonstrate the diversity of such subjects (as well as your specific subject) and thereby encourage audiences to consider how and why canons operate.

- **Promote multimodality.** Because you are not writing a traditional paper-based project, you exemplify the vitality and validity of multimodality. The addition of a research-based argument further reveals how multimodality is not simply subjectivity disguised as substance.

- **Foster global dialogue.** Not only will you develop workplace communication skills, but you will also develop the exchange of ideas worldwide.

(continued)

ASSIGNMENT SHEET (*continued*)

Requirements

As with other academic assignments, this project has certain requisites. To complete this assignment, please:

1. **Create a multimodal final project that enacts the goals and values artic-ulated above and throughout our semester.** Your project's final shape will depend on your choices of (1) subject, (2) medium, and (3) audience. Regardless of the format, your project should be about 2–3 minutes in length. This time limit enables you to create a viable project within our class's time frame and facilitates audience engagement with your topic. Longer projects might not be feasible given the amount of time that we have remaining in the semester, but they will not be discouraged. In addi-tion, this project should serve as the basis for your continued work in this field and others; think of it like a short essay compared to the longer articles and books that you might write later or as an initial statement in the global dialogue and exchange of information.

   - For example, your project might be a relatively simple video featuring a poet's work (e.g., stills of that poet, culture, context) with audio of you reading from that work and from your argument — what we call the "PowerPoint" approach.

   - A more sophisticated video using visual and aural elements contrasting works by "unknown/little known" and "known" authors like Sandra A. Mushi and Chinua Achebe (e.g., interspersing readings with interviews and online resources, simple animation).

   - An animated interpretation of an author's work(s) accompanied (or not) by an introduction to that author and work(s).

   - An aural project like a radio feature that intersperses you reading poetry in the context of a poet's life, times, and other work.

   As you will recognize from this list, we have already explored such concepts and possible projects throughout the semester; having done so, you should be able to create your final project with relative ease.

2. **Include a complete and correct bibliographic list (MLA or APA) of at least five sources at the end of your project.** This requisite

   - demonstrates your research and documentation skills;

   - enables your audience to readily access those sources; and

   - sets an example for other online projects to follow.

   In addition, you might consider adding a list that suggests additional sources for your audiences to pursue. Doing so would further encourage your audi-ences to explore your subjects and, hopefully, additional ones.

3. **Submit two 1- to 2-paragraph progress reports by the dates posted in our calendar.** These documents (1) serve as formal checks on your progress and (2) encourage you to stay focused on your goal. In addition, you may

talk to me informally at any time about your project. As you know, I am always happy to help in any way that I can.

4. **Include a 1- to 2-page rationale statement explaining your choice of sources, audience, goals, and medium.** You should include a hyperlink to your project's online location if you mounted it to such a source.

5. **Include a 1- to 2-page reflective piece in which you communicate relevant aspects of your experience with this project** (e.g., it was more/less rewarding than you had first imagined; the technological issues that helped/ hindered your project; your most/least favorite parts of this project).

Please be honest. Remember to:

Name your files using our class protocol.

Submit copies of your material by the posted deadline.

Grading Rubric			
This rubric modifies traditional rubrics for compositional skills to address the greater complexity of multimodal projects.			
	Capstone	**Milestones**		**Benchmark**
	4	3	2	1
Audience	Exemplary understanding of defined audience and its needs	Adequate understanding of defined audience and its needs	General understanding of defined audience and its needs	Little to no understanding of defined audience and its needs
Context	Thorough understanding of project's context (assignment's requirements and current state of world lit)	Adequate understanding of project's context (assignment's requirements and current state of world lit)	General understanding of project's context (assignment's requirements and current state of world lit)	Little to no understanding of project's context (assignment's requirements and current state of world lit)
Purpose	Clearly defined purpose(s) meeting the project's requirements	Adequately defined purpose(s) meeting the project's requirements	Generally defined purpose(s) meeting the project's requirements	Undefined or loosely defined purpose(s) which does/ do not meet the project's requirements

(continued)

ASSIGNMENT SHEET (*continued*)

	Capstone	Milestones		Benchmark
	4	3	2	1
Design	Exemplary design that reflects your work on this project, your technical expertise with your chosen medium, and your awareness of your project's design on your audience	Adequate design that reflects your work on this project, your technical expertise with your chosen medium, and your awareness of your project's design on your audience, although it may contain ineffective design elements	General design that reflects your work on this project, your technical expertise with your chosen medium, and your awareness of your project's design on your audience, although it contains ineffective design elements which hinder the project's efficacy	Ineffective design that reflects little to no work on this project, a lack of technical expertise with your chosen medium, and lack of awareness of your project's design on your audience
Content	Extremely appropriate, relevant, and compelling content that illustrates your depth of understanding of and research on your subject	Adequately appropriate and relevant content that illustrates your depth of understanding of and research on your subject, although containing a few errors	Somewhat appropriate and relevant content that illustrates your understanding of and research on your subject, although containing several errors	Inappropriate, irrelevant, and unpersuasive content that illustrates your lack of understanding of and research on your subject
Genre and Disciplinary Conventions	Exceptionally well organized, articulate, and thorough presentation of your subject	Adequately organized, articulate, and thorough presentation of your subject, although containing a few errors	Generally organized, articulate, and thorough presentation of your subject, although containing several errors	Little to no organization, articulation, or thoroughness

Sources and Evidence	Extremely appropriate, credible, and relevant sources reflect the depth of your research	Adequately appropriate, credible, and relevant sources reflect the competence of your research, but contain a few errors	Generally appropriate, credible, and relevant sources reflect your ability to research, but contain several errors	Inappropriate, incredible, and irrelevant sources reflect little to no research
Control of Craft	Exemplary development and delivery of material	Adequate development and delivery of material, although containing a few errors	General development and delivery of material, although containing several errors	Little to no development and delivery of material

List of Suggested Topics

Please use this list as the basis for your project, but not as the final determinant. You may adopt one of the following suggestions outright, or you may modify them as you see fit; alternatively, you may create your own approach. Your goal here is to create a project that both (1) reflects your interests, and (2) assumes a final shape that you think is meaningful and useful to your audiences and to yourself. Some suggestions for your project include:

- Design the "perfect" world lit text. You have to choose, organize, and justify your choices and organization in an informed and intelligent way. By this point, you have had sufficient exposure to canonicity and world lit texts to decide how you would want to orchestrate your project. Moreover, you should see how your final project grows out of your earlier work with "accepted" and "denied" texts during our units assignments.

- Nominate and justify your choice of five "noncanonical" authors and their works that should be included in a standardized world lit text or class. You can see how this option grows out of your earlier work nominating authors during our discussion posts.

- Compare and contrast contemporary online and print African literature or a literary genre. While this project may seem relatively straightforward, it (and many of the others listed here) enable audiences who might be resistant to your nominations or revisions to be more receptive since you would be using categories with which they were familiar.

- Compare and contrast a literary genre in a non-Western and a Western culture.

(continued)

ASSIGNMENT SHEET (*continued*)

- Compare and contrast the themes of star-crossed love in a non-Western text and a Western text (e.g., Chikamatsu's "The Love Suicides at Sonezaki" or *The Red Chamber* with something traditional like *Romeo and Juliet*). Yes, a traditional model, but also an effective way of introducing audiences to works that they might not know and encouraging them to see parallels in places that they might not have looked at — or even known about.

- Compare the literary works and legacy of a non-Western and a Western author (e.g., Chikamatsu and Shakespeare, Rumi and Emily Dickinson, Pablo Mir and Walt Whitman). Again, a classic, but these are such fun to do for the reasons that I just cited.

- Compare and contrast themes of domesticity and social mobility in a non-Western and a Western text (e.g., *The Red Chamber* and *Pride and Prejudice*). The fun just keeps coming.

- Analyze how recent Iranian films (re)articulate representations of women relative to gender identities in Islam (e.g., *A Taste of Cherry*, *Baran*, *Gabbeh*, *Osama*). In addition, you would be educating audiences on issues related to Islam, introducing such films to wider audiences, and promoting dialogue about related issues and films.

- Compare and contrast trickster figures from different cultures (e.g., Anansi, Old Man Coyote, Nasrudin, Raven, Trickster Rabbit).

- Compare and contrast examples of recent and earlier Chinese literature.

4. TIME AND TECHNOLOGY

TIME. This assignment is the culmination of a series of smaller assignments designed to

- familiarize students with world literature using traditional thematic units (e.g., African Literatures);
- encourage them to choose an area from which to create their final project (through a combination of exposure to each area's possibilities as well as enabling them to see the need for promoting the subject that they choose); and
- problematize canonicity's exclusivity by promoting porousness.

In addition, I review the final project from our first week of class by emphasizing these goals relative to the final project. By doing so I also encourage students to see that the processes of research involve hits and misses, but that ultimately they can and should gather possibilities from such experiential processes like reading a short story by an Indonesian author, tasting *leche quemada* for the first time, and/or listening to Malian music by Tinariwen.

This project's timeline extends throughout the semester and is divided into two parts.

1. **The Initial or Preformative Phase:** The basis for this final project emerges during the semester's initial twelve-week journey through a range of texts. To help them stay focused on their final projects, I have students complete a short one- to two-paragraph reflective piece at the end of each unit that asks them to consider what final project they might want to do if they were to choose a subject from that unit. Doing so encourages students to consider possible final projects throughout the semester and avoid the scramble at the end of the semester; moreover, it encourages them to consider potential engagement with canonicity and promotion of their subjects as an ongoing enterprise.

2. **The Final or Formative Phase:** Work on the final project exclusively occupies the last third (four weeks) of the semester. During that time period, I meet regularly with students to discuss progress on their projects; I also provide venues for them to share ideas and receive feedback from their classmates as well as review their two short (one- to two-page) progress reports.

Prior to students embarking on their own research paths, I feature available resources that I think are valuable and model their use in my research. For example, we review the tables of contents from online world lit textbooks, noting the authors and works listed there, the frequency of their recurrence, and the ways in which these textbooks parse these authors, their

Literatures Units	12 weeks (3 weeks per unit)	Weeks 3, 6, 9, and 12: Complete unit assignments Submit possible FRP topic
Final Research Project (FRP)	4 weeks	Week 13: determine FRP topic Week 14: first progress report Week 15: second progress report Week 16: submit FRP

works, and the "subject" of world lit. I also talk about my work with international authors and texts, noting challenges and rewards in that process.

In addition, I provide students with an opportunity to survey authors and texts from each unit through one of the most readily accessed sources currently available, *Wikipedia*. Each unit begins with several quizzes based on *Wikipedia* entries for that unit's authors and texts, as well as aspects of the cultures from the areas in that unit. Through these quizzes, students gain

- familiarity with a unit's traditional and contemporary authors, texts, and cultures; and
- firsthand experience using an online, popular venue for such subjects.

While *Wikipedia* entries on authors and texts can be criticized as superficial, they can also be celebrated as intersections of public discourse and traditional research. Another result of these quizzes is students' exposure to a potential venue for their final projects (e.g., the creation of a *Wikipedia* page on their chosen subject) and by extension similar online venues (e.g., existent wikis on their subjects or wikis that students create to disseminate their work on their subjects). Throughout their interaction with this online source, students directly engage with the sorts of rhetorical and argumentative issues involved with disseminating information to general audiences — all topics that we cover in our discussions and that are central to current arguments by multimodal theorists.

Moreover, I expose students to sources for primary and secondary research in ways that extend and enact basic research methodologies. Initially, the focus is on secondary research both to familiarize students with the unit's authors and texts and to foreground the need to understand their subject in depth. After that initial phase, students engage in their own secondary research with the additional goal of helping them see the need (and even pleasure) of creating primary research to disseminate to audiences.

When completing the unit on African literature, for example, I feature resources such as:

1. Africanwriter.com for its access to some of the most interesting and exciting African literature being produced today (often in contrast to "academic" sites like Project Gutenberg's "The Africa Bookshelf").

2. YouTube videos because they provide access to African authors who are using this platform, as well as summative examinations of African literature and potential models for students' work (whether to emulate or counter). Using the phrase "African literature" will provide you with thousands of possibilities, the winnowing of which is fruitful for both instructors and students.

3. Individual sites featuring African poets to demonstrate the range of engagement with these subjects as well as their ephemerality. For example, I show students how link rot in the *Wikipedia* entries for David Diop, Paulin Joachim, and Sipho Sepamla prevents readers from accessing those poets' work; I also show students how individual sites can allow access to poetry otherwise not presented in formal venues like *Wikipedia* as with the site containing Jeremy Cronin's poem "Motho Ke Motho Ka Batho Babang" (A Person Is a Person Because of Other People) but which do not appear among the resources in the *Wikipedia* entry for Cronin.

4. Research repositories like the University of Florida's "African Studies Research" portal.

5. Individual scholars (like Deborah Seddon's "Written Out, Writing In: Orature in the South African Literary Canon") who engage canonicity in African literatures (both as models and as evidence that this assignment manifests wider movements).

6. Links to other world lit classes to show how they approach central African texts, for example, "Three Poems" (www.hpcnet.org/peru /schoolartsandsciences/language/clemente/fall2006/nonwestonline /noteseight3/one/poems) and "In the Cutting of a Drink" by Ama Ata Aido (www.hpcnet.org/peru/schoolartsandsciences/language/clemente /fall2006/nonwestonline/noteseight2/world/drink).

7. Examples of African texts in mainstream media (e.g., *The New York Times*' review of Nadine Gordimer's "A Soldier's Embrace").

Such a review exposes students to the range of resources available to them online and models research behaviors (both the process and products of research). In addition, it demonstrates the range of online venues available for students to use in their assignments and when publishing their own work.

I encourage students to conduct primary research as part of their final research project, whether interviewing authors online, e-mailing inquiries to sources, or administering questionnaires. Given the porous nature of the online environments in which students and texts coexist, such dialogue can prove relatively easy and empowering for many students.

While I have focused on the resources that I feature for the African literature unit (which can also be used as the basis for students' final projects), I have by no means exhausted those resources nor determined the range of potential resources available for this assignment or ones like it.

TECHNOLOGY. Beyond access to the Internet and a computer with basic software, this assignment requires no special technologies. Technology used for this assignment depends primarily on students' choices and skill levels. For example, visual projects might use cameras, software programs, or simple cutting and pasting from web-based sources. Given that flexibility, students can complete this assignment without having to buy additional resources and by using familiar technology. Access, ability, and audience then become the main determinants for technology needed to complete this project.

While they are also determined by students in the contexts of their searches, requisite resources are essentially unlimited given the extent of online resources and their accessibility. In fact, the amount of material could present a problem to students if they have no guidance in their research efforts. However, the vastness of those resources also illustrates central principles of canonicity, and thereby provides students with an unequalled opportunity to define their relationships to it instead of simply being handed a sanitized package of sources.

5. ANTICIPATING STUDENT NEEDS

While I have enjoyed great successes with this assignment, I have also encountered certain difficulties that inform larger issues relevant to multimodal productions by students. Primarily those problems involve convincing students that they have the requisite skills to produce a multimodal project and that the quality of their work is sufficient for publication online.

Such resistance might come as a surprise given assumptions about student facility and engagement with online technologies (e.g., texting, chatting, and otherwise communicating with a wide range of online audiences). My students' comments reveal certain anxieties about posting "professional" content online:

- "Yeah, anybody can put anything on YouTube, but this will have my name on it."
- "I know I could, but I am not sure how good it would be."
- "What if somebody sees it when I am applying to grad school?"
- "I'm not sure if it is good enough."

As these comments reveal, student anxieties about online publishing indicate a devaluation of their own production and dissemination of such production to general audiences. While students have access to sufficient technologies and sufficient time to produce a short project, they tend to view their final productions as lacking sufficient degrees of sophistication requisite to warrant those projects' becoming "permanent" features on the Web. Often they compare their projects' production value with models they had explored during their research. Many students specifically qualify their projects in terms of inadequate production, either their own skill levels (e.g., "I wish I knew more about how to edit videos." "I guess I am not as good at videos as I am at writing papers.") or with related factors like time (e.g., "I wish I had put more time into this thing so it would look better.") and access to technology (e.g., "If I only had a better camera I could have done a better job."). Such anxieties illustrate larger obstacles in the move away from traditional, paper-based compositional models to multimodal models.

In addition, they indicate that students have not realized that multimodal production can be as substantive as traditional, paper-based writing because of the overemphasis on their production's form over its content. Moreover, these statements reveal that students continue to disassociate the personal from the professional aspects of information production. I assume that such perceptions are the result of little to no prior experience with multimodality or its attendant concepts.

In large part, I think that these obstacles result from long-term exposure to the systemic valuation of paper-based linearity so diligently promoted by the majority of current teaching in high school and college classrooms. In this sense, paper trumps multimodality because of its systemic prevalence. If my students had earlier or sustained exposure to multimodality (in their K-12 classes and in our college's other classes), I surmise that they would be less reluctant to create a multimodal project in my class and less anxious about its quality.

While from my perspective, students' anxieties over this project are a result of systemic factors, I cannot discount myself as a factor. If more instructors were enabling multimodal projects in their classes (at my school and nationally), I could analyze my success relative to theirs. Again, we have additional arguments for promoting multimodality.

6. ASSESSMENT TOOLS

Because traditional rubrics cannot adequately assess the possibilities inherent in multimodality, I use a modified rubric. My rubric coincides with the sorts of revisionary, post-Bloomian rubrics assessing creation and metacognition promoted by critics like Yancey (205). Similarly, they approximate the rubrics that Selfe and Selfe promote through their PSA assignments (2008). Moreover, my rubric suggests how multimodal assessments can and should regenerate traditional assessments of composition.

The four basic categories for this rubric are as follows:

1. **Efficacy of communication:** These criteria encompass traditional issues (e.g., the soundness of students' theses, adequacy and use of support, grammatical correctness, and appropriate tone); and non-traditional issues (e.g., the adequacy of students' chosen media to communicate their arguments).

2. **Efficacy of design:** These criteria use the contexts of students' chosen media and audience (e.g., the adequacy of their project's content relative to their stated purpose; the quality of production value, such as the quality, quantity, and integration of visuals in a video-based project).

3. **Fulfillment of audience needs:** These criteria focus on the clarity, comprehensiveness, and concision of the project's message to the intended audience.

4. **Demonstration of research:** These criteria assess the correctness (against MLA or APA standards) of students' documentation and the depth of their research relative to their projects.

Please refer to the rubric included in the Assignment Sheet (p. 383).

7. THEORETICAL BASIS FOR ASSIGNMENT: Remapping World Literature through Multimodality

Since the 1990s, many of us have promoted multimodality as the means to free composition from what Michael Joyce so pointedly calls "the wood-pulp fetishism among the post-lapsarian" (404). In doing so, we have joined the ranks of those seeking to move beyond traditional monomodalities to the possibilities promoted by voices such as Hawisher, Hesse, Johnson-Eilola, Selber, Selfe, Sirc, Takayoshi, Wysocki, and Yancey, as well as by the positions advocated by organizations like the New London Group and NCTE. In the process, we have advocated for multimodality as the primary means for addressing issues with employability, social inequity, and other areas as well as improving students' compositional, argumentative, rhetorical, and metacognitive skills.

More specifically we have promoted the short- and long-term benefits of multimodality for all involved—inside and outside the classroom. Not only do students increase and diversify their compositional skills when they create multimodal projects, they also acquire competencies that they can use and develop throughout their lives and careers. As we have shown, students do so through transmediation, the creative interplay of interpreting original sources and rearticulating them in original representations. For example, multimodality enhances student learning by avoiding the sorts of "narcolepsy" that Taylor identifies as inherent in monomodality. Similarly, multimodality fosters students' metacognitive abilities, as Laist so eloquently argues: "In order to keep from looking like a buffoonish museum curator keeping jealous guard over an inventory of dusty relics or like a hero-worshipping sycophant spreading the gospel of Sacred Stories, it is incumbent upon the survey course instructor to present the meta-narratives which constitute her discipline as living, breathing, unstable, and even dangerous entities" (56). In addition, multimodal projects enable students to explore "the concepts of blurred identity, transgressions, and hybridity" and thereby create "a distinctly postmodern redrawing of the Web" (Hawisher and Selfe 290).

Moreover, multimodality realizes goals beyond the immediate and long-term enhancement of student learning outcomes and instructional design through its extension outside the classroom. As indicated above, multimodality enables and encourages students' engagement with the production and dissemination of information for a wide range of audiences. Instead of seeing themselves as simply consumers of information or as users of information for the immediate requisites of composition projects that engage only the instructor in that class, students come to realize the potential of adding their voices to the global exchange of information — thereby problematizing control of such information by professionals (academic and non-). By redefining such means and goals of production, students promote the democratization of information. Through such multimodality, students come to realize the power and potential of their own production within the classroom; perhaps more importantly, they begin to realize the power and potential of their dialogic exchanges with the world outside the classroom — a world in which they can and should affect positive change by adding their voices.

Achieving such goals, as most of us will attest, is not always easy. In my case, doing so required me to reorient Santa Fe College's world lit class from a traditional to a multimodal focus and to address students' anxieties over such a reorientation. That process and its results inform many of the obstacles we face as we promote multimodality in our classrooms.

As defined by Santa Fe College's course description, LIT2120 World Cultures through Literature is a traditional survey class focused on "selected masterpieces of World Literature from a variety of periods and locations after the 18th Century, with an emphasis on the non-Western world" ("LIT2120 World Cultures through Literature," *SF Catalog*).

When presented with the opportunity to teach this class, I knew I didn't want to reinscribe current world lit within the canon. Instead, I wanted to problematize that canon and help rearticulate newer, more inclusive and relevant canons. I decided that my primary tool in doing so would be multimodality.

I found additional support for my decision after completing a survey of existent world lit texts (both single- or multi-volume works). That survey quickly revealed these sources to be too canonical and/or expensive. For example, a number of these works bundle canonical Anglo-American authors under the rubric of international authorship (e.g., the British romantics) or focus almost exclusively on canonical world literature (e.g., Confucius, Ibsen); by doing so, these works ignore current world lit. In part I reasoned that using such texts would (re)inscribe world lit within the confines of canonicity—something I would not do; those texts would prevent students from significantly engaging the current state of world lit and their potential roles relative to that state. Moreover, I wanted to introduce students to the vitality and variety of online world lit being currently written. Because most of these online sources are (1) free or readily available online, (2) provide students with a wider range of texts than available in print anthologies, and (3) present a range of models that students could follow or oppose in their own projects, I decided that we would use only online sources for our world lit survey.

In addition to increasing students' exposure to such sources, I wanted to promote multimodality's potential to redefine students' roles as producers of information that could affect change outside their classrooms. As the primary means for achieving such goals I chose the students' final research project (FRP). Because this project had been traditionally the capstone for this course, I wanted to maintain its formality while introducing the possibility inherent in a multimodal project. To that end, I switched our class's traditional, paper-based final project to a multimodal one.

> "I wanted to promote multimodality's potential to redefine students' roles as producers of information that could affect change outside their classrooms."
> **Clay Kinchen Smith**

Thus, this project occurred as the result of a sequence of assignments (e.g., one each focusing on African literatures, Asian literatures, American and Caribbean literatures, and European literatures) and a constant focus on canonicity (e.g., how and why it operates, how to [re]construct one—especially one that emphasizes inclusivity). In this process, students are

- exposed to a series of texts from each unit;
- enabled to share those experiences with their classmates (and ultimately with audiences outside the classroom); and
- encouraged to situate those texts relative to the canon and themselves relative to those texts.

Inherent in this process is the redistribution of knowledge from sources (and themselves) to a wide range of audiences; this model informs the specific benefits of this assignment's creation and broadcast (also in its widest senses of meaning) of information on the students' choice of subjects as well as the general benefits of students engaging in dialogue with worldwide audiences.

In short, this assignment uses online sources to

- promote texts by world lit authors that are either marginalized or silenced by current canonicity;
- provide informed access to such texts for a range of audiences; and
- increase the presence of researched content on those venues (and thereby affect ways audiences use them).

In the process, students determine the validity of a range of canons, including the ones that they create with the ultimate goal of promoting texts that they feel should be canonized (whether in the standard canons or in those that the students create and/or promote). And hopefully they also discover sources of pleasure from those texts and their promotion as they enter and shape the dialogue determining such texts.

To do so, students engage in a process that focuses equally on canonicity and multimodality. Students complete a sequence of units designed to expose them to canonicity, specifically:

- the current canonicity of world lit in general and specific areas (e.g., African literatures);
- the range of noncanonical texts available for such categories;
- models for dialogues about canonicity and "other" texts;
- possibilities for (re)defining their relationships with canonical and "other" texts; and
- concepts for promoting "other" texts through multimodal venues designed to reach wide audiences.

In the process, students also explore multimodality through guided concepts and examples, and online examples that they discover as they explore texts for our class.

In doing so, I seek to empower students in ways that are meaningful to them and to the world, as well as provide them with a basis for their final project. In addition, students develop self-directed research skills as they examine and collect examples for the basis of their own final project.

Moreover, I avoided designing this assignment to privilege the notion of the student-scholar — the student who will continue within academia reiterating previous modes of composition and discourse. Instead, I recognize the need to empower those students who will write, think, and otherwise create outside of academia. As Yancey has

> "I recognize the need to empower those students who will write, think, and otherwise create outside of academia."
>
> **Clay Kinchen Smith**

argued, we need to focus as much on the role that composition will play in our students' postsecondary contexts as we focus on empowering the next generation of academics (204). To do otherwise would prevent students from realizing the potential for change inherent in multimodality and in themselves.

Assignment Sequence Leading Up to the Final Project

We begin this process of defining our own canons focused on including marginalized and otherwise silenced authors and their works by examining the standardization of online tables of contents for major publishers' world lit texts and online world lit syllabi that follow such standards.

Next, we use a unit-based approach (nominally organized by traditional geographical units) that enables students to explore the range of literatures produced by and in that unit's area. In the process, students complete summaries, analyses, and critiques on a variety of texts (here used in its broadest sense) from that unit. For example, students create the following:

- one- to three-page analysis of three authors/works chosen by the students;
- one-paragraph summaries of three relevant research texts from the unit area;
- critiques of three examples of films/television/animation from the unit area;
- critiques of three examples of music from the unit area; and
- critiques of at least one food identified with the unit area.

They also answer the following discussion posts for each unit:

- Which five authors would you choose to include in this unit? Why?
- What relevant resource would you like to share with the group?
- What personal discovery/connection have you made with this unit's texts?
- What have you enjoyed the most (or the least) about this unit's literature? Why?

Each unit's assignments also include bibliographic material on the sources covered.

In addition to encouraging students to (re)articulate their own relationships with their subjects, this sequence of assignments meets the traditionalist expectations for "hard" artifacts from student composition and research as well as enables students to communicate with multiple audiences and encourages them to express their (dis)pleasure with their texts. Moreover, this sequence of assignments leading up to students' final project exposes them to a range of media formats and venues (e.g., online journals, YouTube videos, individual Web sites) from which they can determine the shape of their final projects.

Final Research Project (FRP)

By creating and disseminating a multimodal project through an online venue, students use this assignment to engage directly with the issues of canonicity that they have been studying throughout the semester. For this project students choose the area(s) and author(s) that they feel meet their criteria and promote them through media that they choose. As noted earlier, the format and sophistication depend on the students' choices and skills. In many cases, they take the form of more traditional rhetorical and argumentative formats adapted and modified to meet the styles and possibilities of the students' chosen media. For example, they might choose from a formal list that I feature that provides them with models for their own projects. The list of suggested topics (see Assignment Sheet) illustrates some of those options.

While this list is meant to encourage students' final projects, it is not meant to determine them. Although students can and do choose alternatives, many choose these formal organizations because they provide a measure of reassurance: modifying traditional models is less anxiety-provoking than creating a more sophisticated multimodal projects because most students have never produced anything other than linear compositions. As I explored earlier, anxiety over producing a multimodal project can prove daunting for some students because of their lack of experience with such forms.

8. CONCLUSION

As you can see, this project has a transformative potential for students in the classroom and for audiences around the world. Not only can it enable students to create multimodal artifacts, but it can also enable and encourage audiences (both academic and non-) to realize deeper relationships with world literatures and with multimodality. As you can also see, this project faces certain obstacles that illustrate the need for an extensive revision of our K-12 and college compositional systems (e.g., methodologies, criteria) if we want to affect the changes inherent in multimodality.

9. WORKS CITED

Hawisher, Gail E., and Cynthia L. Selfe. "Conclusion: Hybrid and Transgressive Literacy Practices on the Web." *Global Literacies and the World Wide Web*. Edited by Gail E. Hawisher and Cynthia L. Selfe, Routledge, 2000, pp. 279-91.

- - -. *Passions, Pedagogies, and 21st Century Technologies*. Utah State UP, 1999.

Joyce, Michael. "Beyond Next Before You Once Again: Repossessing and Renewing Electronic Culture." *Passions, Pedagogies, and 21st Century Technologies*, edited by Gail E. Hawisher and Cynthia L. Selfe, Utah State UP, 1999, pp. 399-417.

Laist, Randy. "The Self-Deconstructing Canon: Teaching the Survey Course Without Perpetuating Hegemony." *Currents in Teaching and Learning*, vol. 1, no. 2, Spring 2009, pp. 50-57, www.worcester.edu/currents/archives/volume_1_number_2/currentsv1n2laistp50.pdf.

New London Group. "A Pedagogy of Multiliteracies: Designing Social Futures." *Literacy Learning and the Design of Social Futures*. Edited by Bill Cope and Mary Kalantzis, Routledge, 2000, pp. 7-37.

"Position Statement on Multimodal Literacies." *National Council of Teachers of English*, Nov. 2005, www.ncte.org/positions/statements/multimodalliteracies.

Selber, Stuart A. *Multiliteracies in a Digital Age*. Southern Illinois UP, 2004.

Selfe, Cynthia L. "Toward New Media Texts: Taking Up the Challenges of Visual Literacy." *Writing New Media: Theory and Applications for Expanding the Teaching of* Composition, edited by Anne Frances Wysocki, et al., Utah State UP, 2004, pp. 67-110.

Selfe, Richard J., and Cynthia L. Selfe. "'Convince Me!' Valuing Multimodal Literacies and Composing Public Service Announcements." *Theory Into Practice*, vol. 47, no. 2, Mar. 2008, pp. 83-92. *Taylor and Francis Online*, doi: 10.1080/00405840801992223, www.tand fonline.com/doi/full/10.1080/004058408 01992223.

Takayoshi, Pamela, and Cynthia L. Selfe. "Thinking about Multimodality." *Multimodal Composition Resources for Teachers*. Edited by Pamela Takayoshi and Cynthia L. Selfe. Hampton, 2007, pp. 1-7.

Taylor, Todd. "Design, Delivery, and Narcolepsy." *Delivering College Composition: The Fifth Canon*. Edited by Kathleen Blake Yancey. Boynton/Cook, 2006, pp. 127-40.

Wysocki, Anne Frances. "Impossibly Distinct: On Form/Content and Word/Image in Two Pieces of Computer-Based Interactive Multimedia." *Computers and Composition*, vol. 18, no. 3, 2001, pp. 207-34. *ScienceDirect*, www.sciencedirect.com/science/article/pii/5875546150100536.

Wysocki, Anne Frances, et al., editors. *Writing New Media: Theory and Applications for Expanding the Teaching of Composition*. Hampton, 2004.

Yancey, Kathleen Blake. "Delivering College Composition into the Future." *Delivering College Composition: The Fifth Canon*. Edited by Kathleen Blake Yancey. Boynton/Cook, 2006, pp. 199-209.

26

Digital Research and the Public Performance of Scholarship: Web Site Creation within the Literature Classroom

Miranda Garno Nesler
Ball State University

Dr. Miranda Garno Nesler (PhD Vanderbilt University) is an assistant professor of early modern literature at Ball State University in Indiana. Her work on gender, material culture, and education has been published in *Studies in English Literature, 1500–1900*, the *Journal of Narrative Theory*, and *This Rough Magic*. Currently, she is working with the James Shirley Project as the editor of *The Humorous Courtier* (1640).

COURTESY OF MIRANDA
GARNO NESLER

1. OVERVIEW

- **Assignment:** Perform long-term research to analyze and synthesize historical information, and ultimately to produce a scholarly Web site featuring students' independent and collaborative writing.

- **Courses:** Any literature course.

- **Literature:** Any.

- **Technology:** Subscription-based scholarly databases (e.g., JSTOR and Project Muse); field-specific subscription databases and e-archival holdings such as Records of Early English Drama (REED) or Early English Books Online (EEBO); free-access blog space (e.g., Blogger, WordPress).

- **Time:** At least six 50-minute course periods: the annotated bibliography requires one 50-minute session per annotation deadline. The collaborative introduction and individual posts each require approximately two 50-minute in-class workshops at minimum (to introduce the assignment and to allow students to prep); additional workshops may be added if you desire, or the remainder of work may be done outside the classroom. Research presentations can be short or long, with each group running a 10- to 15-minute lecture or a 30- to 40-minute seminar session, depending on the course's design.

2. GOALS OF THE ASSIGNMENT

- Hone students' analytic skills by requiring contact with and interpretation of primary sources that bring past and present into dialogue.
- Heighten student awareness of and participation in current scholarly conversations through the substantive use of critical secondary research.
- Encourage students to blend individual, team, classroom, and online interactions to create a functional product (Web site) that exists after the course ends.
- Educate students toward an awareness of audience needs and effective communication in traditional print and short online written formats.

"From start to finish, I've been impressed with how serious the students were about this project. In the classroom, they engaged in intense debates that brought their external research to bear on the course texts — exploring how economics defines human value in *The Jew of Malta* or *The Merchant of Venice*, and questioning how problematic vocabularies of humanness in Descartes shape modern works such as Peter Singer's *Animal Liberation*. The Web site reflects these nuanced investigations."

Miranda Garno Nesler
Ball State University

3. ASSIGNMENT SHEET

Digital Research and the Public Performance of Scholarship: Web Site Creation within the Literature Classroom

Course: _____

Instructor: _____

Date: _____

Long-Term Research Project: Handout 1

This semester, you will engage in a long-term research project that introduces you to issues of human-animal relations during the sixteenth and seventeenth centuries. Beginning this week, you will sign up for teams focused on three specific themes:

1. Literature and Drama
2. Science and Art
3. Law and Politics

You will collaborate with your team throughout the spring in order to build an independent archive of sources regarding how these cultural fields represented and engaged in the debate about human and animal identities. You will also use this information to supplement class discussion by sharing your knowledge.

The following components of the project will be spaced evenly throughout the semester, and each piece leads us toward the culmination of our work: a live scholarly blog containing collaborative critical introductions from your groups, and a series of independent posts authored by each member of the class.

Component 1: Annotated Bibliography (100 pts total)

The Annotated Bibliography will contain at least 4 entries from each group member. Each entry will be worth 25 points, and entries will be due each Friday throughout the first month of the semester. Entries should be in proper MLA format, should cover scholarly sources, and should be concise, thoughtful, and serve as helpful reference guides. An average annotation ranges from 150 to 250 words. Annotations will be individually assessed; however, you will compile and post a final Annotated Bibliography on Blackboard to assist you and your classmates in researching your midterm paper and your final Web site posts.

Component 2: Collaborative Introduction and Bios (100 pts)

Drawing on your shared research and weekly discussions, your group will compose a collective introduction for your section of the Web site. It should provide

(continued)

ASSIGNMENT SHEET (*continued*)

a brief overview of your group group's theme-related research, as well as a concise discussion of how you chose your post topics and how they tie together. This piece should be between 250 and 350 words. This grade will be shared.

Component 3: Research Meeting (25 pts)

During the semester, your group is required to set up a meeting at the university library with a research librarian to consult about possible sources for your project. You may complete this session at any point during the semester; however, all members of the team must be present. Your librarian should sign a sheet confirming your attendance and participation.

Component 4: Research Presentation (25 pts)

Our last unit will rely heavily on each team choosing its most compelling research discovery (a text, image, historical figure or event, play, poem, etc.) and presenting it to the class. Presentations will be collaborative (each member must have a speaking role) and should range from 10 to 15 minutes. This is your opportunity to introduce classmates to information that hasn't made it into your final pieces, that influenced your discussions and posts, or that brings your work into conversation with that of other groups. Assessment will be shared.

Component 5: Individual Posts (250 pts)

At the end of the semester, you will each need to submit a final researched post to contribute to our Web site. These posts should range between 400 and 500 words, possess at least 3 scholarly sources, and have one relevant image. Along with the post, you should write a brief author bio for the Web site, ranging from 25 to 50 words. Submissions should be e-filed on the day of final exams.

Total Project Points: 500

4. TIME AND TECHNOLOGY

The Web site construction project requires you and your students to have regular access to laptop computers and an Internet connection during class-time. Once a week, students will be required to break into teams to perform and share research, or to construct Web content. As this occurs, you will need to access those pages and guide students toward other content through the use of your own apparatus.

During the first phase of the research project, teams construct an annotated bibliography. Each student is responsible for four entries, generated out of independent research. The teams share and compile that research during weekly in-class sessions. During this process, a portion of meetings center on discussions about assessing the quality of Web research based on a site's structure, dates, and methods. Later in the semester, student teams use their laptops to write and revise collaborative thematic introductions to their fields, and to locate relevant images. On a regular basis, you should guide students back to the Web site to show how and where student content has been formatted for viewing. At least once during the semester, I recommend having students meet with a research librarian who can guide them through a variety of research sources, including but not limited to the following:

- university library card catalog (including onsite, online, and interlibrary holdings);
- scholarly search functions on publicly accessible sites such as Google;
- subscription-based scholarly databases such as JSTOR and Project Muse;
- field-specific subscription databases and e-archival holdings such as Records of Early English Drama (REED) or Early English Books Online (EEBO); and
- relevant blogs.

Prior to the course, I recommend that the instructor select a comfortable, free-access blog space (such as WordPress or Blogger) with which to set up a Web site shell in advance of the project.

This assignment is designed to unfold during a full semester, and each new component builds on the skills students obtained during the previous exercise. Each week, regardless of the stage of the project, students read a shared course text that deals with the semester's theme (e.g., in a course on Renaissance literature, a play such as *Titus Andronicus* or *The Jew of Malta*); they also perform external research that they then use to analyze texts during seminar discussions. At the end of each week, students meet in their teams to use a full class period to draw together research and collaborate on a component of the Web site project.

Knowledge Archive [Week 1]

During the opening week, students attend lectures providing historical/ theoretical groundwork—these involve PowerPoint presentations and lectures on the relevant vocabularies that shape the period's politics, science, art, education, and literature. Lectures are accompanied by roundtable discussions of primary source reading. The aim is to familiarize students with writing from the period and promote their awareness of the period's coexisting cultures and discourses. Once students gain a communal base of knowledge, they can select long-term research teams.

Team Division [Week 2]

Following the first week's lectures on Renaissance history and culture, students sign up for a team based on one of three thematic interests: (1) Literature and Drama, (2) Science and Art, and (3) Law and Politics. Their goals within these teams are to begin broad research that gives them a sense of the period, and then to narrow that research as team members begin locating issues of specific interest.

The Annotated Bibliography [Weeks 3–6]

For the next four weeks of the semester, teams construct annotated bibliographies related to their fields. Students perform research outside of the classroom, using that work to produce one entry weekly. Once a week, teams meet in class to share their research entries, update their bibliographies, and consider how to narrow their focus for the next week. (For example, Team 1 in a Renaissance course might initially research laws on sodomy, bestiality, rape, marriage, coverture, animal trials, livestock ownership, and property dispute. Ultimately they may focus on how the language of legal animal ownership was replicated in marriage contracts.) The final bibliography is a collaborative product from which all team members can draw in their writing; but students earn individual assessment for their entries.

Collaborative Introduction [Weeks 7–12]

In the weeks before and after midterm, the teams meet outside of class and once a week during seminars to reflect on their research, locate an overarching theme under which they will write their individual posts, and gather any remaining necessary research. Once teams have articulated the issues linking their work, they collaborate to compose a researched introduction to guide Web site viewers through the key thematic issues of the period. I recommend reserving at least a week for revisions of the draft. This piece is graded communally and posted on the Web site after students perform post-assessment edits.

Research Presentation [Weeks 13–14]

As team members begin writing their individual blog posts, the team itself performs a brief presentation at the semester's end. The research presentation aims to familiarize the class with all other teams' work and to encourage the active sharing of and listening to scholarly arguments. Groups perform a ten- to fifteen-minute overview of their semester research and raise questions for future inquiry. Each session ends with a roundtable Q&A that empowers all class members to make connections among their research. This assignment constitutes a lower portion of points on the project. In this sense, because it is a lower-stakes and communally assessed assignment, students are more comfortable being exploratory.

Individual Post [Weeks 15–17]

This piece ends the semester. In it, each student composes a concise but well-researched piece presenting an archival finding or critically analyzing a primary text. Two weeks prior to the final deadline, students have the opportunity first to perform a peer review in order to polish their work, and second to meet one-on-one with the instructor to get feedback. Each blog contribution must have proper MLA citation and at least one relevant contemporary image. Posts are individually assessed, high stakes insofar as they constitute a large portion of the course average, and should show the student's ability to use research to engage and inform the larger public. Posts are scheduled to run throughout the coming months, making the Web site live.

My experience in using this assignment has shown that even though the project in its entirety constitutes half of the students' semester grades, the pressure is lowered because the step-by-step nature of the components gives students room to grow, improve, and focus on their work rather than their quantitative grades. The multiple bibliography entries ease students into the practice of locating, assessing, reading, and summarizing external texts. While the independent searches push students to develop strong analytic skills, the team exercises in the classroom provide a support system of peers and instructor so that students can discuss difficulties and celebrate victories. The time spent on this portion of the semester is crucial for the success of the remaining project components; for this reason, I typically plan a flex week so that I can extend the research component if necessary.

5. ANTICIPATING STUDENT NEEDS

As with any collaborative project, friction among team members can occur. In most cases, such discord originates when personalities clash or when certain group members express concern that some members are carrying a greater or lesser load of work than others. This particular project anticipates these difficulties in very specific ways. First, students are at liberty early in the semester to select their own thematic teams following several days of introductory group work that allows them to get to know each other. Second, though the teams work together to build a research archive, the majority of assignments are assessed on an individual level—particularly high-stakes assignments that constitute a high percentage of a student's overall course grade. Collaborative grades are reserved for lower-stakes assignments in an attempt to familiarize students with effective collaboration while relieving them from the pressures of relying fully on others for the bulk of their grades. Meanwhile, individually assessed assignments are combined to create larger shared products such as the annotated bibliography.

In order to stay aware of the teams' work balance, I recommend not only listening in to each group during weekly meetings, but also having at least two consultations with each team at the start and middle of the semester to discuss progress and division of labor. Prior to such meetings, I have found it useful to have individual teammates hand in anonymous, sealed assessments of their team's work to date. This positions you to have an honest awareness of the groups' weaknesses and strengths prior to the consultation.

6. ASSESSMENT TOOLS

In total, the Web site project constitutes 50 percent of the student's course grade, with the remaining 50 percent divided between informal responses and a formal critical paper. To give students the opportunity for growth along the way, points are divided among the components of the larger Web site project into low-stakes collaborative assignments with smaller point values, and higher-stakes individual assignments with greater weight in the average.

RUBRIC 1: Annotated Bibliography   **(100 pts total/25 pts per entry)**

The annotated bibliography will be composed in a team. For each deadline, team members will each bring a new annotation to the table: students will turn in one copy for assessment, and one copy to share and discuss during the team meeting. At the end of the assignment, teams will compile the annotations into one document and provide me with an electronic copy. I will post these on Blackboard for the whole class to share and consult during the ongoing project.

Each annotation will be scored independently based on the following expectations:

A—Proper MLA format with no mistakes. Provides a clear, concise summary and a strong sense of the piece's possible use.

B—MLA format with a few minor mistakes. Provides a summary, but may be slightly verbose or vague. A general sense of the piece's possible value.

C—MLA format with errors. Provides a summary.

D—Consistent formatting errors or lack of effective summary.

F—Plagiarized or incomplete.

RUBRIC 2: Research Presentation   (50 pts)

This presentation provides the group with the opportunity to isolate 1–2 key sources, images, or other research materials to share with the class. In addition to allowing groups to encounter each other's work and enter into a dialogue about critical themes, the research presentation provides a small-scale scholarly conference experience. Teams will be communally assessed on how well they meet the following expectations:

- Each group member has a substantive speaking role during the presentation.
- The presentation meets the minimum research and image requirements, and uses images to clearly exemplify the group's work.
- The presentation possesses a proper MLA works-cited section.
- The presentation is well organized, clear, and presents the class with relevant research and questions for future exploration.
- The presentation meets minimum time requirements.
- Group members participate in the post-presentation roundtable and are prepared to display their expertise in the field of study.

RUBRIC 3: Individual Researched Blog Post   (250 pts)

The individual post is the culmination of your work this semester. It invites you to share your knowledge and interpretation of historical and literary texts, bringing you into dialogue not only with fellow classmates but also with the wider scholastic world. It also requires you to work within rhetorical limits, determining in a small space how to convey meaning effectively through the selective use of research and prose.

Prose (175 possible pts):   A B C D F _____

Writing is clear, concise, grammatical, and eloquent with no typos or errors.

Stays within the assigned word limits.

Contains a clear historical context and/or argumentative interpretation that is clearly based in primary and secondary research.

Makes a unique and important contribution or revelation to debates about the status of humans and animals in the period.

Fits within the group introduction's thematics and shares concerns with other group members' posts.

References at least 4 secondary sources and provides MLA citations.

(continued)

RUBRIC 3: Individual Researched Blog Post (*continued*)   **(250 pts)**

Image or Sound File (50 possible pts):   A B C D F _____

Image or sound exists in the public domain or is the author's intellectual property.

Image or sound is relevant to the prose and aids the author in illustrating key themes or concerns.

Image or sound is properly cited in the bibliography.

Bibliography (25 possible pts):   A B C D F _____

Conforms properly to MLA style.

Appears at the bottom of the post.

Contains citations for all quotations, references, image, and sound.

---

7. THEORETICAL BASIS FOR THE ASSIGNMENT: Digital Research and Public Performance of Scholarship: Web Site Creation within the Literature Classroom

This assignment was the locus of Performing Humanity in the Renaissance, an advanced course for literature majors at a large state university. Seeking to complicate students' perceptions of this alleged golden age, the course emphasized debates about human nature and human identity in seventeenth-century English art, philosophy, law, and science. As students explored representations of these debates in canonical literature, they not only gained an appreciation for the cultural exchanges that shaped and were shaped by literature; they also further considered how such vocabularies about humanity persist in our own lives. My choice of the digital Web site project was partly influenced by a desire to assist students in linking past dialogues about humanness to contemporary discourses that they encountered in social media and online news.

The impetus for this project was also state and university-wide pushes for immersion and technology related projects in the curriculum. The current economic climate has put increasing emphasis on college education as a necessary measure for achieving personal financial success, and the Commission on the Humanities and Social Sciences reports that "the opportunities and rewards open to those who lack this training have declined steadily as the knowledge economy has taken hold" (30). As a result of the government's "Educate to Innovate" campaign, universities have experienced a shift in funding and promotions that prioritizes majors in STEM (science, technology, engineering, mathematics) fields (White House n.pag.). For professors in areas such as English and history, it has become crucial to adapt by bringing more technology into the classroom and providing students with quantitatively assessable skill sets that will not only shape them into well-rounded adults, but will also aid those students in obtaining careers.

> "Technology's presence in the classroom can coincide with traditional humanistic models of pedagogy."
>
> **Miranda Garno Nesler**

As the assignment in this chapter demonstrates, technology's presence in the classroom can coincide with traditional humanistic models of pedagogy while helping departments to meet their universities' strategic plans. In disciplines such as Renaissance studies, digital humanities has provided scholars with opportunities to preserve and share rare manuscripts through databases such as Early English Books Online (EEBO); to generate layered and interactive maps of early cities, such as the Map of Early Modern London (MoEML); and to exchange information or collaborate at a more immediate rate via blogs and Twitter. These possibilities extend to teaching. By using digital platforms in the classroom, we continue encouraging students to hone their analytic and problem-solving abilities, to gain a more detailed awareness of history and culture, and to consider how these skills aid them in becoming economically successful and socially responsible. Digital assignments appeal to students' preexisting digital literacies; and they further demand that students become conscious of how those aptitudes place them within intellectual dialogues beyond both the university and their own Facebook walls, thus "letting them experience firsthand the living work of discovery" (Commission 32).

Incorporating online research and writing in literature classrooms maintains a pedagogical investment in rhetorical growth and scholarly dialogue. The National Writing Program reports, for example, that while "digital tools are blurring the lines between formal and informal writing [. . .] they also [highlight] the benefit of students having more people respond to their writing and the increased opportunities for expression" (n. pag.). This is in part because contact with a wider audience pushes students to engage in humanistic learning practices described in pedagogical texts such as Erasmus's *De copia rerum et verborum*, which taught students to "supercharge texts . . . using methods of rhetorical invention" designed to fit the audience at hand (Mack 31). Such methods shaped the Renaissance classroom and are the origins of the modern American university. Digital projects in our current courses, and this Web site project in particular, provide a similar rhetorical experience.

Within this project, it is key that students interact with a range of research methods and styles. Doing this teaches students to determine the varying reliability of sources—a necessary skill given that "the vast majority of students use either a home computer or a university computer to access research," yet they are not typically "aware of the qualitative distinction between published research and general internet sites" (Hampton-Reeves 1). As students begin identifying qualitative differences among print and digital sources, they become more adept at deciding the most effective ways of making their own work polished, informative, and responsible. For this reason, though I encourage students to privilege traditionally "scholarly" resources such as hardcopy books, journals, and collections (all of which are increasingly searchable and available online), I also urge them to consider publically accessible online resources such as Google Scholar and academic blogs.

It is also important that the students variously work independently, work in teams, and bring both versions of work to bear on roundtable discussion. These are key means through which "the liberal arts train people to adapt and change" in response to new problems (Commission 32). Such dialogues model the practices of advanced scholars, and in my experience they provide the students with a sense of professional engagement. What's more, these abilities prepare students for nonacademic careers wherein employers require interpersonal abilities as part of "a diversity of skills, and not just technical knowledge" (Commission 34).

Finally, I believe that it is significant that students begin with an empty Web site shell rather than contribute to a preexisting site. As students witness new content appearing, I find that they feel a sense of investment (rather than a sense of inferiority compared to professional academic contributors or previous students), and they gain appreciation for how their disparate individual work comes together to build something coherent and new that other scholars may read and contribute to in the future. No longer are they simply writing for a limited or imagined public; they are overtly publicly engaged.

8. CONCLUSION

This assignment was particularly successful at encouraging students to keep up with their reading and discussion because they were constantly aware of the audiences interacting with their work—whether those audiences were classroom peers or Web site readers. As students began to conceive of themselves as specialists in their given fields, they independently sought each other out for advice and feedback in and out of the classroom; and they were eager to share their knowledge during class discussion by bringing additional articles and images to share.

> "As students began to conceive of themselves as specialists in their given fields, they independently sought each other out for advice."
>
> **Miranda Garno Nesler**

I believe that a major reason the Web site design project achieved this is because it allowed students to share their work with an audience beyond the classroom. They were highly aware of the wide readership they would encounter—and of that readership's potential judgment—and they wanted to present themselves professionally. This task became more familiar and more manageable because it required less formal writing that could invite scholars and nonspecialists to learn.

The duration of this project was possible because the course was filled with upper-division majors. In an introductory course, however, I believe it could work if condensed. Such trimming would depend on the goals of the introductory course. For example, if the emphasis is training students in research and writing, the project could be narrowed to the collaborative annotative bibliography and the independent Web post. If the focus is training students to consider how tone and space assists them in relating to an audience, the project could focus on using research from the annotated bibliography to compose a collaborative introduction and a collaborative research presentation.

9. WORKS CITED

Commission on the Humanities and Social Sciences. *The Heart of the Matter: The Humanities and Social Sciences for a Vibrant, Competitive, and Secure Nation.* American Academy of Arts and Sciences, 2013, pp. 30-34.

Hampton-Reeves, Stuart, et al. *Students' Use of Research Content in Teaching and Learning: A Report for the Joint Information Systems Council.* Center for Research-Informed Teaching, U of Central Lancashire, 2009.

Mack, Peter. *Elizabethan Rhetoric: Theory and Practice.* Cambridge UP, 2002.

National Writing Project, "Pew Report Illustrates Impact of Digital Technologies on Student Writing." *National Writing Project Online,* 16 July 2013, http://www.nwp.org/cs/public/print/resource/4162.

White House Office of the Press Secretary. "President Obama Expands 'Educate to Innovate' Campaign for Excellence in Science, Technology, Engineering, and Mathematics (STEM) Education." *White House,* 6 Jan. 2010, www.whitehouse.gov/the-press-office/president-obama-expands-educate-innovate-campaign-excellence-science-technology-eng.

27

Beyond Fanfiction: Creating Remixes in an Advanced Literature Course

Emily Wierszewski
Seton Hill University

Emily Wierszewski is an assistant professor of English/composition at Seton Hill University, a liberal arts institution in southwest Pennsylvania, where she teaches courses in first-year writing, journalism, creative writing, and literature. Her scholarship focuses on applications for multimodal pedagogy, including topics such as assessing multimodal texts and using comics.

COURTESY OF EMILY
WIERSZEWSKI

1. OVERVIEW

- **Assignment:** Students use digital technology to remix literature, then write about the experience.
- **Courses:** Any literature course, including upper level; literature and composition.
- **Literature:** Any work of literature in the public domain (or covered by a Creative Commons license which allows for derivative works) for which there is at least one remix. Some examples of texts used in this class: *Jane Eyre* by Charlotte Brontë (with remixes *Jane Slayre* by Sherri Browning Erwin and *Wide Sargasso Sea* by Jean Rhys, alongside film adaptations), *The Strange Case of Dr. Jekyll and Mr. Hyde and Other Stories* by Robert Louis Stevenson (with remixes *The League of Extraordinary Gentlemen Vol. 1* by Alan Moore and *Mary Reilly* by Valerie Martin, alongside film adaptations), and *The Complete Fairy Tales of the Brothers Grimm* by the Grimm brothers (with *Fables Vol. 1: Legends in Exile* by Bill Willingham and Lan Medina).
- **Technology:** Depending on students' project goals and access, needs range from digital cameras and software (like iMovie to add images or

video to their remix) to web-based interfaces (like WordPress to create blogs or Blurb to create short books).

- **Time:** While reading and analysis of remixes spans the entire semester, work on students' individual remix projects requires about five to six weeks for planning, drafting, feedback, and revision.

> "Show students that literature is a live, collaborative, and evolving art through the use of digital tools and remixing with this assignment."
>
> **Emily Wierszewski**
> Seton Hill University

2. GOALS OF THE ASSIGNMENT

After completing this assignment, students will be able to:

- exercise creativity in reimagining a piece of published literature;
- understand how works of literature are fundamentally intertextual;
- appreciate how remixes depend on references to other texts;
- question standard definitions of literature and think about how technology might alter those definitions;
- develop a sense of the qualities of "good" remixes and strive to create a remix that embodies some of those qualities;
- understand copyright law and how to find and use creative works legally; and
- learn how various technologies can be used to create derivative works of literature.

3. ASSIGNMENT SHEET

Beyond Fanfiction: Creating Remixes in an Advanced Literature Course

Course: _____

Instructor: _____

Date: _____

What's a Remix, Anyway?

Remixing is the process of taking an original work and manipulating it in some way to alter its meaning (for instance, cutting or rearranging content, changing the medium, modifying the tone or colors, building off a small bit of the original text to create something new, etc.). Occasionally, an artist may combine that original work with other works to create new meaning; this is called a mashup. While remixes have always existed, digital technology has facilitated the process. Now more than ever, anyone with a mobile device or computer can quickly and easily produce a remix. As author China Miéville articulated at the 2012 Edinburgh World Writers' Conference, in the digital age "anyone who wants to shove their hands into a book and grub about in its innards, add to and subtract from it, and pass it on, will . . . be able to do so without much difficulty." Remixing has profound implications for our notions of literature, authorship, and intellectual property.

Why Remix?

Remixes are driven by a creative purpose. Often, they are made for subversive or humorous purposes (take, for instance, any number of "fake" Twitter accounts created for political figures, or the classic example of Antoine Dodson, whose animated account during a news report was remixed into a rap song which has had about 105 million hits on YouTube since its release in the fall of 2011). Additionally, remixes can be made to respond to gaps in a work of art or narrative (for instance, Jean Rhys's *Wide Sargasso Sea* is a response to Brontë's *Jane Eyre*. Rhys develops the character of Bertha and explains the reasons for her madness, while she is simply dismissed as a madwoman in Brontë's work).

Project Details

For this project, you will be asked to create a remix of a canonical work of literature we read this semester. The process is broken down into discrete steps:

> **Step 1.** Choose a work to remix. Remember that it must be one of the canonical texts we read from the public domain. This step is closely intertwined with step 2.

Step 2. All remixes are driven by some creative purpose. Why do you want to remix the text you chose, and what will you do to remix it?

Step 3. Articulate your plans in a brief (1 page) project proposal. In the proposal, discuss what technologies you'll use to make your remix and what new meaning you want to create with your remix, including *how and why* it will differ from the original text. Do you want to make a subversive remix, perhaps as a comment on gender or socioeconomic roles in something we've read, as Rhys and Martin have done in their remixes? A remix that changes the tone of the original, making a sad story funny or a children's story into a narrative for adults? A remix that provides a new perspective on the tale or fills a "gap" in the narrative? These aren't the only options, of course, but are meant to get you thinking. It may also be useful to contemplate the creative purposes behind the remixes we've read as a class.

Remember that your remix project is replacing the work of a 10- to 15-page researched essay, so the equivalent amount of work is required. We'll negotiate this during our conference time as we review your project proposal. You'll also assess this work in the accompanying artist's statement (see step 6).

Step 4. Get remixing. Your purpose should guide the production of your remix. Your remix may be constructed in any medium you'd like — text, video, audio, a mixture — and any genre you'd like (poetry, fiction, a Twitter stream, a vlog, a news story, a documentary, etc.). However, you must use at least one form of digital technology beyond a word processor in its production. You should also consult the rubric we derived as a class to be sure your project meets the remix criteria we collaboratively generated.

Step 5. When your remix is complete, you must publish it so that it is publicly available on the Internet (for instance, YouTube for videos, the iTunes store for e-pub books, a Tumblr blog, etc.).

Step 6. You must also compose a brief (2–3 pages) artist's statement accompanied by a works-cited page in MLA format in which you describe the following:

- The underlying creative purpose of your remix. What is your remix's relationship to the original text you chose?
- How your remix "fits" with the criteria of effective remixes we developed as a class (see the rubric).
- The time, effort, and creativity you put into the project. Remember that this project replaces the lengthy research essay, and this is your place to explain the work your remix required.
- How digital technologies factored into the production of your remix. How did they help or hinder your remix?

(continued)

ASSIGNMENT SHEET *(continued)*

- Finally, reflect on the larger implications of this course and project. In an age when technologies are so prevalent, how might our definitions of "literature" and "authorship" shift?

4. TIME AND TECHNOLOGY

In this assignment, students are asked to remix a course reading, using technology to alter it in some way to make new meaning (for instance: removing or rearranging content, changing the tone or medium, building off a small bit of the original text to create a new work, etc.); they are also asked to write about their experiences in an accompanying artist's statement. The form of their remix is purposefully left open to encourage students to consider the varied shapes of remixes. For instance, fanfiction, the practice of creating derivative stories from an original work, is an obvious type of remix. It's grown in popularity thanks to the availability of discussion boards on the Web and sites like FanFiction (www.fanfiction.net). But it's also a type of remixing that can be done without technology and that relies only on print to tell a story. Leaving the assignment purposefully open allows students to imagine possibilities beyond fanfiction and to think about ways to create remixes of literature that incorporate some of their own strengths as writers, remixes that could reach a wider audience (photos, music, video, etc.). As a result, the kinds of technologies that students will need to complete their remixes depend largely on their individual project goals. For instance, some will require digital cameras and software (like iMovie to add images or video to their remix), and some might rely on web-based interfaces (like WordPress to create blogs or Blurb to create short books). It is wise to ask students to articulate a plan for their remixes and anticipate their technological needs before the project gets under way.

Since students are using technology and the Internet to work with intellectual property to create remixes, copyright law is an important consideration both in the preparation of the course and in the students' execution of the assignment. When selecting texts for the entire class to read and later remix, choose canonical works that are available in the public domain so that students do not have to worry whether their remix violates copyright laws (note: the remixes you select for the class to read do not have to be available in the public domain, unless you want to offer that students can remix those derivative works, too). The public domain includes works whose copyrights have expired, as well as works by authors who have chosen alternatives to strict copyrights, such as Creative Commons licenses. A good place to turn for these texts is Project Gutenberg. For instance, in my course students read Charlotte Brontë's *Jane Eyre*, tales from the Brothers Grimm, and Robert Louis Stevenson's *The Strange Case of Dr. Jekyll and Mr. Hyde* (as well as remixes of those texts including, for instance, the first comic in the series *Fables*, which places characters from classic Grimm tales together in a modern context).

When students are ready to create their own remixes, a more explicit discussion of copyright law can generate useful conversations about authorship and intellectual property; this is especially useful if students wish to create mashups (remixes that manipulate both the course readings *and outside materials that do not belong to the students*). For a clear and thorough beginner's guide, try Lawrence Lessig's *Free Culture*, available as a free PDF. Once students understand why they cannot simply use anything they want in their mashups, instructors can use the Web to point students to remix resources that are available in the public domain or that have appropriate Creative Commons licenses (those that permit derivative works). While it is relatively simple to limit Google search results to items that are Creative Commons licensed, the best place to start looking are sites like the Creative Commons search. Students should be encouraged to include their own original work in the remix as well; for example, one of my students created a series of poems from the perspective of Edward Hyde, mixing original content from Stevenson's story with the student's own poetic verse.

Since this assignment is the culminating project in a fifteen-week course, all of the readings, discussions, and activities that occur beforehand are designed to prepare students to execute the assignment. Students should spend the first nine to ten weeks reading and discussing works of literature and their remixes (for instance, beginning with Charlotte Brontë's *Jane Eyre* and moving to remixes like Jean Rhys's *Wide Sargasso Sea*, Sherri Browning Erwin's *Jane Slayre*, and Cary Fukunaga's 2011 film adaptation of *Jane Eyre*). Whenever possible, remixes created with the aid of digital technologies should be brought in for analysis (music, poetry, comics, etc.). Students should be asked to identify and share remixes as well. When discussing remixed texts, classroom discussions may converge on questions like the following:

- How has each remix adopted elements from the original works?
- Do you consider the remix to be successful? Why or why not?
- Should the remix count as "literature"? Why or why not?
- What role (if any) does technology seem to have played in the text's production?

After the first remix has been read, usually around week 2 or 3, students should also be asked to engage in low-stakes, collaborative remixing activities. The activities encourage them both to be mindful about ways they could use technology to remix literature, as well as to apply and rework the criteria for successful remixes they have begun to generate during class discussions. For instance, small groups of students might create Facebook Timelines with interactions between Jane and Rochester by rearranging and updating dialogue from *Jane Eyre*, or create short trailers for their own film adaptations of the book using simple, free animation programs like Wideo or Xtranormal. Remixing activities should continue throughout the semester.

The remix assignment itself should be referenced early on to give students an opportunity to think about their projects, but should not actually be assigned until week 9 or 10 of the course so that students may apply what they have learned. Since student projects will be guided by varying purposes and technologies, it is likely that little class time at this point will be spent focusing on students' individual projects. Rather, the bulk of the time should be devoted to continued discussion of texts, the development of effective "remix" and literature criteria based on those texts, and experimentation with various technologies through in-class remixing activities. Around week 12, a robust discussion about a rubric for the project should also take place. Students should be asked to reflect on the remixes and original texts they have read, including previous class discussions, to negotiate rubric criteria. Having these criteria for efficacious remixes in mind can be helpful for students during the production process, too.

5. ANTICIPATING STUDENT NEEDS

The creative freedom inherent in this assignment's design is both its greatest benefit and its greatest drawback. As aforementioned, leaving the form open requires that students exercise creativity and produce remixes according to their own strengths as students and writers; for example, one of my students who was a journalism major produced a daily newspaper that captured some of Edward Hyde's dark deeds using her knowledge of publication software and experience as the editor of the school's newspaper. The open form also allows students to see the many ways they (and others, with various abilities and expertise) might use technologies to collaborate with others (or the work of others) to create texts, illustrating that literature is a fundamentally social process.

At the same time, the project's open nature creates some instructional issues. One is that it is impossible to specify a standard length for the project. This difficulty can be overcome by simply asking students to draft proposals or to talk with you in a conference in order to negotiate a length or depth for their individual project. A second difficulty has to do with classroom activities. It can be onerous to structure any type of in-class lesson on remixing technologies that will directly help the students with their projects, since there is generally little consistency in the types of projects produced. However, as previously suggested, it helps to expose students to a variety of technological options throughout the term that they can later adopt. Finally, developing grading criteria that can be fairly applied across a wide range of projects may also be problematic. Solutions are discussed in the next section.

6. ASSESSMENT TOOLS

Developing grading criteria for this assignment can be a challenge, given that the types of remixes students produce will vary widely. When generating a rubric, it is therefore helpful to keep learning goals for the assignment in mind. For instance, if you want students to produce remixes so that they can put into practice the "good" qualities of a remix that they discussed over the semester, it is fitting for those qualities to appear on the rubric. Similarly, if you spent a lot of time analyzing texts and remixes from a feminist perspective, it would be logical to include an item addressing this perspective on the rubric if it is required.

It can also be helpful to ask students to negotiate some, if not all, of the rubric criteria. What have they learned about what makes a remix successful, based on course readings, activities, and discussions? Generating a rubric early in the assignment process may also help students be mindful about effective remixing criteria during production. A robust discussion of criteria in my own course led to the development of the rubric below, which is a potential starting point for other instructors.

Rubric: Remix Project	
____/30	The remix is guided by a clear, consistent purpose.
____/20	The remix is the product of great thought and time (determined on the basis of self-reporting in the artist's statement and the instructor's perceptions).
____/20	The remix is creative or unique. It brings original thought or authenticity to the source text.
____/20	The student has experimented with various digital technologies to produce his or her remix.
____/20	The remix references the original in some way but contains noticeable changes. It is distinguishable from the original.
____/20	The student has thoughtfully and thoroughly reflected on the relationship between technology and literature in the artist's statement.
____/20	The student has thoroughly and thoughtfully assessed the success of his/her own remix, according to class-derived remix criteria, in the artist's statement.
____/25	The student has used peer and instructor feedback to revise the remix. Revisions are substantive and purposeful, improving the draft in some way (revisions aren't made simply for revision's sake).

____/25	The project follows assignment requirements outlined in the assignment sheet and meets discipline-specific expectations (MLA, free from frequent or interruptive grammatical errors).
____/200	TOTAL

7. THEORETICAL BASIS FOR THE ASSIGNMENT: Beyond Fanfiction: Creating Remixes in an Advanced Literature Course

This assignment grew out of my experiences as a faculty member at a liberal arts university. While I was educated in rhetoric and composition, I was working in a small department with generalist responsibilities in English. I was assigned to teach my first literature course, and when I turned to scholarship for help thinking about ways to integrate technology into the literature classroom, the resources available underwhelmed me. Yet I wanted my literature students to have the chance to think about the ways the technologies they use every day may impact literary works, just as I often ask my writing students to consider how technology affects nonfiction writing practices. So I brainstormed ways to apply my existing knowledge to this new situation, and realized that the concept of remix—which I had previously explored in writing courses with creative writing and journalism majors—was relevant to the study of literature as well. As I planned the course, I identified two major pedagogical goals. The first was to highlight the intertextual properties of literature through remix, showing students how literature can be a collaborative process that they might add their own voices to through the use of technologies. The second was to encourage students to work with and think carefully about digital technologies and their relationship to literature. Both of these learning goals have theoretical underpinnings.

At the Edinburgh International Book Festival in 2012, novelist China Miéville engaged in a heated debate with other poets and writers about the future of literature in the digital age. He argued that "anyone who wants to shove their hands into a book and grub about in its innards, add to and subtract from it, and pass it on, will . . . be able to do so without much difficulty" (Higgins). One important way digital technology affects literary texts is by allowing people to easily manipulate those texts, to "shove their hands into" books and change them in fundamental ways, as Miéville observes. This transforming process is often referred to as "remixing," and involves altering the work of others in ways that affect that work's meaning.

Digital technology has facilitated the remix process, although it has been enacted and theorized about for quite some time. When it comes to literature, remixing makes the role of collaboration in textual production apparent and creates a "blurring of boundaries between writers, books, and readers" (Higgins). It ruptures canonical definitions of literature, revealing literature as "a profoundly social practice" that we might participate in (Murray 30). Decades ago, Julia Kristeva theorized about literature as a collaborative practice. Her theory of intertextuality suggested that "any text is a mosaic of quotations" and that texts are "common cultural experience[s]" (Bazerman 54). According to Charles Bazerman, Kristeva's theory was meant to emphasize the interconnectedness of readers and writers. Later, Roland Barthes's theory of intertextuality built on Kristeva's work but focused more so on the interconnectedness of texts. Barthes articulated that the author "can only imitate a gesture that is always anterior, never original. His only power is to mix writings" (Barthes 146). Vladimir Nabokov's *Lolita* embodies the concept of intertexuality as Barthes imagined it. The novel bears a striking resemblance to a short story "Lolita" written by a German author in 1916 (Gladstone). While our cultural tendency might be to think about a resemblance between two texts as plagiarism, Ron Rosenbaum suggests that Nabokov was not guilty of plagiarism but was subconsciously influenced by his earlier reading of the German text. Nabokov wrote *Lolita* under the influence of "cryptomnesia," or "the appearance in consciousness of memory images which are not regarded as such but which appear as original creations" (para. 2). Cryptomnesia, or the impact of the texts we read and encounter on our own works, reflects Barthes's pronouncement that the author is never able to create a truly original work but can only build upon what has come before. Nabokov's novel is intertextual in the sense that it was clearly influenced by and "mixed" with the earlier writings of at least one other author—though apparently much of the influence was subconscious.

> "Remixing involves altering the work of others in ways that affect that work's meaning."
> **Emily Wierszewski**

While some have posited that literature has always been intertextual and therefore collaborative in a sense, remixes *depend* on collaboration and intertextuality. Unlike Nabokov (or at least our best guesses about his creative process), when remixers take ownership of and participate in a work of literature, they make conscious choices. They decide which works they want to repurpose (e.g., placing a character from one story into a new one with feminist motives, as Jean Rhys does with Charlotte Brontë's Bertha in *Wide Sargasso Sea*). The remixed text's intertextual properties become critical to its success for, as Diakopoulos and colleagues assert, a remix "cannot exist outside of its network of references to other media" (para. 27). Writers build remixes from existing works, and their message is conveyed in the ways they use and manipulate that work. As a result, remixes can be used productively in the classroom to "evidence the innate intertextuality of *all* literature" and to show students how they, too, can participate in literature (Murray 30).

While technology helps reinforce the fact that intertextuality and collaboration are integral to remixing, remixes can be made without technology. So why should we demand that our students use technology to produce their remixes? As Miéville has hinted, in the digital age the tools needed to create and share remixes are more accessible and simpler to use than ever. For instance, if you wanted to make a video remix of a text in decades past, you'd need access to expensive cameras and editing software, and you could only show the final product to your friends in person on a television screen. Today, you can pick up your phone, record a quick video using a free app like Vine or even the built-in camera, and share your remix almost instantly across platforms with the entire world. Outside of the classroom, our students constantly engage in these kinds of literacy practices facilitated by digital technologies. In recent years, several professional organizations in the discipline of English have clamored for instructors to better integrate these technologies in the classroom. For instance, in 2008 The National Council of Teachers of English (NCTE) drafted the "NCTE Definition of 21st Century Literacies" which specifies that "active, successful participants in this 21st century global society" must be given opportunities to engage with technology in the classroom in many ways, including "to develop proficiency and fluency with the tools of technology" and to "create, critique, analyze, and evaluate multimedia texts."

When teachers integrate technologies for composing remixes in the classroom, they connect to students' personal literacy practices, which can help generate student interest and build on students' existing skill sets. Daniel Anderson, for example, has proposed that English teachers ask students to use "low-bridge" or familiar, user-friendly technologies to "remix" or repurpose existing compositional material (such as images, sounds) in order to "create environments where writers can experience the personal engagement that will translate into motivation" (58). Similarly, Pamela Takayoshi and Cynthia Selfe have noted that students approach multimodal assignments like remixes—which integrate digital technologies and multiple modes of meaning like images, sounds, and writing—with both "implicit, perhaps previously unarticulated, knowledge" about those texts and technologies, as well as a high level of "excitement" (4).

At the same time, when students engage with digital technologies to construct remixes in the classroom, they have to apply academic knowledge and refine their use of the digital tools required to be literate in contemporary times. They learn how to use those tools to accomplish a planned, creative purpose and make meaning. In the case of this assignment, they participate in

> "Remixes can be used in the classroom to 'evidence the innate intertextuality of *all* literature' and to show students how they, too, can participate in literature."
>
> **Emily Wierszewski, quoting Simone Murray**

literature, rather than passively receive it as readers. Anne Frances Wysocki is one of many scholars in rhetoric and composition studies who has advocated for teaching students to use digital and other tools to reimagine new textual arrangements. She writes that "when someone makes an object that is both separate from her but that shows how she can use the tools and materials and techniques of her time, then she can see a possible self—a self positioned and working within the wide material conditions of her world, even shaping that world—in that object" (21). Students exercise agency and learn that contemporary literacy necessitates analysis and production mediated by digital tools when they create texts like this remix assignment, which requires the use of digital tools to thoughtfully rework or remix a text and its conventions.

8. CONCLUSION

When I taught this assignment in my Advanced Study in Literature course, my students applied their knowledge of remixes and remixing technologies to produce a wide variety of successful projects. Some examples included a screenplay for an episode of the popular television show *NCIS* entitled "Blood Red" (a remix of a Brothers Grimm fairy tale), an edition of *The London Sun* newspaper focusing on facts and eyewitness accounts of scandals from *Jane Eyre* and *The Strange Case of Dr. Jekyll and Mr. Hyde and Other Stories*, and a series of humorous public service announcements based on the morals or messages of the texts we had read ("Studies show that 89% of people with poor eyesight mistake a savage wolf as their grandmother and are torn to shreds, sprinkled with oregano, and eaten for a late night snack. Don't mistake a wolf as your grandmother! Get your eyes checked!"). One of the rubric criteria my students generated was creativity, and these examples demonstrate how this assignment requires students to think in innovative ways about original texts, new purposes, and digital tools.

As stated earlier, students often use digital technologies to produce texts like remixes, and bringing these tools into the classroom validates their literacy practices and interests which can lead to student engagement. As one student noted in his or her course evaluation, "I also enjoyed creating the mini-remixes as well as my final remix project." The remix assignment requires that students apply knowledge of course concepts to create a text. Course evaluations validate that all of the students in my course felt the remix assignment was a "hands-on" or "real-life activity." One student observed that the course required students to participate in "creative projects to actively remix the remixes we were reading." The remix assignment is an excellent way to bridge concepts from literature with twenty-first-century literacies and technologies. As they create their own remixes, students must think carefully about how these concepts intertwine.

9. WORKS CITED

Anderson, Daniel. "The Low Bridge to High Benefits: Entry-level Multimedia, Literacies, and Motivation." *Computers and Composition*, vol. 25, no. 1, 2007, pp. 40-60.

Barthes, Roland. "The Death of the Author." *Image, Music, Text.* Translated and edited by Stephen Heath. Hill and Wang, 1977, pp. 142-48.

Bazerman, Charles. "Intertextualities: Volosinov, Bakhtin, Literary Theory, and Literacy Studies." *Bakhtinian Perspectives on Language, Literacy, and Learning.* Edited by Arnetha Ball and Sarah Warshauer Freedman. Cambridge UP, 2004, pp. 53-65.

Brontë, Charlotte. *Jane Eyre.* 1847. Tribeca, 2010.

Brontë, Charlotte, and Sherri Erwin-Browning. *Jane Slayre.* Gallery, 2010.

Diakopoulos, Nicholas, et al. *Remixing Authorship: Reconfiguring the Author in Online Video Remix Culture.* Georgia Tech, 2007.

Gladstone, Brooke. "My Sin, My Soul . . . Whose Lolita?" *On the Media*, 16 Sept. 2005, www.wnyc.org/story/129172-my-sin-my-soul-whose-lolita/. Transcript.

Grimm, Jacob, and Wilhelm Grimm. *The Complete Fairy Tales of the Brothers Grimm.* 1812 and 1815. Translated by Jack Zipes. Bantam, 2003.

Higgins, Charlotte. "China Miéville: Writers Should Welcome a Future Where Readers Remix Our Books." *The Guardian*, 21 Aug. 2012, www.theguardian.com/2012/aug/21/china-mieville-novels-books-anti-piracy.

Martin, Valerie. *Mary Reilly.* Vintage, 2001.

Moore, Alan. *The League of Extraordinary Gentlemen: Vol. 1.* America's Best Comics, 1999.

Murray, Simone. "'Remix My Lit': Towards an Open Access Literary Culture." *Convergence*, vol. 16, no. 1, 2010, pp. 23-38.

Rhys, Jean. *Wide Sargasso Sea.* 1966. Norton, 1992.

Stevenson, Robert Louis. *The Strange Case of Dr. Jekyll and Mr. Hyde and Other Stories.* 1886. Barnes and Noble Classics, 2003.

"The NCTE Definition of 21st Century Literacies." *National Council of Teachers of English*, www.ncte.org/positions/statements/21stcentdefinition.

Takayoshi, Pamela, and Cynthia Selfe. "Thinking About Multimodality." *Multimodal Composition: Resources for Teachers.* Edited by Cynthia Selfe. Hampton, 2007, pp. 1-12.

Willingham, Bill, and Lan Medina. *Fables Vol. 1: Legends in Exile.* DC Comics, 2002.

Wysocki, Anne Frances. "Opening New Media to Writing: Openings and Justifications." *Writing New Media: Theory and Applications for Expanding the Teaching of Composition.* Edited by Anne Frances Wysocki, et al. Utah State UP, 2004, pp. 1-41.

28

Hybrid Bodies and New Media Narratives: Critical Media Literacy in the Literature Classroom

Kimberly Hall
University of California, Riverside

AND

Rochelle Gold
University of California, Riverside

Kimberly Hall is a PhD candidate in the Department of English at the University of California, Riverside. Her dissertation charts the development of an aesthetic of precarity in historical and contemporary social media practices. She is a cofounder of the Critical Digital Humanities Mellon Workshop at UC Riverside and she has taught courses in composition, literature and media, and professional communication.*

COURTESY KIMBERLY HALL

Rochelle Gold is a PhD candidate in English at the University of California, Riverside. Her dissertation research explores formal innovation in transnational print and digital literature from the 1970s to the present. She is one of the coordinators of the Mellon-funded Critical Digital Humanities research group at UC Riverside, and she is the former assistant director of UC Riverside's University Writing Program.*

COURTESY OF ROCHELLE GOLD

1. OVERVIEW

- **Assignment:** Students develop a digital or analog avatar using composite parts from various different media representations of bodies in order to interrogate a cultural norm or anxiety. They create an autobiographical narrative for the avatar, preferably using social media, in order to place the creation within a relevant cultural and social context. Students also

---

*A warm thank you to James Tobias for designing the course that inspired us to develop this assignment, and for your ongoing mentorship in digital pedagogy and scholarship.

produce a metacognitive essay in which they critically analyze and reflect on their creative choices.

- **Courses:** Any literature course; literature and
  composition.
- **Literature:** Adaptable and would potentially work
  well as an accompaniment to a wide range of primary
  and secondary readings (e.g., H. G. Wells's novella
  The Island of Dr. Moreau, and Paul Di Filippo's short
  story "Little Worker," along with literary theory,
  including Donna Haraway's "Cyborg Manifesto"
  and excerpts from N. Katherine Hayles's *How We Became Posthuman*).
- **Technology:** Social media account (e.g., Facebook), digital camera, a
  Web site where students post or link to their hybrid bodies (e.g., the
  course Web site).
- **Time:** Can be conducted in four to seven class sessions, or extended over
  a full semester.

> "Incorporating digital assign-
> ments that require adapta-
> tion and reflexivity in our
> teaching provides an invalu-
> able model of critical inquiry
> for our students."
>
> **Kimberly Hall**
> University of
> California, Riverside

2. GOALS OF THE ASSIGNMENT

The primary goal of this assignment is to help students
develop critical close reading skills through a process
of constructing multimedia objects and narratives. The
secondary goals include implementing critical media
praxis and theory within a literary classroom, and privi-
leging creative and ludic forms of thinking that can be
transferred to analytic essays.

> "Assignments do not need to
> rely on complex technologies
> in order to offer meaningful
> opportunities for student
> learning."
>
> **Rochelle Gold**
> University of
> California, Riverside

3. ASSIGNMENT SHEET

Hybrid Bodies and New Media Narratives: Critical Media Literacy in the Literature Classroom

Course: _____

Instructor: _____

Date: _____

Project: Creating a Hybrid Body

Assignment

The practice of critical close reading allows us to uncover deeper meanings in texts and cultural objects by focusing on how specific elements contribute to the meaning of the work as a whole. This assignment asks you to move from being a reader of texts to a creator of texts and to engage in critical close building. In order to be a successful critical builder, you will need to rely on your close reading skills. For this assignment, you will create a project that interrogates a specific cultural ideology, anxiety, or norm that you are inter-ested in exploring. You might consider one or more of the following broad categories as a jumping-off point for launching your particular project: gender, race, social class, religion, technology, sexuality, age, or ability. Ask yourself: What hopes and/or fears do we as a society have regarding the relationship between one of these categories and our bodies? How has our understanding of that relationship changed over time and how might it continue to change in the future?

Requirements

Create a hybrid body (see description below), create a narrative for the body (give it something to do in some sort of setting), give a class presentation about your hybrid body, and write an essay reflecting on the concept behind your body and narrative. You will also be required to provide feedback on your peers' projects in the form of public and written comments.

Technological Requirements

You must have access to a digital camera and a computer. You are required to post three elements to the course Web site: a digital picture or still of your body, the text of or a link to your narrative, and your reflection essay. You are also required to comment on your peers' work on the Web site.

Due Dates

(all work is due on Friday of the week listed unless otherwise noted)

    Week 3: Submit your proposal to the Web site.

Week 6: Post an image of your hybrid body to the course Web site.

Week 7: Present your hybrid body in class for peer feedback.

Week 8: Post a copy of your narrative or a link to it on the course Web site.

Week 9: Post your reflection essay on the course Web site.

Steps

1. *Build the hybrid body:* Using either digital or analog technologies, create a hybrid body made up of human, animal, and/or machine parts. The body must be pieced together from a series of disparate components and you must choose each component to represent a specific cultural ideology, anxiety, or norm that you are interested in exploring. The only requirement is that your hybrid body must be a compilation of parts that you choose to put together for specific reasons. You can use any elements you wish for the different body parts, but you must be able to speak to what each part represents. You may use analog technologies like bricolage (magazine or newspaper cutouts, sculpture, etc.) or digital technologies like photo editing or digital drawing software.

2. *Write a narrative for the body:* The purpose of the narrative component is to provide a context for your creation by putting it into motion. Give your body a voice and a life outside of the frame of the picture. Possible narration types include a Twitter feed, a profile via Facebook or MySpace, an animation, a YouTube video of some kind, a journal written by the hybrid body, an interview with the body, a sound recording related to the body . . . creativity is encouraged!

3. *Introduce your hybrid body:* The peer workshop is designed as an informal feedback process that provides you with valuable feedback prior to your final submission. Prepare a 3-minute presentation that describes the different elements of your hybrid body, explain which cultural ideals or norms you are engaging, and describe your plans for the narrative. As an audience member you are expected to ask questions or provide comments to help each student make his or her project as strong as possible. You will sign up for your presentation time 2 weeks prior to the presentation dates and you are expected to have a formal presentation prepared on your assigned date.

4. *Reflect on the Process:* Write a 2-page reflection that discusses your process of creating the body and giving it life through the narrative component. Connect this project back to the larger themes of the class and explain how this project informed your understanding of the metamorphic body. You may want to respond to some or all of the following questions: What was the concept behind your hybrid body? What norm, anxiety, or ideology were you trying to represent? What specific choices did you make while building the hybrid body and creating the narrative to represent this concept? What media did you use and why? What were the affordances and limitations of the media you chose? In a perfect world, what media would you have used

(continued)

ASSIGNMENT SHEET (*continued*)

to create your body? How does your work on this project connect with other things we have been reading/viewing/playing in 20C?

This project will comprise 50 percent of your total discussion grade. Please come and see me during office hours if you have questions or run into any problems. I look forward to seeing your projects!

4. TIME AND TECHNOLOGY

We taught this assignment under the ten-week quarter system and found that students needed the full quarter to develop complex and compelling representations and narratives. Our goal was for students to spend a few hours each week both in and outside of class working toward a final product. For the first few weeks of the quarter, we discussed the assignment in relationship to our class reading. We also recommend that you schedule a computer lab working session during the first half of the quarter so that students can experiment with the different types of technologies and bodies that they might want to create.

Students complete the assignment in three stages. First, they turn in the image of the body. Next, the narrative follows within two weeks. Finally, the reflection essay can either accompany the narrative or be turned in within a week of the narrative. However, we recommend giving students an extra week to work on the reflection essay because it is such a significant component of the overall assignment. In order to ensure that students did not wait until the last minute to complete the assignment, we asked students to work on the project in small steps throughout the quarter both in and out of class. Our week-by-week schedule for the assignment is as follows:

Week 1: Introduce assignment in class.

Week 2: Students read Donna Haraway's "A Cyborg Manifesto" for homework.

Week 3: Students turn in one-paragraph proposals for their hybrid bodies.

Week 4: In-class computer lab session.

Week 5: Students brainstorm and discuss ideas for the assignment in class.

Week 6: Students construct their hybrid bodies.

Week 7: Students present their hybrid bodies in class and comment publicly on the work of at least three of their classmates on the course site.

Week 8: Students create narratives.

Week 9: Students write reflection papers.

Week 10: Students present their work to the class.

One benefit of this assignment is the fact that it can be tailored to different levels of technological skill. Our ideal was to encourage students to encounter difficulty not only in their thinking, but also through their technological ability as a way of experiencing the various forms of knowledge necessary for media literacy. All students should have access to a laptop or desktop computer with which they can access social media sites, word processing software or applications, and Internet search capabilities. All images of the hybrid bodies must be uploaded to a course Web site, so students must have access to some sort of digital camera, although many of our students used smartphones for this function. We recommend at least one class period in a computer lab as a working day where students can get feedback on their progress and experiment with different modes of creating their hybrid body.

Below, we've outlined the three levels of technological involvement. You can select the one that best fits with the resources and needs of your classroom:

- *Introductory:* Students create their hybrid body offline using tools like magazines, newspapers, clay, food, or other household materials. Students will still be required to take a digital photo and upload it to the course Web site. The narrative component and reflection can then be completed in a Word document.

- *Intermediate:* Students create their hybrid body offline and share it using a digital photo, but are required to complete the narrative portion in some sort of social media setting. We had great results with students using both Twitter and Facebook, but other acceptable forms would be a blog, a Tumblr account, or an e-mail exchange. The reflection would still be completed in a Word document.

- *Advanced:* Students are required to create their body in a digital format using Photoshop or other editing software. For this level of technological requirement, we recommend at least two classes in a computer lab modeling the tools available to students. Students must then also complete the narrative in a social media format and the reflection piece on a public class blog.

We feel strongly that students should post all of their work to a class Web site so that they can receive feedback and support from members of the whole class rather than just from you. The class Web site can be a space for students to discuss their work in progress with one another, share ideas, and clarify their visions. We recommend that you require students to post a minimum number of comments on the site in order to encourage meaningful peer-to-peer feedback. Depending on your skill level, you can easily tailor standard sites like Blackboard to support these kinds of functions or you can build a Web site just for this project or course. We used the free Lore Web site for this project because of the minimal start-up requirements and costs. A WordPress site could also be a good choice as it provides an easy way to build in a blog function or to follow multiple feeds.

5. ANTICIPATING STUDENT NEEDS

This assignment is a pleasure to teach, but there are some challenges that students and instructors need to navigate over the course of the assignment.

Lack of Technical Skills. This can be a lack on the part of either the instructor or the students. In the case of the former, we recommend using technology that you are familiar with and comfortable using. Even if only one aspect of this project occurs digitally, the requirement of thinking across mediums and platforms generates a lot of positive discussion about how we create our own multiplatform identity and can be a truly effective use of technology. In the case of students having a lack of technical skills, this can really only enhance the assignment because students are being challenged on multiple levels. This obstacle can be overcome by scheduling extra computer lab sessions, in addition to the initial working session, and by limiting the creation of bodies to a particular platform, such as Photoshop, so that these sessions can be tailored to teaching basic use skills.

Lack of Creativity. This happens when students use a limited number of elements to create their bodies, or seem to have thrown their narrative together at the last moment, causing the project to lack depth and critical thinking. The best way to avoid these kinds of pitfalls is to provide enough time to truly develop an idea of what this hybrid body might be, and to have smaller due dates throughout the assignment so that students can receive feedback and change direction if necessary. It would also be effective to meet with students individually at the midpoint in the creation process to check in with them about their progress and any difficulties they might be encountering.

Encouraging a Larger Discussion. Getting students to make the connection between the work required of them for this project and the work required of them for the course as a whole can be challenging in the beginning. This project does require a fair amount of scaffolding so that students make the connection between the two types of work, but we found that this difficulty significantly decreased as the project progressed.

6. ASSESSMENT TOOLS

The three parts of this assignment were considered as a whole and only received a grade at the end of the course. However, we found that students produced much more finely tuned and complex final projects with informal instructor and peer feedback throughout the quarter, particularly because it gave students the chance to take risks and revise in a low-stakes classroom situation. You might want to take this into account as you develop your own grading criteria.

At the end of the quarter, we used the following rubric to holistically assess the hybrid body, narrative, and reflection paper:

- *Creativity:* How creative are the hybrid body and the narrative? Has the student put disparate elements together in an innovative or new way?
- *Focus:* Do the hybrid body and the narrative critically address a specific problem with embodiment or is the focus scattered among too many different ideas?
- *Engagement with course texts:* Do the hybrid body and the narrative engage with or expand upon issues emerging in the course texts?
- *Reflection:* How clearly does the student articulate the theoretical basis for the hybrid body and narrative in the reflection paper? How effectively does the student explain his or her creative choices?

Many students felt anxious about the first stage of this assignment, the creation of the hybrid body itself, because they did not consider themselves to be good artists or because they felt that they lacked the relevant technical skills. We emphasize that students are not being evaluated on the aesthetic merits or the technical complexity of their creation, but that they are being evaluated based on the concept behind their creation. Because the first stage is potentially the most nebulous, one way to make it more concrete would be to require students to include a minimum number of components on their hybrid bodies. This would ensure that the bodies are truly complex hybrids.

Ultimately, we relied heavily on the reflection paper in order to determine final grades as students were given the opportunity to explain the theory behind their creative choices. The most successful final projects all included thoughtful reflection papers that clearly articulated the student's process of critical thinking and demonstrated emerging understanding of the theoretical discussions occurring in the course.

7. THEORETICAL BASIS FOR THE ASSIGNMENT:
Hybrid Bodies and New Media Narratives: Critical Media Literacy in the Literature Classroom

In the age of e-readers, digital archives, and ubiquitous computing, students of literature need to develop a literacy that moves beyond a confined sense of the literary as existing solely in the medium of print. While it is not uncommon for digital media to be portrayed as the evil twin of the literary, our assignment emphasizes that

"Literary studies and new media studies are inextricably intertwined in the twenty-first century."

Rochelle Gold and **Kimberly Hall**

literary studies and new media studies are inextricably intertwined in the twenty-first century. Because contemporary literature is often composed, published, and even read electronically, N. Katherine Hayles argues that literary scholars need to rethink the relationship between literature and digital computing. In *Electronic Literature* Hayles contends, "the belletristic tradition that has on occasion envisioned computers as the soulless other to the humanistic expressivity of literature could not be more mistaken. Contemporary literature, and even more so the literary that extends and enfolds it, is computational" (85).

> "Any form of contemporary critical literacy must engage with literary forms across multiple platforms."
> **Rochelle Gold** and **Kimberly Hall**

Thus, while performing an academic analysis in digital platforms might be a new experience for you or your students, the entanglement that Hayles points to suggests that any form of contemporary critical literacy must engage with literary forms across multiple platforms. We notice that literature students often find applying close reading to mediums other than printed literary texts to be difficult as they struggle with what they should be noticing in a close reading of a new media object. One major reason for this is what Henry Jenkins and his colleagues describe as the "transparency problem" which refers to the fact that "although youth are becoming more adept at using media as resources (for creative expression, research, social life, etc.), they often are limited in their ability to examine the media themselves" (20). Our assignment asks students both to build traditional literary close reading skills and to learn to engage critically with the specific affordances and materiality of digital media objects in order to overcome the transparency problem. We want students to take seriously Hayles's claim that digital computing is inherent to contemporary literature and to use the methodology of close reading on a variety of texts in order to more fully develop a critical media literacy for the twenty-first century.

Our assignment encourages students to build this literacy by putting their everyday digital practices of social writing, experimentation, and play into an academic context. We ask students to engage actively with texts, and in order for them to do so we emphasize the playful nature of reading and writing. Jenkins and colleagues describe contemporary media culture as "participatory" in the sense that readers can easily become writers and that a culture of sharing creative work exists. Our assignment focuses on a particular aspect of participatory culture that is ubiquitous in contemporary culture, and easily engaged in digital platforms: remix.

A number of critics have recently argued for the significance of remix as an emergent form of knowledge construction. Paul Mihailidis suggests that "the act of repurposing information has created a new dynamic in cultural production and social structure online, in which users and peers are democratizing information" (174). Furthermore, Adam Banks contends that remix is a powerful source of creative thinking because it embraces "the wide range of cultural practices, multiple literacies, rhetorical mastery, and knowledge of traditions . . . [that] offer a model for writing that thoroughly weaves together oral performance, print literacy, mastery and interrogation of technologies" (13). Banks refers specifically to the African American tradition of remix, but he argues for the rhetorical agency that all students can locate by utilizing these practices. Because we teach at a large public institution that serves one of the most diverse student populations in the nation, Banks's notion of allowing students of color to "see themselves in the digital story" (5) allows for added valences of individual and cultural agency within this assignment.

> "Banks's notion of allowing students of color to 'see themselves in the digital story' allows for added valences of individual and cultural agency within this assignment."
>
> **Rochelle Gold** and **Kimberly Hall**

In short, this assignment asks students to build their new media literacy through close reading and by engaging with the practices of contemporary remix culture. In the spirit of participatory culture, students use this assignment to develop and share their own creative texts, and utilizing the more familiar methodologies of the literature classroom, students use literary theory and close reading to conceptualize their creations. This assignment provides a space for students to experience both pleasure and difficulty as they engage with technology in a meaningful and critical way.

8. CONCLUSION

This assignment had somewhat uneven results in the actual bodies the students made, but did produce a noticeable improvement across the board in their close reading skills. In one of the most fully realized projects, the avatar, Iam, was made completely from clay and combined different culturally desirable traits in striking and often funny ways. To signal intelligence and coolness, Iam had the bearded and bespectacled head of a Brooklyn hipster. His bulging biceps represented masculine sexuality and his uneven, stretchy legs signaled his flexibility and ability to fit into any scenario or space. Iam had a well-developed Facebook page complete with pictures, friends, and dozens of wall posts, giving him a tangible personality. The student who created Iam was a fantastic student, but one who was overly worried about the mechanics of analysis and argument, rather than the more creative aspects of those processes. This assignment forced her to embrace those elements that often made her uncomfortable, and to think more carefully about how creativity and play might inform effective analytical arguments.

The way that students responded to the creative and ludic elements of the assignment was one of the surprising and most rewarding elements of the project. Although neither of us believe that our primary job is to make this material fun, through the course of the assignment we realized that helping students find pleasure in the work of analysis is one of the most effective ways to push their thinking to a higher level. Even the least successful projects — and these were usually the result of a minimal investment of time on the part of the student — demonstrated a playful and creative engagement with course material and were pleasurable to evaluate. This also helped facilitate some very productive meetings with individual students. We noticed that they felt more comfortable talking through the assignment, and the thinking behind it, at a higher

> "They fully understood the requirements of the assignment, and were able to productively critique one another within those boundaries."
>
> **Rochelle Gold** and **Kimberly Hall**

level, despite the fact that many of them considered this a "fun" assignment. As such, we felt that the creative and ludic thinking and writing required of the students in this lower-stakes project really helped them engage with the more difficult material and assignments with the same approaches, which was the project's biggest success.

We also realized that students were very invested in the project and repeatedly e-mailed us after the quarter to receive feedback on their work. They were also excited to see one another's projects and discuss them, fostering the kinds of critical and engaged peer feedback that we strive for, and often don't achieve, in our peer editing workshops for traditional essays. One of the most outspoken students proudly demonstrated his gaming avatar for the class with an impressive recorded playback from *World of Warcraft*. While this student often overpowered class discussions, this informal peer-review process empowered other students to speak up and to push the presenter to explain his creative decisions. As one of the shyest students pointed out, the body wasn't a hybrid under the rubric of the assignment, and she offered suggestions for how he might revise his work before final submission. Although the students still hesitated to push one another too much on creative decisions, they fully understood the requirements of the assignment, and were able to productively critique one another within those boundaries. Overall we were incredibly pleased with what the students produced, how it helped them develop other significant skills for the course, and the kind of critical community it helped foster. We can't wait to teach this assignment again.

9. WORKS CITED

Banks, Adam J. *Digital Griots: African American Rhetoric in a Multimedia Age.* Southern Illinois UP, 2011.

Haraway, Donna. "A Cyborg Manifesto: Science, Technology, and Socialist-Feminism in the Late Twentieth Century." *Simians, Cyborgs, and Women: The Reinvention of Nature.* Routledge, 1991, pp. 149-81.

Hayles, N. Katherine. *Electronic Literature: New Horizons for the Literary.* U of Notre Dame, 2010.

- - -. *How We Became Posthuman: Virtual Bodies in Cybernetics, Literature, and Informatics.* U of Chicago P, 1999.

Jenkins, Henry, et al. *Confronting the Challenges of Participatory Culture: Media Education for the 21st Century.* MIT P, 2009.

Mihailidis, Paul. "(Re)Mix, (Re)Purpose, (Re)Learn: Using Participatory Tools for Media Literacy Learning Outcomes in the Classroom." *Action in Teacher Education*, vol. 33, 2011, pp. 172-83.

29

Student as Critic in the Classroom: Arguing about Literature, Conducting Peer Review, and Presenting in a Digital Environment

Lesley Broder
Kingsborough Community College, (CUNY)

Lesley Broder is assistant professor of English at Kingsborough Community College in Brooklyn, New York. She teaches online, hybrid, and face-to-face composition and literature survey courses and directs the college's newly established Accelerated Learning Program (ALP).

COURTESY OF LESLEY BRODER

1. OVERVIEW

- **Assignment:** Students choose a literary author or text that they believe should be taught in future sections of an introductory course (in this case, a course on the short story). They write an essay and create a screencast to persuade the English Department chair to consider and agree with their recommendations. In a virtual environment (course or blog space), students begin by drafting an argument essay, then conduct virtual peer review, revise their essays, and, based on their final work, create and share a persuasive webcast, all in an online forum.

  Alternative: Students choose a literary author or text and make a case for their significance for a different audience and context. In an online setting, they draft and, based on feedback, revise a persuasive essay, which they then remix into a webcast.

- **Courses:** Any, including introduction to literature; fiction/short fiction; literature survey courses; literature courses that introduce students to particular genres or time periods.

- **Literature:** Any.

- **Technology:** For the virtual peer review component of the assignment, students can use instant messaging, e-mail, or even text. For sharing drafts and final essays, students can post to a course blog that you can create using free blogging tools, such as WordPress or Blogger. Course management programs, such as Blackboard and Moodle, can serve as alternatives.
- **Time:** Three weeks.

2. GOALS OF THE ASSIGNMENT

After completing this assignment, students will be able to:

- argue persuasively, using textual evidence and reasoning;
- share and discuss a critical interpretation of course readings in an online, public forum;
- synthesize ideas to form a central argument;
- compose a well-organized, developed essay; and
- provide feedback on peers' writing in virtual spaces.

3. ASSIGNMENT SHEET

Student as Critic in the Classroom: Arguing about Literature, Conducting Peer Review, and Presenting in a Digital Environment

Course: _____

Instructor: _____

Date: _____

For this project, you will draft a persuasive "Critic's Choice" essay, work with peer review, and revise multiple times. At the end, you will share your final essay, and, if you'd like, turn it into a video presentation that you deliver online.

Here's the scenario: the chair of the English Department wants to know which literary author should be required reading in next year's Short Fiction class. Your job is to write a persuasive essay arguing why one author you have read this term should appear in all future sections of Short Fiction.

Writing-intensive courses require you to write for different audiences. You have written for me and for each other; now you will write for a different audience.

PART I:
Draft a Persuasive "Critic's Choice" Essay

Review all of your reading and writing from this semester. Which author stands out as one that all students at this school should read?

Write a 1,500- to 2,000-word persuasive essay arguing why each student who takes Short Fiction should read your chosen author.

Go beyond saying you liked the author. Instead, describe what makes this author *essential* reading for this particular course. You may want to consider ideas that others have posted to get you started.

Tips for Making Your Argument

- Refer to the literary terms we have discussed this term.
- Contrast your chosen author to another one on the syllabus. You might also discuss how the author effectively speaks to readers through generations.
- Describe how the author's work reflects the historical moment in which it was written.
- Refer to the theories of fiction that we have reviewed this semester. If you go over to our class wiki, you will find a summary of the authors' theories of fiction for your reference. A wiki can be modified by any of us, so if you

(continued)

ASSIGNMENT SHEET (*continued*)

liked one author's point that I didn't include, go ahead and add it. I would ask that you do not delete any information I have provided.

Guidelines for Drafting Your Essay

- The minimum word count is 1,500 words or 5–6 pages. You can write more if you choose.

- *Draw from your writing this term*. Mine this work for your best writing. If it fits, incorporate it into your final essay. Of course, you shouldn't just dump previous writing assignments into your essay without weaving them into your argument. Look at my comments and build on your early ideas.

- Editing Considerations

  - Contextualize quotations.

  - Don't use texting language.

  - Run a spell-check.

  - Proofread your work, preferably aloud.

PART II:
Conduct Virtual Peer Review

Submit online the **first draft** of your essay to your peer-review partner and me. *Be sure to archive your discussions to submit to me as well.*

Checklist for Conducting Peer Review

As you review the work of others (and revisit your own work), use these questions as a guide.

- ❑ Does the essay have a clear **focus**? Be sure to restate your partner's main point, to confirm that the central message is clear. What is his or her **argument**? How do you know?
- ❑ Are the **supporting examples** convincing to support the **argument**? Is it clear *why* the writer chose the particular author?
- ❑ Is the paper sufficiently **developed**? If not, suggest where the author could include more information.
- ❑ Does the essay's **organization** make sense to you as a reader? Consider:
  - ❑ Overall structure: Does it include a beginning, middle, and end?
  - ❑ Paragraph structure: Does each paragraph focus on a single idea to support the thesis?
- ❑ Do **mechanical errors** get in the way of your understanding? If so, mention this point to the writer, though you **should not** proofread the paper.

Consider your partner's advice and incorporate it into your **second draft**. I will give you feedback before the third and final, public version is due.

PART II:
Share Your Final "Critic's Choice" Essay; Remix and Present It as a Webcast

Post your **third draft** to share with the class and with the chair of the English Department. In addition to the third draft, for extra credit, you can post a webcast of yourself discussing/presenting your essay. Cell phone or digital cameras will allow you to save and then upload a file.

Read your classmates' essays and comment on at least 5 papers. Be sure to specifically comment on their ideas in a constructive and supportive manner.

Grading and Due Dates

This assignment is worth 25 percent of your final grade.

Task/Content	Due Date
❑ Submit **first draft** of your **Critic's Choice** essay to your peer-review partner and me.	
❑ Complete **virtual peer-review** session with your peer-review partner.	
❑ Submit **peer-review transcript** to me.	
❑ Submit **second draft** to me.	
❑ Submit **third draft (public version)** to the class Web site. For extra credit, also submit a video presentation of your essay.	
❑ Comment on at least 5 of your classmates' papers.	
Assignment Point Value	
Virtual peer-review session with your partner	_____/5 pts
Drafted essay	_____/12 pts
Posting your essay to the class Web site	_____/3 pts
Commenting constructively on at least 5 of your classmates' essay posts	_____/5 pts
Total Earned: _____ out of 25 pts	

4. TIME AND TECHNOLOGY

The Critic's Choice essay is a culmination of all the reading, writing, and discussion students have completed during the semester; writing the essay requires reflection and synthesis. Though the assignment can be completed in the last weeks of class, I have found it useful to turn students' attention toward the final project earlier in the term. After the third week of class, I ask them to discuss the assignment in their small writing groups. In online classes, this discussion takes place on a discussion board, but it can also be done in class if face-to-face sessions are available. Students are required to read the final assignment and imagine which author they would choose at this early point in the semester. They don't have to stick to these original ideas, but the discussion gets the students to think ahead and begin to evaluate how the readings work together. Throughout the semester, I refer to the final assignment, both in class lectures and as I respond to student writing, especially when I see ideas that could be useful for this final essay.

The first draft of the essay is due to peer-review partners and you two weeks before the end of class. Students read each other's early drafts and have a discussion about targeted questions, archiving the discussion and submitting it to you. The second draft of the essay is due one week before the end of class. I provide them with feedback promptly, so they can get to work drafting the final version.

For the peer-review portion of the assignment, students might download or use an instant messaging program. The chat programs frequently used in my classroom are freely available from Yahoo, Google, and AIM. Many students already have an account, but it is not difficult to sign up if they are new to chatting. In the past, some students have asked to use texting software like BlackBerry Messenger; using such a tool is an option, but web-based instant messaging will be available to all students, even as various programs fall in and out of usage.

The final, public version of the essay is due on the class Web site the last week of the semester. To share work, I either use an online blog or a course management system. WordPress and Blogger are two easy-to-use options that are free. Students post their essays, and, for extra credit, a webcast of themselves discussing the main points of their argument. I invite my chair to view the students' work and to add comments as well. Sharing these ideas in a public forum and commenting on each other's work is the heart of this assignment. Lively conversation ensues, as most students are interested to see what others have argued.

5. ANTICIPATING STUDENT NEEDS

The Critic's Choice essay was developed for use in the literature elective Short Fiction, a course offered at a large community college in New York City. This writing-intensive, online course can be taken once students have passed Freshman Composition. Each week of my section focuses on one short fiction writer; in addition to reading two or more stories by the author, students read criticism, the author's theories of fiction writing, and, if available, the author's commentary on other writers on the syllabus. This approach helps them gain a deep understanding of each author studied. It is their job, after considering the work of the semester, to act like a critic. They are thus forced to go beyond saying that they liked a story and instead think of their understanding of fiction to make an informed assessment.

When I first assigned this project, I was surprised to see the discomfort some students expressed regarding their ability to make an informed suggestion to the chair of the department. There was a perception of criticism as a skill that was beyond their realm and best left to the experts. Other students felt that choosing a representative author should be my job, not theirs. It is for this reason that it is useful to engage the students in the final project early in the term. The earlier that they see themselves as critics, with the tools and ability to make judgments based on their reasoning, the better able they are to rise to the final task of the semester and publically share their work. Further, if you tailor informal writing assignments with the final assignment in mind, the students will find that they have a lot to draw from as they compose the final paper. Throughout, students are encouraged to make use of the informal and formal writing that they have produced during the semester. Encouraging the students to think toward the Critic's Choice essay will help them to be prepared to draft and share their work by the end of the term.

Another challenge might come from the virtual peer-review portion of the paper. I have used virtual peer review in face-to-face, hybrid, and online classes. Once students begin to talk, the discussions can be productive as long as they have appropriate focusing questions to guide the conversation. Surprisingly, the largest hurdle that students face is finding a time to meet online. This is another reason to introduce the activity early in the semester. Partners can choose one another if you post a sign-up sheet (either virtually or in the classroom) to figure out schedules and availability. One way to avoid the scheduling problem is to allow students to communicate about their papers via cell phones, since most students now own these devices. These conversations, however, tend to be less sustained than conversations conducted in front of the computer, though they tend to occur over a longer period of time.

Students also need some encouragement to translate their work into a multimedia format, which is the extra credit option for the final part of the assignment. In online classes, in particular, where students may not yet have seen one another, it can be intimidating to post a video, though some students are eager to share their work in this way. Many students have access to video through smartphones and other handheld technology; even if they don't own such devices themselves, they often know someone who does. Once they have the file, I always offer to help them edit it or post it online to ensure that others in the class can access the file.

6. ASSESSMENT TOOLS

This assignment, including all the steps that lead up to the final version, is worth 25 percent of the final grade. I break down the assignment into points. Much of the point scale in this grading plan is straightforward; for example, students might earn one point for each substantial comment that is made about a classmate's paper.

When I distribute the assignment to the class, I also make two other documents available. The "Virtual Peer-Review Grading Guidelines" document lets students know what I expect in the peer-review session; "Essay Evaluation Questions" provides the point breakdown and the questions that will guide assessment.

Critic's Choice Essay: Virtual Peer-Review Grading Guidelines

Follow the "Guiding Questions" on Part II of the assignment sheet as you work with your peer-review partner. As I evaluate your virtual peer-review session, I will consider the following elements.

As a writer:

1. Did you submit a developed draft so that your partner had something substantial to critique?
2. Did you respond openly to your reviewer's feedback?

As a reviewer:

1. Did you articulate the author's main point to ensure that the thesis was clear?
2. Did you address each of the Guiding Questions listed in Part II of the essay assignment?
3. Did you focus on the content of the essay, not the mechanical issues?
4. Were you constructive, not destructive, in your critique?

Critic's Choice Essay: Essay Evaluation Questions

Keep these points in mind as you write and revise your essay. I will focus on these items as I give feedback and evaluate your drafts.

1. **Content and Focus.** Does the writer present a clear recommendation to the chair of the department? How well does the writer present his or her argument? To what extent is it persuasive?

2. **Support.** Does the writer use appropriate quotations and examples to help build the argument?

3. **Development.** Has the writer developed the essay fully, and to the required length?

4. **Organization.** Are the ideas arranged logically? Overall: Does the essay have a clear beginning, middle, and end? Within paragraphs: Does each paragraph elaborate upon a single point?

5. **Tone.** Does the writer use a clear, professional tone to address the audience of classmates, professor, and administrators?

6. **Mechanics.** Has the writer proofread the paper so that errors do not get in the way of meaning?

---

7. THEORETICAL BASIS FOR THE ASSIGNMENT:
Student as Critic in the Classroom: Arguing about Literature, Conducting Peer Review, and Presenting in a Digital Environment

Students mingle differently in face-to-face and virtual classrooms, even when the goals for a given course are the same. In some ways, the dynamic can be less personal in online courses because students may never see each other; in other instances, however, online spaces can be more intimate and inclusive — regular group participation is usually a basic requirement in distance learning environments. The assignment I describe here developed in a virtual space, but I have been able to transfer it to hybrid and face-to-face classes. The activity allows students to consult each other throughout the semester, culminating in a final project shared with the entire class, and if desired, with an audience outside the classroom. The instructor can decide the degree to which these activities unfold in virtual spaces.

As barriers to publication have lessened, the Internet has democratized writing so that anyone with an Internet connection can now participate, whether it is to post a 140-character tweet or 140 posts on a blog. Yet, the idea that knowledge is a one-way path still lingers in the college classroom.

It is comfortable for students, even those in online situations, to let the instructor control the flow of information and ideas — to decide what makes a particular reading valid or to judge students' writing. This assignment works to broaden perceptions of the way information and critical judgment can flow by synthesizing the material from the semester for a broader audience than the instructor alone. This point is key to the Critic's Choice essay: the students are the experts and digital technologies make it easier for them to share their ideas.

Over a decade ago, Gunther Kress (2003) considered what happened to meaning and authority as access to such forums for authorship expanded: "The affordances of the new technologies of representation and communication enable those who have access to them to be 'authors,' even if authors of a new kind — that is, to produce texts, to alter texts, to write and to 'write back'" (173). Kress explains what constituted legitimate "knowledge" used to be clearly defined. Nonetheless, "this was based on a relation of knowledge to power, not on one of knowledge to truth. But in that era, power determined truth, so no difficulty arose" (173). Whoever had the power decided what body of knowledge was valid. With multiple modes of information transmission, what now counts as truth now rests with more individuals.

Each step of the essay process redirects the linear flow of information from instructor to student so that students learn from each other and share a final assessment about the course material in a public forum by the end of the semester. An awareness of their audience will help to shape the essay. As early discussions of audience in the composition classroom highlighted, students might consider the real audiences who will read their work or else an imagined, or what Walter Ong called an "invented," audience created by the writer. Even before the digital age, it became clear that students should have both audience types in mind. In this assignment, they know they are writing for you, their classmates, and possibly the chair of the department; but if their work is available on an open public forum, they can also imagine the readers who might stumble on their words.

A second facet of the assignment involves students' virtual collaboration about their drafts. Research on virtual peer review, notably by Beth Hewett, who compared virtual and face-to-face peer review, and by Lee-Ann Kastman Breuch, who devoted a book to the subject, highlight that online peer review is a different experience from face-to-face peer review. Breuch notes "virtual peer review is most effective when writers take control of technology" (146). While research on virtual peer review has room to grow, it is likely that this method is increasingly used in classrooms as distance learning programs expand and communication technologies become mobile. The assignment lets students "take control of the technology," both for sharing writing with a larger audience and for communicating virtually.

8. CONCLUSION

This multipart assignment encourages students to compare texts and make independent judgments regarding what they have read. Students might be stretched beyond their comfort zone, but if they have completed the work of the semester, they should be prepared to make these evaluations and to share their ideas publically. I have used this assignment for various survey courses and have had successful results, though I would suggest that it works best for courses that cover a range of material so the students have a number of texts from which to choose.

One semester, a student became agitated in her online writing group that the essay was impossible; how could she be expected to know the "right" answer to this question? It didn't seem fair, she thought, that I would be grading students on something without telling them the answer ahead of time, especially since it was an introductory course, taken by students without special training. I posted her concern for the entire class, and we discussed how the assignment required them to make a claim and use evidence to support that claim. The answer would not come from me, but from their critical reading. Despite these concerns, I am always surprised about the positive energy that comes when they share their work publically. The student who was apprehensive ended up debating a classmate about the merits of Edgar Allan Poe. After being immersed in their own viewpoints, they are interested to see the different approaches their peers have taken. It seems that the principles that apply in exclusively face-to-face classrooms apply to this assignment as well. If students have worked together in peer-review activities earlier in the semester, they will know the expectations for the final project. The sharing portion of the assignment will unfold smoothly if participants are familiar with the selected software before it is time to post and share work.

Although this assignment describes a specific class — an online, writing-intensive, short fiction elective — it could readily be adapted to work with other literature electives. Students could review the work of the semester and, based on the knowledge they have acquired, decide which writer (or text) is essential to understanding the particular genre or time period covered in the course. Reframing their role and their peers' roles can be unsettling at first, but it ultimately gives them confidence and opens up a space for independent thinking. Furthermore, this assignment is designed to be flexible so that it can be adapted to the resources of the class. It works well for hybrid or fully online courses. Classes that always meet face-to-face could incorporate this assignment for work assigned outside the classroom.

Blogs and course management systems are useful tools to help you transmit content, but they also allow students to participate in the flow of knowledge as they consider a wider audience than the person who will give a grade. A key decision when adapting this assignment will be how wide the audience will be — the options range from keeping posts within the class, within the college community, or opening it to the Web. Whatever platform is chosen, the assignment is a success if students move away from viewing you as the one who should be handing out judgments for student consumption.

9. WORKS CITED

Breuch, Lee-Ann Kastman. *Virtual Peer Review: Teaching and Learning about Writing in Online Environments*. State U of New York P, 2004.

Hewett, Beth. "Characteristics of Interactive Oral and Computer-Mediated Peer Group Talk and Its Influence on Revision." *Computers and Composition*, vol. 17, 2000, pp. 265-88.

Kress, Gunther. *Literacy in the New Media Age*. Routledge, 2003.

Ong, Walter J. "The Writer's Audience Is Always a Fiction." *PMLA: Publications of the Modern Language Association of America*, vol. 90, no. 1, 1975, pp. 9-21. JSTOR, doi: 10.2307/461344, www.jstor.org/stable/461344.

PART FIVE ASSIGNMENTS

Archives

Archives

30

Special Collections for All: Open, Digital Archives to Public Writing in the Literature Classroom

Ryan Cordell
Northeastern University

Ryan Cordell is assistant professor of English at Northeastern University and core founding faculty member in the NULab for Texts, Maps, and Networks (nulab.neu.edu). His scholarship focuses on convergence in antebellum American mass media. Cordell collaborates with colleagues in English, history, and computer science on an NEH-funded project (viraltexts.org) using data mining to discover borrowed texts across archives of antebellum texts. He serves on NITLE's Digital Humanities Council and as vice president of the Digital Americanists scholarly society. He is coeditor-in-chief of centerNet's journal, DHCommons (dhcommons.org), and he also writes about technology in higher education for the group blog ProfHacker at the Chronicle of Higher Education (chronicle.com/blogs /profhacker/).

COURTESY OF RYAN CORDELL

1. OVERVIEW OF ASSIGNMENT

- **Assignment:** Write and produce a new historical episode and paper.
- **Courses:** Upper-level literature courses, especially those that incorporate American, British, or world literatures.
- **Literature:** American literature; British or world literature can be used, but would require a blog or wiki.
- **Technology:** The History Engine (historyengine.richmond.edu).
- **Time:** Three to four weeks.

2. THE GOALS OF THE ASSIGNMENT

By completing this assignment, students will:

- develop skills in writing for public, online audiences;
- gain facility researching primary historical sources;

453

- improve their ability to integrate secondary sources with primary research; and

- enrich their understanding of a specific historical event and its significance to a literary work.

"This assignment allows students to do real scholarship and contribute that work to an ongoing public humanities project. When students see a writing assignment as a contribution to a public resource, they take it more seriously and devote more effort to it than when it simply seems like a classroom exercise."

Ryan Cordell
Northeastern University

3. ASSIGNMENT SHEET

Special Collections for All: Open, Digital Archives to Public Writing in the Literature Classroom

Course: _____

Instructor: _____

Date: _____

New Historical Assignment

One of the challenges of new historical criticism is that it requires a real and deep knowledge of history. There's nothing worse than an essay that talks vaguely about "people back then" or "THE PAST." New historical arguments should be grounded in specific, thoroughly researched events, people, movements, and so on. In order to help you write an effective new historical critique, this assignment will unfold in two parts.

Part 1: Writing an Episode for the History Engine

The History Engine (historyengine.richmond.edu/pages/about/what_is_the _history_engine) describes itself as

> an educational tool that gives students the opportunity to learn history by doing the work—researching, writing, and publishing—of a historian. The result is an ever-growing collection of historical articles or episodes that paint a wide-ranging portrait of life in the United States throughout its history, available in our online database to scholars, teachers, and the general public.

For the first half of this assignment, you will research and write an episode that springs from a historical observation drawn from your reading of a literary text. When composing your History Engine episode, you will focus on a specific historical event related to your chosen literary piece—the literature itself need not, and likely will not, be mentioned in your episode.

The History Engine provides extensive guidelines about both how to research (historyengine.richmond.edu/pages/students/research) and how to write (historyengine.richmond.edu/pages/students/writing) an episode for the site. They even provide a style guide (historyengine.richmond.edu/pages/students /style_guide) and a citation guide (historyengine.richmond.edu/pages/students /citation_guide). You will use the historical periodicals archives listed below to find primary sources for your episodes; we'll talk more about how to do this research in class.

Archives

- *Making of America* collection at the University of Michigan, quod.lib.umich.edu/m/moagrp/

(*continued*)

ASSIGNMENT SHEET (*continued*)

- Making of America collection at Cornell University, digital.library.cornell.edu/m/moa/
- Nineteenth Century in Print collection from the Library of Congress, memory.loc.gov/ammem/ndlpcoop/moahtml/snchome.html
- Chronicling America collection from the Library of Congress, chroniclingamerica.loc.gov/
- HathiTrust, www.hathitrust.org/
- Google Books, books.google.com/

This part of the assignment will be complete when your episode is published on the History Engine. The purpose of this part of the assignment will be to help you flesh out your understanding of a *highly specific historical event* that will, in the second part of the assignment, help you more fully understand your literary work. This part of the assignment will also help you think about your writing as aimed at a broader audience than your instructor. As the History Engine says,

> A final important difference is that your instructor will not be the only person reading your final product. You will make an important contribution to understanding the American past by uploading your finished episodes to the *History Engine* database.

You will actually add to a resource used by students around the world in their history classes. When you complete your episode, you'll be a published historian.

Technical notes: When you first visit the History Engine, you'll need to register for an account. Use the registration code provided in order to be placed into my class. This way, I'll be able to see all of your episodes, and visitors will know which episodes were published by our class.

Part 2: Writing a New Historical Critical Essay

From here, the remainder of this assignment should feel more familiar. You will write an essay that demonstrates how the historical dimension you explored in part 1 of the assignment is important to our understanding of your chosen literary work. You may think more broadly than you did in your History Engine episode, reflecting on the historical phenomenon your History Engine event was part of, rather than only the single event you wrote your episode about.

As you write, remember the distinction we've drawn in class between *topics* and *research questions*. In part 1 of this assignment you investigated and wrote about a *topic*; in part 2 you must move toward interpretation, and demonstrate why this topic should matter to a scholar studying your chosen literary work. Your paper shouldn't merely point out each allusion to your chosen event in your chosen poem, story, or novel. Instead, your paper should present an argument about how that historical event should inform our interpretation of the literary work — why, in other words, should a reader of your chosen work care about this historical context? How does an understanding of that history allow you to develop a "thick description" of the literary work in question?

Your new historical essays must incorporate **at least 4 research sources**, which could include historical newspapers, letters, critical studies, historical studies, and so on. You will have used at least two sources in part 1; for part 2 you must expand your critical background even further.

4. TIME AND TECHNOLOGY

TIME. This assignment works best when staged deliberately over the course of three to four weeks. From my experience with this exercise thus far I've learned just how infrequently undergraduates have researched or cited primary historical sources (which is, of course, a major reason why I want them to do so). In practice, however, this means I must teach them what primary sources are, where and how to find them, and how to use them responsibly and effectively. As you plan your assignment, then, consider scaffolding it through the following stages:

1. Five to seven days before the episode drafts are due, schedule one entire class period in a computer lab. Alternately, if your students have laptops, you could ask them to bring their laptops to class on that day. During this lab session, sketch out the distinction between primary and secondary sources. Then, spend some time showing students databases for each kind of source. Students may have used JSTOR or Project Muse to retrieve scholarly articles before, but it's worth showing those databases—or others to which your library subscribes—during this session. Make sure also to spend some time walking students through archives of historical primary texts. You might come in with a research question for the class to investigate together in these databases. Then give students some time to begin researching their own topics while you are available to help. If your library has subject librarians who could help during these sessions, you might invite them to take part in this session.

2. Once your students have chosen their historical topics, you should spend some class time discussing or even workshopping their developing ideas. You could devote an entire class to this activity or set aside blocks of time at the beginning or end of a few classes. During these times, you could review some published History Engine episodes as a class, discuss the challenges they are facing during research and writing, or even look together at one or two of their episodes in progress. Your goal for these sessions should be modeling your hopes for their writing and giving students a clear sense of how they should be progressing in the assignment.

3. If your students struggled during the first lab session, you might consider scheduling another lab three to five days before the first draft of their episodes is due. This session should be a working session only—they research and write while you offer guidance and (if necessary) technical support.

4. Drafts of students' History Engine episodes should be due well before their literary analysis papers. In my class I always schedule seven to ten days in between the two assignments. Episodes will be brief—a

few paragraphs apiece — and can be read quickly. Students can also revise them quickly, and they will need to do so. Before they post their episodes to the official Web site you should give them at least one chance to revise. In my classes I work with students until I feel the episodes are both clearly written and well researched before clearing students to post their episodes to the History Engine itself.

5. Once students' episodes meet your standards for publication, they should add them to the History Engine using your course code. This way, their work will be aggregated under your course so you (and their peers) can easily find it.

6. Finally, you should accept drafts of students' new historical papers well after their episodes are complete and posted. Of course, you may decide not to include the second stage of this assignment at all, focusing instead on the historical writing that literature students rarely get to practice.

As you can see, this assignment does require careful scaffolding to work well. I have found this kind of staged assignment beneficial for both students and for myself, as I can help students develop their work in small increments rather than spending hours commenting only on final drafts. The work students produce benefits from this level of attention, and they emerge from the unit much more secure in their ability to research and analyze both historical materials and the historical nuances of literary works.

TECHNOLOGY. This assignment requires no special technology or software beyond a computer with a web browser. It can be completed on students' laptops, on their personal computers at home, or in computer labs. You might consider reserving a computer lab for at least one day of class, during which time you can introduce the assignment at the Web sites students will use to complete it. Those Web sites will be of three kinds.

1. Digital Archives of Primary Historical Materials. My classes usually center on nineteenth-century American literature and culture, and so the archives I use in this assignment include mostly nineteenth- and early twentieth-century materials. They include:

- Library of Congress's Chronicling America newspaper collection (chroniclingamerica.loc.gov/)
- Library of Congress's Nineteenth Century in Print periodicals collection (memory.loc.gov/ammem/ndlpcoop/moahtml/snchome.html)
- University of Michigan's Making of America periodicals collection (quod.lib.umich.edu/m/moagrp/)
- Cornell University's Making of America books and journals collection (digital.library.cornell.edu/m/moa/)

I also refer students to the historical materials available through the HathiTrust Digital Library (www.hathitrust.org/) and Google Books (books .google.com/). I recommend these archives because they are open access (i.e., free to use for anyone who wishes). Your school may also subscribe to paid archives of historical material, and you could include those archives in your version of this assignment. It may help to talk with your subject librarian about the archives of your course's time period and/or region that can be available to your students.

One great benefit of this assignment is that it helps students move beyond simple Google or *Wikipedia* searches in their research. While a Google search might reveal historical texts scanned for Google Books, it will not delve into these rich archives of historical materials. Google and/ or *Wikipedia* might help students determine what historical moment they want to research for this assignment, but they will then have to take the next step and delve into a more scholarly archive to find the required primary and secondary sources.

Though I will refer in this article to archives useful in American literature courses, this assignment could be easily modified to fit courses in other literary areas, periods, or regions. You may need to explore archives of primary documents more closely related to your course's content. Fortunately, the National Endowment for the Humanities' Office of Digital Humanities compiled a list of humanities archives as part of their Digging into Data challenge. That list can be found at www.diggingintodata.org. Here too your subject librarian may be of help.

2. Archives of Secondary Sources. Technically students' secondary sources needn't be digital—they could cite print journal articles or books. In my experience, however, students most frequently turn to digital archives of scholarly articles such as Project Muse (muse.jhu.edu/) or JSTOR (www .jstor.org/) to research secondary sources. Many institutions subscribe to these two databases, and for many classes these resources will be sufficient. You may want to talk with your subject librarian about the secondary sources available to students, and modify the assignment accordingly. Students could also use Google Scholar (scholar.google.com) to find secondary sources, though Google Scholar sometimes links to resources to which your school may not subscribe. Students can get frustrated when they find relevant resources they cannot access.

3. An Open, Online Publication Platform. This platform could be a (public) course blog or wiki. You could even ask students to create or improve the *Wikipedia* entry for their chosen topic. I ask students to publish their historical research as episodes on the University of Richmond's History Engine platform (historyengine.richmond.edu/). According to the project's own description,

The core of the [History Engine] project is student-written episodes—individual snippets of daily life throughout American history from the broadest national event to the simplest local occurrence. Students construct these episodes from one or more primary sources found in university and local archives, using historical context gleaned from secondary sources to round out their analysis. Students then post their entries in our cumulative database, giving their classmates and fellow participants around the country the opportunity to read and engage with their work. . . . The HE also gives students a more intimate experience with the process of history. Participants who work with the *History Engine* project learn the craft of an historian: they examine primary documents, place these documents in a larger historical context using secondary sources, and prepare cogent analysis of their sources for the public eye. These students go into the project fully aware that future classrooms will engage with and critique their work.

The History Engine offers many benefits to both you and your students that make it an ideal platform for a public writing assignment:

- First, the History Engine provides careful documentation for teachers (historyengine.richmond.edu/pages/teachers/getting_started) that explains, step-by-step, how to bring a class through a History Engine assignment. This documentation also links to other schools using the History Engine so instructors can see how their colleagues elsewhere are using the project in their classes.

- Following on the last point, the History Engine allows you to register their classes on the site. Once a class is registered, the site gives you a code that your students can enter when they register for accounts. You can easily follow your students' work through their administrative interface, which allows you to see a list of all the episodes contributed by particular classes.

- Perhaps most compellingly, the History Engine provides detailed documentation for students. This documentation explains what a History Engine episode entails (historyengine.richmond.edu/pages/students /goal), how to research primary and secondary sources (historyengine .richmond.edu/pages/students/research), and how to write and format History Engine episodes (historyengine.richmond.edu/pages/students /writing). These detailed reference pages save me significant preparation time and student handholding, as I can confidently refer students to the History Engine's own documentation rather than repeating that information in conversations or e-mails.

- The History Engine's guidelines help students understand the rigor required of real scholarly work. History Engine episodes require students to write clearly and factually, and to incorporate at least one primary and one secondary source into their writing. A History Engine episode is similar to an encyclopedia article, which is a genre in which many literature students have never written. The site's writing guide can help students understand the form and rhetoric of effective historical writing.

Finally, the History Engine is a collaborative project with contributors and users from colleges and high schools around the country. As such, it has a built-in audience that could be hard to replicate for an individual course blog, wiki, or Web site. When students contribute to the History Engine they join a national community of students in history and literature classes.

5. ANTICIPATING STUDENT NEEDS

The most salient and likely difficulty you will encounter with this assignment comes from its public nature. As I wrote above, some students will be anxious about presenting their work publicly. Indeed, there are some professors who worry about unintended consequences when students write outside the controlled environment of the classroom. In a world of easy Google searching, some worry that public student work could have ramifications when students apply for jobs, run for office, or — perhaps most worrisome — ask out a potential significant other.

Of course, part of the reason I assign this particular activity is because I want my students to have the experience of writing for a wider public. A History Engine episode is in many ways a safer genre to post publicly than an academic argument might be. There are less likely to be political or social opinions explicitly expressed in a History Engine episode that could endanger a students' reputation with, say, a future employer who Googles his or her name. Indeed, I would hope that a future employer would be impressed to see his or her employee's research and writing abilities. Nevertheless, you might consider offering anonymity for students nervous about posting their work publicly — allowing them to use a pseudonym, perhaps, when posting to the History Engine.

6. ASSESSMENT TOOLS

I have only assigned this writing in a portfolio-based classroom, in which student's grades were based almost entirely on a body of work they submitted after significant revision at the end of the semester. As such I've not developed intricate grading rubrics for each stage of the assignment, and have focused instead on developing students' writing through focused, staged comments on their work. However, as you prepare to grade this assignment you might consider the following concerns and questions:

- What are *your goals* for students in using this assignment? How can you evaluate students' work to reflect those specific goals? In my classes I use this assignment primarily to teach research skills, and so I would weigh students' use of effective evidence more heavily than other features of their papers, which would be the focus of different writing assignments.

- Will you grade each part of the assignment separately or as a package? For instance, how would you evaluate a student who wrote a careful and insightful History Engine episode and a mediocre new historical essay? While the two halves of this assignment are closely intertwined, it might make more sense to evaluate them separately. After all, the goals for each half of the assignment differ, and separate grading rubrics might reflect those differences. In my case, the History Engine episode is ultimately graded as a pass/fail part of the assignment. Students must revise the episode until it is ready for publication on the Web site. They either achieve this goal and receive full credit for completing the episode, or they do not. Because I treat the episode as pass/fail, I do commit to working with students through many revisions if necessary to bring their episodes up to the site's standards. Students' new historical essays are developed for their final class portfolios.

- How will you evaluate informative, historical writing? Students' History Engine episodes will follow a genre — the encyclopedia entry, really — that we rarely see in literary studies. Before talking with students about this assignment, review some other students' History Engine episodes and make sure you understand the genre you are assigning. Though we might say "everything's an argument," the argument of a History Engine episode will be more muted and implicit than much literary writing. Again, this challenge could be solved by evaluating the History Engine episode as pass/fail, rather than with a letter grade.

Because this assignment differs in kind from much of the writing students do in literature classes, it will benefit the entire class (including you) if you make clear what your goals for the History Engine episodes are, and how you plan to evaluate them. Some students will be nervous about publishing their writing in a public forum, but you can ease this anxiety by clearly outlining how that public work will translate into private assessment.

7. THEORETICAL BASIS FOR THE ASSIGNMENT:
Special Collections for All: Open, Digital Archives to Public Writing in the Literature Classroom

This assignment was developed for use in a sophomore-/junior-level course within the English major at a small liberal arts college. The course, "Literary Theory and Writing," is a gateway course to the upper-level courses in the major. In it, students are expected to gain some familiarity and facility with many of the theoretical schools that have shaped the past decades of literary study: New Criticism, reader response theory, feminist theory, postcolonial theory, and so on. The course is reading- and writing-intensive, requiring students to compose five research papers over the course of the semester, to revise all five at least once, and to revise three papers further for inclusion in a final portfolio.

The assignment asks students to engage in real, substantive historical research and to publish their work as public scholarship using the University of Richmond's History Engine platform. In the second stage of the assignment, students develop a new historicist essay that brings that historical topic into conversation with a literary work, showing how thinking historically can change readers' perceptions about a given poem, story, or novel. The dual structure of the assignment helps students first learn to ground their ideas in primary historical evidence and secondary critical work before making historicist claims about literature. The primary aim of this assignment within the course, then, is to convey particular methodological principles and practices to students entering the profession of literary studies.

The assignment also gives students insight into new, electronic forms of scholarship within humanities fields, a secondary but not inconsequential benefit for students as they move into upper-division courses. Often discussions of "classroom technology" focus on gadgets: SMART Boards, laptops, tablets, or e-readers. Such conversations can exclude teachers and students at schools without the resources to invest in the most current devices. What is perhaps even more troubling, however, is how focusing on the *stuff* of technology can distract from the more transformative and democratizing affordances of the digital age. These affordances include widespread, open access to primary historical and cultural sources; the ability to connect students across disciplines and institutions; and opportunities for students to easily share their work with their peers, wider scholarly communities, and the public.

> "Focusing on the *stuff* of technology can distract from the more transformative and democratizing affordances of the digital age."
>
> **Ryan Cordell**

Engaging in primary research pushes students to think beyond the generalizations about "life back then" that professors often encounter in the classroom. Preparing their research for a public Web site challenges students to think of the potential for their writing to have life (and repercussions) beyond the walls of the classroom.

The assignment grew from and attempts to model two pedagogical principles.

Real, Substantive Undergraduate Research Can Transform Students.

As the movement toward undergraduate research over the past decades has shown, students can engage in meaningful research throughout their college careers. What's more, students benefit significantly from undergraduate research experiences, which have been correlated with increased satisfaction and retention during their undergraduate years, as well as to professional success in college and beyond. Discussing his studies of SURE (Summer Undergraduate Research Experience) surveys, David Lopatto summarizes that students reported "gains on a variety of disciplinary skills, research design, information on data collection and analysis, information literacy, and communications." Lopatto also cites "professional advancement through opportunities such as scholarly publication, becoming part of a learning community, and relationships with mentors and peers" as benefits stemming from undergraduate research, along with more difficult to measure benefits such as "growth of self-confidence, independence of work and thought, and a sense of accomplishment." This assignment provides many of these same benefits to students, asking them to develop independent research and writing skills and to publish a document that could ultimately benefit other students and scholars.

This assignment also helps expand the idea of undergraduate research to include humanistic work. In the first years of the undergraduate research movement, such experiences were limited primarily to the sciences, where students could participate in laboratory experiments. In a report to the Council on Undergraduate Research, Mark Schantz marks the "individualistic" nature of most humanities work as a barrier to undergraduate research projects, which tend to flourish in collaborative "laboratory models" in which the instructor can guide the research while undergrads make significant, though typically small, contributions.

The growth of digital archives, however, offers new opportunities for undergraduates to engage in the kinds of primary source research that once required access to special collections libraries (and perhaps the travel funds to visit those libraries). The growth of open-access archives online can be thought of as "special collections for all" that allow undergraduates in literature, history, and other humanities classrooms across the spectrum of institutions to engage in the kinds of research that were once restricted to a few privileged schools. Chris Blackwell and Thomas Martin claim of classics students preparing texts for their Perseus Project, "the closer we can bring our students to the real sources of knowledge — the ancient remains, the papyri and parchment — and the real reward of scholarship — the joy of producing a piece of work that one knows will be discovered and read with interest and pleasure by people we may never meet — the closer we can bring students to the experience of being true scholars, working beside other scholars, the more enthusiasm we find."

Undergraduate students in American literature can realize some of the same benefits their students gained working with "papyri and parchment" through working with primary sources — newspapers, magazines, books, among others — in online archives. This assignment asks students to practice the true research skills of the profession rather than mimic those skills.

Bryan Alexander and Rebecca Frost Davis identify this kind of work with "applied learning," which they describe as "another of the key learning outcomes for liberal education identified by AAC&U" (Association of American Colleges and Universities). "By giving students a limited amount of information," they argue, "and some guidance, faculty can limit the scope and scaffold the learning process" in undergraduate research projects, after which "students will be ready for more independent research."

> "This assignment asks students to practice the true research skills of the profession rather than mimic those skills."
>
> **Ryan Cordell**

Writing in Public Can Dramatically Improve Student Writing.

When Blackwell and Martin describe "the real reward of scholarship—the joy of producing a piece of work that one knows will be discovered and read with interest and pleasure by people we may never meet," they touch on another principle of this History Engine assignment: that writing in public and for the public can benefit student engagement with writing assignments. Though we often ask students to write *as if* they are composing for—to paraphrase language common to syllabi and essay assignments—"an educated lay audience," this audience is usually imagined. Students understand this fact, and so inevitably turn from asking "what would an educated lay audience need to understand about my topic?" to the less ambitious but more germane question, "what does my professor want to see in this essay in order to give me an A?" As professors we're often frustrated by students' utilitarian approach to writing assignments. However, when students post their writing in public forums such as wikis, blogs, and specialized Web sites, that imagined public can become an actual public. Describing a public Web site designed by students in a Shakespeare course, Mary Hocks argues that "students can make their ongoing work and learning purposeful by directing it toward this particular situation and their audience of both professionals and students. By publishing it online as public discourse and new knowledge in the field," Hocks argues, "students have an immediate sense of their impact on audiences." When students realize that their writing may be seen by readers besides their professor and outside of the confines of one course, they attend to their writing more carefully. Indeed when students write for the public, the conversations that happen around their writing shift dramatically. Questions of tone, rhetorical effectiveness, and accuracy largely overtake—though never entirely supersede—questions about credit and assessment. This is not to say that public class writing cannot or should not be assessed, only that students' priorities shift in positive ways when they are asked to write for a wider audience.

8. CONCLUSION

This assignment gives students the chance to engage in substantive scholarly research and share their work with an authentic, online public. In my experience with the assignment, students rise to both challenges, producing History Engine episodes that make valuable contributions to the project's database. What's more, the essays that follow from students' History Engine episodes are often written with more nuanced understanding about students' chosen historical periods. They write, in short, about historical ideas that are grounded in precise evidence. More colloquially, I've seen far fewer unsubstantiated claims about "life back then" since I began requiring this extra research and writing step from my students.

Perhaps most importantly, however, students can research and publish these papers using one of the most basic digital tools available today—a Web browser. "Technology" not only describes shiny gadgets, it also describes changes in information access and usability that can dramatically change classrooms in a range of institutions around the world. Of course, to use these resources effectively students must be trained to move beyond a simple Google search when researching a topic. Whether they're preparing for graduate school or for careers in the private sector, then, literature students need practice exploring and evaluating vast digital archives. Nearly all students can now find their own special collections libraries online, and we should help them learn how to take full advantage of that fact.

9. WORKS CITED

Alexander, Bryan, and Rebecca Frost Davis. "Should Liberal Arts Colleges Do Digital Humanities?" *Debates in the Digital Humanities*, dhdebates.gc.cuny .edu/debates/text/25. Accessed 19 Nov. 2013.

Blackwell, Christopher, and Thomas R. Martin. "Technology, Collaboration, and Undergraduate Research." *Digital Humanities Quarterly*, vol. 3, no.1, 2009, www.digitalhumanities.org/dhq/vol/3/1/000024/000024.html.

Hocks, Mary E. "Understanding Visual Rhetoric in Digital Writing Environments." *College Composition and Communication*, vol. 54, no. 4, June 2003, pp. 629-656.

Lopatto, David. "Undergraduate Research as a High-Impact Student Experience." *Peer Review*, vol. 12, no. 2, 2010, www.aacu.org/publications-research /periodicals/undergraduate-research-high-impact-student-experience.

Mark S. Schantz. "Undergraduate Research in the Humanities: Challenges and Prospects." *CUR Focus*, vol. 29, no. 2, 2008, www.cur.org/assets/1/7/winter 08schantz.pdf.

31

Reading with Your Ears:
Using Poetry Sound Archives

Karen Weingarten
Queens College, CUNY

AND

Corey Frost
New Jersey City University

Karen Weingarten is an assistant professor of English at Queens College, City University of New York. She teaches and writes about American literature, feminist theory, digital writing, and critical methodologies. Her work has been published in *Feminist Studies, Radical Teacher, Literature and Medicine*, and other journals. Her book, *Abortion in the American Imagination* (Rutgers University Press), was published in 2014.

COURTESY OF
KAREN WEINGARTEN

Corey Frost is an assistant professor of English at New Jersey City University. He has a wide range of experience at universities in Canada and the United States as a teacher of literature, composition, creative writing, and English as a second language, and as a writing across the curriculum coordinator. He has also published three books of fiction and poetry and has performed his work across North America and internationally.

COURTESY OF COREY FROST

1. OVERVIEW

- **Assignment:** Students create a self-recording of a poem read aloud, listen to the same poem read aloud by the poet through online sound archives, and write about similarities and differences between the two readings and the readers' interpretations.
- **Courses:** Poetry; literature courses that incorporate poetry.
- **Literature:** Poetry.
- **Technology:** Audio recording devices (students can use their own smartphones in many cases); online audio collections; speakers for playback in the classroom.

- **Time:** Two to four class meetings of about one hour and fifteen minutes each, or at least two hours of class time total.

2. GOALS OF THE ASSIGNMENT

By completing this assignment, students will:

- know what is involved in close reading;
- recognize basic terms used to analyze poetry;
- understand the importance of the aural aspects of poetry; and
- see how the performance of a poem can affect its interpretation.

"This lesson takes advantage of an impressive online archive of poets reading their poems. We ask students to use this resource and recording technology to help them reflect on the aural components of poems as a method of close reading."

Karen Weingarten
Queens College, CUNY

3. ASSIGNMENT SHEET

Reading with Your Ears: Using Poetry and Sound Archives

Course: _____

Instructor: _____

Date: _____

Part One

Choose a poem from the list below. Then write a short paper that presents your interpretation of the poem. Briefly, what is the poem about or what is it trying to say or do? Try to find evidence in the poem itself to make your argument. However, you can use any of the literary approaches we have covered to make your argument.

Your paper should be 1 or 2 pages long, double-spaced, in 12-point Times font or its equivalent. It should have a thesis statement and all quotations should be cited in MLA format. Don't forget to introduce the title and author of the poem in your introductory paragraph.

Please bring 3 copies of your essay and a copy of the poem to class on the due date.

List of possible poems:

Elizabeth Alexander, "Gift"

W. H. Auden, "Friday's Child"

Amiri Baraka, "Black Dada Nihilismus"

Gwendolyn Brooks, "We Real Cool"

Robert Frost, "The Road Not Taken"

Allen Ginsberg, "A Supermarket in California"

Louise Glück, "Witchgrass"

Langston Hughes, "The Negro Speaks of Rivers"

June Jordan, "Poem for a Young Poet"

Tan Lin, "Broken Sonnets"

Audre Lorde, "The Black Unicorn"

Adrienne Rich, "Letters to a Young Poet"

Gertrude Stein, "How She Bowed to Her Brother"

Wallace Stevens, "The Poem That Took the Place of a Mountain"

Dylan Thomas, "Do not go gentle into that good night"

Derek Walcott, "Origins"

William Carlos Williams, "Shoot it Jimmy!"

William Butler Yeats, "The Lake Isle of Innisfree"

Part Two

Find a quiet space and record yourself reading the poem you wrote about for part one. As you record yourself, pay careful attention to where you pause, what words you emphasize, and how you control the rhythm of your voice — every choice you make in reading the poem, in other words. Then write a 1- to 2-page reflection that describes your experience of recording the poem. What performance choices did you make? Did you make mistakes or have any difficulty with any lines in particular? Did you use an accent or a persona? Did you try to convey any emotion? These are just a few of the questions you might consider. Please upload your recording to our class blog or bring a copy of the recording to class on a flash drive.

If you have any issues accessing recording equipment, please let me know immediately and we will work something out. The equipment you use to record does not need to be high-tech, as long as your voice is relatively clear on the recording. (Think back to the Whitman recording we heard; your recording should try to be at least as clear as that!)

Part Three

Find the recording of your poem by the poet on either Poets.org (www.poets .org) or PennSound (writing.upenn.edu/pennsound). Then write a 4- to 5-page essay that compares your recording to the one by the poet. What does comparing the two recordings reveal about how our appreciation and understanding of a poem can be affected by the way the poem is performed?

When writing part three of this assignment, you're welcome to make use of the writing you did in part one and part two. Remember to double-space your essay and use 12-point Times font or its equivalent. Your paper should have a thesis statement that summarizes your argument. MLA format should be used for all citations.

4. TIME AND TECHNOLOGY

We begin the unit by introducing students to Walt Whitman's late poem "America." Since the poem is only six lines, it can be easily read out loud in class, and since it has many pauses and some punctuation that may seem unusual, it presents some interesting issues regarding how the text should be spoken. It begins, "Centre of equal daughters, equal sons, / All, all alike endear'd, grown, ungrown, young or old. . . ."

We first ask students to read it to themselves, and then we ask one student to volunteer to read it out loud to the class. During about half an hour of discussion we have students analyze the poem. Some questions you might ask them to consider are the following:

> How is America presented in the poem?
>
> Who are the daughters and sons and what does it mean that they are all alike?
>
> Why are certain nouns capitalized?
>
> Who is Mother?
>
> What does it mean that she is "Chair'd in the adamant of Time"?

This discussion could go in different directions, with different levels of sophistication and guidance depending on the students' experience with poetry and literary analysis. In Introduction to Literary Studies, this assignment is preceded by study of other work by Walt Whitman, which helps students understand the poem, but without such preparation it will be helpful to spend some time unpacking the poem and giving students guidance on how to read it before moving on to the next step.

Once students have a grasp of the poem's intentions, we move on to a discussion of its form. We ask another student to read the poem out loud again, paying particular attention to punctuation. Then we ask them to discuss the following:

> This poem is free verse, but what can we say about the rhythm of the poem?
>
> How do the line breaks affect the rhythm?
>
> How do the commas affect what words and ideas are emphasized?
>
> Does the capitalization have an effect on how you read the poem?
>
> Why are "endear'd" and "chair'd" spelled without the final *e*?

Finally, we end the class by introducing and then listening to Walt Whitman's recording of the first four lines of the poem, available on Poets.org.

For the next class, students are asked to read Ed Folsom's short essay about this wax cylinder recording of uncertain origin, along with Walter Benjamin's "The Work of Art in the Age of Mechanical Reproduction." Benjamin's essay is relevant because it introduces the concept of a work of art's "aura," while Folsom's essay demonstrates the academic interest in proving whether the Whitman recording is authentic. These readings are optional, and you'll have to decide if your students are able to deal with the specialized diction and references that may seem obscure in the Benjamin essay. Both essays in conversation set up the discussion for the next class, which focuses on whether this recording, ostensibly of Whitman reading his poem, changes our understanding of the poem, and how a recording of a poem by its author might provide insight into the poem that isn't available from the printed page. This discussion lays the groundwork for the essay students ultimately write about poetry and sound. The conversation over two days of class about Whitman's recording of "America" serves to introduce students to the theoretical questions that will serve as the foundation for their papers.

The actual essay prompt, presented in the assignment sheet above, is made up of several stages. First students are asked to choose one poem to write about from a list of poems that we provide. These poems have been chosen because audio recordings of the poets reading them are available on PennSound or Poets.org, although initially we do not inform the students of that. Part one of the assignment asks them to perform a brief analysis of the poem of their choice in a one- to two-page essay. We ask that they include a thesis statement that reflects their interpretation, but we are open to various approaches to analyzing the poem. They are given a week to write this short paper and asked to bring three copies and a copy of the poem to class on the due date so that the paper can be peer-reviewed. This review process is in place to help students draw out their analysis and get feedback on their interpretations. If you have less time to implement this assignment, this step could be replaced with a short classroom discussion of the poem or poems.

In part two of the assignment, students record themselves reading a poem of their choice. In addition to the recording, they write another one- to two-page essay reflecting on their performance. This part of the assignment asks them to consider every choice they made in producing the recording—how quickly they read, where they paused, what they emphasized or de-emphasized, whether they made mistakes or had difficulty with any lines, if they adopted an accent or posture, if they tried to convey any emotion, and so on. They are also asked to bring a copy of their recording to class (or post it online). During the follow-up lesson, some students are asked to share their recording. After that, the students are told that each poem has also been recorded by the poet, and that the recordings are easily available online. (If students discover this prematurely it's not a problem, but we prefer not to mention it in advance, so that students will not be tempted to model their performance on the poet's performance.) Then both recorded versions (the student's and the poet's) of a poem are played back-to-back for the entire class (this can be repeated for several poems if there is time). Students are asked to compare them, keeping in mind the choices they wrote about in their short reflective paragraphs. This discussion serves to model for them the type of argument they will develop for the unit's final essay.

Part three, finally, is an assignment to write a longer (four- to five-page) essay that consolidates some of what students have discovered about performing poetry. The students will be expected to locate their poet's recording of the poem online so that they can compare it to their own. By this point in the activity, students should already have a sense of what they'd like to say about the effect of oral performance on their chosen text. They can base their longer paper in part on the writing they have already done.

The assignment can be done over a couple of days if students are already comfortable analyzing poetry. However, if, like us, you are working with relatively inexperienced students, we recommend first introducing students to poetry analysis before embarking on this assignment. The initial discussion of Walt Whitman's poem, which we spent an hour and fifteen minutes on, could really be done in less time, and the additional class that we spent discussing the Folsom and Benjamin essays could be omitted. Since these discussions model the kind of responses expected in the essay, they serve an important purpose especially for students who are less experienced with poetry analysis, but they could be simplified and shortened. On the other hand, the process as described above may take up additional time if your students need more in-class work improving their analyses of individual poems. You might also need to spend some class time helping students record their poems or troubleshooting any recording issues they've encountered. If you follow all the steps outlined above then the assignment will take four classes, or about two weeks if your classes meet twice a week.

The technology required for this assignment is fairly standard in tech-enabled or "smart" classrooms, but even if your classroom doesn't have the equipment built in, it shouldn't be difficult to arrange. You will need a computer with an Internet connection in your classroom that will allow you to stream recordings of poetry, and you will need speakers loud and clear enough to be heard by your entire class. Your students, on the other hand, will need to have access to some kind of audio recording equipment. Most laptop computers are equipped to make digital audio recordings, or your students may own other devices that they can use, such as iPods, iPads, digital cameras, or camcorders. Some of them may be able to use their smartphones to record themselves. Ideally, they will create a digital file of their recording (MP3 files are the most versatile), but if that's not an option any recording device that can be used for playback in the classroom, such as a tape recorder, will do. You can ask them to upload their digital files to a class blog, individual blogs, or a public media-sharing Web site such as YouTube or Google Drive, so that the files will be easily accessible online. Alternatively you can ask them to bring their recording to class on a thumb drive or e-mail it to you. Just be sure to do a sound check before class—if you are using your own computer for playback, make sure that you can access and read all the files—so that no time is wasted on software or hardware glitches.

This assignment relies on online audio recordings of poetry, of which it seems there are a nearly limitless number, but the sites in the by-no-means-exhaustive list that follows represent some of the more popular, well-known, well-organized, and easily accessible collections of recordings.

- PennSound (writing.upenn.edu/pennsound): This site, directed by Al Filreis and Charles Bernstein and housed by the Center for Programs in Contemporary Writing at the University of Pennsylvania, has a voluminous grab bag of recordings, many from reading series or radio shows. The featured poems are mostly, but not exclusively, contemporary.
- Poetry Foundation (www.poetryfoundation.org): A tidy, well-organized site that can filter searches for poems by title, region, subject, and other categories, including poems available as text, sound, or both.
- Academy of American Poets (www.poets.org): Another well-structured site, it serves as a multipurpose poetry-promotion resource and includes a relatively small but wide-ranging audio archive with recordings of many famous works.
- Ubuweb (www.ubu.com/sound): This impressive site features text, audio, and video of avant-garde writing and art in all its forms, from every period—including a great selection of sound poetry.
- The Internet Poetry Archive (www.ibiblio.org/ipa/index.php): A very small but well-designed site featuring the work of a handful of world-renowned poets.

5. ANTICIPATING STUDENT NEEDS

Before beginning this assignment, it is preferable that students are exposed to some basic principles of close reading, so that they can comfortably practice it throughout the assignment. Robert Pinksy's *The Sounds of Poetry: An Introduction* is a good companion piece for this kind of work, but there are many books out there with varying approaches to the sound of poetry. In our course, students have also been exposed to various approaches to or theories of literary criticism (e.g., historicist, psychological, or structuralist approaches), which means that they understand close reading as just one tool in the literary critic's tool box.

In addition, because this assignment consists of several steps, a student might not complete some steps or might miss some classroom discussions. We often require that students who miss peer review take their drafts to the Writing Center to make up for the missed in-class time. If they miss hearing the recordings in class, they can be directed to the recordings online. Also, even though most personal computers and smartphones these days have digital recording capabilities, there may be students who don't have access to any device that will allow them to record themselves. If this is the case for some of your students, you might want to set up studio time outside of class (or at the end of one class) and ask the media center at your institution for simple recording devices students can use to record their readings, with help from you or the media center. Additionally, you might find, when students bring their recordings to class, that there are compatibility issues (depending on how they recorded themselves and what they're using to transport the recording). One way to circumvent this issue is to ask students to upload their recording to a class blog (if your course has one). This method forces them to troubleshoot any technical issues before class time. (For other ideas on how to use a blog in your literature course, consult the rest of this book!)

6. ASSESSMENT TOOLS

This assignment has multiple parts, so it's important to emphasize to students that they need to keep up with each task or they'll find completing the final project more difficult. You can choose to assign a grade only for the final project, but grading each component or emphasizing that each component will be factored into the final grade helps ensure that students will complete each step. Regardless of how you choose to assign grades, we recommend that students be given feedback on each step so that any issues they might have are caught before the final paper is drafted. Some components of the assignment — like the recording of the poem — can be integrated into a participation grade rather than marked separately, but keep in mind that if a student fails to complete the recording then she or he won't really be able to fully complete the assignment. It's important to emphasize to the students that they are not being graded on the "quality" of their performance, as some may otherwise feel inhibited about their lack of expertise in this regard. The recording is only an exercise intended to provoke ideas for the essay, not an end in itself. The final grade should depend on what aspect of the project you think is most important for the overall goals of your course and whether the assignment is included in an introductory literature course, a survey of poetry, a senior seminar, or a creative writing course.

Below we list components of the assignment that we think would benefit from receiving a separate mark, and we also include advice for marking each part. If you choose to allot 100 points to the total assignment, we provide a recommendation for how much each part could be weighed.

- Part One: Short Interpretation of the Poem (1 to 2 pages) — 25 pts
Advice for marking: The final mark for this assignment should evaluate the attention the student gave to the analysis of the poem. Did the student incorporate terms and ideas that were introduced in class? Does the student's thesis statement make a coherent and provable argument about the poem? Did the student come up with an argument about the poem's meaning that is supported by evidence from the poem?

- Part Two: Recording of Poem and Reflection (1 to 2 pages) — 25 pts
Advice for marking: The mark for this assignment should assess the effort and attention given to the performance. How well did the student use the available technology? Did the student take the time to create a thoughtful and faithful performance of the text? Does the written reflection about the recording process demonstrate that the student thought carefully about it? While it would be unfair to penalize students who don't have access to high-end recording technology, part of the assignment is learning to use the available technology and troubleshooting any issues, so a clearly audible recording should be a minimum expectation. Students should be reminded to consult with you if they have trouble meeting this expectation.

- Part Three: Analysis Comparing the Two Recordings (4 to 5 pages) — 50 pts
Advice for marking: This component of the assignment is the longest and most substantial and should therefore be graded as such. When grading, ask yourself: Does this paper have a clear and coherent argument? Is it reflected in the thesis statement? Does the student conduct a thorough comparison of the two recordings of their poem? Is an analysis of the poem incorporated into the argument? Does the student demonstrate an understanding of how the performance of a poem impacts its interpretation? (Note: it's possible that a student might argue that a poem's performance doesn't impact its interpretation, and that's an acceptable argument. However, if they take this approach, then they should still be able to coherently prove their argument with evidence from the recordings.)

7. THEORETICAL BASIS FOR THE ASSIGNMENT:
Reading with Your Ears: Using Poetry Sound Archives

In the long history of poetry, audio recordings are a fairly recent development. Originally poetry was created with the human voice and reproduced via the human memory, without the mediation of any technology. Eventually, though, poets who wanted to address audiences at a distant remove — in space or in time—were compelled to make use of the first poetry recording technology—writing—which over time established a literal monopoly. It wasn't until 5,000 years later, give or take a few centuries, when Edison invented the wax cylinder phonograph, that writing was challenged by a rival technology. For the first time, it was possible to capture and convey the actual sound of poetry in its original medium, the human voice. The technology quickly evolved beyond wax cylinders, but even those early audio recordings were inarguably better than writing at preserving poetry as a vocal phenomenon. So much better, in fact, that a five-millennia history of writing poetry could have been abandoned at that point as a temporary inconvenience.

Except, of course, that in the meantime poetry evolved quite a bit itself, and many people, poets foremost among them, became rather attached to writing. Even into the twenty-first century, teaching poetry has generally still referred to teaching the printed text. Good poetry teachers make sure to fill their classrooms with the sound of poetry read out loud, and some of them may be in the habit of playing the occasional recording of a poet performing his or her own work, but for the first hundred years after the technology was invented, despite many gradual improvements, audio recordings were not as accessible, as convenient, or as ubiquitous as print. At least partly as a result of these technological limitations, attending to the sound of poetry has not been the norm in the pedagogy of poetry. In the last decade, however, new technology has intervened again, because digital audio makes it easy to record and share poetry performances, and the Web makes it easy to access poetry recordings that previously would have been difficult for the average student to come by.

The assignment outlined here begins with a look at one such recording, a scratchy thirty-six-second clip rescued from a nineteenth-century wax cylinder that is believed to reproduce the sunny, avuncular voice of an elderly Walt Whitman. As Ed Folsom explains, the circa-1890 recording was essentially buried in collections for decades, coming to light in the mid-twentieth century and then being rediscovered by scholars (though not conclusively authenticated) in the early 1990s. In the 1950s, it was played on the radio, and in 1992, according to Folsom's article, one could send a check for $10 to the University of Iowa and receive a cassette in the mail. But students today can hear this recording instantly, on demand, on the Web site of the Academy of American Poets (www.poets.org), just one of a number of sites with rapidly expanding archives of poetry recordings.

The question remains, though: What advantage does it bring us, as scholars, students, or lovers of poetry, to hear Whitman's voice—if it is his—or any other poet's voice, reading their own poetry? This is one of the questions that our assignment is meant to address. It asks students how their experience of poetry is affected by listening to it rather than reading it, how listening to a recording differs from listening to a live performance, and how one person's reading may sound different from another's. These are questions that have been attracting more and more attention from scholars who are reengaging with poetry as an oral phenomenon, beginning with Charles Bernstein's landmark anthology *Close Listening: Poetry and the Performed Word* (1998), and continuing more recently in Lesley Wheeler's book *Voicing American Poetry: Sound and Performance from the 1920s to the Present* (2008). A parallel trend in recent poetry criticism is to emphasize the social function of poetry, and to acknowledge the interdependence of poetry and poetry scenes. For example, editors Maria Damon and Ira Livingston reframe poetry criticism as a form of cultural studies in *Poetry and Cultural Studies: A Reader* (2009), which juxtaposes diverse essays, both historical and current, that promote a common understanding of the social import of poetry and poetry studies.[1]

PennSound is a preeminent example of how online audio poetry archives contribute to both these movements within poetry criticism. In the site's fifth podcast, director Al Filreis talks about the pedagogical uses of poetry sound files with Steve Evans, who says at one point that his students often tell him that hearing the recording "humanizes" the poem for them (Filreis). Evans audibly puts the word in quotation marks, as it is here. We've heard the same comment from students, but what does it mean, exactly? The human voice may be a good emblem of humanity, but it's not a prerequisite for human poetry. Perhaps what students are drawn to in the recording is not the voice itself but what it represents: the imagined physical presence of an actual person. In poetry performance, the live event depends on the presence of the poet, while recordings are premised on the poet's absence; nevertheless, the recording still allows for a kind of social contextualization that one doesn't get from print. In the recording one hears not just a poem but a space in which the poem exists: the background noise of the room, the idiosyncrasies of the performer's voice, the passion—or impassivity—with which the poem is read. Furthermore, "live" recordings, as opposed to studio recordings, often capture a significant part of the performance context—introductions, applause, laughter, slips, and asides—along with the performance itself. Online archives can further enhance the listener's sense of participation by incorporating photos and background information as well as interactive discussion threads, blogs, and so on, and by allowing listeners to download and pass recordings on to other sites and other ears.

> "In the recording one hears not just a poem but a space in which the poem exists."
> **Corey Frost** and **Karen Weingarten**

---

[1]Other examples would be Joan Shelley Rubin's *Songs of Ourselves: The Uses of Poetry in America* (2007), Joseph Harrington's *Poetry and the Public: The Social Form of Modern US Poetics* (2002), or Daniel Kane's *All Poets Welcome: The Lower East Side Poetry Scene in the 1960s* (2003).

Using online archives of audio poetry recordings in the classroom can accomplish two things, then. First, it encourages students to do a little close listening themselves, to read with their ears and hopefully notice aspects of the poem that their eyes failed to catch. Secondly, it can make it easier for students to understand the context that generated the poem, and to grasp that poetry is not just an object but also an event. As the students say, it "humanizes" the work: rather than thinking of poetry as something people make, written in isolation and read in isolation, students are able to experience it as something people *do*.

8. CONCLUSION

Poetry is a notoriously difficult genre to teach to undergraduates, and this may have something to do with it being often introduced to students only as a printed text, not as spoken word. In fact, the popularity of poetry readings, poetry slams, and other forms of spoken word performance over the last couple of decades has shown quite clearly that exploring performance is one way many students become engaged with poetry. Therefore, it makes sense for us to try as much as possible to emphasize the sound of poetry when we teach it, and luckily, this has become very easy to do. There's nothing wrong with the old-fashioned approach, of course—poems being read out loud by teachers and students—but hearing the author of a poem read his or her own work does add another dimension of richness to the experience of the poem, and to the experience of teaching and studying the poem. For students who are somewhat familiar with Whitman's work, for example, it can be quite an unexpected pleasure to suddenly hear his voice, brimming with personality in the recording as though he were still alive. The inimitable performance styles of Gwendolyn Brooks, Langston Hughes, and W. B. Yeats all stood out for our students as adding a dimension to the poem that was not apparent in the text alone. In our experience teaching this lesson and assignment, we found that although our students often struggle with reading—and even listening to—poetry, the exercise of recording a poem helped them in their close reading; they spoke of being forced to rethink the way they had understood a particular word or line. It also gave them a sense of intimacy with their chosen poem and helped them understand why the poem was written in the first place. Similarly, audio recordings connect writers and readers not only through language but also through a sense of shared place. Once students had the experience of recording a poem, they were eager to hear how the poet's own reading compared to theirs. Without any goading, they became close listeners. As a bonus, this lesson has students listening to a recording together, rather than reading silently to themselves. The upshot of this group activity is that the people in the classroom are connected too, which, we discovered, also had a positive effect on our students' understanding and appreciation of poetry.

9. WORKS CITED

Benjamin, Walter. *Illuminations: Essays and Reflections.* Edited by Hannah Arendt, Translated by Harry Zohn, Schocken, 1968.

Filreis, Al. "Podcast #5 — Steve Evans on Recorded Poetry." *PennSound*, media .sas.upenn.edu/pennsound/podcasts/PennSound-Podcast_05_Evans.mp3. Accessed 10 Feb. 2016. Sound recording.

Folsom, Ed. "The Whitman Recording." *Walt Whitman Quarterly Review*, vol. 9, 1992, pp. 214-16.

Whitman, Walt. "America." *Poets.org*, www.poets.org/viewmedia.php/prmMID /20157. Accessed 10 Feb. 2016.

32

Into the Archives: Using Early English Books Online in the Early Modern Literature Classroom

Nichole DeWall
McKendree University

Nichole DeWall is an assistant professor of English at McKendree University, where she teaches medieval and early modern literature, as well as drama and composition courses. Her research focuses on teaching Shakespeare and representations of disease in Shakespeare's plays. She recently published "Into the Woods: William Shakespeare's *A Midsummer Night's Dream* and Peter Weir's *Dead Poets Society*" in *Verse, Voice, and Vision: Cinema and Poetry* (Scarecrow, 2013) and "'Like a shadow, / I'll ever dwell': The Jailer's Daughter as Ariadne in *The Two Noble Kinsmen*" in the *Journal of the Midwest Modern Language Association* (2013). She frequently participates in the Shakespeare Association of America's seminars and workshops.

1. OVERVIEW

- **Assignment:** Students select one archival text from Early English Books Online (EEBO) and complete a reflection paper, presentation, and longer essay (optional) about its relationship to a canonical text from the course reading list.
- **Courses:** Upper-level English; early English.
- **Literature:** English literature written between 1475 and 1700.
- **Technology:** Early English Books Online (EEBO) or alternative; a learning management system (e.g., Blackboard).
- **Time:** In-class time requires approximately three hours depending on course enrollment; substantial time should be set aside for writing outside of class, especially if students choose to pursue the longer EEBO research essay.

2. THE GOALS OF THE ASSIGNMENT

After completing this assignment, students will be able to:

- interrogate the difference between "literary" and "nonliterary" texts;
- better understand early modern print culture and the history of the book;
- experience the exhilaration and frustration of conducting research with primary materials;
- become more attentive to the critical moves particular to the new historicism; and
- broaden their views of early modern culture as a whole.

"Although it's not terribly fashionable to admit these days, I believe that the thoughtful study of literature has the ability to make us better humans: more empathetic, more alive, and more able to appreciate beauty."

Nichole DeWall
McKendree University

3. ASSIGNMENT SHEET

Into the Archives: Using Early English Books Online in Early Modern Literature

Course: _____

Instructor: _____

Date: _____

Throughout this course, we will attempt to move away from overgeneralized assumptions about the early modern period (e.g., "women back then" or "people during that time") and instead move toward complicated and nuanced readings of early modern literary texts. Drawing upon your knowledge of critical literary theory, this assignment asks you to search, select, and write about one archival text from Early English Books Online (EEBO) that seems to participate in the same conversation as an assigned canonical text. You will then share your findings with your peers through an informal writing assignment and presentation. Later in the semester, you will have the opportunity to develop your work with EEBO into one of your longer research essays.

As I described during our first class session, EEBO is a database of archival documents used by scholars of the early modern period. Here's the description of this resource from EEBO's Web site:

> From the first book published in English through the age of Spenser and Shakespeare, this incomparable collection now contains more than 125,000 titles listed in Pollard & Redgrave's *Short-Title Catalogue (1475–1640)* and Wing's *Short-Title Catalogue (1641–1700)* and their revised editions, as well as the *Thomason Tracts (1640–1661)* collection and the *Early English Books Tract Supplement*. Libraries possessing this collection find they are able to fulfill the most exhaustive research requirements of graduate scholars — from their desktop — in many subject areas: including English literature, history, philosophy, linguistics, theology, music, fine arts, education, mathematics, and science.

I recommend that you begin your work on this assignment early in the semester by moving through the following steps (many of these steps will overlap in the recursive process that is archival work):

Familiarize yourself with EEBO. The introductory tutorial found on EEBO's home page provides a good overview of the database (eebo .chadwyck.com/marketing/eebo_demo1.htm). For a guide to conducting searches, go to ProQuest's web page (www.proquest.com/en-US/catalogs /databases/detail/eebo.shtml) and download the PDF called "Search Guide: Early English Books Online" under Training Materials.

Sign up for a presentation time. You will notice that our reading schedule is divided into five units: The Early Sixteenth Century (1485-1550); The Later Sixteenth Century (1550-1603); The Early Seventeenth Century

(1603–1625); The Mid-Seventeenth Century (1625-1660); and The Restoration (1660-1785). We will spend approximately 5 class sessions reading and discussing the material from each unit. On the 6th day of each unit, you and three of your classmates will give presentations that describe the findings of your EEBO projects. Since the texts on our reading schedule are unfamiliar to you at this point, you may wish to skim the headnotes for each assigned work in your textbook to see what most appeals to you before choosing a presentation time (or you may simply choose at random).

Carefully read your chosen assigned text. Although you will read your chosen assigned text in the course of our normal reading schedule, you may wish to read it ahead of the class to allow for ample time with EEBO. As you read, note any moments in the text that seem particularly intriguing, confusing, or provocative. You may wish to jot down 2 or 3 research questions along the way that will guide your EEBO searches (e.g., Why are Polonius and Laertes so determined to protect Ophelia's virginity?).

Choose an archival text from EEBO. You should choose a text that seems to be in dialogue with your chosen assigned text. Some pairings that students have found instructive in the past include:

- *The Taming of the Shrew* and the anonymous conduct manual *A mery dialogue, declaringe the propertyes of shrowde shrewes, and honest wyues* (1557)
- *The Faerie Queen* and a map of Ireland from William Camden's *Britannia* (1586)
- *Hamlet* and passages from Robert Burton's *The Anatomy of Melancholy* (1621)

Many of the texts in EEBO's collection are already transcribed into fully searchable, SGML/XML-encoded texts; if yours is not, you may wish to transcribe a page or two of your document for greater ease of reading.

Write a 2- to 3-page response paper. Your paper may be informal in tone, but should be carefully supported with evidence from both your EEBO text and your chosen assigned text. You will need to include a works-cited page, as well ("How do I cite a title from EEBO?": eebo.chadwyck.com/help/faqs.htm#2). Please include the following sections in your paper:

    General description. Briefly describe your EEBO text: date of publication, complete title, and author (consult the *Dictionary of Literary Biography*). Include the text's permanent URL so that your classmates can look at it for themselves. Which assigned text are you pairing with your EEBO document?

    Research process. Describe your research process. What questions did you use to guide your searches? Did your questions change as you went along? What was the most difficult part of the process? What was the most rewarding?

(*continued*)

ASSIGNMENT SHEET (*continued*)

Genre. Based upon what we've discussed in class this semester, describe the generic qualities of your EEBO text. How would you categorize this work? Also consider whether you would classify it as "literary" or "nonliterary." Why?

Connections. Describe the connections that you have made between your EEBO text and your chosen assigned text. Has working with your EEBO text changed the way you view your chosen assigned text or early modern culture as a whole? Support your observations with textual evidence.

Theory. Which theoretical approaches informed your work with EEBO? You may quote passages from your textbook to frame your discussion. You may also analyze the theoretical underpinnings of the assignment itself, particularly the way it draws discrete boundaries between canonical and archival texts.

Feedback. What questions do you still want to explore with your EEBO text? Is there anything in particular that you would like your peers to pay special attention to as they read it?

Post your response paper on our Blackboard page. This should be done at least 24 hours before our class meets.

Present your findings (10 minutes). This is not a presentation in the formal sense. Since your peers will have already read your response paper and looked at your EEBO text, you may spend this time fielding questions and leading a general discussion about your process.

Write a 1- to 2-page reflection. After your presentation, write an informal reflection on your entire experience working with EEBO and receiving your peers' feedback and attach it to your response paper. Also indicate whether or not you may wish to pursue your EEBO project further by developing it into one of your 2 longer research essays.

Submit your response paper to me for assessment. I will grade your response paper based on the rubric that I distributed with this assignment during our first class session.

4. TIME AND TECHNOLOGY

To complete this assignment, students will need the following resources.

ACCESS TO EEBO. Unfortunately, not every institution of higher learning can afford to subscribe to EEBO; my small liberal arts college, for example, does not have a subscription. My students can, however, travel to a nearby research university's library to access the database.

Even if your school does not have an EEBO subscription, a less expansive collection of EEBO texts (25,363 compared to 125,000) is accessible to institutions that partnered with the University of Michigan's Text Creation Partnership (TCP) during Phase I of the EEBO-TCP project (2000-2009). A list of Phase I members is available at www.textcreationpartnership.org /partners/. Happily, all Phase I texts became open and freely available to the public on January 1, 2015. A more modest version of this assignment can also be carried out using an online repository of medieval and Renaissance manuscripts called Digital Scriptorium (scriptorium.english.cam.ac.uk/). Unlike EEBO, however, Digital Scriptorium is not a searchable database; it also offers a more narrow selection of texts.

If modifying this assignment for slightly later time periods, the Eighteenth Century Collections Online (ECCO-TCP) is freely available to the public (www.textcreationpartnership.org/tcp-ecco/).

Because EEBO's collection includes texts in literature as well as science, education, medicine, music, and religion, this assignment could easily be adapted for classes in disciplines other than literature.

A LEARNING MANAGEMENT SYSTEM. This assignment asks students to post their EEBO reflection papers on their school's learning management system before coming to class (we use Blackboard). If your school does not utilize a learning management system, students could circulate their work via e-mail instead.

A COMPUTER LAB (OPTIONAL). You may wish to reserve a computer lab early in the semester to guide students through some basic searches on EEBO. However, since EEBO's Web site offers excellent online tutorials that students can view independently, you may find that most students don't need a group computer lab session.

I also recommend the following:

Plan for Overall Time Needed. Plan to spend approximately thirty minutes of instructional time early in the semester for general setup and brief lectures on early modern printing and the history of the book. Student presentations will take another two and a half hours spread throughout the course of the semester (this calculation assumes three or four students on any given presentation day). If students choose to pursue a longer EEBO research essay, they should allow substantial time for drafting, revision, and polishing.

Start Early. I discuss this EEBO project during the first class meeting, and often distribute hard copies of the assignment then as well (or draw their attention to it on Blackboard). If I have time during that first session, I often pull up the EEBO Web site on the projector and show students a few of the archival documents that I have worked with in the past (the ones with images are especially intriguing to students). Students are often interested enough to watch the introductory EEBO tutorials on their own during that first week of class (or you may choose to assign them as homework).

You may also wish to consider setting aside ten minutes during the first few class periods for mini-lectures on the history of early modern print culture. Introduce students to terms like *folio*, *quarto*, *commonplace books*, *broadside*, and *ballad*. You can also copy a small section of an EEBO text and ask students in groups to transcribe it in order to introduce them to black type and variant spellings. One short lecture should be devoted to citing texts from EEBO.

Because their initial forays into the database can be intimidating to students, you may choose to move one entire class session to a computer lab before the first round of EEBO presentations takes place. Ask students whose presentations are coming up to conduct a few EEBO searches while the class watches on the projector unit. Classmates may offer suggestions about how to modify these searches for greater return. After these demonstrations, allow students to explore the Web site on their own and encourage them to watch the online tutorials if they haven't already done so.

Make the Most of Your Learning Management System. This assignment saves valuable in-class time by having students distribute their work on Blackboard before the class period begins. Students post their reflection essays on the online discussion board at least twenty-four hours before their presentations; they also include the persistent URL to their EEBO document so their classmates can prepare questions ahead of time. The reflection essay assignment also asks student presenters to identify specific areas on which they would like to receive feedback, so the relatively short ten-minute presentation usually begins at a much higher and more specific level than if a learning management system had not been utilized.

Work with Librarians. Lastly, I recommend giving a copy of this assignment to your subject librarians before the course begins. They can serve as valuable and time-saving resources to your students throughout the semester.

5. ANTICIPATING STUDENT NEEDS

To a certain extent, this assignment is difficult by design. The difficulty students experience when working with these archival texts is what begins to disrupt their sense of easy familiarity with early modern culture. This is most likely the first time that students have encountered blackletter type and variant spellings, for instance. It may also be the first time that students confront the notion that early modern texts — including towering, canonical ones like *Hamlet* — are potentially unstable and often unreliable. Students often express feelings of frustration and bewilderment as they move through this assignment, so be prepared to explain exactly why you think this project is worthwhile despite (and because of) its difficulty.

You may wish to extend your office hours or set aside a few extra blocks of time throughout the semester to work with students individually on their EEBO projects. Because students often find their work with EEBO frustrating at first, it is helpful to work with them one-on-one before complete exasperation sets in. Reassure them that every scholar experiences frustration during the messy, complex, and time-consuming endeavor that is archival research. Offer to help transcribe a few passages together; sit at a computer and guide them through a few searches. The goal is not to eliminate frustration for your students: one objective for this assignment, after all, is for them to realize how unsettling and strange it feels to work with early modern texts.

In my experience, students also express reluctance to share their written work with their peers before they have received feedback from me. I usually offer to look over their reflection essays if they get them to me at least seventy-two hours before their presentations. Simply providing students with some quick written or verbal comments seems to go a long way in reducing their anxieties. I encourage the three or four students who are presenting on the same day to circulate and provide each other with feedback on drafts of their reflection papers before they post their essays on Blackboard. You may also recommend that students utilize your school's writing resource center.

6. ASSESSMENT TOOLS

This assignment grew out of my desire to integrate a wider variety of assessments into my literature classes. I had gotten stuck in a "four critical essays per semester" rut, and needed to allow my students to demonstrate their learning in different ways. This EEBO project does not produce a formal written product; rather, students generate around five pages of informal, reflective writing based on their experiences and peer feedback. Therefore, I consider this a relatively low-stakes writing assignment and weigh it accordingly. Students do have the option of later pursuing a longer, formal critical essay based upon their work with EEBO.

That said, when done well this assignment requires a good amount of time and a high degree of effort. Students must read assigned texts on their own and understand them thoroughly enough to develop EEBO search queries. In their reflection papers, they must make informed judgments about genre and discuss the theoretical approaches that inform their methods. Moreover, this assignment asks students to lead discussions and field questions, which can be daunting tasks for some.

In order to keep students motivated over the course of this multiphased assignment, I recommend awarding a certain number of points for various stages of the project. The breakdown that I use is as follows:

Response paper (2–3 pages)	40 pts
Post response paper on Blackboard (24 hours prior to class)	5 pts
Presentation (10 minutes)	20 pts
Reflection paper (1–2 pages)	35 pts
	(100 pts, total)

The best way to make transparent your expectations for this assignment is by showing students samples of EEBO projects that have earned As, Bs, and Cs during previous semesters. Obtain permission from these former students, of course, and offer to keep their documents anonymous. I post this small archive of past EEBO projects on Blackboard and encourage students to refer to them early and often.

7. THEORETICAL BASIS FOR THE ASSIGNMENT:
Into the Archives: Using Early English Books Online in the Early Modern Literature Classroom

Since its inception in 1998, the Early English Books Online (EEBO) database has altered dramatically the way early modern scholars conduct research. Archival projects that in previous generations required expensive travel to rare books collections or long hours in the microfilm room can now be carried out on laptops. The searchable, full-text transcriptions of many texts made possible through EEBO's ongoing collaboration with the University of Michigan's Text Creation Partnership (TCP) make the initial stages of many archival projects much less labor intensive. And because EEBO's corpus includes a wide variety of texts from many disciplines (English literature, history, philosophy, linguistics, theology, music, fine arts, education, mathematics, and science), scholars may now more easily pursue collaborative and interdisciplinary lines of inquiry with one another.

While EEBO's impact on scholarship has been generally acknowledged (Gadd; Kichuk; Pack; and Steggle), less discussed is the way in which the database has the potential to change the way we teach in the early modern classroom. (The notable exceptions here are Crowther, Jordan, Wernimont, and Nunn; and Lindquist and Wicht.) This assignment attempts to bridge the gap between scholarly practice and pedagogy by asking students to pair one frequently taught, canonical early modern literary work with one EEBO archival source. Students complete an informal writing project that discusses how their EEBO text participates in the same cultural conversation as their assigned literary text; students then present their findings to their peers both virtually and face-to-face. This assignment asks students to participate in the scholarly discourses that surround genre, the literary canon, and the relevance of new historical criticism.

The assignment stems both from general pedagogical principles as well as those more specific to the teaching of early modern literature and culture.

Active Learning

Active learning, defined broadly as "any instructional method that engages students in the learning process" (Prince 223), has been linked consistently to positive student learning outcomes. According to Prince, instructors who utilize active learning methods such as collaborative, cooperative, and problem-based learning are able to engage students more effectively than passive, lecture-based courses. Therefore, in my classroom I attempt to move away from lecture as often as possible. This assignment does incorporate brief mini-lectures (approximately thirty minutes total), but it mainly asks students to actively pursue their own investigations into the EEBO databases. As a result, my students report that they feel like scholars. Students also report that they feel actively invested in their peers' EEBO projects as well as their own.

Decentralized Authority

Most college instructors today attempt to move away from what Barr and Tagg call the "Instruction Paradigm" in which they "transfer or deliver knowledge from faculty to students" and toward a "Learning Paradigm" in which "a college's purpose is not to transfer knowledge but to create environments and experiences that bring students to discover and construct knowledge for themselves" (15). This is often easier said than done, however, in classrooms that focus on earlier literary periods. Because students are often so befuddled by middle and early modern English, they rely on their instructor to make sense of the language for them. In the Shakespeare classroom in particular, many students are skeptical about their ability to say anything that hasn't already been said about "The Bard." In contrast, this assignment encourages students to become experts on their EEBO texts and to share their expertise with their classmates. As Crowther, Jordan, Wernimont, and Nunn argue, "digital resources like EEBO allow students and teachers alike to see how earlier generations of scholars have found new things to say about an old, but still evolving, body of literature" (2). As a result, students often feel less intimidated by the course material, and they become less dependent on instructors to make meaning of it for them.

Because EEBO's collection is so expansive, it is more likely than not that students will discover archival texts that are unfamiliar to their teachers. As a result, in their reflection papers and during their presentations, students teach the entire class—including the instructors—about something new and often unexpected. This enacts one of the fundamental principles of collaborative learning, in which the "instructor and the students [are] placed on equal footing" (Faust and Paulson 3). By its very design, then, the instructor's authority is decentralized, and the vertical power structure that so often forms in the early modern classroom shifts to one that is much more horizontal.

8. CONCLUSION

Perhaps the most important aspect of this assignment is its ability to complicate my students' notions of Shakespeare's "universality." Students often enter the early modern literature classroom convinced of Shakespeare's "timelessness." These convictions are almost always imported from high school teachers and are not wholly inappropriate: during Shakespeare's era, Ben Jonson's "Not of an age, but for all time" certainly expressed a similar idea. Yet notions of Shakespeare's universality tend to encourage a too-easy sense of familiarity with the early modern period, one that discourages the kind of deep and nuanced literary readings that we hope for from our students. The ubiquity of Shakespeare and the Renaissance in popular culture can be a curse in this respect, as well. As Derval Conroy and Danielle Clarke write in their introduction to *Teaching the Early Modern Period*, "the sense of familiarity engendered by the presence of the Renaissance in popular culture presents as many challenges as solutions. In fact, the greatest obstacle that early modern teachers face is that their period is already known, always already familiar" (1). According to Conroy and Clarke, we should attempt to teach our students in a way that will "facilitate engagement with the specifics of a particular historical moment" (1).

To this end, I tell my students at the beginning of each semester that part of my job is to "make the familiar strange," and that this EEBO assignment is one of the primary ways I hope to accomplish this goal. Working with EEBO tends to disrupt students' sense of easy familiarity with the early modern period. Students have usually only experienced the works of Shakespeare and his contemporaries in what C. W. Griffin calls "sanitized texts, whose goal is to remove as many barriers as possible" (105). In contrast to their "sanitized" classroom editions, EEBO texts feel raw, chaotic, and foreign: they are relics of a different and distinct culture. When students work with EEBO, they feel alienated from a culture that they thought they always and already knew. Above all, I value this assignment's ability to challenge my students' assumptions about the early modern period and its literature.

9. WORKS CITED

Barr, Robert B., and John Tagg. "From Teaching to Learning: A New Paradigm for Undergraduate Education." *Change*, vol. 27, no. 6, 1995, pp. 12-25.

Conroy, Derval, and Danielle Clarke. Introduction. *Teaching the Early Modern Period*. Edited by Derval Conroy and Danielle Clarke. Palgrave Macmillan, 2011, pp. 1-7.

Crowther, Stefania, et al. "New Scholarship, New Pedagogies: Views from the 'EEBO Generation.'" *Early Modern Literary Studies*, vol. 14, no. 2, Special Issue 17, 2008. Pp. 3.1-30.

J. L. Faust, and D. R. Paulson. "Active Learning in the College Classroom." *Journal on Excellence in College Teaching*, vol. 9, no. 2, 1998, pp. 3-24.

Gadd, Ian. "The Use and Misuse of Early English Books Online." *Literature Compass*, vol. 6, no. 3, 2009, pp. 680-92.

Griffin, C. W. "Textual Studies and Teaching Shakespeare." *Teaching Shakespeare into the Twenty-First Century*. Ohio UP, 1997, 104-11.

Kichuk, Diana. "Metamorphosis: Remediation in Early English Books Online (EEBO)." *Literary and Linguistic* Computing, vol. 22, no. 3, 2007, pp. 291-303.

Lindquist, Thea, and Heather Wicht. "'Pleas'd By a Newe Inuention?' Assessing the Impact of Early English Books Online on Teaching and Research at the University of Colorado at Boulder." *The Journal of Academic Librarianship*, vol. 33, no. 3, 2007, pp. 347-60.

Pack, Thomas. "Bringing Literature Alive: Early English Books Online Reshape Research Opportunities." EContent, vol. 22, 1999, pp. 26-28.

Prince, Michael. "Does Active Learning Work? A Review of the Research." *Journal of Engineering Education*, vol. 93, no. 3, 2004, pp. 223-31.

Steggle, Matthew. "'Knowledge Will be Multiplied': Digital Literary Studies and Early Modern Literature." Chapter 4. *A Companion to Digital Literary Studies*. Edited by Susan Schreibman and Ray Siemens. Blackwell, 2007, *Wiley Online Library*, doi: 10.1002/9781405177504, onlinelibrary.wiley.com /book/10.1002/9781405177504.

33

Thinking through Making: Curating a Victorian Poem in the Context of Its Cultural Moment

Lorraine Janzen Kooistra
Ryerson University

Lorraine Janzen Kooistra is professor of English and codirector of the Centre for Digital Humanities at Ryerson University, Toronto. In 2013 she received the Provost's Experiential Teaching Award and a provincial Teaching Award from the Ontario Confederation of University Faculty Associations for her innovative digital pedagogy.

COURTESY OF LORRAINE
JANZEN KOOISTRA

1. OVERVIEW

- **Assignment:** Curate a poem in a digital exhibit shared online with classmates and beyond the classroom to a wider online community of nineteenth-century scholars and interested citizens.
- **Technology:** NINES, the open-access Networked Infrastructure for Nineteenth-Century Electronic Scholarship (www.nines.org); blogging software, like WordPress; instructor-approved scholarly databases, like American and British Periodicals Online, NINES and the Rossetti Archive, and the Victorian Web.
- **Literature:** Victorian, romantic, or American literature.
- **Time:** Full semester (thirteen weeks).

2. GOALS OF THE ASSIGNMENT

- Students access and successfully navigate archival fonds in digital databases and effectively use their findings in support of a critical argument.

494

- Students establish an effective research question to guide a literature review and select, summarize, and annotate judiciously chosen secondary sources.
- Students critically situate and analyze a Victorian poem in the visual or material context of its publication, gaining insight into the historical particularity of interpretive practices.
- Students develop online publishing and editing skills and gain insight into the professional practice of digital scholarship by working collaboratively and incrementally and by contributing their work to an online scholarly community.

"The assignments and experiences I design for my classes aim to empower students with the understanding that they have ideas that matter, ideas that can contribute to public knowledge, ideas that have ethical and social impact."

Lorraine Janzen Kooistra
Ryerson University

"As a Victorianist, I want to inspire my students with the excitement of the past, and with an understanding of how the past continues to live and breathe in the present."

Lorraine Janzen Kooistra

3. ASSIGNMENT SHEET

Thinking through Making: Curating a Victorian Poem in the Context of Its Cultural Moment

Course: _____

Instructor: _____

Date: _____

Creating a Digital Exhibit, Online Abstract, and Annotated Bibliography on Victorian Visual and Verbal Culture

The Digital Exhibit is an experiential opportunity in online scholarly publishing that aims to give you insight into Victorian visual/verbal culture while developing skills in primary and secondary research; critical thinking and analysis; and writing and editing. In addition to developing these practical skills, the use of online digital tools also facilitates new ways of examining and understanding Victorian literature and culture.

You will participate in an international virtual scholarly community, the Networked Infrastructure for Nineteenth-Century Electronic Scholarship (NINES; www.nines.org). Each of you will have a log-on and password on NINES, which gives you access to over 100 peer-reviewed sites containing electronic archives of primary material and scholarly commentary, essays, and journal articles. NINES also provides access to digital publishing tools.

You will prepare both the Online Abstract and Annotated Bibliography* and the Online Digital Exhibit using the NINES Exhibit Builder** tool. These two assignments will also draw on the NINES e-resources as well as those available through other course-approved scholarly Web sites, such as the C19 Index available through Ryerson University Library and Archives; and open-access resources such as the Rossetti Archive; the Victorian Web; and the Database of Victorian Wood-Engraved Illustrations (I will provide a list of approved sites). I also encourage you to consult print and manuscript resources as appropriate.

To facilitate these linked projects, some class hours will be held in the computer lab. The TA (curatorial tutor) will also hold drop-in office hours to assist any individual or group requiring further help in locating resources or building exhibits. My office hours are also available for this purpose.

---

*See Blackboard for further information on Annotated Bibliographies. There will also be class time devoted to this topic.

**See Blackboard for further information on the NINES Exhibit Builder. There will also be class time devoted to using the Exhibit Builder, collection, annotation, and linking tools.

Select One of the Following Poems for Your Digital Exhibit

Dante Gabriel Rossetti, "A Portrait"; "Body's Beauty"; "Soul's Beauty"; "The Blessed Damozel"; or any of his "poems for pictures" or "double works of art" (see Rossetti Archive), such as "Mary's Girlhood (For a Picture)," "Venus Verticordia (For a Picture)"; "Pandora (For a Picture)"; "Proserpina (For a Picture)"; and so on. *Note: All of DGR's poems have associated paintings by him.*

Christina G. Rossetti, "The Round Tower at Jhansi, June 8, 1857," in *Once a Week* (Aug. 13, 1859): 140; "Maude Clare" in *Once a Week* 1.19 (Nov. 5, 1859): 381; "A Birthday" in *Macmillan's Magazine* 3.18 (April 1861): 498; "If" in *The Argosy* 1.4 (March 1866): 336. (See C19 Index, British Periodicals in RULA; note that the poems "Maude Clare" and "If" are illustrated.)

Alfred Tennyson, "The Lady of Shalott"; "The Charge of the Light Brigade" in *The Examiner* (Dec. 9, 1854): 780; "The Grandmother's Apology" in *Once a Week* 1.3 (July 16, 1859): 41; "The Victim" in *Good Words* 9 (Jan. 1868): 17; "The Defense of Lucknow" in *Nineteenth Century* 5.26 (April 1879): 576. (See C19 Index, British Periodicals; "Grandmother's Apology" and "The Victim" are illustrated.)

Elizabeth Barrett Browning, "The Runaway Slave at Pilgrim's Point" in *The Liberty Bell By Friends of Freedom* (Jan. 1, 1848): 29 (C19 Index, American Periodicals); "A Musical Instrument" in *The Cornhill Magazine* 2.7 (July 1860): 84 (C19 Index, British Periodicals).

Michael Field and/or Walter Pater, "La Giaconda." These poems are on the *Mona Lisa*, which first achieved international acclaim in the nineteenth century. Note that Pater's piece on "La Giaconda" is in prose. However, W. B. Yeats included it as a prose poem in his edition of *Modern Verse* in 1936.

The Online Abstract and Annotated Bibliography Assignment

DUE: _____   WEIGHT: 20%   MODE: INDIVIDUAL

The research you do for the Annotated Bibliography is designed to help you write with authority on your selected Digital Exhibit topic. It is also designed to help you familiarize yourself with the methodologies of digital humanities scholarship using the NINES Exhibit Builder and the e-resources available via NINES and other online scholarly sites, such as the C19 Index, and other approved scholarly Web sites and databases.

Each member of the group will take responsibility for a targeted aspect of the research, but both will be responsible for following up on any further research that may be required. Each individual will use the NINES Exhibit Builder to collect and annotate primary and secondary sources using electronic archives as well as print material.

(continued)

ASSIGNMENT SHEET (*continued*)

When the assignment is completed, group members will share their research to build a collective knowledge base and delegate responsibility for follow-up research.

Tasks for Preparing the Annotated Bibliography Online

Week One: Study the requirements of the Digital Exhibit Assignment (below).

By Week Two: Select a Victorian poem from the list provided; browse e-resources to help you choose one you're interested in. (*Be ready to identify text in class.*)

By Week Three: Do some preliminary research/archival browsing to determine a relevant visual/material context or practice associated with this text. These include but are not limited to the following: periodical contexts; illustrations or paintings based on the text; and world events (abolitionist movements; the Indian "mutiny"; the Crimean War; the "woman question," reform bills, etc.). In addition to these contexts, you may also consider the visual representation of these events in print media, photography, visual art, and drawing practices; and the influence of technologies of reproduction, such as wood engraving, or technologies of vision, such as stereoscopes, panorama, magic lanterns, advertising, fashion, and so on. If in doubt about a relevant visual/material context or practice, consult me.

Week Three: Working with your research partner, establish a preliminary guiding research question about the relationship between the text and its visual/material/cultural context.

Weeks Three–Five: Using approved scholarly electronic resources, supplemented by print materials, find and select materials that will help you develop detailed historical and critical knowledge about your text and its context and allow you to answer your question.

Week Five: Abstract/Annotated Bibliography due in NINES classroom group.

Required Components of the Online Abstract and Annotated Bibliography

(The sections outlined follow the Exhibit Builder Template layout options.)

Section One: Illustration + Text *or* Text + Illustration.

This is the "Abstract" portion of this assignment. Start by identifying your selected Victorian text and associated visual/material object or practice. Upload a visual image that represents the visual material/object or practice that you've selected. In your paragraph annotation, provide your guiding research question, rationale, and approach to the text and its visual/material context. Be sure to clarify the targeted aspect of the research you're responsible for. The sources for both text and visual/material object need to be indicated in a footnote. If the resource comes from an electronic archive, the footnote should include a link to the resource.

Second Section: Illustration + Text; Text + Illustration; *or* Text only

This is the annotated "primary research" section of this assignment. In this section, you will include (upload if available electronically) at least one *primary* source related to the selected text and/or visual/material object (i.e., an archival resource, such as the original periodical publication; a letter; diary entry; nineteenth-century review or news article; visual study for an illustration or painting; etc.). If it is an electronic resource, the archival object should be linked; either way, it must be sourced in a footnote in MLA format. The accompanying paragraph annotation should clearly identify the primary material and its context; provide a brief summary of its contents; and explain how this primary material will help you situate your text in its context in relation to your research question.

Third and Fourth Sections (Please Begin a New Section for Each Resource): Layout as Above

These two sections are the annotated secondary research parts of this assignment. In each of these two sections, you will upload/link at least one scholarly, peer-reviewed source (total of 2) related to the text and/or digital object, and specifically related to your targeted research with respect to the guiding research question. You will write a separate paragraph annotation for each scholarly resource, summarizing its main idea and commenting on how this secondary material will help you situate your text in its context in response to your research question. Each scholarly resource will have a footnote identifying the source in appropriate MLA format; if the resource is electronic, a link to the article will be included.

Final Bit: Hyperlink to Your Partner's Abstract & Annotated Bibliography Exhibit

Digital Exhibit in Victorian Visual/Verbal Culture Assignment

DUE: _____   WEIGHT: 30%   MODE: COLLABORATIVE

Working with your partner, choose one of the following topics and prepare a critically astute and informative exhibit that shows how a specific aspect of this text's original visual/material context offers insight into its historically particular meanings. Each exhibit must include at least one visual object and draw on both primary and secondary sources. Direct quotations are to be avoided; students should credit all ideas gained from other sources in footnotes, but use their own words and ideas as much as possible. Historical and critical context should be clear, as should the authors' critical approach to the text. The commentary should be about 2,000 words in length (total).

(continued)

ASSIGNMENT SHEET (*continued*)

Note: *All exhibits that meet the established criteria and achieve a minimum grade of B+ will be published online on NINES and available to nineteenth-century scholars and interested citizens around the world. As you prepare your exhibit, keep these potential users in mind.*

Tasks for Preparing the Digital Exhibit

Week One: Choose a Victorian text from the list provided.

By Week Two: Choose a Victorian material/visual object or cultural practice associated with the selected text.

Weeks Three–Eight: Research the history of the text in relation to the material/visual object or cultural practice associated with it. (You may need to do further research when your Annotated Bibliography and your partner's are returned, based on the feedback you receive. You need to build collective knowledge on your text, object, and approach.)

Weeks Seven–Ten: Working in pairs, create a digital exhibit that presents the text in the context of an aspect of its visual/material culture. Each individual author will be responsible for half the commentary, but both will be responsible for editing the completed commentary, footnotes, and links, as well as the visual objects and layout.

Week Eight: Partners to exchange their drafted commentaries for peer review, and revise their commentaries based on feedback.

Week Nine: Peer-reviewed and revised commentaries due in class for uploading; images, links, footnotes, and layout plan finalized.

Week Ten: Digital Exhibit is due in the NINES classroom.

The digital exhibit will be historically focused and critically insightful. Its aim is to bring a Victorian text to life by situating it within its conditions of production and reception. Analyzing it in relation to a material/visual object or cultural practice should bring new critical insight to the text under scrutiny.

Weeks Twelve and Thirteen: Presentations and self-assessments due.

Exhibit Presentation and Self-Assessment (5 + 5 = 10%)

Each group will have the opportunity to present their Digital Exhibit to the class and discuss its various aspects. Each group member will speak briefly about his or her contribution. Group members will also be asked to prepare an honest assessment of their contribution to the project, and their partner's contribution, using the standard rubric provided.

4. TIME AND TECHNOLOGY

This assignment is structured to be completed over a thirteen-week term, as a series of scaffolded assignments. The three-hour class was divided into a two-hour lecture on content, and a one-hour workshop on methodology. The latter was sometimes held in a computer lab, so that I could demonstrate tools and students could have a hands-on opportunity for developing their skills and applied knowledge, with further opportunity for one-on-one assistance from me and the TA. It is not difficult to reduce the assignment to be completed over a shorter period, and it is certainly not necessary either to use a computer lab or to have a TA to assist with student questions. I have modified the curation assignment for different classes to make it a single component (equivalent to an end-of-term research essay, but in a different mode). While I was very glad to have the assistance of a TA for my first foray into digital exhibit building with students, I have not found this to be a requirement, so long as I adapt the assignment for the new circumstances and respect the limitations of my own instructional time.

5. ANTICIPATING STUDENT NEEDS

While we know that the twenty-first-century professional workspace combines individual and collaborative modes of working, creating, and communicating digitally, we also know there are social challenges associated with each of these activities. The same is, of course, true of collaborative assignments. Some students resist collaboration, preferring to work alone; others embrace it as a way to get good grades on a hardworking colleague's coattails. Because this class was relatively small, I was able to give students the option of building their exhibit alone rather than with a partner, on the understanding that some collaborative peer-review processes still had to be followed. To ensure that partners pulled their weight within groups, I built in a number of assessment mechanisms (by myself, students, and peer partners) requiring students to be accountable for their contributions. I also stressed that all scholarly work is, at bottom, collaborative, since the publishing process requires every author to respond to, and incorporate, the feedback of a variety of individuals, including peer reviewers, editors, proofreaders, publishers, and (ultimately) readers. The act of publishing depends on social interaction, just as teaching and learning are, in essence, about human social relationships.

Students' individual access to computers is rarely a problem today, given the laptop loans available through university libraries as well as the open computer labs students can use on campus. The wired classroom is also becoming the norm at most institutions. However, economic realities do come into play with issues of access to databases. The technology required in any digital humanities project will always pose potential difficulties, and much will depend on the quality of your institution's infrastructure and technical support. If the server is too slow, or intermittently down, students will experience more frustration than success in completing a digital assignment. Other problems might arise if access to electronic resources is too severely limited. Not all university libraries are able to make significant investments in e-resources, and while NINES offers open access to archival material, some of the secondary material returned in a NINES search is only available to users if their institution subscribes to the proprietary database holding the resource (such as Project Muse). Another potential challenge may be the (limited) technological skill and knowledge of the students and you. I have found that, while students are generally very adept with computer interfaces and online publishing tools of various kinds, they are less adept at working with electronic resources and databases that require more than a simple Google search. However, I prefer to view this as a teaching opportunity, rather than a potential difficulty. And the same goes for questions of copyright and "fair use" that come up in the process of building and publishing the exhibits.

The greatest potential difficulty of this assignment comes down to the time that must be devoted to it. While I have found the pedagogical rewards to be great, and the student results extremely gratifying, I have not discovered any way to get around the time-consuming aspects of this assignment for the instructor. Since each student or group essentially creates their own project and approach, individual feedback, guidance, and support are essential, and virtually continuous from the first to the last week of term. The process of designing the series of skills workshops, creating evaluation rubrics for each assignment, and assessing both individual and group work is also demanding.

6. ASSESSMENT TOOLS

The challenges (as well as rewards) of this scaffolded digital assignment lie in its collaborative methodology and public visibility; both require a high degree of ethical practice, transparency, and accountability. Like most postsecondary institutions, my university has a policy governing group work and evaluation, restricting its weighting to 30 percent of the individual student's final grade. I therefore built a number of individualized grading mechanisms into the collaborative project. First, the online Proposal and Annotated Bibliography was an individually graded assignment. Although students worked collaboratively to select their text and visual object and to create a research question about the relationship between them, each had to take primary responsibility for targeted research of one aspect of their project (either the verbal text or the visual object) and create an Annotated

Bibliography of relevant secondary sources. Students were also required to hyperlink this assignment to their partner's in the NINES classroom; the idea here was that they were to read each other's research in the process of gaining a collective knowledge base about their project. Second, for the final Digital Exhibit, students were individually responsible for the content of their section of the Critical Commentary (about 1,000 words), and collaboratively responsible for the Introduction and Conclusion, image selection and layout, and the overall editing—that is, both the formatting and writing style of the exhibit. In practical terms, this meant that twenty of the thirty points allotted for this assignment were individual, while only ten points were assigned for collaborative work. The other collaborative grade was given to the Group Presentation on the exhibit, weighted at 5 percent, bringing the total percentage of group work evaluation to 15 percent.

Evaluation Form: Curated Digital Exhibit in NINES	
Group No. Creators: Project Title: Date: Grade: ____/30	
Curatorial Commentary	
• **Information** (Marks Possible: 5). The **Victorian text(s) is clearly contextualized and presented in relation to a visual and/or material object and/or cultural practice with regard to a clearly identified historically particular moment.** Creators of the verbal text(s) and visual object(s) are clearly identified and the relation between the creators and the objects under scrutiny is specified. The Commentary provides accurate information, where relevant, about intended audience, place, time, medium, format, genre, style, and the like. All necessary information is located in the Introduction and the Commentary provides additional information/analysis in a sequence that serves the content of the Commentary in an organized and easy-to-follow fashion. Information is accurate and comprehensive and of high quality (i.e., well chosen and presented, with no extraneous or redundant details).	
Comments	**Score**

(*continued*)

Evaluation Form: Curated Digital Exhibit in NINES *(continued)*

- **Critical Insight** (Marks Possible: 10). The (collective) **critical approach to the Digital Exhibit is specified in the Introduction and used to organize the analysis in the Commentary,** with clear links between individual paragraphs and/or sections. If used, subheads help to organize the material logically. The Curatorial Commentary demonstrates how a specific aspect of the Victorian text's original visual/material context offers insight into a historically particular meaning. Excellent commentaries will develop a critical approach that brings exceptional insight into the ways in which the text makes its meanings and addresses its audience at its historical time and place in relation to the selected visual/material object and/or cultural practice.

Comments	Score

- **Source Credit** (Marks Possible: 5). Although direct quotations are used sparingly, all information gathered from primary and secondary sources receives appropriate credits in footnotes. The footnotes present full bibliographic information about the source credited in correct style. Where appropriate, links are made to the relevant digital documents and/or objects.

Comments	Score

Total Score: _____/20

Digital Exhibit

- **Images and Layout** (Marks Possible: 5). The exhibit is identified by an appropriate thumbnail image and title (of no more than 60 characters). Both partners' names appear under the title. Within the exhibit, the images have been selected carefully, located and sized appropriately, and credited accurately. The selected images support the Commentary and overall critical approach. The layout is pleasing and visually attractive.

Comments	Score

• **Verbal Text** (Marks Possible: 5). The Commentary, captions, and subheads (if applicable) are error free, grammatically correct, and formatted correctly. The overall writing quality is very high in terms of cohesion, clarity, style, diction. The verbal text is a pleasure to read.	
Comments	**Score**
Total Score: _____/10	

I posted all marking rubrics and assignment information on Blackboard, so that students always knew what the expectations were and how they were being evaluated, but I suspect the single most significant grading consideration in this assignment was that all exhibits that met the publishing criteria — that is, received a B+ or better — would be made available beyond the NINES classroom to interested readers around the world (as an administrator of the Classroom group, I had access to this function for each exhibit). To this end, when partners exchanged drafted copies of their critical commentaries for feedback, or edited the exhibit as a whole, they were guided by the evaluation rubric, and knew what to aim for. Many were keen to cite their online publication on their résumés, rightly seeing it as a significant accomplishment. Thus, both the process of writing and revision, and the final assessment, had meaning and purpose beyond simply achieving a grade in a class assignment and a credit in a course. I also encouraged students to take responsibility for their own learning by involving them in the assessment process.

On the first day of class, when I went over the linked Digital Assignments, I explained that students would also be required to submit a self-assessment, using the rubric provided. Group members were responsible for keeping attendance records for each other at designated Skills Workshops, and for providing an honest evaluation of their own and their partner's attendance, ranging from 0 ("I never saw this person") to 5 ("Attended all 5 skills workshops"). They were to give a separate assessment of the actual contribution to the project of each group member, ranging from 0 ("Contributed nothing") to 5 ("Excellent contribution: on time, accurate, informative, took initiative"). My job was to review these self-assessments and assign a final grade for participation (out of 5); my assessment was final, and I reserved the right to assign a 0 to students who either did not submit a self-assessment, or whose self-assessment did not show thoughtful consideration and accurate representation. The self-assessment was due on the day of the group presentation.

Since the Digital Exhibits were submitted online to the NINES e-classroom, I had no papers to return with my feedback. Instead, using the rubric I'd previously posted, I sent each student an individual assessment articulating the strengths and weaknesses of the information, critical insight, and source crediting in their Curatorial Commentary, and including the collaborative evaluation of their Digital Exhibit's presentation of images and layout, and quality of writing and formatting. The assessment document arrived in the student's inbox as a PDF attachment to an e-mail that indicated, where applicable, that the exhibit had met publishing criteria and would be made available on the Web, pending my receipt of permission by return e-mail. My final task was to go into the administrative end of the NINES classroom and select those exhibits that met the criteria for publication for general access to Internet readers. I should stress that this was a back-end activity: *all* the exhibits remained in our designated e-classroom, and continued to be accessible for reading by members of the class.

For the purpose of sharing their research findings, students were given the following instructions to include four components when preparing a five-minute presentation:

1. A clear introduction to the exhibit, identifying yourselves as authors; the Victorian text(s) and visual/material object(s) and/or cultural practice(s) they examined, the historical moment you investigated, and your critical approach. Don't forget to name the creators of the text and visual object as well, and any other pertinent information, such as publication context or art medium.

2. High-resolution image(s) of the visual/material object(s) and/or cultural practice(s) your exhibit presents.

3. Each presenter should offer *one* critical insight that he or she gained about the text/object/historical moment. Don't try to present the whole exhibit; whet our appetites to go online and read your commentary by sharing what you consider to be the most exciting or interesting insight your exhibit offers.

4. Presenters should offer at least *one* self-reflexive comment about something they learned in the process of (primary and secondary, digital and print) research, writing and revision, and/or building the exhibit (i.e., about the *experience* rather than the *subject* of building your exhibit).

Please do not read off the screen; speak directly to the class. Your goal is to interest us so much in your project that we'll all want to go to the NINES Classroom to read your Digital Exhibit.

Presentation Evaluation Form		
	Mark	COMMENTS
Introduction. Clearly identified text(s), visual/ material object (and/or cultural practice) and critical approach.	/1	
Content 1. Each individual clearly explained one critical insight he or she gained about the material.	/2	
Content 2. Presenters reflected on something they learned through the experience of building their Digital Exhibit.	/1	
Presentation. Image(s) presented were clear with good resolution. Presenters spoke to and engaged the class. Kept within the 5-minute time limit.	/1	
TOTAL	/5	

Peer Evaluation/Self-Assessment (Marks Possible: 5). Average score received from team members, as adjudicated by professor.

Comments	Score
	/5

7. THEORETICAL BASIS FOR THE ASSIGNMENT:
Thinking through Making: Curating a Victorian Poem in the Context of Its Cultural Moment

In his now-famous essay "What Is Digital Humanities and What's It Doing in English Departments?" Matthew Kirschenbaum concludes:

> Whatever else it might be, then, the digital humanities today is about a scholarship (and a pedagogy) that is publicly visible in ways to which we are generally

unaccustomed, a scholarship and pedagogy that are bound up with infrastructure in ways that are deeper and more explicit than we are generally accustomed to, a scholarship and pedagogy that are collaborative and depend on networks of people and that live an active, 24-7 life online. Isn't that something you want in your English department? (9)

My own answer to Kirschenbaum's question is a decided yes! As codirector of my university's Centre for Digital Humanities (http://www.ryerson.ca /cdh), member of a number of online editorial boards, and longtime participant in born-digital projects, bringing digital humanities pedagogy into the English classroom allows me to integrate the research, teaching, and administrative aspects of my academic life. Even more importantly, as I've discovered, digital humanities pedagogy provides a public, collaborative, and creative approach to teaching and learning that excites and motivates students. In an age in which students are constructed as consumers and large class sizes encourage a factory approach to undergraduate education, digital humanities pedagogy can reset the paradigms of engagement by addressing students as knowledge producers who think through making.

"Thinking through making" is Alan Galey's apt description of work in the digital humanities (qtd. in Davies and Osborne). While researchers may build scholarly e-resources from the ground up, undergraduate students can tap into the excitement of critical making by using some prefabricated (but customizable) building tools provided through the Networked Infrastructure for Nineteenth-Century Electronic Scholarship (NINES), an open-access site. These include an electronic classroom with hyperlink functions; a personal workspace with access to search, collection, tagging, and annotation tools; a wealth of primary materials in digital archives and peer-reviewed secondary sources in electronic databases; and exhibit-building tools for online publishing. Cited by Cathy Davidson as an example of what she calls "Humanities 2.0" at work, NINES realizes some of the enormous potential of Web 2.0 by uniting peer-reviewed repositories with open access and user participation. As Davidson notes, this paradigm shift raises critically important issues for teaching and learning. An open repository such as NINES "challenges the border between disciplines as well as between professionals and amateurs, between scholars and knowledge enthusiasts [or, I would add, professors and students]. It raises questions of privilege and authority as well as ethical issues of credibility and responsibility, privacy and security, neutrality and freedom of expression" (480). In the NINES classroom, students *work* through these issues and address these questions practically and theoretically precisely because they are "thinking through making."

In my third-year course in Victorian literature and culture in winter 2011, students completed two linked assignments in the NINES classroom: an online Proposal and Annotated Bibliography; and a Digital Exhibit in Victorian visual/verbal culture. By creating the Proposal and Annotated Bibliography using the NINES Exhibit Builder, students gained experience in locating and incorporating primary and secondary e-resources using the customizable template, and became accustomed to working within a collaborative model. In the culminating Digital Exhibit, students analyzed a Victorian poem (usually in its first, periodical publication) in relation to a contemporary visual or material object or cultural practice in order to offer insight into its historically particular meanings. All exhibits that met the publishing criteria (posted on Blackboard) were eligible to be published online and made available to Victorian scholars around the world, subject to the author's written permission. Thus students were positioned as contributors to, rather than simply consumers of, scholarly knowledge of Victorian materials. They were part of the NINES community, networked with Victorian scholars and knowledge enthusiasts around the world.

As I explained in the material I gave out, the linked assignments provided an experiential opportunity in online scholarly publishing that aimed to give students insight into Victorian visual/verbal culture while developing skills in primary and secondary research; critical thinking and analysis; and writing and editing. In addition to developing these practical skills, this digital humanities project also aimed to facilitate new ways of examining and understanding Victorian literature and culture by taking advantage of the powerful search engines, electronic resources, and interactive building tools of Web 2.0. By building a Digital Exhibit that critically situated a Victorian text in relation to a visual object, students were encouraged to see how the past continues to live in the present, and to connect our own "picture-oriented, digital-centric culture" (O'Gorman xvi) with the dynamic visual/verbal world of nineteenth-century print culture. At the same time, students were encouraged not only to recognize but also to *experience* "the textual condition" as textual theorist Jerome McGann has described it: profoundly social, historically particular, and constantly changing (*Textual Condition* 9–10). As with all digital humanities projects, the work students produced would be directed at a public community of readers; be built collaboratively; and integrate visual material with verbal texts in a critically insightful way.

There were two simple but crucial underlying pedagogical principles motivating this assignment: (1) students are producers, not merely consumers, of scholarly knowledge; and (2) humanities courses in the twenty-first century have an obligation to prepare students to be thoughtful contributing citizens by teaching digital literacy in addition to our traditional mandates of textual literacy, cultural literacy, critical thinking, and close reading.

1. Students Are Producers, Not Merely Consumers, of Scholarly Knowledge

Our traditional model for training students to think and write critically while demonstrating their cultural knowledge and analytical skills is the literary essay. Theoretically, this format offers a vehicle that allows students to *essay*—that is, to *try*—scholarly writing. We train students in formulating the thesis as a debatable interpretative claim and in building a persuasive argument through penetrating close readings of the literary text, thoughtfully enhanced with an apt theoretical framework, careful historical positioning, and judiciously selected secondary sources. However, for a variety of reasons, the twenty-first-century undergraduate essay has degenerated from a critical thinking tool for student learning to a measurement tool for administrative purposes. Despite a general consensus among composition theorists that effective writing requires a specific purpose and audience, the typical undergraduate essay has no real purpose other than to collect a grade en route to completing course requirements, *precisely because it has no audience*. In most mid- to large-size universities with which I'm familiar, undergraduate essay marking has become primarily the responsibility of anonymous markers or TAs. Under these conditions, the student is not producing knowledge, demonstrating cultural literacy, or persuasively developing an argument using close reading skills: she or he is simply submitting an assignment, and getting a grade.

On the other hand, as Mark Sample observes, by incorporating *public* writing into the English classroom, it's possible to instill in "students the sense that what they think and what they say and what they write matters — to me; to them; to their classmates; and, through open access blogs and wikis, to the world" (404). Characterized by their public visibility rather than their disappearance into the black hole of the marking bag, Digital Exhibits have a clear audience and purpose. Aiming to publish on the Web for a global community of readers interested in their material, students become motivated to write clearly, edit painstakingly, and source ideas carefully, because the stakes of publication matter to them. They are knowledge producers whose creative and intellectual labor is being shared in a permanent and public, rather than ephemeral and private, forum. Their online publication also has another purpose that moves it beyond the classroom and the course: as an authored work students can feature in their resume or e-portfolio, it becomes meaningfully connected to their long-term career aspirations.

2. Humanities Courses in the Twenty-First Century Have an Obligation to Prepare Students to Be Thoughtful Contributing Citizens by Teaching Digital Literacy

Like all humanities subjects, English classes have traditionally focused on training students in textual literacy, cultural literacy, critical thinking, and close reading skills. The students sitting in our courses today, however, are accustomed to living much of their social and academic lives in virtual space — and this is likely to remain true for their working lives as well. Knowing that, regardless of their chosen career, almost all their communication, research, and creative work postgraduation will take place in online environments of various types, it behooves us to train students in digital literacy. And this includes not only a knowledge of how to locate, evaluate, and use material available online, but also how to communicate and publish material online by using effective writing strategies, digital tools, and ethical practices. As Alexander Reid points out, "If we think of the humanities educational mission as one that is founded on literacy, not just in the sense of basic reading and writing literacy, but in the sense of a broader cultural literacy, then the growing need to teach digital literacy impacts all humanities faculty" (354). Indeed, Reid anticipates "a time in this century when digital research tools and born-digital scholarly composition were as common as close reading and essay writing are today . . ." (362).

In my view, it is not only the methodological skills of digital research and writing that are pedagogical imperatives for the twenty-first-century classroom, but also the underlying practice of digital humanities work in general: a practice that is socially collaborative, outward-looking, and community-building in its commitment to public visibility and open access, and critically creative in its juxtaposition of media, voices, times, and places. "Thinking through making" in building a Digital Exhibit raises questions of authorship and audience, credibility and authority. It aims to make both students and instructors critically aware of our social, economic, and political roles and responsibilities in the production and dissemination of knowledge.

8. CONCLUSION

Given the challenges (real and potential) noted above, what's digital pedagogy doing in my English classroom? Partly, I suppose, I have made a "wager" as a humanities scholar and teacher. Alexander Reid puts the case before us in stark terms: "Either," he writes, "we believe that the humanities can survive as an essentially print-based intellectual practice or we believe the humanities will need to adapt to contemporary communication and information technologies" (363). Digital pedagogy — "thinking through making" in the e-classroom — requires the highest possible quality of research, writing, and critical thinking from students, while enabling them to take up their roles as knowledge producers with social, intellectual, and ethical obligation to readers and makers. And if, as McGann posited over a decade ago in *Radiant Textuality*, "the next generation of literary and aesthetic theorists who will most matter are people who will be at least as involved with *making* things as with writing text" (19), I want my students to be ready to take up this twenty-first-century critical challenge.

The students enjoyed this opportunity to learn about each other's research and conclusions, and were particularly excited to discover the different interpretive directions the same poem could generate by being read through a different context. Unlike an individual essay, in which a student's topic and analytical reasoning generally remains unknown to their classmates, having been read by only one person (the marker), the Digital Exhibit assignment provides students with the opportunity to be part of an intellectual community of knowledge producers and learners. For some students, this was the highlight of the term's work.

9. WORKS CITED

Davies, Marian, and Zachary Osborne. "Defining the Digital Humanities." *Ontario Library Association, ACCESS*, Winter 2010, www.accessola2.com /images/infocentral/ACCESSWinter2010_vol16_no1.pdf

Davidson, Cathy N. "Humanities 2.0: Promise, perils, Predictions." *Debates in the Digital Humanities.* Edited by Matthew K. Gold. U Minnesota P, 2012, 476-89.

ENG 633 Digital Exhibits. *NINES, Nineteenth-Century Scholarship Online*, www .nines.org/groups/ryersonde>.

Kirschenbaum, Matthew. "What Is Digital Humanities and What's It Doing in English Departments?" *Debates in the Digital Humanities.* Edited by Matthew K. Gold. U Minnesota P, 2012, pp. 3-11.

McGann, Jerome. *Radiant Textuality: Literature after the World Wide Web*. Palgrave, 2001.

- - -. *The Textual Condition*. Princeton UP, 1991.

NINES, Nineteenth-Century Scholarship Online, www.nines.org.

O'Gorman, Marcel. *E-Crit: Digital Media, Critical Theory, and The Humanities.* U of Toronto P, 2006.

Reid, Alexander. "Graduate Education and the Ethics of the Digital Humanities." *Debates in the Digital Humanities.* Edited by Matthew K. Gold. U Minnesota P, 2012, pp. 350-67.

Sample, Mark L. "What's Wrong with Writing Essays." *Debates in the Digital Humanities.* Edited by Matthew K. Gold. U Minnesota P, 2012, pp. 404-5.

Index